A Collection of Hayne Letters

Edited by

Daniel Morley McKeithan

GREENWOOD PRESS, PUBLISHERS
WESTPORT, CONNECTICUT

To
Greta and Jimmie

CONTENTS

PAGE

CONTENTS ix

CONTENTS xi

PAGE

FOREWORD

Paul Hamilton Hayne (born at Charleston, South Carolina, on January 1, 1830; died at Copse Hill, Georgia, on July 6, 1886) was the most conspicuous Southern professional man of letters in the first twenty-one years following the Civil War. His poetry appeared in nearly all the leading magazines, Northern and Southern, and he was everywhere known as "the laureate of the South." He also wrote multitudes of reviews and critiques for many Southern magazines and newspapers, as well as biographical sketches and historical essays. He composed about five hundred poems; over four hundred of them appear in his *Complete Edition* of 1882, but a number remain uncollected. Many of them are conventional, weak, bookish, or sentimental; especially unsuccessful are some of the narrative poems and those treating worn-out classical themes. But at his best he was a true artist, and often wrote lyrics of nature, love, and friendship with feeling, imagination, and charm. Of the nineteenth-century Southern poets, Hayne was the fourth best, after Poe, Lanier, and Timrod (or Poe, Timrod, and Lanier, for the best hundred lines of Timrod are as good as the best hundred lines of Lanier); and Hayne wrote as much poetry as the other three combined. His comparatively long career, his identification with and his championing of things Southern, his contemporary fame, his wide acquaintance with Southern writers and leaders of his time, and his experiment as a professional poet in a region where the experiment had never been tried before make him an important figure in the history of the life and thought of the South between 1855 and 1886.

He had no interest in business or in the practice of law,

> The sordid zeal with which our age is rife,
> Its mammon conflicts crowned by fraud or chance,

and after the war he resolved to live by his pen or starve. Never were the times more inauspicious for such an experiment. The South had undergone a tragic revolution and everything was out of joint. Poverty was widespread; it was nearly universal among the best citizens in the South. Nor was the state of the nation sound. The period has been variously called the Tragic Era, the Gilded Age, the time of the Great Barbecue. Thinking was materialistic; moral and artistic standards were low. Most editors preferred poetry that was conventional, sentimental, and insipid; and Hayne was forced to write what he could sell. Moreover, he was hampered by ill health, poverty, depression over what seemed to him the universal ruin of the South, and the suffering of personal friends, such as Timrod and Simms. Yet in spite of all handicaps he succeeded in making a living, meager though it was, and in producing far better verse than did most of the magazine writers of his time.

Hayne belonged to an old and distinguished Charleston family, and as the only child of a widowed mother he expected to inherit a comfortable home and a competent fortune. But his home and library were burned during the war, the family plate and silver were stolen, banks failed, and most stocks and bonds became worthless. After the war he worked for several months on the editorial staff of the Augusta *Constitutionalist*. Fortunately, he owned eighteen acres in the pine woods sixteen miles west of Augusta, on the Georgia Railroad. There, on a windy hill, he built a cottage and moved in 1865 with his wife, mother, and only child. After experimenting with several names—such as "Hayne's Roost"—he called his home "Copse Hill." (It is still standing, though in a deplorable state of disrepair. It should be restored and preserved as a literary shrine.)

The only income he had other than that from his writings was about four hundred dollars annually from investments in South Carolina (what remained of his mother's property), but high taxes consumed from a third to a half of the total amount. He contributed to all Southern magazines which were able to pay him and to many that could pay nothing. Northern magazines often paid him fifteen or twenty dollars—and sometimes as high as fifty cents a line—for longer poems and from seven to ten dollars each for sonnets. But Hayne was ill much of the time, no poet is in the mood for composition every day even when well, and he could find no market for much that he wrote. Some of the unsalable verse and prose was sent to Southern magazines which he knew could not pay, but, on the other hand, his very best essays and some of his best verse appeared in Southern magazines. No doubt during many months his income was absolutely nothing. His first four volumes of poetry (dated 1855, 1857, 1860, and 1872) were published, according to his statement, at his own expense; his volume of 1875 sold "slowly, slowly"; and his *Complete Edition* (1882) was published partly by subscription and brought him very little money, if any at all. He probably made nothing from any of them—at least it is certain that he lost money on the first four.

In politics Hayne was conservative. Even before the war he was disturbed by demagoguery, in the South as well as in the North. After the war when he saw the disgraceful spoliation of his native state by carpetbaggers and the worst element of the population—done under the protection of the Federal Government and in the name of democracy—he came to doubt the democratic theories of Jefferson and to exclaim, "Republics are impossibilities!" As a Charleston aristocrat, he believed in the rule of the best men. What he was really protesting against was demagoguery, the suppression of the best element of the population, and Negro dominance.

Hayne was a prolific letter writer, partly because this was one way to maintain contact with the outside world, and he was lonely and needed companionship with kindred spirits. He corresponded with Tennyson, Swinburne, Jean Ingelow, Philip Marston, Holmes, Bayard Taylor, Longfellow, Stoddard, Stedman, Whittier, Moses Coit Tyler, John Esten Cooke, Joel Chandler Harris, Margaret J. Preston, Lanier, Timrod, Simms, Francis Orray Ticknor, Charles E. A. Gayarré, and many lesser lights both in and out of the writing profession. Hayne wrote literally hundreds and hundreds of letters, many of which do not survive, and many of which remain in private homes—in trunks and attics, or concealed in desks and books. Perhaps those here collected provide a good cross section of his correspondence, and no doubt there would be little point in publishing all of his letters even if a complete collection could be made.

Of the 245 letters in this collection, 229 are by Hayne himself, 11 are by his wife, Mary Middleton Michel Hayne (Nos. 93, 94, 136, 137, 144, 199, 205, 216, 232, 239, and 245), and 5 are by his son, William Hamilton Hayne (Nos. 157–161).

With regard to the arrangement of the letters I considered three plans: (1) a chronological arrangement, (2) a grouping with respect to addressees, and (3) a preservation of the library groups. I thought first of the chronological arrangement and still think that in some respects it would have been the best (as in the case of a reader who wished to follow the events in Hayne's life year by year). I rejected it only because I thought that most readers would prefer to examine as a unit the letters addressed to the same person. Plans two and three, as it turned out, were practically the same, so I adopted plan three and provided cross references in the case of the letters to John Esten Cooke and John Reuben Thompson, which appear in two groups.

After practically every letter I have tried to give adequate notes, even when such a plan necessitated a certain degree of repetition, the purpose being, of course, to save the reader's time. Some cross references have been provided to avoid excessive repetition.

In the table of contents I have listed the libraries which have granted me permission to publish the Hayne letters included here. To the officials of these libraries I hereby express my gratitude and thanks. Microfilm copies were obtained of the letters in the New York Public Library, the Library of Yale University, the Library of Harvard University, the Henry E. Huntington Library, the Craigie House, the Boston Public Library, and the Library of Columbia University. Of the letters in the Library of Congress, in the Library of the University of Virginia, and in the Library of the University of North Carolina I obtained photostats. I had access to the original Hayne letters in the Library of The University of Texas. I am especially grateful to Dr. Otto Kinkeldey for typed copies of the Hayne letters in the Library of Cornell University. Acknowledgment of debts to various scholars and librarians who have helped me will be found at appropriate places in the notes. Dr. Robert Adger Law and Dr. E. Merton Coulter examined the manuscript, made helpful suggestions, and recommended its publication. To Dean A. P. Brogan and the other members of the Research Council of The University of Texas I am grateful for making the publication of this volume possible.

DANIEL MORLEY MCKEITHAN

Austin, Texas
February, 1944

I. NEW YORK PUBLIC LIBRARY (NOS. 1–29)

PAUL HAMILTON HAYNE to RICHARD HENRY
STODDARD

Charleston (S. C.) Jan 1st 1854 [1855]

My Dear Stoddard;
—Your letter of the 26th ult, I have this moment received.
I cannot delay a reply, for your communication is so friendly,
so genial, so affectionate, its contents have gone to my heart,
& I must at once thank you *fervently*, and *sincerely* for your
warm interest, & your really valuable advice. That some of
the poems in my liliputian vol. have pleased you is quite eno'
to satisfy my present ambition. I have such perfect confidence
in your sincerity (how few we meet in life, of whom we may
truly say this!) that your opinion is worth much, *very* much
to me. As for the "pitching in" God knows you have done it
with a tenderness I could never exercise towards myself. I
feel the imperfections of my venture keenly, but still I *do*
experience a gradual increase of power, & with the blessing of
my better Genius I trust to achieve *something* yet.— I rejoice
to hear that you are engaged upon a new prose work, as much
for my own sake, & the sake of the Public as for yours. Should
you die to morrow Stoddard (which may the Gods avert) you
could still know that you had not lived in vain. I never take
up your poems without having *some* chord of my poetical
nature touched, not superficially, or lightly, but by the breath
of a beautiful inspiration— I can never tire of reading the
"Household Dirge," the "Two Gates," the magnificent description of Jenny Lind's singing, & parts of the "Castle in the Air,"
which I have always maintained is one of the most elaborate
pieces of pure imaginative art, ever written on *our* side of the
water— Indeed it is altogether unique. "The Squire of Low
Degree," caught my eye about a week ago. I read it one evening to my wife (who by the way is quite well, & begs to be
especially remembered to Mrs Stoddard, & yourself) before a
blazing *wood*fire in my study— (you never have wood fires
in N York I fear) and was gratified as I almost always am

with what you write. I envy the Flemish fidelity of your descriptive powers. I use the term *Flemish* as conveying the idea of the singular — and to me wonderful accuracy— with which you bring a picture before the mind's eye— so that one feels *palpably* in the presence of the object delineated. This is exemplified with marked success in your poem in Graham's— The opening lines, the— "royal sunlight flushed the room" are as rich as the sunlight itself, & the last 17 lines struck me as possessing a mournful, & touching melody above all praise. — When do you purpose publishing another vol of *poems?* Surely during the last 4 years you have written eno' to fill a respectably sized book. I live in hope of its speedy appearance. I cannot tell you, my dear S. how disappointed I was in not being able to stop in NYork on my return South. But I had outstayed my time, & had not a moment to spare. Besides, one of my relatives was quite sick, & I had to hasten home. I was anxious not only to meet Mrs Stoddard, & yourself, but to make the acquaintance of your gifted friend Bayard Taylor, whose "Poems of the Orient" I saw in proof, & thought *very fine.* One is inclined to think that Taylor must have been stolen when an infant from some Arab tent, & brought over to our colder clime, which however, has been utterly unable to subdue the latent fire of his heart & intellect. His dedication to you was equally appropriate, & beautiful. From the post-mark on your letter, I presume you are now in Boston. I wd' give a great deal to be with you. During my two months sojourn there during the last summer, I met with *so* much kindness, & sympathy, that I can never forget the good old city. Whipple has been a sort of father to me. I am told that he has reviewed me in Graham with great good nature, & kindly interest. He is not only the acutest critic, but one of the most estimable of men. Have you seen Fields' wife? Isn't she a fine-looking woman. I saw our Publisher married, resplendent in a blue coat, & brass buttons, & looking quite handsome, & diabolically cool— Madame was a little— a very little agitated. From all I can hear, the union promises to be propitious, but promises—especially *these* Sort of promises— are very deceitful— Pray Stoddard, have you seen a cousin of mine— Miss Ada McElhenney— in your city of late. She has totally abandoned her friends, & I would like to know now, & then, something about her. When you answer this, tell me about your health. You looked quite thin when we met, & I thought seemed feeble. I fear the Custom House duties are too hard for you— Terribly uncongenial they *must be.*

I write this letter, my dear Richard, with the full intention of re-opening our pleasant correspondence. Let me hear from you whenever you find it convenient, & keep me informed of your literary doings, & intentions. I am almost utterly alone (so far as *mental* sympathies are concerned) & an occasional word from you will really be a charity— With warmest regards to Mrs Stoddard, and an earnest hope for the success of your forthcoming stories—

Believe me

Most Truly Yrs—

Paul H. Hayne

Richard H. Stoddard Esq—
  Nyork

[Richard Henry Stoddard (1825–1903), native of Massachusetts, spent most of his adult years in New York. In his youth he worked at many jobs, became a molder in a foundry, and was mainly self-educated. He contributed poems, literary criticism, and sketches to nearly all the leading magazines of his time. He worked in the New York Custom House from 1853 until 1870 and served as literary editor of the New York *World* (1860–1870) and of the New York *Mail and Express* (1880–1903). He collected his poems in volumes from time to time, especially *Poems* in 1852, *Songs of Summer* in 1857, and *The Poems of Richard Henry Stoddard (Complete Edition)* in 1880. Some of his other works are *Footprints* (1848), *Adventures in Fairy-Land* (1853), *Life, Travels, and Books of Alexander von Humboldt* (1860), *The King's Bell* (1863), *Abraham Lincoln: a Horatian Ode* (1865), and *The Book of the East* (1867).

The first letter is clearly dated, but 1854 is an error for 1855:

(1) Hayne's "liliputian vol." came out in 1854 and is dated 1855 (*Poems.* Boston: Ticknor and Fields, 1855).

(2) Stoddard's "The Squire of Low Degree" (beginning "The royal sunlight flushed the room . . ."), which Hayne had already seen in *Graham's Magazine*, appeared in XLVI (January, 1855), 66–69. (The poem was collected in *Songs of Summer* (Boston: Ticknor and Fields, 1857), pp. 149–59. Stoddard dedicated the volume to George H. Boker.)

(3) Hayne implies that four years had passed since the publication of Stoddard's last volume of poems. Stoddard's *Poems* (Boston: Ticknor,

Reed, and Fields, 1852) was "entered" in 1851. (Stoddard dedicated the volume to Bayard Taylor, "whom I Admire as a Poet, and Love as a Man." This volume contains "A Household Dirge" (pp. 96–8), "The Two Gates" (pp. 63–4), "To a Celebrated Singer" (pp. 59–62), and "The Castle in the Air" (pp. 3–20).)

(4) The review of Hayne's *Poems* which he had heard would appear in *Graham's Magazine* appeared in February, 1855 (XLVI, 192–3).

(5) Fields' wedding, which Hayne had attended, occurred in 1854, apparently early in November (see *James T. Fields: Biographical Notes and Personal Sketches* [By Mrs. Annie Fields], Boston, Houghton Mifflin and Company, 1881, p. 51).

Bayard Taylor (1825–1878), Pennsylvania essayist, playwright, critic, traveler, poet, journalist, diplomat, lecturer, novelist, translator, orientalist, was becoming famous at the time of this letter because of the publication of his *Poems of the Orient* (1854). In other letters Hayne speaks of Taylor's *The Picture of St. John* (1866), *Lars: A Pastoral of Norway* (1873), and his translation of Goethe's *Faust* (2 vols., 1870–1). Stoddard and Taylor first met in 1848 and immediately became intimate friends. At that time Taylor was a journalist and Stoddard was a molder. Later the two poets and their families lived in the same house for several years. Through Taylor, Stoddard met many other men of letters, including Buchanan Read and George Boker.

The idea that Taylor was really an Arab stolen in infancy Stoddard embodied in his poem " 'Poems of the Orient' " (*Songs of Summer*, p. 49).

Edwin Percy Whipple (1819–1886), Boston critic, author, and lecturer, began his review of Hayne's *Poems* (in *Graham's Magazine* for February, 1855, pp. 192–3) with this sentence: "This volume, the product of a young poet of South Carolina, is one of great promise as well as fine performance."

James Thomas Fields (1817–1881) became, in his early twenties, a junior partner in the Boston publishing house of Ticknor, Reed, and Fields, which became Ticknor and Fields after the retirement of Reed in 1854. In 1859 the *Atlantic Monthly* was bought by Ticknor and Fields, and Fields was the editor from 1861 until 1870. He married Annie Adams (1834–1915) in 1854, a cousin of his deceased first wife. Annie Adams Fields was vivacious and charming and, like her husband, became the author of several volumes.

Jane McElhenny (1836–1874),—the name is sometimes spelled with one *n* followed by *e*—a cousin of Hayne, was born in Charleston and when a child was taken to the North by her grandfather after her parents had died. In 1855, when she was 19, her literary career began with love poems in the New York *Atlas*, under the pseudonym of Ada Clare. From then until her death she was a celebrity, admired for her beauty and intellect and sometimes abhorred for her unconventional ways. She wrote sketches, fiction, and criticism, as well as poetry, visited Paris, returned to reign as queen of the New York Bohemians at Pfaff's, became the mother of an illegitimate son (supposedly by Louis Moreau Gottschalk, pianist and composer), and appeared on the stage in New York, San Francisco, Memphis. and elsewhere. At first her stage career was a failure because her roles were too ambitious for her mediocre talent, but later she did somewhat better in minor roles. At the time of her tragic death in 1874 she had been for several 'years the wife of a fellow actor. Two of her most loyal friends were the poets Walt Whitman and Charles Warren Stoddard. See Albert Parry, *Garrets and Pretenders: A History of Bohemianism in America* (New York: Covici-Friede, 1935), pp. 14–37.

Stoddard's "forthcoming stories" is probably a reference to *Town and Country; a Book for Children* (New York: Dix. Edwards. and Company, 1857).]

No. 2

PAUL HAMILTON HAYNE to RICHARD HENRY STODDARD

Marietta (Ga.) July 28*th* 1855

My Dear Stoddard;

It is so long since I have heard of, or from you that I write with some solicitude to inquire how you are in "mind, body, & estate"— Last summer it was my misfortune to see you but a moment, & as I doubt whether I shall be able to visit New York again for years, I have determined to write occasionally, in order that I may be informed of your health, prospects &c. You will be surprised to observe that I date this letter from the backwoods of Georgia. I am here to try if a light, dry atmosphere will be beneficial to my mother, whose constitution has been feeble for a long time, & is unable to stand the terrible summers in C—. What are you doing in a literary way? Sometimes at long intervals I find a poem in Putnam attributed to you. Are you the author of the exquisite little piece beginning "There are gains for all our losses &c"— Indeed, Stoddard I must tell you, & I speak sincerely, that you are nearer to me as a Poet than any of our younger bards. I think in a word that you far surpass them all, particularly in a certain delicate purity of artistic finish, in which American verse is so wretchedly deficient. I tell you this not to flatter God knows, but because I know sympathy is dear to us all. Can you inform me who is the author of a critique in

the July no. of Putnam entitled recent American poetry. I
think it exceedingly clever, & spicy, but am sorry the Author
should be so severe upon Alice Carey.— There is no denying
that the choice of her subjects has been very unfortunate, but
the Critic is unmerciful. What he says of your friend Bayard
Taylor is not at all to my fancy. The truth is I have observed,
both in Boston, & New York a determination amongst certain
persons systematically to underrate T— *as a Poet*. A gentleman of cultivation & intelligence (one you know) in the former place told me that he looked upon T. as one who had
made himself a Poet by *travel*, denying him any claim to
original genius, as if anything on earth could have created a
power, not constitutionally his— For myself I look upon all
this as damnable cant, & I think that the elevation of Mr Parsons at the expense of T. in the last Putnam is absurd, altho,
characteristic eno' of the one-sided criticism of a clique. Are
you engaged at present upon any work of length. Mrs Stoddard told me last summer, if I do not mistake, that you had
abandoned "Proserpine". The subject altho, a fine one presents peculiar difficulties, and would be so especially addressed
to scholars that I think it would be possible to choose a topic
more felicitous. What say you to composing a Poem upon
Sappho? The struggle in *her* case between genius, & love, the
passion of art, & the passion of affection might be worked up
to a superb antithesis; besides the subject would just suit you.
Think of it at any rate. My life at present is very quiet, and
uneventful. I am living at a farm house some miles from the
little village of Marietta, a place which twenty years ago was
surrounded by Indians. It is dull eno' at times, but by the
aid of a few choice volumes I am enabled to endure the solitude. I think it is such a location as would benefit you greatly.
Your position in the Custom House must be very irksome
during the summer, & I have no doubt you must often long
for quiet, and seclusion. I am sure that city-life wd' kill me in
6 months. I could never muster up the moral strength to resist
its manifold temptations— If I lived in New York I should continually be patronizing the Saloons, billiard tables &c & getting
elated upon champagne. Heidsick is a drink for the Gods, &
not all the liquor laws in the world shall ever be able to abolish

it. In fact how can rulers expect to *legislate* people into *moral-ity*. Of course grog shops should be blown up, annihilated, but as Hawthorne has it, so long as mankind have the power to to [*sic*] bring back the jovial feelings of youth, & to experience all its glorious enthusiasms for quarter of an hour, so long will the[y] use this power, or abuse it. I hear nothing about me now but politics—slavery, & antislavery ad nauseam. Fat old gentlemen catch me by the button, & want to know with a fierce look what I think about Nebraska. My days are ren-dered wretched by such persecution. Who the deuce cares whether the President cuts the throats of the democracy, or the democracy cut his— Thank God! I shall have a prospect in time of living in Florence under a quiet despotism—When ready to cross the Atlantic may I trouble you for a letter to Thomas B. Read.? *Apropos* of R. what is your opinion of the "New Pastoral"—? It seems to me exceedingly sweet, and touching in parts, but it lacks unity of interest. I dare say I ha· e myself to blame in this. I merely state an impression. A little more than two months ago I had the pleasure of receiv-ing a visit in Charleston from Alex. Galt who had been five years in Florence, & who told me he was intimate with Read. I was glad to hear from him that Read was esteemed as an Artist no less than a Poet, that he had taken several successful portraits, & had realised something handsome pecuniarily. Galt himself is a sculptor of eminence. You might have noticed at the Grand Exhibition in your city the head of a *Bacchante* (an exquisite bust) by him— Do you continue to correspond with our friend Jas. Fields? You of course heard of his mar-riage. I *hope* it will be a happy one, but entre nous the lady is not much to my humble taste. She intrigued a good deal I am told about this very affair. In a word she laid regular siege to F's heart, and caught him at last by starving out the gar-rison— If correctly informed it was altogether a work of cal-culation—on one side at least. Such marriages are usually productive of misery in the end— Speaking of wives let me say that my own little woman is quite well, & sends her kind regards to Mrs S. & yourself— We have not yet been cursed— with children for which the Saints be praised— Do, my dear Stoddard let me hear from you soon. It will be a positive

charity to send me news of the great world in this, my banish-
ment from civilized life—

Believe me, *Ever Truly* Yrs
Paul H. Hayne—

P. S. Writing as you do for Putnam, you can of course tell
me upon what principle that mag. is conducted. I mean do the
Editors admit contributions *impartially* or is it a clannish publication, or one confined to writers of *established reputation*.

[*Putnam's Monthly Magazine* was published (under varying titles and
subtitles) in New York (1853–57, 1868–70, 1906–1910). Charles F. Briggs
(who had edited the *Broadway Journal* with Poe) was the first editor
(1853–57, 1868–69). George William Curtis was an associate editor from
1853 until 1857. The article "Recent American Poetry," in the issue for
July, 1855 (VI, 48–58), is a review of recent volumes by Alice Cary,
Thomas William Parsons, Bayard Taylor, Elizabeth C. Kinney, and
Erastus W. Ellsworth. Alice Cary is handled rather severely, and Parsons
is praised more highly than the others reviewed. Only faint praise is given
to Taylor, who the critic says is still a traveler to him rather than a good
poet. Stoddard is not discussed in the article, probably because he had not
recently brought out a volume of poems.

Stoddard's "There Are Gains for All Our Losses" was collected in *Songs
of Summer* (p. 5).

Alice Cary (1820–1871), Ohio poet and prose writer, lived in New York
(with her poet sister Phoebe Cary) after 1850. The name was often
spelled *Carey* in the magazines.

Thomas William Parsons (1819–1892), Boston dentist, wrote poetry
and translated Dante.

The "drink for the Gods" which Hayne refers to is a champagne of
good quality.

Hawthorne speaks in a number of places of the restoration of youth
through the drinking of an elixir. Hayne may have been thinking of "Dr.
Heidegger's Experiment."

Nebraska was the huge area between Missouri and Iowa and the Rocky
Mountains. The Kansas-Nebraska Act (1854) repealed the Missouri
Compromise and provided for the organization of two territories in the
region (Kansas and Nebraska), each to have the right to settle the question
of slavery within its borders. Two effects of the act (to which President
Franklin Pierce had given his approval) were the bloody struggle for the
control of Kansas and the formation of the Republican Party.

Thomas Buchanan Read (1822–1872), Pennsylvania poet and painter, is
now best remembered for his Civil War ballad "Sheridan's Ride." In his
later years he spent much time in Europe and was in Florence from 1853

until 1855. His *The New Pastoral* appeared in 1855 (Philadelphia: Parry and McMillan). In *Recollections Personal and Literary* (New York: A. S. Barnes and Company, 1903, pp. 205–212) Stoddard tells of a week-end he and his wife spent with Read and his family at Bordentown, New Jersey. He thought Read erred grievously by trying to be both poet and painter.

Alexander Galt (1827–1863), Virginia sculptor, studied in Italy and for years had a studio in Florence. He worked for the Southern cause during the war and died of smallpox while modelling a statue of Stonewall Jackson. Among his works are the bust of Rutledge in the Supreme Court (Washington, D. C.), *Thomas Jefferson* (at the University of Virginia), and the ideal figures *Sappho, Aurora, Bacchante, Hope,* and *The Spirit of the South.* (See *The South in the Building of the Nation,* XI, 380–1.)]

No. 3

PAUL HAMILTON HAYNE to RICHARD HENRY STODDARD

Marietta (Ga.) August 24*th* 1855

I was very much pleased my dear Stoddard at the reception of your note of the 15*th* which reached me this morning— I am well nigh bored to death in this cursed place, which is without society, or amusements of any kind, & consequently your communication which would have been welcome at any time, is doubly so just now. You ask me whether I have abandoned verse-making. By no means. The "divine itch" as you aptly call it, has become I fear constitutional. I have engaged to write regularly for Graham, and the "Home Journal"; and attempted to propitiate Putnam, but my peace offering was courteously returned, accompanied by a curious note to the effect that I have not yet reached the standard of merit necessary to admit me as a contributor. I trust I may be able in time to do better— I am neither offended nor mortified, but intend to labor & study. Success will come most probably in the End. Upon the general merits of Curtis' article on "Recent American Poetry" I fully agree with you. Like everything its author writes it is exceedingly clever, but I must still hold to the conviction that *Taylor* has been depreciated, & *Parsons* overrated. Of course I have seen the "Poems of the Orient". In fact Fields showed me some of them *in proof*. "The Desert Hymn to the Sun" struck me as peculiarly fine— Surely there is inspiration in *that*. And the dedication is full of beauty, & feeling. How proud you ought to be of the friendship of a man like Taylor!— "Birds", & "summer & autumn" in the July no. of Putnam have pleased me as all your minor pieces invariably do. You have estimated yourself properly. Few, very few bestow the labor limaë so patiently upon poems of two or three verses, & "verily you shall have your reward"— Still do you not think my dear Stoddard that there is some disadvantage in accustoming one's self to such rigid brevity, & may not a poem however excellent, & complete in itself lose a certain portion of its effect by being too epigramatic? Poems of this class leave a vague impression of sweetness, but there is a lack of *body* about them which causes the impression to be transient. I only allude to poems of from 2 to 3 stanzas. What you say of Smith & his school is very true. Every acute critic fathomed Smith's depth at once—if not swayed by prejudice— Do you remember Whipple's "scorcher" on the "Life Drama" which appeared in the Lit; World? & how bitter the Editors of the "Home Journal" who swore by the great Alexander, were about it—?— Well! all sensible people acknowledge now that he was right. I am taking your advice, literally going back to first-principles in my poetical studies. Having had little to do this season I have reviewed our English Poets from Chaucer down i.e., I have read such authors as may be considered the representatives of different periods, & schools. I believe the study has been instructive; but I have waded thro. a great deal of dull stuff, & am amazed at the quantity of inanity which once passed with the Public as genuine inspiration. Since my last letter (I tell you this my dear Stoddard in the *strictest confidence*) I have encountered a great danger. You know that old appeal de Dieu is much more common at the South than it is with you, & that it is well nigh impossible for a gentleman if *publicly* affronted to avoid the ordeal. While engaged in a game of billiards with a friend, I was so unfortunate as to be subjected to a wanton, & brutal affront from a person whose position in society compelled me

to notice his conduct—& to resent it. .Accommodation was out
of the question, & the next morning we fought with pistols. I
gave him a trifling wound, & escaped entirely myself, & what
is unusual in these cases, the matter has been completely hushed
up. Not one of my family, nor indeed any one else (except
the parties immediately engaged) even suspect the occurrence
of this rencontre. I merely mention the circumstance to show
how alarmingly uncertain is our tenure of this sweet life— I
felt the bullet whistle by me in a damned uncomfortable prox-
imity. As Byron says somewhere in Don Juan there is something in the click of a trigger when you know the weapon is
about to bear upon your person "at ten steps off, or so", which
is more thrilling than agreeable— I trust that I shall not be
so unlucky as to get into such—a scrape again— The night
before a duel is to one who thinks, & feels a period of agony—
To a Bachelor it may be different; but in any case it is bad
eno'— It grieves me that your health continues precarious.
Deeply, & profoundly can I sympathise with those who suffer
from bodily maladies. I have been at various stages of my life
a martyr to ill health. Once when 17 years old I was attacked
by a severe fever of a nervo-billious kind which played the
deuce with my constitution. It's [sic] effects will follow me to
my grave— You, I think suffered from too much physical exertion just at that period of life when the muscles needed wholesome development, not hard, & straining work. I am sorry to
hear of Miss M's failure— Of course she is nothing to me now,
but I feel for anyone in so shocking a position. If you can
procure any critique upon her debût let me have it, & you
will really be conferring a favor upon all of us. Give me at
your leisure one or two details of her first appearance, & say
whether it was a regular break down, or only a weak & imperfect performance. The father of this girl was a man of
genius, & the soul of honor. Fortunately he is dead.— And so,
my dear fellow there is a young Stoddard in the family. I
thoroughly envy you. No such fair prospect for me. In all
likelihood "that little wee wife of mine" will continue the
only jewel of my household. But she *is* a jewel indeed. Our

joint love to Mrs Stoddard & the baby— When time offers write me more fully, & Believe me, affectionately yrs.

P. H. H.

P. S. Have you seen the vol. of poems by young Bulwer—?—

[*Graham's Magazine*, Philadelphia monthly, ran (under a variety of titles) from 1826 until 1858.

The Home Journal, a New York weekly, was founded in 1846 by Nathaniel Parker Willis and George Pope Morris. For the first nine months its title was *The National Press: A Home Journal*, and in 1901 it was changed to *Town and Country*.

George William Curtis (1824–1892), of Rhode Island, was an author, critic, orator, and editor (associate editor of *Putnam's* 1853–1857, political editor of *Harper's Weekly* 1863–1892, and editor of the "Easy Chair" of *Harper's Monthly* 1859–1892).

"And the dedication is full of beauty": the reference is to "Epistle from Mount Tmolus," addressed to Stoddard. In his *Recollections Personal and Literary* (p. 247) Stoddard commented: ". . . the 'Epistle from Mount Tmolus' with which it [Taylor's *Poems of the Orient*] opened, and which was addressed to myself . . . , was a beautiful compliment, of which any one might have been proud . . . , this poem about our poetic friendship. . . ."

Stoddard's "Birds" and "Summer and Autumn" were collected in *Songs of Summer* (pp. 15 and 41).

Alexander Smith (1830–1867) was the Scottish poet and essayist. His *Life Drama and Other Poems* (1853) occasioned a controversy over its merits. It was reviewed, mainly unfavorably, in *The Literary World* of New York for June 11, 1853 (XII, 472–4), and the issue of July 9, 1853 (XII, 547–8) contained "Alexander Smith's Poetry. (From a subtle review from the pen of E. P. Whipple, in *Graham's Magazine* for July)."

Hayne gives another account of his duel in the letter to Moses Coit Tyler dated February 26, 1874 (No. 168).

The reference to Byron is to *Don Juan*, IV, stanza 41.

"Miss *M's* failure": see the note on Jane McElhenny following letter No. 1. Her failure was as an actress. The critics said her arms were too thin and her voice too shrill, but Jane could "take it" and persisted.

Stoddard's first son was born in June, 1855, and died in December, 1861. His name was Wilson, but Stoddard called him Willy. A second son was born in 1859 and died within a few months. A third son (Lorimer) was born in December, 1863, and lived until 1901. He became a successful dramatist. Stoddard's wife died in 1902, the year before his own death.

Hayne's only child (William Hamilton) was born March 11, 1856 (died 1929).

Edward Robert Bulwer-Lytton (1831–1891), first Earl of Lytton, statesman and poet, brought out a volume of poems in 1855 under the pseudonym
of Owen Meredith.]

No. 4

PAUL HAMILTON HAYNE to RICHARD HENRY STODDARD

Charleston, Sep 17th 1856.

My Dear Stoddard;

After the lapse of Heaven knows how many months, I feel
the spirit of correspondence, strong within me. I wish to know
how the world has treated you & yours since we met. I stop
to shake hands with you sometimes (whenever you give me
a chance) in the magazines, & some very pleasant interviews
of this kind I have enjoyed; still I could desire to see you in
the flesh, to discuss matters over a bottle of any respectable
liquor, & dispense for once with this eternal cold void of distance which plays the very deuce with all genial communion.
I cannot forget the delightful episode in my rather flat & unprofitable existence which introduced you to my acquaintance;
I often recur to it now, & only regret that the Fates seem to
have interposed to prevent a recurrence of the same. However I suppose we shall meet in the satisfactory region of
"somewhere", & at the definite period of "sometime"!

Meanwhile I rejoice to hear that you are preparing to make
your second bow before the Public in November. I shall
eagerly look for your book. *Pray send me an early copy.*—
Does the "Search after Proserpine" come out in the present
vol?—

I am curious to see what you have made of a theme at
once so attractive & so difficult. During the last year I have
read some exquisite little poems by your wife in the "Home
Journal"— You are fortunate Stoddard in having by you for
life so congenial a companion— Tell Mrs Stoddard she should
write oftener, that I mean no idle coxcomb flattery when I say
that her lyrics have been to *me* at least very charming.

And how is your boy?— I too can boast of a son, a six monther who has just cut his first teeth, an olive complexioned, black eyed, lively little scoundrel, the light & joy of the household—"a *son*-shine" as Hood hath it "in a shady place"—

I suppose it was the young Stoddard who suggested the Children's Prayer in the last "Lit Messenger"—a picturesque & sweet poem the style of which I like. It is as Thompson says in the best vein of Leigh Hunt.

—*Apropos* of magazines we are about to start a *monthly* in Charleston much upon the plan of Blackwood, which I really think is likely to succeed. It is to be a Joint Stock Concern, & to commence with considerable capital. We shall pay *liberally*, & *promptly* for everything. I have been appointed one of the Editors, & take this opportunity of requesting you to become *a regular Contributor*— The Politics won't suit you I suppose, but what of that—you are no Politician, but a Poet whose audience is humanity everywhere. Our first no. will appear in December, & for this number may I not look to you for a Poem? Write of course upon any topic you like, & send me the M.S. by 1st November—i e. if my proposal meets your assent. We will cheerfully pay you anything you ask— Have you visited Boston of late?— If so, how are our friends in that vacinity?— Has marriage dashed the luxuriant gayety of Fields—? Do Whipple's great eyes gleam large, & luminous as of yore— In brief, what report can you make of the Athenians?

—Do my dear fellow write me at your Earliest convenience. Answer such of my queries as you think deserving of reply.

My wife's special regards to Mrs Stoddard, & the boy, to which please add my best wishes for the happiness & prosperity of your whole household—

I am Most Truly Yrs:

Paul H. Hayne

[Stoddard's *Songs of Summer* is dated 1857 but was "entered" in 1856. It contains "The Search for Persephone" (pp. 175–92). This was Stoddard's third volume of verse (*Footprints*, 1848; *Poems*, 1852). *Footprints* was a complete failure: "one copy was sold; the edition was committed to the flames" (Stoddard's *Recollections Personal and Literary*, p. 111).

Stoddard's wife (Elizabeth Drew Barstow Stoddard, 1823–1902) wrote poems, sketches, stories, and novels.

Thomas Hood (1799–1845) was the English poet and editor, best remembered for "The Song of the Shirt" and "The Bridge of Sighs." His sonnet "The World is with me, and its many cares" ends:

> I gaze upon a little radiant face,
> And bless, internally, the merry boy
> Who "makes a *son-shine* in a shady place."

"The Children's Prayer" appears in *Songs of Summer* (pp. 112–115).

John Reuben Thompson (1823–1873) was the editor of the Richmond *Southern Literary Messenger* from 1847 until 1860.

Russell's Magazine, Charleston monthly, of which Hayne was editor, ran from April, 1857, until March, 1860.]

No. 5

PAUL HAMILTON HAYNE to RICHARD HENRY STODDARD

Charleston Oct *3rd* 1856.

My Dear Richard;

Yours of the 25th gave me sincere pleasure. It was satisfactory in more ways than one. In the *first* place I rejoice to hear of your health, & happiness; in the second place, your consent to become a regular contributor to my Magazine, I consider most excellent news. Remember, I shall depend upon you—! You can, if you choose, give me something *every* month—& especially, have a story, *and* poem ready by *the middle of November.* As I said before, *make your own terms.*

Many thanks for the promise of an early copy of your poems. Flattery between us would be folly, & therefore you will not suspect me of acting the hypocrite, when I repeat what I have often intimated before that your verses touch me nearly—there is real genius in them, & a new book from you I regard as a delightful event— I like your style both of Art, & of Thought. So, keep your promise ab't the new vol. "The Search after Proserpine" you *ought* to have finished. Fragments of poems may be beautiful, but somehow they always leave an impression of unconcentrativeness (is there such a word?)—

Putnam refused the Children's Prayer!! Well! Putnam be d—d. Graham refused it!! Graham be d—d. Thus it is with Mags, & their Editors! The latter are too frequently under the influence of small prejudices, & smaller cliques. In the article of poetry they are forever falling into ridiculous blunders. As for Putnam I nurse a very pretty hatred against the entire concern. It begun with loud professions of nationality; it ends with abolitionism, & a studied contempt for everything Southern. Pray, is Mr Geo. Curtis still the Editor? His late tirade against the manners & *morale* of the Southern people was a piece of antithetical stupidity. He sacrafices [*sic*] truth to epigrammaticism, decency to point!— We are *not* all the licentious brutes he seems disposed to represent us. One of these days I hope to welcome Mr*s* Stoddard & yourself in Charleston, & then you can judge how far M*r* Curtis'es [*sic*] statements are correct.

To return to pleasanter topics. I have made up a portion of the table of Contents for the 1st no, of the Periodical.— There are two brief, but pungent papers upon general Politics, (you are too sensible I know, to mind *them*) written by men of power in their line—a Review of Macaulay's 3rd & 4th vol*s* of the His of England, an Essay upon Matthew Arnold, & poems by your humble servant, and others:—the no: however is by no means full—a story & poem from your pen are *absolutely needed*. With regard to the *form* of the Magazine, I have thought *Putnam* a pretty good model. For the *first* year we c'ant have so much matter in it, but hope to Enlarge with enlarging patronage.

You inquire what "I am doing in the verse way"— Nothing *very* important, but a good deal miscellaneously. In fact, since the publication of the sadly immature vol. which stands deservedly last upon the list of Fields' poetical issues, I have written eno' to fill another book of (say) 150 pages. I hope, I pray, that the next work of this class bearing my name may meet with your approbation, & the approbation of other good judges.— "Set a thief to catch a thief"— Let Poets be the Judges of each other— With all their proverbial irritability they are, when above the chances of jealousy, the only true Critics of such works of Art as are founded upon the higher processes of the Imagination.

I never see the National Magazine. C'ant you make them send me a copy. Say that I shall notice it in the Charleston papers, & mail them (the Publishers) the notice regularly—

By the way Stoddard, you are more conversant with the ways of the Book Trade than I am. Advise me in the following case. When Ticknor & Fields published my poems I paid them $180 cash [,] the full cost of the edition which only consisted of 500 copies— Of course the work has had no sale at the North, but here in Charleston more than a hundred copies were disposed of. After the usual deduction upon each vol, am I not entitled to the surplus.?— I have written to Fields asking him ab't it. A very small matter, but one's rights should be regarded.

[Written at the top of the second page of the letter:]

P. S. Wife's love to Mrs S—& the boy of whom we are glad to hear such glowing accounts. Have you called him Richard Henry? Write me soon, & at length if you can. What has become of *Bayard Tailor* [*sic*]?

> Believe me my dear fellow,
> Ever affectionately yrs
> P. H. H.

[According to Frank Luther Mott (*A History of American Magazines,* II, 423), Parke Godwin, an associate editor of *Putnam's Monthly Magazine* in charge of politics, supported the Republican Party and attacked slavery and the South, occasioning rejoinders in such Southern magazines as *De Bow's Review* for February, 1857 (XXII, 129), the *Southern Literary Messenger* for March, 1857 (XXIV, 236), and *Russell's Magazine* for April, 1857 (I, 82–5).

In the back of Stoddard's *Songs of Summer* there is a supplement of twelve pages entitled "New Books and New Editions Published by Ticknor and Fields." In the section headed "Poetry" (pp. 8–9 of this supplement) the last item is "Paul H. Hayne. Poems. 1 vol. 16 mo. 63 cents."

The New York *National Magazine* was a Methodist monthly published from 1852 until 1858.

In connection with the sale of Hayne's first volume, it is interesting to note that his chief support—almost his *only* support—came from Charleston.

Hayne published six volumes of poetry: *Poems* (Boston: Ticknor and Fields, 1855), *Sonnets and Other Poems* (Charleston: Harper and Calvo, 1857), *Avolio: A Legend of the Island of Cos* (Boston: Ticknor and Fields,

1860), *Legends and Lyrics* . . . (Philadelphia: Lippincott, 1872), *The Mountain of the Lovers* . . . (New York: E. J. Hale and Son, 1875), *Poems of Paul Hamilton Hayne (Complete Edition)* (Boston: D. Lothrop and Company, 1882). The first four (and possibly the fifth) were brought out at Hayne's expense. The last was at least in part a subscription edition made possible through the efforts of Colonel John Garland James, President of the Agricultural and Mechanical College of Texas. Before the war Hayne could well afford to pay for the publication of his volumes. But after the war his remaining property (or his mother's) brought in only about $400 a year, from a third to a half of which had to be paid in taxes. Consequently, he had to support himself and his. family (wife, son, and mother) with his pen. This was a herculean task for a poet. The surprising thing is not that he did not make more money from his poetry but that he managed to make a living at all. If he had been a writer of fiction his task would have been much easier.]

No. 6

PAUL HAMILTON HAYNE to RICHARD HENRY STODDARD

Charleston Nov *7th* 1856.

My Dear Stoddard;

Your last letter enclosing three poems (for wh' accept my thanks), one from your own pen, the others by Mr*s* Stoddard, to whom my special acknowledgements are due—was not rec*d* until yesterday. I have been absent for 10 or 12 days from Charleston, which will account for the delay—x I wish you, my dear fellow, to write me something more elaborate— a poem for example like the "Fisher & Charon", in the last Putnam— Let it be just *half* as long, and a third as good, & I am willing to pay you the *highest magazine price.*

Our Periodical appears positively on the 1st March, when all accepted contributions shall be *promptly paid for*— I want a long poem (as intimated above *one half* the length of the "Fisher & Charon["]) to begin with— Let it be ready—with a prose paper if possible—by 1st of February, or say, a few days sooner— You wish to stand well (you say) at the South *poetically;* I promise you the amplest opportunity of doing so— As for our "infernal institution," as you mildly call it, we will discuss *that question*, my dear Richard, when I shall have the honor (as I hope to have one day) of entertaining Mrs S. & yourself under my humble roof-tree in Carolina, with said "infernal institution", right under our eyes— I fear that the argument, if attempted between us in our present relations would simply be a *geographical*, not a *political* discussion.

I am so busy just now, that you must really excuse this hurried, & execrable scrawl. Say, if you accede to my propositions, & write as soon as convenient—

Very Truly & affectionately yr Friend;

P. H. Hayne—

["The Fisher and Charon" appeared in *Putnam's Monthly Magazine* for November, 1856 (VIII, 493–98), and was collected in *Songs of Summer* (pp. 126–39).

Stoddard calls slavery the South's "infernal institution," while in *Russell's Magazine* Hayne calls it her "peculiar institution."]

No. 7

PAUL HAMILTON HAYNE to RICHARD HENRY STODDARD

Charleston Dec 15th 1856.

My Dear Stoddard;

You must excuse my delay in replying to your last letter. I have just recd it. Having been for some time in the upper part of the State lecturing, the letter remained on my desk in Charleston. Enclosed, you will find Mrs Stoddard's poems. I regret that she cannot let me retain them, but hope she may be induced to contribute something more. The Maga appears in *March*. I am keeping a space open for your promised Poem, & shall really feel hurt, & disappointed—if you d'ont [*sic*] let me have it— Mention your own terms. I have been re-perusing your *"Fisher & Charon"*. My deliberate opinion— an opinion I am ready to sustain anywhere, & against all challengers—is that no such perfect piece of blank verse has ever been written by an American. You have therein surpassed yourself— Not to dwell upon individual lines, I wd' especially refer to the descriptions of the river Lethe, & the rush of ghosts to the Styx. These passages are glorious. Indeed the whole conception is wonderfully striking— I say all this from the fullness of *entire sincerity*.

Why is your book delayed so long? I had expected to receive it at least a month ago— Let me remind you that I was promised a copy—. I also have a small vol. in press composed mainly of that most unpopular species of verse—the Sonnet.

There is much truth undoubtedly in what you say of Simms. He has no tact—discretion, or judgment, [.] But if you knew the circumstances of his career—what, from boyhood he has had to contend against here, your surprise at his Conduct would be vastly modified. There is great nobility at the bottom of his nature, but the surface is not pre-possessing.

To me he has always been a kind friend— & I regret his failure deeply.

You ask after my wife, & boy— They are both well *now*, but the *latter* nearly met his death of *croup* some nights ago— We were terribly alarmed.

Your friend Boker's Dramas are very vigorous, and artistic. Many of his Sonnets too, strike me as among the best things of the class that I know. The Sonnet is a favorite of mine. Generally, it is much misunderstood.

I hope you will be able to decypher this scrawl. I have sprained my wrist, & can hardly hold a pen.

Wife & self unite in love to Mrs Stoddard, and the baby— Say to Mrs S. that I can hardly forbear quarrelling with her in consequence of the abrupt withdrawal of her poems.

She should not have so served me—

> Write soon, & Believe me dear Richard,
>
> Yrs Ever,
>
> P H Hayne.

P. S D—n sectional difficulties. What have *we*—(I and you), to do with Politics. Many a pretty fellow has been ruined by that accursed trade already. Let it alone. Let it alone—

[Harper and Calvo, of Charleston, who brought out Hayne's second volume (*Sonnets and Other Poems*, 1857) at Hayne's expense, would properly be called job printers rather than publishers. · For advertising Hayne probably had to depend solely upon reviews.

William Gilmore Simms (1806–1870), novelist, poet, editor, critic, playwright, biographer, historian, was the leading prose writer of Charleston, as Henry Timrod (1828–1867) was the best Charleston poet. Hayne was the most loyal friend and champion of the two. Simms was editor of *The Southern Quarterly Review* of Charleston from 1849 until 1855. Because of financial difficulties of the magazine and a quarrel with the publisher, Simms gave up the editorship, after which the magazine was moved to Columbia, where it continued until February, 1857. This may explain Simms's failure referred to.

George Henry Boker (1823–1890) was the Philadelphia poet, dramatist, and diplomat. His best play is *Francesca da Rimini* (1855). His best collections are *Plays and Poems*, two volumes (1856), and *Poems of the War* (1864). Stoddard met Boker in 1848, through Bayard Taylor, and their acquaintance rapidly developed into an intimate friendship. In the third letter below Hayne tells of meeting Boker in Philadelphia. See also Jay B. Hubbell, "George Henry Boker, Paul Hamilton Hayne, and Charles Warren Stoddard: Some Unpublished Letters," *American Literature*, V, 146–165.]

No. 8

PAUL HAMILTON HAYNE to RICHARD HENRY STODDARD (AND NOTE TO ELIZABETH DREW BARSTOW STODDARD)

Charleston Dec 30*th* 1856.

My Dear Richard;

Yours of the 24*th* I have rec*d*, & I need scarcely say, *read* with great pleasure— You are *now* my *only* Northern correspondent, & your epistles are equally novel, & interesting ·to me— Send me your book at once, directing it to the care of Jno Russell[,] King S*t* (Charleston)— Follow this direction, & I c'ant fail to receive it— I am anxious to see your new publication. I expect a great deal from it. Indeed, Stoddard, you have achieved a permanent place among our American poets— And depend upon it, the position is unique, original, entirely *your own*. One of these days I shall do you justice in our So Maga— If you *can* (apropos of the Magazine), let me have your poem by the *5th* February, it will suit *exactly;* we come out on the *1st March*—

You speak of having been *lazy*— I think, considering your duties in the *Custom House,* that you have been industrious enough— For God's sake d'ont overwork yourself—! Your constitution is *not* Herculean, & you c'ant stand it—

The strictures on the *Sonnet* I sent you, seem to me correct in the main; "meek peace" is *not* good, & *"patience" is* good; unfortunately I cannot have an opportunity of correcting it now; the M. S. is out of my hands— About the impropriety of "crowning" a stream with "sleep" I confess myself doubtful. The figure is old. It occurs in the 3rd Book of the *"Fairy Queen"*. In Sir Philip Sidney's "Arcadia" (unless I am much mistaken) it is used more than once— Of course a bad image, comparison, a metaphor ca'nt [*sic*] be bolstered up by mere authority, but *is* the idea incorrect *per se.?*— It is an open question—

I have almost finished a notice of Geo Boker's "Plays & Poems", wh' perhaps you may like—Boker is *the* Dramatist of America— Apart from his constructive power, his *style* is the most direct, vigorous, & idiomatic I know—

I *am* about to publish as you suppose a new vol, of verses—a very, *very* small vol; It consists mostly of *Sonnets,* & is a simple *brochure*— The fact is I am just beginning to know what Poetry *should be,* & certainly, after this, I shall print nothing that does not at least possess *grit.*

Yrs Faithfully;
P H Hayne—

[At the bottom of the same letter:]

My Dear Mrs Stoddard;

Is it possible that I could have been guilty of the rudeness, & *injustice* of *not* saying distinctly that in my opinion your poems were *excellent,* especially the Lyric in seven quatrains? It was a simple inadvertence for which I beg you to pardon me— *Anything* from your pen My dear Madam, I shall be most happy to receive— I am *sincere* in saying this;

therefore pray *believe me*— How is your little boy—?— I long to see the youth, & (D. V) *intend* to see him next summer—

Pray, have you read Mrs Browning's last work, "Aurora Leigh"? Tell me what you think of it?

Believe me,
Most Truly Yrs
P. H. Hayne

[John Russell was the Charleston bookseller who assisted Hayne in editing and managing the magazine which bore his name. The intellectual men of the city often met at his shop in the 1850's for informal discussions.

"The strictures on the *Sonnet* I sent you": the sonnet may be "Pent in This Common Sphere" (*Complete Edition*, pp. 26–7). The thirteenth line reads:

Gleam by the drowsy streamlets sleep hath crown'd . . . .

Hayne's review of Boker's *Plays and Poems* and Stoddard's *Songs of Summer* appeared in · *Russell's Magazine* for April, 1857 (I, 90–92). Hayne's *Complete Edition* (p. 268) contains a sonnet with this title and headnote: "To George H. Boker. Addressed to George H. Boker, of Philadelphia—after the perusal of Sonnets contained in his 'Plays and Poems.'"

The sketches, poems, and stories of Stoddard's wife (Elizabeth Drew Barstow Stoddard) appeared in the *Atlantic*, the *Knickerbocker*, *Harper's*, *Appleton's*, and other magazines.

Elizabeth Barrett Browning's *Aurora Leigh* (1856) was reviewed in *Russell's Magazine* for June, 1857 (I, 274–5).]

No. 9

PAUL HAMILTON HAYNE to RICHARD HENRY
STODDARD

Charleston Jan 3rd 1857

My Dear Richard;

I answered your last in full, directing my reply to *No 52 E 24th St*. Now, I am by no means certain that this is your direction, as your letter apprizing me of the same has been mislaid. Therefore let me repeat some things contained in that communication—

1*st:* You must not fail to send me by the 5*th* February (at latest) the *Poem* I engaged. (Pray write it in blank-verse if convenient—of course this is simply a suggestion.)

2nd. Let me enroll your name among the names of my *regular contributors.*

3rd, Mail me your book, care of *Jno Russell*[,] *King St*[.,] *Charleston.*

4*th* Tell your wife that she must write for me. Her last poems were most acceptable—

Best regards to young Richard & Mrs S—
Believe me Ever yrs—
P H Hayne

[The name of Stoddard's son was Wilson.]

No. 10

PAUL HAMILTON HAYNE to RICHARD HENRY STODDARD

Charleston 10*th* Feb. 1857.

My Dear Richard;

x I have just returned from a long, arduous, & disagreeable canvassing & lecturing tour in the upper part of *So,* the lower part of N*o* Carolina— Such a time as I had of it! In Charlotte, (look on your map, & see where that is), the thermometer fell to within one degree, & a half of *zero.* Our houses are not like yours, hermetically sealed, & therefore I suffered,—toes, hands, feet, & especially my very elegantly turned-up *nose,* were shockingly victimized— Your last note (that of Feb 3*rd*) reached me at Columbia. I find here at home your poem, together with *two* long, kind letters, and a brief lyric from Mrs Stoddard— Thanks for them all— Of course I accept the *two poems with pleasure,* & accede without demur to your terms. The inexcusable indolence of Carlisle has put back our periodical abominably— Neither the money-matters, nor the printing-matters are as yet arranged— Do not I beseech you my dear fellow, suppose for one moment that the concern is failing at the very outset— Nothing of the kind— It is simply *delayed*.

What you say about my appreciation of your poems is, I trust correct— I d'ont know whether the warm personal attachment I feel towards you has re-acted upon my estimation of your autorial claims, but certain it is, that I love your verse—& love it heartily—. Let me say at once what I intend doing. Just so soon as practicable I shall write a careful, impartial, & *analytical* critique upon *Boker* & *yourself*. I like Boker *as a man*, altho somehow I am always thinking that He regards *me*, (to use a Milesian vulgarism), as the smallest sort of *"potato"*— I was out of sorts when we met in Philadelphia, & was intensely stupid whenever I conversed with him— I defer what I have to say in regard to your "Songs of Summer," until I can compose the Review alluded to. Considering your unquestionably unique position in American Poetry, & considering your special claim upon *them*, the Putnam clique have snubbed you shamefully— I know not what *your* opinion of Howadji Curtis may be, but, (with the amplest allowance of *his* great ability), I thoroughly, and conscientiously *detest him*. At the bottom of all his brilliancy he is a *snob*.

The idea of patronizing *you*, of patronizing—(or at least *by comparison*, faintly *praising* Geo Boker)—& then falling on his knees before the author of *Passion Flowers*, who vigorous as she may be, is a sort of rhyming Mrs Caudle who takes the whole world into confidence, wailing her individual woes *ad nauseam* (& many of the these[?] are *erotic*),— is *monstrous*.

The fact is, Stoddard, that you must quit these cliques, & write for *me*. A modest request is'nt it. Well! *after* the *maga* has taken firm root, you will as the papers say, find it "to your advantage"— I am free to confess that for the *first year* I can afford to purchase from you but *two* or *three long poems*, like the one just sent me—but briefer lyrics you must compose *ad libitum*. My collections of *Joint-Stock* are tardy, but the money is sure in the end. You sh'ant lose anything pecuniarily by "Russell's Magazine", & hereafter I promise you shall *gain by* it. "The laborer is worthy &c"[.]

I will mail you a check, (with $10 for *Mrs* S—) the moment I can. Pardon a little unavoidable delay— I am sure that you have no suspicions of me upon *this* score—

Did you receive my book of "Sonnets"—?— I wrote to Carlisle entreating him to send you a copy, but he's untrustworthy about such things, & I should'nt be surprised to find that my request was neglected. If so, I will immediately remedy the negligence.

My Review comes out in Russell's *Second* number, and is headed Geo. H Boker, and Richard Henry Stoddard—

—Might I venture to send a copy of my poor verses to Boker? Answer this soon,

> & Believe me Truly & affectionately *Yrs.*
>
> P. H. H.

P. S. Let me say emphatically that your Poem is noble *noble;* I wish that I could afford to pay $100 for it without more gammon— Mrs S' lyric is warm in coloring, & original in conception, a quaint, unique, suggestive piece for wh' I feel much obliged— Say to her that I shall answer her kind note tomorrow. Nothing but a stress of business prevents my replying now—

> P. H. H.

[F. L. Mott says (*op. cit.*, II, 489): "W. B. Carlisle, a Charleston journalist, was announced as co-editor [of *Russell's Magazine*] with Hayne; but he proved a disappointment to Russell and Hayne, and after the second number Russell himself became an associate editor."

See the note on the last letter but one for a reference to Hayne's critique on Boker and Stoddard.

"Howadji Curtis": Hayne takes this name for George William Curtis from the latter's *Nile Notes of a Howadji* (1851) and *The Howadji in Syria* (1852).

Passion Flowers, a collection of lyrics published anonymously by Ticknor, Reed, and Fields (Boston) in 1854, is by Julia Ward Howe (1819–1910), best remembered for her war song "Battle-Hymn of the Republic."

Mrs. Caudle's Curtain Lectures, by Douglas William Jerrold (1803–1857), appeared in *Punch* in 1845 and in book form the following year.]

No. 11

PAUL HAMILTON HAYNE to RICHARD HENRY STODDARD

Charleston *22nd* Feb 1857

My Dear Richard;

I rec*d* yours of the 17*th* yesterday—. My time is so limited just now, that I have leisure only to beg that the exquisite Persian anacreontic contained in your letter may be given to me.

Pray write *immediately*, and say whether I may take it, (on your own terms)—for if you consent, it shall appear in the *first* no— Pieces of this, & a similar length are what I especially desire during the first year.

I know that you will let me have them as reasonably as you can afford to, for as I said before our Stock comes in slowly at *first*.

+ The check for "Herod Agrippa &c" you may expect soon. I shall register the letter containing it, so that there can be no mistake.

X Say to *Mrs* Stoddard that I shall write to her, the moment the printer's Devil condescends to grant me a little peace. I wish to say many things to her in reference to divers matters interesting I believe to us both.

Believe me Ever Truly

P. H. Hayne

P. S. A notice of the "Sonnets" from your pen— I should of course feel grateful for—

[The poems in *Russell's Magazine* are unsigned, but I recognize these as Stoddard's (and there may be others by him):
"Oriental Lyrics," I (April, 1857), 81.
"Herod Agrippa and the Owl," I (May, 1857), 123–27.
"From the Persian of Sadi," I (August, 1857), 426.
"Lines. *(Oriental)*," I (September, 1857), 533.]

No. 12

PAUL HAMILTON HAYNE to RICHARD HENRY STODDARD

Charleston April 20*th* 1857

My *Dear Richard;*

Why the deuce do you commence your last letter with the formal address of "My dear *Hayne*"—?— D'ont address me by my surname again— In *three days* from date, you will receive a check for $60—would to God it were a check for *thrice* the *amount*—

The reason why the poem of "Herod Agrippa & the Owl" was *not* published in the first no: of "Russell's," is briefly this: Contrary to my *express orders* (I was absent in the country at the time), the Foreman actually printed the poem as the very last article in the number— Now, I was determined to make it the poetical "*leader*," & consequently preferred that it should come *first* in the 2nd number, to it's occupying a subordinate position in the *1st*— In the *July* no: of the Magz I intend to publish a careful & elaborate review of *Boker,* & *yourself.* I hope you'll like it—

I owe you many thanks for the beautiful notice of my *Sonnets* which appeared in the "Home Journal"— Ah! if I could believe all that—but—&c; Knowing that *you* are perfectly sincere I yet look upon myself—*(poetically)* as a "poor devil"— No doubt the Magz (Russell's) must seem to you a rather *barbarous* affair—but—my dear Richard, we were *Compelled* to pitch into Putnam— D'ont think me so blind as to suppose that I am unaware of the fact that we are sure to get the very *devil* in return— We are fully prepared for *it:* or even for for [*sic*] that silent *contempt* which is worse than "*the devil*"—

Pray present my best regards to Mrs Stoddard, (whose poem comes out in the June no:) & also, *remember* me (!!)

to the *"baby,"* whose acquaintance (God willing) I shall make
next summer—

Most Truly & affectionately Yr's

P H Hayne

[The cooling of the friendship between Hayne and Stoddard, fore-
shadowed in this letter, was due, I think, to these causes: Hayne's in-
ability to accept and promptly pay for as many poems as he had invited
Stoddard to contribute to *Russell's Magazine;* certain inconsequential
affectations of Hayne which may have irritated Stoddard; Stoddard's well-
known tactlessness, which sometimes amounted to rather brutal frankness; Stoddard's strong feeling against the South's "infernal institution"
and the spirited defense of the South and her "peculiar institution" in
Russell's Magazine, though Hayne did not wish to debate the question
with Stoddard, insisting that the two of them were poets and should not
quarrel over politics. No doubt Stoddard did not feel that it was merely
a political question. When their correspondence was renewed for a while
after the war, Hayne sent Stoddard poems to dispose of for him to Northern
magazines. Hayne later did the same thing in the case of Moses Coit
Tyler. But whereas Tyler was glad to do what he could to help Hayne,
Stoddard may have felt that Hayne should not have made this request of
him. Apparently it was Stoddard who broke off the correspondence.
See Hayne's references to him in the letter to Whipple dated March 13,
1872 (No. 32), and those to Tyler dated December 10 and December 16,
1878 (No. 194 and No. 195).]

No. 13

PAUL HAMILTON HAYNE to RICHARD HENRY
STODDARD

Charleston May *2nd* 1857.

My Dear Richard;

I have been too busy of late to write, so pray excuse my
protracted silence. The *$60* dollars, owing you for "Herod
Agrippa", which is the leading poem in the May no: of
Russell's Magaz, (I hope you have rec*d* it), was duly paid
last week to the Adam's Expressman— Is it not all right?
Pray inform me immediately.

"Herod Agrippa" is a noble poem, & *must* attract general
attention—

+ I have only leisure now to ask how you are, & to thank you for your Contribution—

> Ever Affectionately yrs
> P H Hayne

No. 14

PAUL HAMILTON HAYNE to RICHARD HENRY STODDARD

> *Charleston Feb 28th 1858*

My Dear Stoddard;

I know by your *silence,* by the fact that my *last* letter has remained *unanswered,* that something in my conduct has given you *serious,* & *lasting offence.* I now write to say in *all sincerity* that *no offence* was designed, that if any hasty expression of mine appeared *unjust,* or *insulting,* I *heartily regret it.* Towards Mrs Stoddard, & yourself I may say with truth, that ever since 1852, I have entertained feelings not merely of *respect,* but of *sincere affection.*

You *alone* of *all* my Northern friends, seemed to possess the warm blood, & the *high* soul of the *South.* With *you* alone could I experience entire *sympathy,* and therefore, I can no longer rest contented with this cloud glooming between us.

Will you not accept my *apology,* and reply to the present communication? If you do not forget & forgive whatever may have appeared unwarrantable in my conduct then, I have utterly mistaken your character, & shall never attempt again to comprehend *any* human *soul.*

Pray answer this note, & let me know among other things, to what extent I am your debtor for the Eastern Songs &c published in *"Russell's Magazine".* You will not, I think, misunderstand my motive in writing this letter. There are *few* whose friendship I value, but *of* the few I can afford to lose not *one.*

> Ever Truly Yrs
> Paul H Hayne

No. 15

PAUL HAMILTON HAYNE to RICHARD HENRY
STODDARD

Charleston March 29*th* 1859.

My Dear Stoddard;

You must pardon my *long* silence. For more than a year past, I have *not* been in a condition to correspond even with my *best friends*. Without referring to my *own health* which has been (at times) very feeble, I have only to tell you that my wife, (whom I am sure you remember with kindly feelings), has been repeatedly at death's door,—to excuse my *seeming* neglect. Thank God! we are *both* better *now*. Something resembling health, & strength, has re-visited me, & in company with the blessed boon, hope, & buoyant feelings are mine once more. My disease has been a *cross* between the *liver*-complaint common in these low latitudes, and the *lung*-complaint, which is common at the North. But I have fought against both *liver* & *lungs*, & have succeeded, if *not* in *conquering*, at least, in keeping the enemy *at bay*. Do not pronounce me egotistical. Thus much I felt bound to say, in order to explain my protracted silence. Now, I *beseech* you to renew the old correspondence. Altho *years* have elapsed, it appears to me as if I had parted from you *only* yesterday. And believe me, Stoddard, when I say that I have always looked upon you as a *true friend*. Brief as our intercourse— our *actual personal* intercourse—has been, there are few individuals in this world towards whom all my better & higher feelings have been more thoroughly drawn out. For God's sake d'ont laugh at me, & declare that I am a sentimental fool.

Have you stopped writing for the magazines.? It is very rarely that I see your name among the contributors to our popular periodicals. Of course, you take the "Atlantic!" Are you able to inform me by whom a poem in the last (April) number, called "A Prayer for Life," is written?—

Accompanying this letter, I send you a very imperfect performance of mine own, which was delivered before the *"Carolina Art Association"* of *this City*, together with a "legend" versified from Leigh Hunt's *"Indicator."* Tell me how you like, or *dislike* them.

I hope your little boy is well. Ours has grown wonderfully of late, and his *health* is almost *perfect*. O! how I long to see Mrs Stoddard, & yourself once more!! If the stars favour me, I shall visit NYork in *August*, & then our old pleasant acquaintance shall be renewed.

With best regards to your wife, I
remain *Dear Stoddard*,

Faithfully Yours,

Paul H Hayne

["A Prayer for Life": it appeared in the *Atlantic Monthly* for April, 1859 (III, 419–423). The index to the *Atlantic* issued in 1889 attributes it to G. S. Burleigh.

For "Ode. Delivered on the First Anniversary of the Carolina Art Association, Feb. 10, 1856," see Hayne's *Complete Edition*, pp. 9–13. The year 1856 is an error for 1859. The Carolina Art Association held its first anniversary at Hibernian Hall, Charleston, on February 10, 1859. Nathaniel Russell Middleton, President of the College of Charleston, was the main speaker. The Charleston *Daily Courier* announced on February 10, 1859: "Paul H. Hayne, our gifted young laureate, will pronounce an original poem on the occasion." The issue for the following day (February 11) devoted one and a half columns to Middleton's address and Hayne's poem. I quote from the article: "On the conclusion of the address, Mr. Paul H. Hayne arose and delivered an original ode. This exquisite production fell on the ear of the enchained auditory like notes of sweetest music." That was written in the Oratorical Age.

In *Russell's Magazine* for April, 1859 (V, 30–37), appeared "Avolio— A Legend of the Island of Cos." Hayne wrote this footnote: "The authority for this Legend will be found in a paper called 'The Daughter of Hippocrates,' which first appeared in Leigh Hunts' [*sic*] 'Indicator.'" This poem gave its title to Hayne's volume of 1860. For the *Complete Edition* (pp. 178–87) Hayne rewrote the poem and gave it the title "The Vengeance of the Goddess Diana."]

No. 16

PAUL HAMILTON HAYNE to RICHARD HENRY STODDARD

Charleston (S. C.) Aug 28th 1859.

My Dear Stoddard;

—It is a long, a *very long* time, since I have heard *of,* or *from* you. But notwithstanding *this,* I look upon you *as a friend.* It would be altogether *absurd* in me to expect you to correspond regularly with a man, whose home is a *thousand* miles from *yours;*—particularly, when I reflect upon the engrossing nature of your business in NYork. But although the remembrance may have become, to *you, dim,* if not *wholly obliterated,* of the brief communion between us in *1855,*— *I* am not ashamed to confess that I revert to that period as one of the happiest episodes of a life, *not* perhaps, very brilliant, or, entertaining.

Often, & often, I have wished to see you Since;—to tell you how much comfort, and pleasure I have derived from your *poetry,*—& with what *sincere* longing, I have yearned to meet Mrs Stoddard & yourself, *once more.*

The position of a literary man at the *South* is anomalous, & by no means agreeable.. You will not accuse me of a want of *patriotism,* when I declare, that the condition of things amongst us,—is *Such,* as to *compel* a poet (for example), to publish *abroad,* if he desires his vo*l* to receive the *slightest* degree of attention. For *two years* I edited (with great pains & labour) "Russell's Magazine"—but *not one cent* have I rec*d* in payment. In 1857, (of course, at my *own* expense), I published a small book (chiefly of *Sonnets*), which you were kind enough to review only *too* favourably in the *"Home Journal."* *Three hundred copies,* were issued by Messsr. *Harper & Calvo* of this city, *more* than *100* of which, now burden the Shelves of my *library.*

There's encouragement for you!!

Pray, forgive this *egotism.*

I trust that *Mrs Stoddard,* & yourself are in good *health.* And *how* is the little *boy,* to whom you addressed that manly & feeling poem (composed in the *"In Memoriam"* verse,) which appeared in your last volume?— But *perhaps,* your family has increased;—perhaps, in *addition* to the "eldest son, and heir," you have been blessed with a sweet *daughter!*— *If* so, I may be allowed to sympathise with, & warmly to congratulate you. For *myself, dear Stoddard,* I have but *one* child—, a boy. He is *really* a noble little fellow, full of spirit, vigour, and enthusiasm.

Altho he c'ant understand them,—I sometimes read aloud to the urchin pieces from Tennyson, & from our *own* poets, &c. He opens his *eyes,* and claps his *hands,*—but *there* his demonstrations of approval—cease.

Do not fail to answer this letter. I am sincerely anxious to hear something of you, both in a *literary,* & *social* point of view.

Apropos, of *literature,* I have now in the press of *"Ticknor & Fields,"* a volume of poems (likely to occupy about *200* pages *duodecimo*)—, which are *certainly* much better than any of my former verses. *This,* I know, is but small praise;— nevertheless, I entertain *some* hope of the success of the book;—*i. e.* I hope, the Northern journalists *may* rank me as a *respectable,* if not a *brilliant* singer.

Have you heard from *Boker lately?* A report reached me yesterday that he is in *Europe. My wife* (whose health is very feeble), begs to be kindly remembered to *Mrs Stoddard;* Present my *best regards* to her,—& Believe me,

Ever Yours,

P. H. Hayne

[Letter No. 30 shows that Hayne was in New England in the late summer and early fall of 1853. In the letter to Stoddard dated July 28, 1855 (No. 2), Hayne says he had seen Stoddard the preceding summer and doubted whether he would visit New York again in years. In No. 31 (written in 1859) he implies that he had not been to Boston since 1854. But in several later letters he says he visited in the North (New York and New England) in 1855, though he may have been thinking of 1854. In 1859 he took his sick wife to a medical specialist in Philadelphia. In 1873 Hayne and his son visited New York and Boston. The most valuable new personal acquaintance he made was with Moses Coit Tyler. On this journey they visited Poe's grave in Baltimore, Timrod's widow in Washington, and John Russell in Charleston. In 1879 Hayne and his wife went to the North again and saw Stedman and others in New York, Longfellow at Cambridge, and Whittier at Oak Knoll. According to Albert Mordell (*Quaker Militant: John Greenleaf Whittier*, Boston and New York, Houghton Mifflin Company, 1933, p. 283), "Hayne visited Whittier a second time in the summer of 1885, not long before his own death."

By publishing "abroad," of course Hayne means in the North.

The failure of an editor to receive a salary was nothing unusual. In discussing the situation in the 1840's Mott says (*op. cit.*, I, 512): "Most reviews, however, both secular and religious, paid little or nothing to their editors." Simms became editor of the *Southern Quarterly Review* in 1849 at a salary of a thousand dollars a year, but he had trouble collecting it. This salary equaled that of most of the Northern editorships of the time, and was larger than the income of many college professors.

The sale of the second volume of Hayne's poetry seems to have been at least as good as that of his first volume, published in Boston. The latter, Hayne said, did not sell in the North and over a hundred copies were sold in Charleston. The sale of the second volume was between one hundred and two hundred copies.

Stoddard's second son was born in 1859 but died within a few months.

"I sometimes read aloud to the urchin pieces from Tennyson": Hayne's son (William Hamilton Hayne, 1856–1929) became a poet of considerable ability.

Hayne's third volume (*Avolio: A Legend of the Island of Cos*, Boston, Ticknor and Fields, 1860) came from the press before the end of 1859.]

No. 17

PAUL HAMILTON HAYNE to RICHARD HENRY STODDARD

Charleston, Dec 3rd 1859.

My Dear Stoddard;

It was *really* a great pleasure to me, when, (opening a letter recd from NYork yesterday,)—I found your well-known signature at the end thereof. True! you have not written for an age, but it is quite eno' for me to learn that you are *still*, "as much my friend, as if you wrote every month, or week."— I am *not* punctilious, Heaven knows, in the matter of correspondence. Once convinced that the person to whom I write, does not keep silence because of *indifference*, or want of affection, I feel perfectly content, & am willing to address to him a *dozen* letters, without receiving any definite reply.

It was only very *recently* that I heard your name mentioned in connection with the authorship of "Humboldt's Life". The book I have not *yet* procured, but (D V), I propose getting it this very morning, & reading it with care.

—I rejoice but, of course, am in no wise, *surprised* to hear of its generally warm reception by the Public, & the ˙Press. As for the "notice" in the *"Columbia,"* (*not* the *Charleston*) *"Courant,"*—pray cease to experience the *slightest "annoyance"* on *that* account. Mr Howard H Caldwell, the Editor, & a scion of one of our respectable up-country families, is a man of *some talent*, and many accomplishments, but in attempting to be a *critic*, & a *poet*, he has failed in both vocations. A book of verses was issued for him in Boston, *two* years ago, which met with the "damnation" of cold "praise", or, hot abuse, & ever since, Caldwell, spoiled by the flattery of friends at home, & by his own vain heart, has nourished a bitter hatred of everything Northern, or "Yankee," as *he* elegantly terms it, which he displays in a weak way by *striving* to depreciate the claims of some of your *best* writers. Soon after his "notice" of you, he admitted into his paper a series of the most stupid, & malignant articles, the purpose of which was, to prove that Oliver Wendall [*sic*] Holmes' admirable *"Professor at the Breakfast Table,"* is a very mediocre, & vastly over-estimated work (!!) "The Courant" has, however expired; like an angry snake—, of its own superabundant venom. x x x Thank you for having read my vol, and telling me the truth—what I *feel* to be the truth—about it. So long as you think I have *some* of the right stuff in me, which *may* hereafter, be worked up into really artistic fabrics—I am *more* than *satisfied*. You are right in your belief that I *labor* on my verses. Therefore, when I find in them such grave faults as those pointed out by you in the first passages of "Avolio," I confess, that for a moment, I experience a sensation *akin* to dismay. Please tell me frankly; did *you ever* encounter in any *elaborate* piece of yours *after* publication, artistic blunders, or errors of expression which disappointed, & vexed you?— I mean in any poem, which, *previously,* you deemed free from such mistakes? because you had written & re-written,—& studied, & rë-studied the language, rhythm, metre, & everything about it?— If so, did you not feel angry and annoyed?. But, *"courage! mon* ami!" I say to myself. ["]After all, Stoddard, & other friends in whom I put hearty trust, tell me to work on, & I may yet achieve something."— So, I buckle on the harness once more,—& take the field cheerfully. Enough of this egotism.

I am glad to hear of your continued good health, & glad too, be assured, to observe how steadily you rise in the world of Letters. 'Tis a good thing for a poet to write *prose* occasionally. It strengthens his muscles. Mr*s* Stoddard, & the boy also, are well you say. Thank God for *that,* my dear fellow. as [*sic*] for my own "wee wife," the poor little thing has been suffering for years. I carried her to Philadelphia last summer, placed her under Dr Meig's care, & hoped to see her recover. Alas! upon our return, there was another relapse, & ever since, her health has been radically bad.

My *boy* is, however, a picture of hearty Childhood. He is *3* years and *8* months old, eats—, oh! Lord! *how̧* he *does* eat!— and has the lungs of a young Stentor, which are exerted for the benefit of his "distressed parents" every morning, in the shape of a sort of oration, or disquisition upon "every thiñg", which he begins regularly at 5 o'clock *A. M.* & continues with amazing loquacity, until we are both *thoroughly* roused, & literally *shaken* out of any disposition to sleep again.

Now, 5 *A M* in Winter *is* early, & morning naps are proverbially "sweet." Reflect, therefore, upon the nature of the sacrifice, we (the *aforesaid* parents), are called upon to make! By the way, if you will only consent to mail me your son's daguerreotype, (I never *could* spell that word), I shall, confess myself greatly your debtor, & will (if you desire it) return the compliment, by sending you a similar likeness of my own boy.

When you write, furnish me with your present direction, the *no* of the Street &c. My wife's *best* regards to Mr*s* S., &

yourself. She beg's [*sic*] you to *kiss* the little Stoddard for her; & moreover, unites in my request with reference to his picture.

Believe me now, as always,

Most faithfully your

— *friend,* —

Paul H Hayne.

P. S. Pardon my alluding *again* to so delicate, & disagreeable a topic, but can you tell me anything of *"Ada Clare"*. I see she contributes to the *"Saturday Press."*

Apropos, of this spirited journal, I wonder *who* the *Editor* is: Aldrich, or, Clapp?

Yrs P. H. H.

[In his *Recollections Personal and Literary* Stoddard admits that several of his friends (including Bayard Taylor) had occasion to complain of his failure to write, and adds that they would not call him a man of letters. In the same work he says (pp. 253–4): "While living with Taylor [for two years in the late 1850's] I was temerarious enough to undertake a popular life of his friend Humboldt. I succeeded after a fashion, and, helped by an introduction which he contributed, the venture was successful." The title is *The Life, Travels, and Books of Alexander von Humboldt* (New York: Rudd and Carleton, 1860). Stoddard further comments (*op. cit.*, p. 299): "My poetry is my best work, but one cannot live by poetry, which must be to most poets its own exceeding great reward. I taught myself to write prose. . . ." Hayne wrote prose too but was determined to live by his poetry mainly, and succeeded after a fashion, though the struggle was intense. But Stoddard's testimony should serve as an adequate reply to those critics who assert that the struggle of Southern poets is due solely to intellectual darkness south of the Mason-Dixon line.

Howard Hayne Caldwell (1831–1858) was a South Carolina poet and journalist. His two volumes of poetry were *Oliatta and Other Poems* (1855) and *Poems* (1858). The second volume (Boston: Whittemore, Niles, and Hall) was reviewed in *Russell's Magazine* for April, 1858 (III, 36–47). The critic was sympathetic but frankly pointed out the faults of Caldwell's poetry. In another letter Hayne says that Simms wrote this review.

After Hayne and his wife moved to Copse Hill (in the pine woods sixteen miles west of Augusta, Georgia), Mary's health was much better than his. He had tuberculosis. I am uncertain how early it developed, but he complains of having the "lung" trouble in the 1850's.

Henry Clapp (1814–1875) is best known as the king of the New York Bohemians at Pfaff's and as the founder and editor of the New York *Saturday Press* (1858–1860, 1865–1866).

Thomas Bailey Aldrich (1836–1907), the story-writer, poet, novelist, essayist, playwright, critic, and editor, was on the staff of the *Saturday Press* at the beginning, but left it after a few months. In New York he did critical (and sometimes editorial) work on the *Evening Mirror,* the *Home Journal,* and the *Illustrated News;* in Boston he edited *Every Saturday* (1865–1874) and the *Atlantic Monthly* (1881–1890). Hayne met Aldrich in Cambridge in 1873.]

No. 18

PAUL HAMILTON HAYNE to RICHARD HENRY STODDARD

Charleston, Feb. 14*th* 1860.

My Dear Stoddard;

—Your welcome note of the 9th has just been placed in my hands. The enclosed letter to Henry Timrod, I will keep for him, until his *return* to the city. He is now sojourning *somewhere* (I know not *where*), in the upper part of this State, & were I to mail your communication to him, it wd' be all *guesswork.* He would probably fail to receive your letter, for which I should feel sorry, because *Timrod* entertains a *very high* opinion of your capacity, & *nothing could* please him more, than any commendation coming from *you.*

I cannot tell you how *sincerely* gratified I am, to find, that my friend's vo*l* has not merely satisfied, but "charmed" you. Timrod possesses more ability, (*native,* & acquired,)—than *all* the other *young* poets of the *South,* placed together. For *myself,* (loving the man as I would a *brother*)—, *his* successes are *my* successes, *all* his triumphs—*mine.*

I wish—(if you can possibly manage it—) that you would give a brief notice of T—'s vo*l* in the New York "H. Journal," or, the "*Sat Press.*" By so doing, you will have contributed much to the encouragement of a young man of *real genius.*

Timrod (*not* "*Nimrod*[""])—(by the way he is especially sensitive about his name)—, is the son of a bookbinder of this city, who *was* (for he perished in the Florida war of 1828) a gentleman of *extraordinary talents,* which raised him far above the level of his trade, and gained him reputation among the *Literati* of the town, & the State.— His son is quite equal to the father. To turn to a different topic—, let me ask you what is the literary position of the *"Sat Press"* edited by Mr Clapp.? I observe that "Ada Clare" has become a regular Correspondent. Does she rank at all in the *"Literary* world of NYork"?

You kindly express a hope that "I & *mine"* are well. Would to God, it were possible to answer truthfully in the affirmative. But the fact is, that my poor little wife—(I believe you really liked her Stoddard)—, has, for 5 years been called upon simply—, *to endure.* Women (generally) at the South, break very soon. Our climate is a villainous one. In summer, altho the *heat* is never very intense—, there is a *something* (God knows *what)* in the atmosphere—, which enervates the vital energies, and leads to the worst descriptions of chronic diseases. I have proved *this* to my *mother* over & over again, but—she *will not* remove from the thrice accursed place.

I wish you to send me your "life of *Humboldt."* A few copies came to Charleston, while I happened to be absent, and they have all been sold. My purpose in preferring this request is, to make a full notice in some prominent Southern journal of your book. It is true, I had a chance of *somewhat* hastily perusing it, but *that* has only served to "whet my appetite."

If you send the book to *me personally* Care of "Russell & Jones" of Charleston, I will assuredly receive it.

What are your friends B. Taylor, & Aldrich doing *now?* Is the *latter* still connected with the *"Sat Press."?*

—I do not perceive his name under the Editorial head. *Apropos* of Mr Aldrich, how can I procure a copy of his *poems,* which (if I mistake not) were issued *not* long ago, in NYork? Can *you* send me one copy, also directed to "Russell & Jones," or, (better still) thro the Charleston P Office? I will remit to you *at once* the amount of postage, &—now that I reflect on it—, you had better send the "Life of Humboldt" in the same way. Please not to forget these requests. x x My wife begs

to be *especially* remembered to Mrs *Stoddard & yourself*—
With best regards to your wife, I am as ever

Faithfully

P H Hayne

[Hayne's estimate of Henry Timrod (1828–1867), his old classmate,
is correct; and his loyalty and readiness in acknowledging Timrod's
superior genius and talent are admirable. In 1873, nine years before a
collected edition of his own poems appeared, he collected the poems of
Timrod and wrote for the edition a memoir which is still the best
biography of his friend.

Timrod's *Poems* (Boston: Ticknor and Fields, 1860) was the volume
that "charmed" Stoddard. Timrod's best poems were written later and
most of them were collected by Hayne.

William Henry Timrod (1792–1838) was a Charleston bookbinder of
literary tastes and abilities. He published *Poems, on Various Subjects*
(1814) and contributed to several magazines. He served in the Florida
War of 1836 as a captain of the German Fusileers. (Hayne's error of
1828 for 1838, the date of the elder Timrod's death, is just a slip of the
pen.) Simms knew him well and both Simms and Hayne thought well
of his poetry. (See Jay B. Hubbell, *The Last Years of Henry Timrod
1864–1867* (Duke University Press, 1941), pp. 165–178).

The *Saturday Press* was notable for sparkle and sophistication. Although
it did not pay well, most writers of the time were eager to appear in it.
Mark Twain's "Jim Smiley and His Jumping Frog" appeared in it
November 18, 1865.

"Ada Clare": see Jane McElhenny in the notes following letter No. 1.

John Russell and James C. Jones were booksellers at 251 King Street,
Charleston.

Thomas Bailey Aldrich's *The Ballad of Babie Bell and Other Poems* appeared in 1859.]

No. 19

PAUL HAMILTON HAYNE to RICHARD HENRY
STODDARD

Ga R R. July 18*th* 1866.

Dear Stoddard;

Two weeks ago, I answered your long, affectionate letter,
directing my reply to the "Round Table" Office. I ventured
to enclose 5 small poems, asking you (if possible), to dispose

of them for me to the different periodicals &c. Now, I enclose 2 more, which you can hand to "the Galaxy," i. e. my
dear friend, if you have the time. Never would I have had
the conscience to bother you thus, but my position here
is well nigh *desperate.* One barrel of flour, & a box of what
sailors call "hard tack," stand between me, & starvation.
Jolly, is'nt it?

My purpose in sending these verses to you, is simply that
you may say a few words on my behalf to the publishers,
with whom I am wholly unacquainted.

It would be (to *you* I'm not ashamed to confess it),—a
real *charity.*

Heaven bless you, & yours, & keep you from the "slough
of Despond," in which I am now sinking, deeper & deeper.

Always Truly & affectionately Yours,

Paul H Hayne

My address is;

Box 260 Augusta

P. Office

[For a letter from Hayne to Stoddard dated July 1, 1866, see *American
Literature,* IV, 195–99 (ed. by Harry Shaw, Jr.).

The Round Table (1863–1869) was a New York weekly. Stoddard was
an assistant editor for a time.

The Galaxy (1866–1878) was a New York semimonthly which became
a monthly after its first year.]

No. 20

PAUL HAMILTON HAYNE to RICHARD HENRY
STODDARD

Sunday Sep 8*th* 1866.

Dear Stoddard;

Here are 2 *Sonnets,* which, if you think them of any
account, I hope you'll print for me in the "Literariana" of
the R. Table.

Of course, I offer them for *nothing*, &c.

Please send me your Lincoln ":Ode," & believe me,

Always Faithfully,

Paul H Hayne

[*The Round Table* had a section entitled "Literariana," made up mainly of miscellaneous items concerning books, magazines, authors, editors, and publishers. It often published poems which correspondents had sent in.

Stoddard's *Abraham Lincoln: a Horatian Ode* appeared in 1865. (See Stoddard's *Complete Edition*, pp. 276–83.)]

No. 21

PAUL HAMILTON HAYNE to RICHARD HENRY STODDARD

Sunday Oct 21*st* 1866.

My Dear Stoddard;

Please d'ont bother yourself further about those verse-trifles I sent you.

Keep them, or such as may suit your purpose, & issue the same in your "Literariana." I *give* them to you, together with the enclosed rhymes, always provided of course, that they d'ont fall below the "R. T." standard.

What a stupendous piece of conceit, & folly that letter of Reade's was, "anent" his new Tale!

Why the fellow must be crazy with arrogance, & vanity!

Is G. Gaunt so *deuced* wicked? The *notoriety* gained by the work will make its author's fortune.

I wish you could come & see me here in the quiet woods, during these fine autumnal days. We could have such a jolly time, hunting the *partridges* (which abound), & after a morning of sport, smoking our pipes, & paying tribute to *Bacchus*, in scurd [?] *Claret* (somebody sent me a *dz* bottles lately), or good *old Rye*, if you prefer, (as *I* do,) the more potent cordial.

I am very serious, & *heartily* in earnest with regard to this invitation: A cot bed I can spare you, & in the department of the *cuisine* why potatoes, bacon, eggs, &c can at least be had. Can't you get off for a week or two?—

By the way, I send another & longer piece *("De Profundis ad Altum")* which you are welcome to, for the R. T.

Always, old friend,

Believe me

affectionately & Truly Yrs

P H Hayne

P. S. C'ant you manage to mail me your long poem, the one translated into German? I am *very* anxious to see it, & your wife's *Tales*.

[*Griffith Gaunt, or Jealousy,* by the English author Charles Reade (1814–1884), ran serially in the *Atlantic Monthly* from December, 1865, through November, 1866. It was widely attacked as immoral. The titular hero marries a second time, bigamously, when he suspects a love affair between his first wife and a priest. *The Round Table* for July 28, 1866 (III, 472), called it "indecent" and "morally unfit for introduction into families." Reade sued the editors for $25,000 damages but got only six cents. (See Mott, III, 322–23.) Stoddard's *The King's Bell* (1863) was translated into German.]

No. 22

PAUL HAMILTON HAYNE to ELIZABETH DREW BARSTOW STODDARD

"Copse Hill," G*a* R. Road:

March 6*th* 1869.

My Dear Mr*s* Stoddard;

It is nearly *15* years since I had the pleasure of seeing you last. During that weary period, the mysterious Powers who rule our mortal fates have not been kind to me.

I have suffered from ill-health, from loss of friends, & finally, loss of fortune. The *war* ruined me. My home in Charleston was burnt. Bank stock, securities, Bonds, all "went by the board," & even our family-silver, including many curious *antiques,* became the spoil of Sherman's enterprising soldiers.

Thus, stripped of everything, I removed from the sea-coast of Carolina to the pine-barrens of Georgia.

Here my little family, *wife*, mother, & child, reside in a Lilliputian Cottage, on the top of a windy hill, with a small garden to yield us *vegetables*, & the tiniest *income* between us and starvation!

Still, we are not unhappy. My *morsel* of a wife has developed noble qualities of endurance, ingenuity, & patience. I work hard with the pen, and—all things considered—, we manage to make the very best of a hard life, & to triumph over untoward Circumstances.

Your kind heart will pardon this egotism.

Let me inquire concerning your own affairs, & Stoddard's.

The papers & magazines inform me that you have published 3 or 4 novels. Not a *single copy* of your works—so far as I can learn—, has been sent to the benighted South. *Who* were your Publishers? I ask, because I feel *exceedingly anxious* to procure *one* of your Tales at least.

Our acquaintanceship—tho brief—, is a charming memory to me, and I desire to see what you have done in the great world of art.

Stoddard kindly mailed me *his* last Poem, "The King's Bell", which we all read with a *genuine* delight. It is an admirable work of art, full of *pathos*, & inculcating a noble philosophy.

From what your husband wrote me, I am aware that you have been burdened with domestic afflictions. May I inquire how many children you have living now?—Briefly, *Dear Madame*, if the leisure offers, tell us how you are circumstanced at present—. No *idle* curiosity prompts the question.

My *wife* unites with me in kindly remembrance.

By the way, is *Stoddard* engaged upon any new work? His late verses in "Putnam's" assure me that the marvellous delicacy of his fancy has not declined—, that the brightness & purity of his genius remain in their fullest force.

I am *very, very* lonely here. Won't you be merciful, & answer this letter?— A single word from the outside world cheers me to a degree which any City denizen would deem extravagant. With earnest regards to Stoddard,

I am Faithfully Yours,

Paul H Hayne

Address, P. O. Box 635, Augusta Ga

[Elizabeth Stoddard's novels are *The Morgesons* (New York: Carleton, 1862), *Two Men* (New York: Bunce and Huntington, 1865), and *Temple House* (New York: Carleton and Company, 1867).

At the time of this letter the Stoddards had only one living child, a son named Lorimer, born in December, 1863. Their first-born son (Wilson, whom they called Willy) had died in December, 1861. In 1859 a second son had died in infancy.

Stoddard's "An Invocation" appeared in *Putnam's Monthly Magazine* for February, 1869 (III, 169).]

No. 23

PAUL HAMILTON HAYNE to RICHARD HENRY STODDARD

"Copse Hill," G*a* R. Road:
May 6*th* 1869.

My Dear Stoddard;

During the last 8 or 10 months I have written you several times, but I fear that my communications miscarried.

Having no P. Office here, we are compelled to rely upon the different Car-Conductors to post our letters.

Consequently, the said epistles, *go too often* to the dirty, & dismal domains of "Limbo," or perhaps, fairly to the devil!

I trust that better luck may attend my present effort, as I am exceedingly anxious to procure from you (if possible), a copy of the vo*l* you entitled *"Songs of Summer,"* published ages ago by Ticknor, & Fields.

Frankly, I'm too confoundedly *poor* to *purchase*, and am in no way ashamed to acknowledge my *impecuniosity*.

If therefore, you can— (without trouble or loss), *mail* me the book desired, I shall thank you with *all* my *heart*.

Believe me, I have a *special* reason for making this request. Altho my letters may not reach you, I can still in this "ultimate, dim Thule," hold some sort of communication with your spirit. Of late I've read with pleasure some exceedingly dainty verses from your pen in *"Appleton's Journal,"* and also in *"the Galaxy."* I had the honor of being near you in the *latter* magz, I mean among the "Choir of Songsters," as the Editor called them.

The "Nation", I perceive, in alluding to these pieces, spoke of the Poets *en masse* as *"more* than *minor,"* an elegant phrase which may possibly suit *me, & others,* but which was a simple *impertinence* as *applied* to *you!*

No doubt, however, you have long learned to *smile* at the malignity, or stupidity—as the case may be—of the *"more* than *minor"—Critics!.*

Let me hope that Mrs *Stoddard* is *well.* My *wife* sends her *best* remembrances, (recalling gently [?] those far off shores of her youth, upon which for a moment, we met, only to *part*).

My best regards likewise to your wife. We reside here, in the country of middle G*a,* upon a little farm of 18 acres, about *one acre* of which is cultivated. 'Tis a life of strange *monotony;* yet I have become so accustomed to *Solitude,* that a removal would shock me inexpressibly.

Drop me a line, *my old friend,* & Believe me,

Always Faithfully,

Paul H Hayne:

Address,

P. O. Box 635, Augusta, G*a*—

[Stoddard had sent Hayne a copy of *Songs of Summer* (1857) soon after publication, but Hayne's home and most of his books were burned during the war.

Stoddard's "Love Thy Neighbor" appeared in *Appleton's Journal* for April 3, 1869 (I, 16), and his "What's My Love Like?" appeared in the issue for April 10, 1869 (I, 49).

In the *Galaxy* for May, 1869 (VII, 729–34) appeared a number of poems grouped under the title "A Choir of Songsters." Among them was Stoddard's "Drifting" (p. 730), and the very next poem was Hayne's "Dolce For Niente." The *Nation* for April 29, 1869 (VIII, 335–37), contained an article entitled "The Magazines for May." In the discussion of the *Galaxy* (p. 337) occurred this sentence: "The rest of the *Galaxy* is all readable, except the 'Choir of Songsters,' in which some dozen or so of the minor, or more minor, poets sing for us in not very sweet contention." (The phrase "more than minor" does not occur in it.)

The New York Public Library has a copy of Hayne's "Sonnet" ("In yonder grim, funereal forest lies"), in Hayne's handwriting, together with the envelope, which Hayne addressed to "Mr. Richard Henry Stoddard, Literary Ed: N. Y. *Mail and Express*, New York City." The same sonnet, revised, is found in Hayne's *Complete Edition* (p. 154). The envelope bears the postmark "Atlanta Ga Jan 17," but no year is given. Stoddard became literary editor of the New York *Mail and Express* in 1880, and Hayne's *Complete Edition* came from the press about November, 1882.]

No. 24

PAUL HAMILTON HAYNE to JOHN REUBEN THOMPSON

Fort Sumter, (Charleston Harbor) Feb 15*th* (1862)

My Dear Friend;

Your kind note reached me some days ago. I take the first opportunity of replying. It is indeed, as you say, "a long & weary time" since we corresponded with each other. But in the terrible war, we are now waging, all *personal* interests & feelings must, for the nonce, be merged. x x Severe trials await us. The capture of "Roanoake Island" gives the enemy great advantages. How, in Heaven's name did it happen that only 2000, or 3000 men were left to maintain that important position?— But 'tis useless to complain *now*. We must fight to the last, & if need be, perish "red-handed". Your company the "Richmond Blues" have immortalized themselves. As for young *Wise*, he died an enviable death.

I have been at this post (Sumter) for *four* months. The chances are, that we shall soon be attacked in force. The Errickson Battery, & the mortar fleet of Porter, we have reason to believe, will pay us their respects.

Apropos of the chief object of your note, I enclose several poems, which may suit the forthcoming volume. Timrod's "*Ode*" is superb, uniting the thoughtfulness of Wordsworth, with the fire of Byron. For myself, I have written but *one* war-poem as yet. *That*, together with other productions, I'll send you in a week's time, perhaps in 3 or 4 days.

Your "brave, beautiful boy" *Willie* is (*I* think) quite as "brave" & "beautiful" as ever. Even now he often speaks of "M*r* Thompson". D'ont fear! he w'ont forget you, for the youth has a marvellous memory.

By the way, you had better look out, all of you, at Richmond! "The folds of the Anaconda" (Yankee phrase) *seem* gathering about the country, the "old Dominion" especially. But the blood of the Cavaliers, can *never succomb!*.

In these doubtful times, I must send you my blessing. If we never meet again, think *Oh! John*, that in me you have lost a *true friend*. God be with you.

Yours always,

Paul H Hayne

[John Reuben Thompson (1823–1873) was the Virginia editor, critic, and poet. He edited the *Southern Literary Messenger* from 1847 until 1860. In May, 1860, he joined the staff of the Augusta weekly *Southern Field and Fireside* but was back in Richmond early in January of 1861, and there he remained until the summer of 1864. During most of this time he served as a state official and did editorial work for the Richmond *Record* and the *Southern Illustrated News*. The end of the war found him in London, where he had gone to work for the Confederate cause. He remained for over a year longer, and returned to Richmond in the fall of 1866. After the spring of 1867 he lived in New York. In 1868 William Cullen Bryant made him literary editor of the New York *Evening Post*. He held this position until his final illness.

Roanoke Island in on the coast of North Carolina. In the Battle of Roanoke Island (1862), Captain O. Jennings Wise, formerly editor of the Richmond *Enquirer*, was mortally wounded. He was the son of Henry Alexander Wise, Confederate general, who had been governor of Virginia.

The attack upon Charleston "in force" came in 1863.

The *Monitor* was sometimes referred to as Ericsson's floating battery, after John Ericsson (1803–1889), Swedish engineer in America, who had designed it. The *Monitor* (a Federal ironclad with a revolving gun turret) fought a famous battle with the Confederate ironclad *Merrimac* on March 9, 1862. Later it was ordered to join the fleet blockading Charleston, but on December 30, 1862, it foundered off Cape Hatteras while on its way south.

Rear-Admiral David Dixon Porter (1813–1891) served under Admiral Farragut as commander of a mortar flotilla which attacked the approaches to New Orleans in April, 1862. His main work was in connection with the opening up of the Mississippi River and (in 1865) the capture of Fort Fisher, near Wilmington, North Carolina.

The Timrod ode was probably "Ethnogenesis," which had been composed in February, 1861.

Willie (William Hamilton Hayne) was nearly six years old at the time of this letter.

See the letters to Thompson in the University of Virginia group (Nos. 64–70).]

No. 25

PAUL HAMILTON HAYNE to [?] (FRAGMENT)

(p 5)

Can we ever forgive the infernal people, who have reduced us to such wretched vassalage?.

My chief delight in editing the "So Opinion" is to have *some* opportunity of abusing the Puritan, & indeed the whole Yankee Race!

I know not how long this may be permitted. Some fine morning we may all be quietly clapped in a Yankee Bastile! But what does it matter? Life is worth but little now, & I d'ont see that we need care very particularly about consequences.

Pray give our *united love* to Cousin Lucy, & kiss "Douselka" [?] for us. *Willie* often speaks of his "Cousin Francis". He has grown much, & is fond of his books.

Always Faithfully,

Paul H Hayne

[The tone of this fragment indicates that the letter was written to another Southerner who resented as strongly as Hayne did the plan of reconstruction imposed upon the defeated South. It was not the defeat, by the way, but the reconstruction measures that occasioned Hayne's resentment and that of all other Southerners. The letter may possibly have been addressed to the Virginia author and Confederate soldier John Esten Cooke (1830–1886). If so, "Cousin Lucy" is Lucy Mann, "Cousin Francis" is Cooke's wife, and "Douselka" is their infant daughter (Susan Randolph Cooke, born July 11, 1868). This is merely a conjecture. (See

John O. Beaty, *John Esten Cooke, Virginian,* Columbia University Press, 1922.)

The Richmond *Southern Opinion* ran from June 15, 1867, until May 1, 1869. Hayne was literary editor during the whole period. He not only wrote a column of "Literary Notices" but also edited a column entitled "Reminiscences and Anecdotes of the Late War." The editor and owner was H. Rives Pollard, who, according to Hayne, died "owing me nearly all my salary, of which I have never since recd a solitary cent!" (See *Whittier Correspondence from the Oak Knoll Collections 1830–1892,* ed. by John Albree, Salem, Massachusetts, Essex Book and Print Club, 1911, p. 205.) Pollard offered a prize for the best poem on "The Confederate Dead" and published the prize poem in the first number (June 15, 1867). He offered another prize (one hundred dollars) for the best poem "In Laudation of the Deeds, Valour, Sufferings and Sacrifices of the Confederate Soldiers." Hayne won this prize and his prize poem was published in the second number (June 22, 1867—first page, first two columns). For the poem see Hayne's *Complete Edition,* pp. 67–71. The only issue of *Southern Opinion* which I have examined is that of June 22, 1867. Hayne's column headed "Literary Notices" is devoted exclusively to Swinburne. The column entitled "Reminiscences and Anecdotes of the Late War" relates anecdotes concerning General Jackson and General Barksdale and the Battle of Bull Run. There is no word of abuse either of Puritan or Yankee. In fact, Hayne earnestly desired and worked for reconciliation, as witness these poems in his *Complete Edition:* "The Stricken South to the North" (pp. 299–300), "The Return of Peace" (pp. 300–04), "Union of Blue and Gray" (pp. 310–11), "Reconciliation" (p. 325)—and many others. In a few poems he protested against the harsh measures of reconstruction, but that was only natural and merely indicates loyalty to the South. (See the *American* for January 21, 1882 (III, 231–33), for an interesting article by Eugene L. Didier of Baltimore entitled "Living American Authors. Paul Hamilton Hayne." Didier probably obtained his information from Hayne himself.)]

No. 26

PAUL HAMILTON HAYNE to WILLIAM CULLEN BRYANT

Augusta, (Geo), Oct 22*nd* 1877.

My Dear & Honored Master;—

Indeed, you have been *"My Master"* in all *important* matters of *Poetic art,* & *Study* for many years! Now, I write to ask of you a *special favor.*

It is, that when the enclosed *Ode, ("Unveiled")*, (to be published in *"Scribner's Magz"*, altho I know not precisely *when*), shall finally appear, I may have *your permission to dedicate the Lyric to you!*—

That is, if you really *deem it worthy*.

Will *you not* glance over the verses, so that I may receive your candid opinion? This "Ode" to "Nature" came from my *heart of hearts*—

Ah! great & true Poet!—our Wordsworth of America! how rejoiced I would be, to associate your noble name with a production I have endeavored to make *not wholly unworthy of* it!!

With *profound respect,*

I am Ever Yours,

Paul. H. Hayne.—

P O Box 275.—

Augusta (Geo)

P S. The *Messrs J B Ford & Co* wrote me not long ago, to the effect that they wanted my likeness, to accompany a *revised & enlarged edition* of your *Poetical Selections,* now being issued by them; I mean *one* of the vol*s* of your *"Library of Poetry & Song"*. Of course, I complied with their kind request.

[On the back page of the letter:]

\# *Pardon* my sending the *Poem written in pencil!* My hand is *sprained,* & it is very difficult for me to use a *pen!*

[Hayne's "Unveiled" appeared in *Scribner's Monthly* for January, 1878 (XV, 383–86). There is nothing about the dedication on those pages, but in the index to the volume occurs this notation: "Unveiled (Dedicated to William Cullen Bryant)." On January 10, 1878, Hayne wrote Whittier that he had received fifty dollars for the poem, the largest sum he had ever received for a single poem, and added: "For shorter pieces I receive from 5 and 8 to 10 dollars." The poem has 146 lines. (See *Whittier Correspondence from the Oak Knoll Collections 1830–1892*, ed. by John Albree, pp. 199–201.) In his later years Hayne often received as much as ten dollars for sonnets and sometimes as much as fifty cents a line for longer poems.

J. B. Ford and Company of New York published *A Library of Poetry and Song Being Choice Selections from the Best Poets,* with an introduction by Bryant, in 1870. The first edition contained no selection from Hayne. In 1876 the publishers asked Bryant to enlarge and revise it. Later editions contained Hayne's "Love Scorns Degrees" and "Pre-existence."]

No. 27

PAUL HAMILTON HAYNE to [?]

"Copse Hill", Georgia
May 16th 1882

My Dear Sir;

Your courteous letter of the 8*th* inst. has just reached me. Owing to a mistaken direction it went to the "Dead Letter Office."

Of course it affords me pleasure to comply with your request, & to send you herewith, (1*stly*) an extract from my Sonnet to *Marston,* (& 2*ndly*) a full letter from my old friend *Wm Gilmore Simms.*

Most of his letters are pasted in a blank book.

The one I enclose is the exception. I had *already* cut the signature out for some Autograph seeker years ago.

Thanks for your kind offer to send me Mr Longfellow's *auto.* if I did not chance to have it. But we were in correspondence, & therefore I do not need it.

Believe me *dear Sir*
Respectfully & Truly,
Paul H Hayne

Address P O Box 275 Augusta Georgia.

[A correspondence journal of Hayne that I have examined indicates that he frequently heard from autograph hunters and that he usually replied promptly.

Philip Bourke Marston (1850–1887) was a blind English poet.]

No. 28

PAUL HAMILTON HAYNE to [THE EDITORS OF
THE *CRITIC*?]

"Copse Hill" Geo
15th Sep '84

Gentlemen;

Many thanks for your cordial note of the 6th inst.

It will of *course,* afford me pleasure to receive "The *Critic*",
which I *truly* value as a journal of marked independence, &
talent.

> With best wishes
> Very Faithfully
> *Paul H Hayne.*

P. S. By the way, *what* a *Cad* that fellow Buchanan must
be!!

I read your paragraph about him! Respecting the *man's un-
doubted powers,* I *once* wrote him a letter the tenor of which
would have drawn a reply from *any Gentleman.*

But he preserved a sullen silence.

[The *Critic* was a New York weekly edited by Jeannette L. Gilder and
Joseph B. Gilder.

Robert Williams Buchanan (1841–1901) was a Scottish poet, dramatist,
and novelist who lived in London. The *Critic* for September 13, 1884
(p. 127), contained a brief paragraph about him. He was in New York
at the time in connection with the production of one of his plays. The
paragraph ridicules him because of his outspoken dislike of America and
his complaint about bad cooking.]

No. 29

PAUL HAMILTON HAYNE to [?] (FRAGMENT)

By the way, would you believe, that my article recommend-
ing the His, has been most savagely, & rudely attacked by

several Georgia journals? The race of fools, has assuredly not died out.

Very Respectfully

P H Hayne

[The New York Public Library has only this fragment of the letter. I do not know to whom it was written or to which history it refers.]

II. LIBRARY OF YALE UNIVERSITY (NOS. 30–41)

PAUL HAMILTON HAYNE to EDWIN PERCY WHIPPLE

New Haven Sep: 6*th* 1853—

My Dear Mr Whipple:

I should have written long since to beg your pardon for the very abrupt manner, in which I parted from you, on the evening we were all assembled at your house. Fearing that after your kind attentions to a "stranger," you may think him ungrateful, I now write to thank you for the courtesy, which rendered my brief visit to Boston, the most delightful—week of my life— I longed to grasp you by the hand before we parted. But the thing was impossible—you were besieged by *three* clergymen, *one* of them I understood half mad from the toothache. Of course, I knew that thus surrounded by the votaries of the Church, & hallowed as it were by their presence, it wd' not have been becoming in a "sacrilegious dog," like me, to intrude upon, & disturb your meditations. During my sojourn here, I have read thro the two volumes of your reviews & essays. Indeed Sir! you must permit me to add my feeble applause to the public voice that has already commended them so loudly— Sympathy (however humble) wd' never be ridiculed by a man like you, and intense sympathy I may surely claim to feel with most of the views, so gloriously set forth in the volumes you gave me.

To return to the state of siege in which I left you. How did it terminate? By a capitulation upon *your* part, of course— you are not one to deny the "benefit of clergy." It was really ludicrous to see the very puzzled air, with which your priestly guests were received. But they were strangers, & you took them in. You know the consequences. About the first week in October I shall visit your city again. Will you be in Boston at that time?— I wrote to Mr Fields yesterday, to learn when I should meet him in New York—

With best regards to your wife, whose eye I hope has recovered from the effect of her boy's filial affection—

I remain

Most Truly Yrs—

P. H. Hayne—

[Edwin Percy Whipple (1819–1886), author, critic, and lecturer, lived in Boston after 1837. The volumes mentioned by Hayne were probably *Essays and Reviews*, 2 vols. (Boston: Ticknor & Co.), 1851 (first issued in the winter of 1848–1849).

James Thomas Fields (1817–1881), author, editor, and publisher, was a partner in the famous Boston publishing firm of Ticknor, Reed, & Fields (Ticknor & Fields, after the retirement of Reed in 1854). His firm published—at the author's expense—Hayne's first and third volumes (*Poems*, 1855; *Avolio; A Legend of the Island of Cos. With Poems, Lyrical, Miscellaneous, and Dramatic*, 1860).]

No. 31

PAUL HAMILTON HAYNE to EDWIN PERCY WHIPPLE

Charleston, Sep. 10*th* 1859

My Dear Friend;

I was *truly* delighted to receive last evening, your letter of the 7th inst, which convinces me that I am not wholly forgotten among my former kind friends, & acquaintances in Boston. Ah! I have longed, and *longed* to visit you once more,—but difficulties of the most unexpected & provoking description have *always* arisen to prevent it,—until *now* I almost despair of ever seeing you again in *this world*. But thank God!—the *"mind's* eye" has not been dimmed, & Memory is faithful to *her* trust; so that I am enabled to see you *all* in imagination, & to pass many a happy hour in the *"Albion"*, with Woodman, & Whipple, and old McRenzie [McKenzie?] (by the way, is the old man dead?)—, & Gilman, & Lowell, and Richard Henry Dana, the younger, as in those *pleasant, pleasant* days about the latter portion of the summer of *1854*. It is *not* easy for me to realize that since that time, *five years* have gone by. *After* we have reached the age of 24, or thereabout, how rapidly our lives appear to slip on!

I have often marvelled, what the sensations of a person, retaining (in the main) his mental integrity must be—, who has managed to reach the age of 80, or 90 years.— A few nights ago, (*apropos* of this subject), I met the last *survivor* of one of our most ancient Revolutionary families, (a man, whose three score years & ten, have been *more* than surmounted). He talked with the *liveliest* interest of Rutledge, & McDuffie; told us some pregnant anecdotes of Dr Cooper, the associate of *Tom Paine*, and a partial believer in his religious (!!) views; spoke of Washington, with whom he had *dined* at *"Mount Vernon"*,—and closed with a reference to my unlucky ancestor, commonly mentioned in school histories as the "martyr Hayne!"— Entirely oblivious of the presence of one of the family, the old gentleman (whose name 'tis needless to mention)—, went on to draw a sort of comparison between *Isaac Hayne* (who was hung), and *Gen Robert. Y. Hayne*, who, according to *his* opinion (, he had been a violent "Union man" during the ["] *Nullification* difficulties" of 1830–1) *ought to have been hung!!* It was an amusing tirade;— but I have *never* seen so curious an exhibition of the characteristics of an old man's memory. Of the events of 1798–9 &c, he spoke as if referring to events of yesterday, whilst, as regarded *more recent affairs*, his intellect was a perfect blank. He did'nt remember the death of a beautiful granddaughter who died 2 months before, but his tears flowed like a flood, when some allusion was made to his uncle who was buried— God *only* knows how long ago!

You refer to Mr Field's [*sic*], and his European tour. I had the *great satisfaction* of receiving from him a full, & *eminently interesting* letter *just* (I *think*), after my last communication addressed to yourself. *Fields* writes in the highest possible spirits, as indeed, one is *bound* to do, whose time has been passed in the society of some among the greatest of mankind. Most *especially*, do I envy him his acquaintance, & companionship with *Tennyson!* It is hardly necessary for me to ask what you think of *his* (T—'s) last book, the *"Idyls"*? Among other interesting items,—Fields mentions the fact, that he enjoyed the inestimable privilege of hearing *Tennyson* read "Queen *Guinevere*". But probably I am detailing stale news. If *so*, pray pardon me.

x —————— . . —————— x

Enclosed, I send you my *"Dedicatory Sonnet."* As I said *before*, whatever its artistic, or poetical imperfections, regard it as *an expression* of *sincere & earnest feeling.*

With my *best regards* to *Mrs Whipple*, Believe me,—*My dear friend,*—as

Ever Truly Y*rs*

Paul H Hayne

[The Albion Hotel, Boston, was located at the corner of Beacon and Tremont streets.

Horatio Woodman (1821–1879), Boston lawyer, lived for a time at the Albion Hotel and later at Parker's Hotel. He arranged dinners for the literary men at the Albion, serving as business manager, and founded the Saturday Club.

Arthur Delevan Gilman (1821–1882) was an architect of Boston and New York (after 1868). He may be the Gilman to whom Hayne refers.

James Russell Lowell (1819–1891) and Richard Henry Dana, Jr. (1815–1882) were original members of the Saturday Club.

I am unable to identify "old McRenzie" (or McKenzie).

There were two distinguished brothers of the Rutledge family in Charleston in Revolutionary times. John Rutledge (1739–1800) was the governor and most gifted leader of South Carolina during the first part of the Revolution. After the war he was a member of Congress for a number of years and was appointed Chief Justice of the United States Supreme Court by Washington and held one term, but the Senate rejected the nomination because of his denunciation of the discriminations against the South in John Jay's treaty. Edward Rutledge (1749–1800) was a signer of the Declaration of Independence and was governor of South Carolina at the time of his death.

George McDuffie (1790–1851) was a South Carolina lawyer, representative, governor, and United States senator.

Thomas Cooper (1759–1839) was an English philosopher, lawyer, and scientist who came to the United States in 1794. He taught at the University of Pennsylvania and for fourteen years at South Carolina College, beginning in 1820, during most of which period he was president of the institution.

Isaac Hayne (1745–1781) was a colonel of South Carolina militia in the Revolution. He was captured by the British and hanged on August 4, 1881. See *D. A. B.* for details.

Robert Young Hayne (1791–1839) was a member of the state legislature, attorney general of South Carolina, United States senator for two terms, governor, mayor of Charleston, and railroad president. As governor during the Nullification controversy, he supported the policy of South Carolina.

In 1859 James Thomas Fields (1817–1881) traveled in Europe for pleasure and business. He made the acquaintance of many notable writers and "rounded up" some of them for his publishing house.

Four poems of Tennyson's *Idylls of the King* appeared in 1859: "Enid," "Vivien," "Elaine," and "Guinevere." The American edition was *Idyls of the King*, Boston: Ticknor & Fields, 1859.

Hayne's volume of 1860 (*Avolio; A Legend of the Island of Cos*) was dedicated (in a sonnet) to Whipple.]

No. 32

PAUL HAMILTON HAYNE to EDWIN PERCY WHIPPLE

"Copse Hill," March 13*th* *(1872)*

My Dear Friend;

Both your last notes have safely arrived.— Many thanks! The *merest touch* of your handwriting always delights me—; for verily, in all this Country, *South or North,* where could I find a more generous friend than *yourself.*

You d'ont know, you'll never *imagine* (excuse *tautology!*), my fervent gratitude for that *last* exquisite critique from your pen!

You "builded better than you knew" in writing it. In truth it has done me *immense* good everywhere [?]. Your 1*st* note concludes with a sentence to the effect, "that you will *always love me, provided I keep* clear of the *"Ku Kluck"!"*

Then, assuredly, I am *certain* of your *"love",* until the end of this mortal chapter! So far from *joining* the *"Ku Kluck",* why— God bless your soul! my friend— I never *have* even *seen* a member of that mysterious confraternity, altho for *6 years* a resident, in the county, which of all others in G*a* was held up to execration as a place delivered over to the Devil & all his *abominations!*

One day the *real truth* as to this *"Ku Kluck"* matter *must* appear! It will amaze *many!* x x x x *Did* I say *anything* against Stoddard's *critique?*— If so, it must simply have been suggested by the *involuntàry contrast* drawn between *your review & his.* But what you urge on behalf of *tired* Critics &c, is all too true to be gainsaid.

Stoddard meant a kindness, & I would seem conceited, (which God knows, I *am far from being)*—were I to "look the gift horse in *the mouth.*"

x x x The initial no of your *"Globe"* came duly to hand. W'ont you get the *Publishers* of this paper to mail me the *tri-weekly or weekly—Edition?* I'll *notice* the . . . [one illegible word omitted] especially in my own periodical.

It grieved me to hear of our mutual friend M*r* Woodman's fallen fortunes. *Now,* I can measurably comprehend why he ignores, & *has* for *years*—my letters! But, with his shrewdness, business tact, energy, and indomitable resolution, is'nt it likely that he will recover himself, and again be *"even with Fortune?"*—

Ah, I truly *loved Woodman,*—& in his *misfortune* (of course, I'd never allude to *that,* by even the *ghost* of a *hint!*), I am determined to try him once *more* with an affectionate letter. May I address it *to your care?*—

Please hand to *your wife,* with my sincere regards, the enclosed *violets.* They may bring a *"waft"* of Spring, while Spring *delays!*

Heaven bless you.

Ever Yr's

Paul H Hayne

(P O Box 635 Augusta Ga

[A part of the third page of this letter overlaps with the second page, and is written vertically across it, with the result that several words are hard to make out.

Whipple's critique of Hayne was probably a review of *Legends and Lyrics* (Philadelphia: J. B. Lippincott & Co., 1872).

Copse Hill is in Columbia County, near the border of Richmond County, in which Augusta is located.

It is interesting and amusing to note Hayne's side-stepping of the Ku-Klux Klan issue. I have no doubt that he sympathized with its aims and purposes during the reconstruction period. But he had no connection with it, and there would have been no point in his arguing about it with Whipple.

Richard Henry Stoddard (1825–1903) had probably reviewed *Legends and Lyrics* in one of the New York magazines or newspapers. Evidently this old friend of Hayne had turned against him, although Hayne tried repeatedly to maintain their friendship as of old.

The *Union List of Newspapers* gives the date of the first issue of the Boston *Daily Globe* as March 4, 1872. Whipple was the literary editor. There was also a weekly *Globe* from 1872 until 1892. (There had been an earlier Boston *Daily Globe* in 1832–3.)

Horatio Woodman speculated in Western land. (See notes on the preceding letter and the letter (No. 112) to John Sullivan Dwight, dated January 29, 1879.)]

No. 33

PAUL HAMILTON HAYNE to JOHN ESTEN COOKE

Charleston (S. C) Sep 16, '56

My Dear Sir;

Enclosed I send you a brief advertisement, which will inform you of a literary project now in the course of development in S. Carolina. I propose in connection with Mr Carlisle (a man of great tact & cleverness), to start a new monthly magazine in this City upon the plan of Blackwood, which shall be an exponent of Southern genius both in literature & politics. We design to commence with ample Capital, & to pay for *every article*. The Courtenays (a very successful, & Enterprising firm) have undertaken the business management, & never before I may truly say in the history of Southern Literature has an enterprise of the kind commenced under auspices so favorable. I therefore have no hesitation in proposing to you the composition of a brief serial novel *(upon your own terms)* to run through 6 numbers, & written of course upon *any* subject you like. I may say without the slightest intention of flattery that your present position as an author (true in every sense to Southern life & character), necessitates this appeal, & I am sure that you will not disregard it—

Pray mention our plan in Virginia, & let me hear from you when convenient—

Believe me Dear Sir,

Most Respectfully &

Truly Yrs:

P H Hayne—

[John Esten Cooke (1830–1886) was the most prolific and prominent author of Virginia in his generation. His best work was in the novel, but he also wrote short stories, articles, poetry, and history.

The new monthly was *Russell's Magazine* (April, 1857–March, 1860), of Charleston, edited by Hayne. W. B. Carlisle, Charleston journalist, assisted at first but, proving unsatisfactory, was soon replaced as associate editor by John Russell, bookseller, at whose store the intellectual men of the city often gathered, and who gave his name to the magazine.

William Ashmead Courtenay (1831–1908) and his brother (S. G. Courtenay) conducted a bookselling and publishing business in Charleston from 1850 until 1860. He was mayor of Charleston from 1879 until 1887. In 1893 he went into the cotton manufacturing business at Newry (Oconee County), South Carolina.

The serial novel contributed to *Russell's Magazine* by John Esten Cooke was *Estcourt; or, The Memoirs of a Virginia Gentleman.* The terms agreed upon were $300. Hayne was able to pay only $50, for the magazine did not prosper. Hayne offered to make himself personally responsible for the remaining $250, but Cooke declined the offer. See John O. Beaty, *John Esten Cooke, Virginian* (New York: Columbia University Press, 1922), p. 64, and Hayne's letters to Cooke in the Library of Congress group (Nos. 42–46).]

No. 34

PAUL HAMILTON HAYNE to JOHN ESTEN COOKE

Charleston, May 8th '60

My Dear Friend;

Be assured that your long, affectionate, & most welcome letter of the 11th *of April,* should have been answered long ago, if circumstances had only permitted. But *again,* I am compelled to write in a lugubrious, desponding strain. God seems to have marked *both* of us out, for affliction.

Since the reception of your letter, my wife has become (daily) more feeble; and, in order that my troubles should be complete—, my *mother* has also been visited by a *serious sickness.*

As for *myself,* altho I have never communicated the matter, even to those nearly connected with me—, I feel that my life "is'nt worth six months' purchase!". I have had *two* severe attacks of *hemorrage* [*sic*] lately, which, of course, are proofs of a bad condition of the bodily-system.

—You must really pardon this exhibition of *selfishness. Why* should I write to you, if I have nothing pleasant to communicate?— Well! we all pine for sympathy, & the egotism of human nature forbids that we should spare *even* our friends!

In my last letter, I spoke of Mr *Mann,* somewhat disrespectfully. I am bound to say, that a farther acquaintance with that gentleman, has convinced me how wrong my first hasty impressions were! . .

He appears to me, *now,* as courteous, & able, a little *too* peremptory in his style of correspondence,—but nevertheless, possessed of sterling, & admirable—qualities.

—The intelligence you gave me of Thompson's acceptance,—of the editorship of the "*F. & F.*," was exceedingly agreeable. By the *merest* accident, I met Mr Gardner, (the *Proprietor* of the journal referred to),—who, at once, confirmed your tidings, & added, that *Thompson* had consented to take up his abode in the city of *Agusta* [*sic*].

I fear, *(Entre nous),* that our friend *T*—, will find *Agusta* the dreariest place in the world. However, it happens to be near *Charleston,*—& I hope to see *T*—*n* frequently *here.*

The IXth vo*l* of Appleton's "Cyclopædia", contains, I observe, 4 or 5 articles from your pen. I have read with the *liveliest* interest the papers on *P. Henry* & *W. Irving.* They are masterpieces of biography,—& I have taken occasion to notice them in the next "*F & F*".

Whenever the opportunity offers, I design contributing to that journal an elaborate review of *your* works &c. How does the book on "*So poets & poetry*" progress?—

In *haste*, but also, in
Sorrow, & deep anxiety,
I remain
Yr*s* always,

P H Hayne

[The afflictions of John Esten Cooke to which Hayne refers may have included any of these: his mother and his brother (Philip Pendleton) died in 1850, he was profoundly grieved by the death of his father in 1854 (he also paid some debts left by his father), he was caused some grief by an ill-fated love affair between 1855 and 1858 (he also suffered from neuralgia of the teeth), two other brothers (Henry Pendleton and Edward St. George) died about 1859 or 1860.

Southern Field and Fireside (1859–64), of Augusta, Georgia, was edited by William W. Mann (until May, 1860), who had contributed letters from Paris to the *Southern Literary Messenger.*

For information about John Reuben Thompson (1823–1873), of Rich-mond, see the notes following letter No. 24.

In the closing 1850's John Esten Cooke wrote a number of biographical sketches for Appleton's *New American Cyclopoedia*, edited by George Ripley and Charles A. Dana. Among them were sketches of Madison, Monroe, Marshall, several members of the Lee family, Jefferson, Washington Irving, and Patrick Henry.

John Esten Cooke and John Reuben Thompson had been asked by a New York publishing house to bring out *The Poets and Poetry of the South,* "a work which was well under way when the war interrupted it, but was never completed." See Beaty, *op. cit.,* p. 66.]

No. 35

PAUL HAMILTON HAYNE to [?]

"Copse Hill," near *Augusta* (Geo)
Dec 5*th* 1870

Dear Sir;

Some time ago, you were kind enough to write me *favorably* concerning a Poem, *("Daphles"),* which I had summoned up the courage to mail you.

Now, with that diffidence which one cannot but feel when presenting an imperfect production to the *first poetic Artist* in America, I venture to send you another, and more elaborate story in verse, the *plot* whereof is, of course, familiar to you; since it comes from *Chaucer*.

I may hope, that whatever the faults of the narrative— it does not at least, belong to that careless class of Works, the pages of which one instinctively touches *au bout du doigt*, and then passes on.

I enclose some *violets*, the *first* of the season *here*. Whether when they reach you, verses *and* violets may not equally prove dry and *perfumeless*, I cannot tell;—but my sanguine temper prompts me to hope otherwise.

With profound respect & esteem,
I am *Dear Sir*,
Faithfully Yours,

Paul H Hayne.

P. O. Box 635, Augusta
  (Geo)

[As early as the date of this letter Hayne was or had been in correspondence with Bryant, Whittier, Lowell, and Longfellow, and it is possible that he may have referred to any one of them as "the *first poetic Artist* in America." I think the letter was certainly sent to one of the four. He had sent a copy of the poem to each of the last three, and probably to Bryant also.

"Daphles. An Argive Story" and "The Wife of Brittany. [Suggested by the Frankeleine's Tale of Chaucer.]" appear in *Complete Edition*, pp. 89–100 and 118–137, respectively.]

No. 36

PAUL HAMILTON HAYNE to [THE EDITORS OF THE *GRAPHIC* AND *HEARTH AND HOME*]

Augusta, Dec 18*th* 1874.:

Gentlemen;

I *have been* doing, and I *am* continuing to do, all in my power to advance the interests of your publications in the

South, by frequent notices of both "the *Graphic*", & "*Hearth & Home*". Associated as I am, with several able & prominent journals of this section, my opportunities are considerable, & I shall not neglect them, in your favor.

The fact that my friend & correspondent, *Miss Jean Ingelow*, has a serial novel,—or is about to have one—, in "*Hearth & Home*", only adds to my interest in your "weekly",—rely therefore, upon my efforts to make our people acquainted with its claims to patronage.

Continue—(if you choose)—, to mail your Periodical, & the "*Daily Graphic*" to my present address, *P. O Box 635, Augusta* Geo, & Believe me

Most Respectfully

Paul H Hayne.

[The New York *Graphic*, established in 1873, was issued daily except Sunday by the Graphic Company, editors and publishers.

Hearth and Home, New York weekly (1868–1875), was bought by the New York Graphic Company in June, 1874.

Jean Ingelow (1820–1897) was an English poet and story writer. Hayne corresponded with her.]

No. 37

PAUL HAMILTON HAYNE to [CHARLES W. SQUIRES]

Augusta, Georgia,
April 18*th* 1875.

Dear Sir;

In March 1873, I recd a *very courteous* note from you, requesting me to mail you "*my autograph & a sentiment*".

This I at once did, & no doubt the communication reached its address. You were kind enough in y'r note to refer to my poems in high terms of commendation; and therefore, I write you now to say that a new vo*l* of mine will appear from the press of *Messrs E J Hale & Son, No 17 Murray St NYork, on* or *about* the *1st* of May next.

The title is, "*The Mountain of the Lovers, With Poems of Nature & Tradition*" [.]

Besides several legendary Tales, a number of Lyrics &c &c, it contains those *"nature pieces"* which attracted your notice in *"The Atlantic Monthly"*.

Now, my *Publishers* desire me to have the forthcoming vo*l* *announced* far & wide. I have—more on *their* account than my *own*—complied with this request; but being an utter stranger to the people of *Albany*, I can only turn to you, and request your help in the matter.

Should you be acquainted with any of your *Editors*, perhaps you could embody the information given, and thus inform your Public, briefly, that such a *work* is soon to be issued, &c.

That is all I ask. Please drop me a line,
& Believe me Faithfully,

Paul H Hayne.

P O Box 635 Augusta
Georgia.

[One of Hayne's diaries indicates that he wrote a letter to "Chas. W. Squires, Exchange Building Albany (New York)" on March 29, 1873. (For this information I am indebted to Miss Nannie M. Tilley, Manuscript Department, Duke University Library, in a letter dated June 26, 1942.) This letter to Squires is preserved in the Henry E. Huntington Library, but it is merely addressed to "My Dear Sir." I do not have permission to publish it but have compared it with the Yale letter above. Obviously both were written to the same person. E. Elizabeth Barker of the Harmanus Bleecker Library, Albany, New York, informs me (in a letter dated July 21, 1942) that Charles W. Squires was a broker or banker of Albany, New York.

Hayne's information about his forthcoming volume is correct: *The Mountain of the Lovers; With Poems of Nature and Tradition*, New York: E. J. Hale & Son, 1875.

Hayne's nature poems that had appeared in the *Atlantic Monthly* since the publication of *Legends and Lyrics* are these:

"Aspects of the Pines" 30:351 (Sept., 1872)
"Forest Pictures" 30:662 (Dec., 1872)
"The Voice in the Pines" 31:53 (Jan., 1873)
"The Wood Lake" 31:405–6 (April, 1873)
"Golden Dell" 32:425–6 (Oct., 1873)
"The Woodland" 34:474 (Oct., 1874)
"Visit of the Wrens" 34:717–19 (Dec., 1874)
"After the Tornado" 35:322 (March, 1875)]

No. 38

PAUL HAMILTON HAYNE to HEZEKIAH BUTTERWORTH

"Copse Hill," Georgia Rail Road,
November 27th 1879

Address:

P. O. Box 275,
Augusta, Ga.

Dear Friend;

I reached home with my wife about 3 weeks ago, & so many & onerous have my duties been since, that I *literally* now take the first opportunity of writing you.

Enclosed please find two pieces for "Youth's Com*p*," which I trust may suit your columns.

With *best remembranc*e from my *"winsome Marrow"*, (who *never never* can forget all your kindness), & with a *Brother's* love from myself—

I remain, *dear Butterworth*
in haste, but Faithfully &
affectionately
Your obliged friend,

Paul H Hayne.

(Over)

Drop me a line *in reply to this.* Say *if the poems please?*

[Hezekiah Butterworth (1839–1905) was one of the editors of *Youth's Companion*, Boston weekly, from 1870 until 1894. He was also a popular writer of fiction and non-fiction. In 1879 the circulation of the magazine was over 100,000 and was increasing annually. Twenty-three of Hayne's poems appeared in it between January 9, 1879, and January 26, 1882. No doubt other poems of his appeared in it before and after that period. After this letter was written the next two poems of Hayne to appear in it were "The Broken Chords," January 1, 1880 (53:6), and "England," February 26, 1880 (53:68).

When he wrote this letter Hayne and his wife had recently returned from a three-month trip to the North, including Boston.]

No. 39

PAUL HAMILTON HAYNE to WILLIAM ROUNSEVILLE
ALGER

"Copse Hill," Georgia Rail Road,

Address:

P. O. Box 275,
Augusta, Ga.

May 9th 1881

My Dear Sir;

. . . . When a man has derived *great instruction*, no less
than *pleasure*, from the works of another, I think that he
should, (if practicable), *specially* acknowledge such a debt to
his Benefactor. Now, your elaborate, careful, learned, and
beyond all things, *impartial* treatise upon *"The Future Life,"*
has for years past, been my daily companion;—and I can
truly affirm, that a more *suggestive production*, I have never
studied.

Could you see my copy, you would remark upon every
page; & all along the margins, *notes*, quotations, references
to numberless other essays, touching upon similar themes,
ancient & modern;—in fine, a series of *"Marginalia"* of stun-
ning variety, and every conceivable degree of pertinence!!

In the unusual combination of eloquence & richness of
style, with the *sternest logic*, your Book seems to me unrivalled.

It contains whole pages of pure, exalted poetry; and then
suddenly one encounters passages which for rigid, uncompro-
mising argumentation, would have satisfied the highest logical instincts of *Mill*, nay! of *Mill'[s?] more than Master,*—
Bacon himself!!

Therefore, in brief, but *earnest* phrase, *thank you* for the
intellectual benefit, the instr[uction?] & frequent consolation,
I have derived from your really great work.

My own copy is marked *"Sixth Thousand"*, *W. J. Widdleton, Pub: 1869.*

Has any *other* edition appeared since the date mentioned?—

xxx. It would gratify me to receive some answer to this; & to learn something of yourself—*personally; especially* in regard to your *health*, which a year or two ago, the papers spoke of, as frail & uncertain. Here, *truly* I can sympathise with you; because during 25 years, (a sad quarter of a century), I myself have not known a solitary day of strength, or freedom from pain, & lassitude. And *now*, I stand, as it were, face to face with Death!. liable to be "swept, at any moment, from all attempts at a *theoretical* solution of the great problem of a future life, into the *real* solution itself"!! Yet, there are seasons when I ask of the *spirit, does* "a real solution" *await* any of us? . . *What* if at Death's mysterious touch, we *merely sink into oblivion?—a sleep never ending?—* The question is morbid, and only obtrudes itself in moments of *mental* sickness, or unnatural depression.

Generally, my faith in immortality is *(Laus Deo!)*, assured!

xxx My courteous friends, *Messrs Roberts & Bros*, have just mailed me a copy of your last essayical work. Needless to say, I shall read it with care, & attention.

—By the way, during my last visit to Boston in 1879, I promised myself the rare pleasure of making your personal acquaintance;—but alas! untoward Circumstances prevented it! I was forced to cut short my visit after seeing once more, however, such old friends as *Prof. Longfellow*, Dr *Holmes*, Mr Whipple, and a few others.

Let me not trespass unduly upon your leisure:—Interested by your work in yourself;—knowing that you are as far as possible removed from that order of Thinkers, strongly characterized by old Burton, as *"Eunuchi Sapientiaë"*,—I have ventured thus directly to address you;—sure that my motives will be both comprehended, and appreciated.

Most Respectfully & Cordially Yr's

Paul Hamilton Hayne.

[William Rounseville Alger (1822–1905), Boston author, wrote *A Critical History of the Doctrine of a Future Life*, New York: W. J. Widdleton. The fourth edition was dated 1866. Hayne's copy, dated 1869, must have been the fifth or sixth. Hayne says his copy was marked "Sixth

Thousand." Possibly each edition, or printing, was limited to one thousand copies.

Roberts & Bros., Boston publishers, brought out a good many of Alger's books. Possibly the later work referred to by Hayne was *The School of Life*, 1881.

Mill and Bacon were the great English philosophers, John Stuart Mill (1806–1873) and Francis Bacon (1561–1626).

Robert Burton (1577–1640) wrote *The Anatomy of Melancholy* (1621). In the "Dedication" of *Don Juan* Byron calls Castlereagh an "intellectual eunuch."]

No. 40

PAUL HAMILTON HAYNE to [?]

"Copse Hill", Geo Nov 7th 1885

My Dear Sir;

Many years have passed since I had the pleasure of meeting you in Boston; but I vividly recall our meeting, & your courtesy. By the present mail I venture to send you a copy of the *"Savannah Sesqui-Centennial* Ode",—now for the first time *correctly* published—, and if you deem it worthy I shall be grateful for a notice in your columns.

By the way, if you choose to mail me *occasionally,* the "weekly" or "tri-weekly" edition of your journal, I may serve its interests at the South.

With best regards,
Cordially Yrs

Paul H Hayne.

Address
    P O Box 275
    Augusta Geo

[The unidentified correspondent to whom this letter was addressed was apparently the literary editor of a Boston newspaper.

The sesqui-centennial celebration of the settlement of Georgia was held at Savannah in February, 1883. Hayne wrote an ode for the occasion by request. He attended but because of a throat ailment could not read his poem. Portions of it were read by General Henry R. Jackson.

Alexander H. Stephens made the principal address, which was his last
public appearance. See Hayne's letter to Moses Coit Tyler dated January
31, 1886, in the Cornell group (No. 204).]

No. 41

PAUL HAMILTON HAYNE to [?]

23rd Nov . . . 1885.

My Beloved Friend;—

Did you ever read Russell Lowell's "Ode"—his "*Hartford*
[*sic*] *Commemoration* Ode"?— Referring to the Yankee heroes
returned from the war, he says,

> "They come transfigured back
> Secure from change in their high-hearted ways,
> Beautiful *evermore, & with the rays*
> Of *morn on* their *white shields of Expectation!*"

—Now, on p 6 of my Savannah "Ode" are these lines,—
"Pierced oftimes by *Hope's* sublimest ray *Flashed o'er the
morning hills of Expectation.*"

—Do you think anybody can rightly accuse me of copying
here another's image? Are not the fancies different? Please
tell me *frankly*.

An old *college* boy of your's [*sic*] *Thos Gibson* of the "*Augusta Evng News*" dined with us yesterday, and spoke most
lovingly of you.

Enclosed I send you an article of mine about *Miller,* published in "*Wilmington* [N.C.] Star".

> In haste, but
> Ever affectionately
>
> *Paul H Hayne.*

P. S. These Atlantians are going very foolishly to work concerning "*Prohibition*". *Extremes* are always *fanatical.* I've
told Avery so frankly. He, & his friends are unconsciously
cutting the throat of true *Temperance.* Will men never learn

the wisdom which dwells *alone* in the "golden mean".?—
Naive "liquor laws" have but *one* final result;— *to Drunken-
ness is added Hypocrisy:*

[A note from the Library of Yale University indicates that this letter
was sent "probably to Miss Rutherford." I do not know the basis of this
opinion. It seems to me more likely, for reasons that appear below,
that the letter was sent to some professor or former professor at the
University of Georgia. Mildred Lewis Rutherford (1851–1928) was
principal of the Lucy Cobb Institute at Athens from 1880 until 1895 and
taught English there during that period and until 1899. In the 1890's
she published a number of books containing sketches of authors. Her
father, William S. Rutherford, was for more than thirty years professor
of mathematics at the University of Georgia. I quote as follows from
a letter (dated December 3, 1941) to me from Mr. T. W. Reed, Registrar
of the University of Georgia:

"Thomas Reuben Gibson was graduated from the University of Georgia
in 1876 with the degree of Bachelor of Arts. He was born in Augusta,
Georgia, in 1857. For a number of years he was a journalist in that
city. At one time, he was U. S. Consul to Beirut, Syria. He died there
in 1894. He entered the University of Georgia from Thomson, Georgia.

"The professor of English in the University of Georgia during his
college days was Dr. Eustace W. Speer, long since dead. Miss Rutherford
was not teaching at Lucy Cobb Institute during Mr. Gibson's college days,
though later on she was principal there. Chancellor Andrew A. Lipscomb
was the executive head of the University up to 1874. Dr. Henry H.
Tucker was chancellor from 1874 to 1878. Other professors who may have
taught Mr. Gibson were W. H. Waddell, Henry C. White, L. H. Char-
bonnier, William Rutherford, Wm. M. Browne, C. P. Willcox, all of them
long since dead."

Hayne may have been in correspondence with several of these professors, but the only one with whom I am certain that he did correspond
was Dr. Andrew Adgate Lipscomb (1816–1890), Methodist minister,
author, and lecturer as well as professor. After he left the University
of Georgia (where he may have known Thomas Gibson when the latter
was a freshman or sophomore), he taught for a short time at Vanderbilt
University and then retired to live in Athens until his death. The *D. A. B.*
says that as a teacher he was held in "affectionate veneration." In the
Augusta *Evening News* for July 13, 1886, Lipscomb quotes from a letter
which he had received from Hayne in January, 1886, and adds that this
was one of the weekly letters which he had been receiving from Hayne.
He was, therefore, probably a correspondent of Hayne in November,
1885. Lipscomb delivered a series of lectures on Shakespeare in Augusta
under the auspices of the Hayne Literary Circle in March, 1886, at which

time he publicly paid tribute to his "especial and admired friend, Paul Hayne" (Augusta *Evening News*, March 25, 1886).

The lines quoted somewhat inaccurately from Lowell's "Ode Recited at the Harvard Commemoration July 21, 1865" are found at the end of the eighth section.

Miller is probably the poet Joaquin Miller (1841–1913).

The Wilmington (N. C.) *Star* was a newspaper to which Hayne sometimes contributed in his later years.

Isaac Wheeler Avery (1837–1897), who had been a colonel in the Confederate Army, was a prominent Georgia leader and journalist after the war. The *D. A. B.* says: "For a number of years he was editor-in-chief of the *Atlanta Constitution* and for a short time owned the *Atlanta Herald*." He was a pallbearer at Hayne's funeral. The Augusta *Chronicle* for July 11, 1886, says: "Col. I. W. Avery, of Atlanta, . . . and his family came up yesterday to attend the funeral of the gentle poet, Paul Hayne. The friendship between the two men was a close and fraternal one, in which the families warmly shared."]

III. LIBRARY OF CONGRESS (NOS. 42–49)

No. 42

PAUL HAMILTON HAYNE to JOHN ESTEN COOKE

Charleston Feb 10th 1857

My Dear Sir;

I have just returned from a long, and exceedingly arduous canvassing tour through this State & No Carolina— I may truly say that every moment of my time was occupied, otherwise I should have written to you 'ere this. Forgive the apparent neglect— Our magazine has been somewhat delayed, & the payments to the Joint-Stock come in slowly— Nevertheless my candid opinion founded upon extensive observation is, that we shall ultimately, and gloriously succeed— To confess the truth, (this sub rosâ), my colleagues—especially Mr Carlisle, has not seconded my efforts as vigorously as he ought to have done—as I had a right to expect that he wd' do—but *thro all* obstacles I shall please God! fight the Maga through— Only my dear Mr Cooke, *you,* in common with all Southern authors, must stand by me— After the first year we can make it worth your while even *pecuniarily—*

Meantime, you may look for a check covering the amount wh' we agreed upon for the first intallment of "Estcourt"—

My absence alone has caused the delay— Is the novel progressing? Pray let me hear from you, & Believe me Dear Sir,

Ever Truly Yrs,

P H Hayne

[See letters No. 33 and No. 34.

John Esten Cooke (1830–1886), native of Richmond, younger brother of Philip Pendleton Cooke, was an officer under Lee during the Civil War. Both before and after the war he was a voluminous writer: fiction, sketches, essays, poetry, biography, and history. *Estcourt, Henry St. John, The Pride of Falling Water, The Craniologist,* and *Canolles*—all mentioned in Hayne's letters—are works of fiction. (See John O. Beaty, *John Esten Cooke, Virginian,* Columbia University Press, 1922.)

Russell's Magazine (April, 1857–March, 1860), Charleston monthly, was edited by Hayne, assisted (in the first two numbers) by W. B. Carlisle,

Charleston journalist, and then by John Russell, Charleston bookseller, after whom the magazine was named. (See Mott, II, 488 ff.)

Estcourt: or The Memoirs of a Virginia Gentleman began as a serial in the first number of *Russell's.* Three hundred dollars had been agreed on as the price to be paid, but the magazine did not flourish and Hayne paid only fifty dollars. He was painfully embarrassed about the situation and offered to make himself personally responsible for the debt, but Cooke refused the offer. (See Beaty, *op. cit.,* p. 64.)

For a letter from Hayne to Cooke dated May 22, 1858, see *The South in the Building of the Nation,* XI, inserted between p. 464 and p. 465. It is a facsimile and shows Hayne's handwriting at its best. It accompanies the sketch of Hayne by L. W. Payne, Jr.]

No. 43

PAUL HAMILTON HAYNE to JOHN ESTEN COOKE

Charleston, (S C) Nov 4*th* 1859

My Dear Mr Cooke;

—I have this moment rec*d* your kind letter of the 1st Nov. I never mention, or think of "Estcourt" without feeling embarrassed, & almost ashamed. The reflection *will* Come, that *I & I* alone induced you to contribute the work to "Russell's Magz." You will recollect that some time since, I offered, in fact, I *beseeched* you to permit me to make myself in *some way,* responsible for the payment which is due you. I *now* repeat my former request; *i. e.* let *me* assume the *debt,* & give you some *(written),* guarantee for its payment. xxx Frankly, I am a poor man *myself*—;—but then, should I live, I must finally inherit an independent property, so that any legal acknowledgement of the debt in question will positively ensure you payment at some future day. You *will,* (I speak most *sincerely*) do me a great kindness by suggesting some mode of settlement in this matter.

—You speak of publishing *"Estcourt"* in a separate vo*l,* and write to ask if there is *any objection! My dear Sir,* how *can* you dream of such a thing? We have no earthly claim upon the tale, unless the fact of having issued it in "Russell," *without* paying for it, constitutes a claim!—&c

—May *the good Gods* grant you better luck in the publication of *"Estcourt"* in book-form, than attended it, (I allude

wholly to its *pecuniary success*)—, when issued in "Russell's
Magz."—

—I have read *"Henry St John"* with the most *vivid interest, & delight*. In the Dec number of *"Russell"*, (the editorship of which, after *twice* abandoning it, circumstances have
constrained me to *resume pro tem*)—, you will see an elaborate, & I trust, *satisfactory* review. *The* work, (*one* of your
very *best*, & a noble historical novel beyond doubt)—, has
been everywhere successful. *Two* favourable notices have
already appeared in So Carolina papers,—*one*, in the "Mercury", written, (I presume), by Mr Simms, & the *other* in
the editorial department of the Columbia *"Courant,"* conducted by Mr Howard H Caldwell. The *first* of these, (the
"Mercury" article)—, is a genial, glowing, & yet strictly
analytical criticism; the *second*,—perfectly just in its conclusions, is unfortunately defaced by a side hit at our mutual
friend, *Simms*.— I do not hesitate to say, that H. H. Caldwell is a man in whom I have *no confidence whatever*.—
He has conceived the *bitterest* enmity against *Simms*, because
the *latter* reviewed *his poems* in *"Russell,"* with a touch of
severity,—& the consequence is, he permits *no* opportunity
of abusing him (S), to pass unimproved. In this most hon-
ourable warfare, Caldwell is assisted by an obscure literary
adventurer, who edits the lighter department of the N.
Orleans "True Delta".— The person's name is *Overall, & he
too* is incensed against Simms, because a poem by Jno Wilson Overall, entitled *"The Death of Mirabeau,"* was noticed
contemptuously in the *So Quarterly Review*. I regret to say,
that these detractors have found allies *even* in the city of
Charleston! xxxx. You kindly inquire after my vol of verses.
In a few days it will be published by *"Ticknor & Fields"* of
Boston. As for the "sale" thereof, I expect, absolutely *nothing*. If it gives me a slight sprinkle of reputation, I shall be
more than satisfied. Please let me hear from you as soon as
possible, & believe me My *dear Mr Cooke*,

Ever Truly Yours,—

Paul H Hayne

P S. Will you visit Simms at his plantation this winter?
If so, *when?*

[John O. Beaty (*John Esten Cooke, Virginian,* Columbia University Press, 1922) does not mention *Estcourt* in book form.

Cooke's *Henry St. John, Gentleman* was published in 1859 (New York: Harper and Brothers).

William Gilmore Simms (1806–1870) was the most versatile and industrious of the Charleston writers, and by far the best of them in prose.

Howard Hayne Caldwell (1831–1858) was a South Carolina poet and journalist. His *Poems* (Boston: Whittemore, Niles, and Hall, 1858) was reviewed in *Russell's Magazine* for April, 1858 (III, 36–47). The review is sympathetic but frankly points out the faults of Caldwell's poems.

John Wilson Overall, New Orleans journalist, was on the staff of the New Orleans *True Delta* in the late 1850's and edited the comic weekly *Southern Punch* in Richmond in 1863–64. In the *Southern Quarterly Review* for October, 1852 (VI, New Series, 533–4), there was a brief and unfavorable notice of a pamphlet of fourteen pages, published in Mobile, containing a poem by John Wilson Overall entitled *The Funeral of Mirabeau.* Simms was editor of the *Southern Quarterly Review* from 1849 until 1855. *Russell's Magazine* for January, 1859 (IV, 373), had an editorial by way of reply to a slur at Simms which had recently appeared in the New Orleans *True Delta*—"Mr. Simms is not a poet, for he lacks the essential element of a poet—imagination." No doubt this was the voice of the aggrieved Overall. Simms was as generous to Caldwell and Overall as those more than minor bards deserved, but they were right to this extent: Simms's poetry is not his best work; he is at his best in prose romance, or the historical novel.

Hayne's third volume, *Avolio: A Legend of the Island of Cos* (Boston: Ticknor and Fields), is dated 1860, but it was issued before the end of 1859.

Simms lived on his father-in-law's plantation ("The Woodlands") near Midway, which is nearly equidistant from Charleston and Augusta.]

No. 44

PAUL HAMILTON HAYNE to JOHN ESTEN COOKE

Charleston,
Thursday 17*th* May 1860.

My Dear Friend;

—Accept my *best,* & *warmest* thanks for your sympathising letter of the 14th inst.

When I reflect upon the troubles, thro which *you* have gone during the last winter, my conscience reproaches me for having so persistently obtruded my *own* afflictions upon your notice. It was selfish, and unmanly. Forgive me.

Your theory of life is *true*. About us on every hand are signs, corresponding to inward monitions, which say, "Prepare to die!". For my own part, I confess, that I contemplate dissolution, with feelings strangely compounded of awe, & curiosity. But enough of this gloomy strain.

You ask me to tell you the news. Since the great Democratic Convention left us, *Charleston* has been *more* than usually dull, and dreary. *Apropos* of that convention, I *must* say, that I never saw, (of course, there were illustrious exceptions), a *dirtier*, & more *blackguard* set of fellows; half of the members were drunk, and the remainder could hardly be called sober. In sad earnest, what, *mon ami!* is to be the fate of this great Republic?

Are we not drifting headlong to the Devil? Has not Jefferson's famous dogma in reference to the natural equality of mankind, upon which our Government is founded, been proved untenable, & worthless? Speaking of *Jefferson*, let me congratulate you, upon the *full*, *able*, & *satisfactory* life of him, issued, (from the "Cyclopœdia")—in the May no of the "Messenger."

I have also read with lively interest your articles on *P. Henry*, and *W*. Irving. The Publishers paid you a handsome Compliment, in selecting you as *Irving's* biographer,—& *nobly* have you performed your task.

I spoke of these matters in a former *letter*,—but you'll pardon the tautology.

In the last "*F & F*," your name was introduced in the discussions of "*the Whittington Club*." Doubtless, you have seen the article.

Thompson, I observe, has finally left the *S. L. M.* His valedictory is peculiarly graceful, & appropriate. I cannot say how glad I am, that *T*—, has consented to edit the "*Field & Fireside*"[.]

Mann possesses, beyond question, some good qualities, & *some* ability,—but my literary intercourse with him, has been, upon the whole, *unpleasant!*

He appears to have a nervous apprehension of being *over-reached*, in all his literary negotiations.

The liberty, moreover, which he takes with one's *MSS*, degenerates into absolute *licence.* When, for example, I have been at the trouble of reading a book carefully, to extract its *"cream,"* Mr Mann nullifies my labour by omitting the most important *extracts;* simply because, he does'nt think I have a right to charge for them.!!! *You* know that the labor of *compressing* the thoughts of others is *harder* than original composition.

I am *eagerly* expecting the first installment of the *"Pride of Falling Water."* But let me beg you not to *overwork your-self.* This is the common, & always fatal mistake of most literary men.

Write whenever you can,

& Believe me,

Ever Faithfully *yrs,*

P H Hayne

[Cooke's troubles included the recent death of several close relatives, personal illness, and an unhappy love affair. (See Beaty, pp. 62–3.)

The Democratic National Convention which met in Charleston April 23, 1860, was exceedingly stormy and split into Northern and Southern wings over the party platform and the nomination of Stephen A. Douglas, the two wings adjourning to nominate candidates later at Baltimore and Richmond.

Cooke contributed sketches of Jefferson, Patrick Henry, Madison, Monroe, four Lees, Washington Irving, and others to Appleton's *New American Cyclopoedia,* edited by George Ripley and Charles A. Dana. (See Beaty, pp. 64–6.) Beaty agrees with Hayne (p. 65) that "the invitation to write the paper on Irving was a very particular compliment to Cooke's tact as well as his ability."

John Reuben Thompson (1823–1873) had been editor of the *Southern Literary Messenger* since 1847. In 1860 he became editor of the Augusta *Southern Field and Fireside* (1859–64), a literary and agricultural weekly edited (until May, 1860) by William W. Mann, but returned to Richmond early in the following January. *The Whittington Club* was a series of articles written for the magazine by Hayne.

Cooke wrote *The Pride of Falling Water* in 1860 for the *Southern Field and Fireside.*]

No. 45

PAUL HAMILTON HAYNE to JOHN ESTEN COOKE

Forest Station, Ga R R, July 24th
1866.

My Dear old Friend;

It gave me *real* pleasure to receive your kind letter, which arrived yesterday. How like a voice from the *Past*, it seemed!, a reminiscence of those pleasant times, when life had somewhat of a glory, & charm! *Now* everything is dark with me! Your wish in reference to the results of the war upon me personally, I truly appreciate—, but oh! *mon ami*, I have had a terrible time! To be brief, I am a *Beggar!*

Our house in Charleston was burnt to the ground. *All* the *Banks* have failed, & inevitably every *Bond*, all *Stocks* &c, have taken to themselves wings, & are no more to be seen, or relied upon. A few hundreds of Interest money I can still expect, but even the old Family Silver & Plate, fell into the remorseless clutches of Sherman, & his myrmidons—I am therefore, at present rusticating in a miserable building— termed by *especial* courtesy—a Cottage, situated 16 miles from Augusta on the Central Ga. R. Road, "moiling", when ill health permits—upon ephemeral essays, & verses for the various magazines, Yankee, & Southern. Until *very* recently, I had to live, (with my small family, thank the gods! it *is* so small!!), "from hand to mouth," just grazing the lantern jaws of Starvation—, but the generous kindness of certain friends, has placed us for *5 or 6* months above the fear of absolute want. Indeed, *just now*, if you could stop, & see me, I actually possess the means of treating you with a tolerable degree of hospitality; i. e. you are welcome to a cot-bedstead, some fair Claret, a couple of Cans of Oysters, & *Fresh Salmon,*—a modicum of good smoking *Tobacco*, & by "Bacchus," I might even offer you a "tap" of antique Cognac, or a little generous "mountain dew!!"— Truly, I feel rich, & somewhat puffed up with a pardonable pride!! Could'nt you manage to give wings to that stout "grey steed" of yours,

& fly over on a friendly evening visit? What a jolly night we might make of it!! Concerning your Circular, "the Heroic Women of the South," I promise to do *all* in my power. For the Augusta "Constitutionalist," (now partly edited by Jas R Randall), I'll prepare a proper notice, & will moreover mail copies of your paper to other journals the Proprietors of which are known to me.

Please, *my dear friend,* send me some of your recent *essays, books* &c &c. I should be *so* glad to read them, & (if agreeable to yourself), give a brief notice of the same, here & there. Jno R. Thompson, wrote me, last week, from *London.* He says, that *since* our great National defeat, *all* Confederates are treated quite *de haut en bas* by *Bull,* & his compeers! The mean rascals!, but of course; this was to have been expected. As a People, the English are *intensely selfish.* However, they'll soon be cutting their *own* throats on the Continent. D—n it!, *let them!!* xx You inquire very kindly about *my* Literary projects &c. I can only say, that the events of the last 5 years, have debarred me from carrying out many a fair intellectual plan. "Nathless," I have a goodly pile of *MSS,* (with *one* long poem to head them), which (God willing), I trust to publish—whenever the chance occurs!! A somewhat

[Written vertically in the margin:]

indefinite hope, no doubt!, but still—a hope! God bless you, My *Dear Cooke,* & (with the hope to hear from you at somewhat more length soon) I remain now as Always,

Your faithful friend,

Paul H. Hayne

[The income from Hayne's (or his mother's) South Carolina property amounted to about four hundred dollars a year, of which from a third to one half had to be paid in taxes.

Beaty says (p. 96) that about 1866 Charles B. Richardson of New York offered Cooke two thousand dollars "for a work on the 'heroic women of the South,'" but that Cooke abandoned the project because "no interesting material could be assembled."

James Ryder Randall (1839–1908), native of Baltimore, was teaching in Louisiana when he wrote "Maryland, My Maryland" in 1861. After the war he went to Augusta and was a journalist there (and in Washington) for most of the remainder of his life.

John Reuben Thompson went to London in 1864 to work for the Confederate cause and remained there over a year after the war ended. From 1868 until his death he was literary editor of the New York *Evening Post*, William Cullen Bryant's newspaper.]

No. 46

PAUL HAMILTON HAYNE to JOHN ESTEN COOKE

"Copse Hill" Ga R R
(16 miles from Augusta, Geo
March 16*th* 1877

Dear Old friend;

Your P C. came yesterday, & I at once write to acknowledge your cordial communication.

Somehow, the *briefest note* of yours always *inspirits me!* There's a *tonic* in the very wave of your pen;—& a geniality not to be repressed, or mistaken, trickles, as it were, out of your inkstand, carrying warmth & encouragement to your far-off friends!

I'm heartily glad you liked my S. C. lyric; *heartily glad & grateful* to find that you think I've "done my *literary devoirs*" gallantly! . . . But the idea of your saying that "you yourself are doing *nothing!"*

Why, you work like *"20 horses rolled into one!"*— No man in America can show a fuller record! Novels, essays, biographies, histories, miscellaneous tales, poems &c &c—flow from your brain with a magic facility.

Indeed, your industry amazes me!

x x. I felt sure that *"the Craniologist" must be* your work! Let me tell you that *therein* you have "made a *decided kit,"*—the entire story being of its kind nearly perfect. *"Canalloes,"* [*sic*] I'll read, you may be sure, with avidity. Nay! I'll do *more* than *that.* I'll *notice* the work, and try to increase the sale in this section of Country. x x Thanks again for your kind invitation to visit you. Alack! my dear *Cooke,* I would *fly* to *Millwood,* were the thing possible; but I could as reasonably expect, just now, to fly up into heaven!

But we'll hope for better days! *My wife* joins me in thanking you for all your unselfish courtesy, & kindness, *to her husband!*

She often talks of Mr Jno Esten Cooke, as one of the *very few real Southern gentlemen, left to show what the manners & morale of the South once were!*

x   —By the way, I *enclose* for your amusement *two* political trifles.

Thinking of the Country, & its degradation, one feels simply *desperate!* Thus much *for Republics! Jefferson,* Washington, all of them, were mistaken! Republics are *impossibilities!*

Ever affectionately

Paul H Hayne.

[The "S. C. lyric" referred to may be "South Carolina to the States of the North" (*Complete Edition,* pp. 297–99).

Cooke's "A Craniologist" appeared in *Harper's* for January, 1877, and his *Canolles* was published in Toronto (Belford Brothers) in 1877.   The latter had appeared in 1876 in the Detroit *Free Press.*

Millwood was Cooke's post office, a village near his country home, called "The Briars."]

No. 47

PAUL HAMILTON HAYNE to ROBERTS AND BROTHERS

"Copse Hill" Ga R. Road
(Dec 21*st* 1866.)

To Messrs Roberts & Bro—

Gentlemen;

Your *very* polite note of the 15*th* has just reached me,   x I must again thank you for your liberality & kind consideration.

No doubt the pc*k* you speak of will come in time, & be assured that I shall not fail to notice these books properly.

Of course the Book of Sonnets is worthy of *special* mention. I intend to write *two reviews* of it at least, which shall be duly mailed you.

By the way, you allude to a *blunder* in having credited certain Sonnets to W H, & to Henry Timrod. This is *no* blunder *at all,* since there are *two* Timrods, (father, & son), who have composed beautiful Sonnets, & the initials you mention are perfectly *correct!*

I allude to this matter, because otherwise you might be led into the error of making some false correction.

Believe me, Gentlemen,

Faithfully yours,

Paul H Hayne.

[*The Book of the Sonnet,* edited by Leigh Hunt and S. Adams Lee, two volumes, 1867, was published simultaneously in Boston (Roberts and Brothers) and London (Low). It is devoted to the history of the sonnet with examples by English and American poets. Both Hayne and George Henry Boker of Philadelphia assisted with that part of the work dealing with American sonneteers.

The father of Henry Timrod (1828–1867) was William Henry Timrod (1792–1838), of Charleston. He was a bookbinder, soldier, and political writer as well as a poet.]

No. 48

PAUL HAMILTON HAYNE to ROBERTS AND BROTHERS

Augusta (Ga); Aug 2*nd* 1867

To *Messrs Roberts & Bros, Boston;*

Gentlemen;

I must heartily thank you for the many new works, all valuable, & interesting, which you have sent me. Already, I have prepared very careful reviews of *several,* & they shall all receive due attention in time.

Both in the "*So* Opinion," Richmond, (of which I am Literary Editor), & in the Augusta papers, I shall criticise in all fairness, the books you may desire noticed. Moreover, my intention is, to draw the *special attention* of So *Litterateurs* to the high character of your *Firm.* As the "*R. Table*" said the other day, your *very name* is a guarantee of the ability & value of the productions, bearing your *imprimatur.*

Miss Ingelow's 2nd vo*l* has arrived safely. So soon as I am able I will criticise the book *especially*. Miss Ingelow is a favorite of mine. She possesses real genius.

By the way, I have now in the printer's hands a long notice of your "Myths of the Middle Ages." It is a most curious & entertaining work.

Who do you think I heard from, at length, only 4 days ago? Why, our friend, *S. Adams Lee,* whom I had thought *dead & buried.* Far from this, his health has improved, & he talks about preparing a vo*l* on the *"Experiences of an Opium Eater,"* (from which I shall strenuously dissuade him), besides writing *Lectures* &c.

How did you succeed with "the Book of the Sonnet," I mean in England? Surely, for *Hunt's sake,* his *posthumous* performance *ought* to have been welcomed there! Besides, Hunt's Essay is *intrinsically* a gem.

You are kind eno' to mail me sometimes a copy of the Boston "Transcript" containing notices of your forthcoming books &c. Pray continue to do so. These notices help me essentially.

And now, I beg you to believe, in all sincerity, that I desire, (in my small way), to advance the interests of your House.

I would like *(entre nous),* to see you eclipse *"Ticknor & Fields,"* who like Jeshurun have "waxed fat," & are "kicking," it seems to me, rather arrogantly.

Besides, this firm is becoming day by day so intensely *radical.*

Why c'ant *"the Atlantic,"* let our poor, wretched, undone *South* alone? In God's name have we not suffered sufficiently?

Please let me hear from you.

Always Faithfully,

Paul H Hayne

Bx 260
Augusta P. O.

[Written at the top of p. 3 of the letter:]

Soon I will send you notices of your books.

[Written at the end of the letter:]

Please remember to send your Works to me, Care of Geo Oates, Broad St Augusta (Ga).

[Hayne was literary editor of *Southern Opinion* (1867–1869), a Richmond weekly edited by H. Rives Pollard.

The *Round Table* (1863–1869) was a New York weekly.

Jean Ingelow (1820–1897) was an English poet and story writer, with whom Hayne corresponded.

S. Baring Gould's *Curious Myths of the Middle Ages* was issued by Roberts and Brothers in 1867.

At the time of this letter Ticknor and Fields owned and published the *Atlantic Monthly*. In a letter to R. H. Stoddard dated July 1, 1866, Hayne wrote (*American Literature*, IV, 197): "Like yourself, I am far from being in the 'good books' of Ticknor & Fields. To the latter[,] *once* a personal friend, I wrote, stating my position, & sending him a few brief poems for his monthly. He replied politely, but coldly, remailing the MSS."

Jeshurun is a poetic name for Israel. *Deuteronomy* xxxii.15 begins: "But Jeshurun waxed fat, and kicked. . . ."]

No. 49

PAUL HAMILTON HAYNE to LOUISE CHANDLER MOULTON

My address is P. O. Box 275,
Augusta Geo.

March 3rd 1879

My Dear Madam;

I wrote to the Editor of the "N Y Independent",—my friend Dr Ward—, asking for the address of Mr Philip Bourke Marston; and he tells me to *direct to your care.*

Will you, therefore, have the courtesy to forward the enclosed for me, and thus greatly oblige *one*, who—*en passant*—has often read & admired your beautiful Poems.?

Most Respectfully Yrs

Paul Hamilton Hayne.

Would you inform me whether this had reached you?

[Louise Chandler Moulton (1835–1908), wife of a Boston journalist and publisher, contributed poems, tales, and sketches to the leading magazines and newspapers. Her "beautiful Poems" often appeared in the same magazines as Hayne's. After 1878 she lived much in London, making friends of the leading English writers, including Philip Bourke Marston (1850–1887), blind English poet, whose works she edited. Until his death, Hayne kept up his correspondence with Marston.

Hayne often contributed poems to the New York *Independent* edited by Henry Chandler Bowen and William Hayes Ward.]

IV. LIBRARY OF HARVARD UNIVERSITY (NOS. 50–63)

PAUL HAMILTON HAYNE to JAMES RUSSELL LOWELL

Charleston Dec, 28*th* 1859.

To the Editor of the "Atlantic Monthly."

Dear Sir;

I trust you will not look upon me as intrusive & presumptuous, if I venture to offer you my *heartfelt thanks* for the *indulgent & kindly* notice of my verses, which appeared in the Jan n*o of "the Atlantic"*.

I possess, & have read all the issues of "the Atlantic" from its initial number, & having never found in its Editorial department a prejudiced, or unworthy statement, or the manifestation of narrow-minded, sectional bitterness—it was natural that I should anticipate any review of my own humble vo*l* with a mingled feeling of anxiety, & confidence, *anxiety* lest the book should be viewed as falling far beneath the standards of your criticism; and confidence that whatever the result, *I* should be justly treated.

Now, when your notice actually came, I can hardly tell you the relief it afforded me; what you say of *censure*, is so courteously put, & I *know* so *completely* deserved (for *I* too, since the publication of "Avolio" &c perceive with mortification, that *many* pieces are unworthy)—; and yet, your encouragement seems so *hearty & sincere*—, that I am deeply touched & thankful for it. Why cannot a young author—living as I do in an eminently "uncongenial atmosphere", (oh! you know not *how true* your conjecture on *that* point is!) make of his generous critic a confidante, at least to the degree of tendering his acknowledgements, and expressing the sense of pleasure, & new force, which have been imparted to him? There are *seasons* when a cheering word from those whose powers we respect, & whose truthfulness is patent,— comes to one, situated as I have been—with somewhat of the appeal to fresh life & courage, which the author of that beautiful Eastern poem in your Magz, describes as accompanying "*Abdel-Hassan's*" sight of the "green palm-crest" in the desert.

At all events, such was, I honestly declare, the effect of your "notice" upon *my* spirits.

I *will* "persevere", (as you tell me, *My dear Sir*) "in self-culture"; and if ever again by God's help I am enabled to stand before your noble & just tribunal, perhaps you will learn that the council [*sic*] so kindly given—has not been *utterly* in vain.

Pray, do not think me an unworthy son of the soil that bore me, because I have partially confessed to the justice of your remark in regard to the *unliterary character* of the Southern People. But ah! Sir, to a young literary aspirant, it is very hard to know that his *very profession* is looked upon with contempt, or, at best a sort of half-pitying patronage by those he would fain delight, & satisfy. And yet such is the fact, a fact that cannot be denied. With a sincere rëiteration of my thanks, I remain,

Your obliged servant;

Paul. H. Hayne.

[James Russell Lowell (1819–1891) was poet, critic, essayist, editor, Smith Professor of Modern Languages at Harvard, and diplomat. He was editor of the *Atlantic Monthly* from its beginning in November, 1857, until May, 1861. Of all the New England writers whom Hayne met personally (the list includes Lowell, Emerson, Longfellow, Holmes, Whittier, and Whipple, among others) Lowell seems to have come nearest to overawing him. In their relationship—which was not very intimate—there seems to have been as much humility on the part of Hayne as there was on the part of the young Howells, whereas there was in both cases a slight touch of condescension on the part of Lowell. He was, however, very kind and generous to Hayne.

In the *Atlantic Monthly* for January, 1860 (V, 123–4), appears the review of Hayne's *Avolio; A Legend of the Island of Cos* . . . , Boston: Ticknor and Fields, 1860. The volume had come out before the end of 1859. The review contains these sentences: "There is a great deal of real poetic feeling and expression in this volume, and, we think, the hope of better things to come. . . . There is a tone of sadness in the volume, as if the author were surrounded by an atmosphere uncongenial to letters.

. . . Mr. Hayne need only persevere in self-culture to be able to produce poems that shall win for him a national reputation."
"Abdel-Hassan" appears in the same issue of the *Atlantic* (V, 70–4). It is unsigned. *The Atlantic Index* (1889) ascribes it to B. R. Plumly.]

No. 51

PAUL HAMILTON HAYNE to JAMES RUSSELL LOWELL

Sunday, Aug. 11*th* 1860.
(Aiken So Ca).

My Dear Sir;

I thank you *sincerely* for your note of the 5th inst, which reached me *yesterday*.

I am *glad* that the Sonnet, sent to *"the Atlantic"*, has met with your approval, & is accepted.

Let me take this opportunity of *again* thanking you for the *beautiful* notice of my verses which appeared in your magz some months ago.

I value your criticism *very highly*, & shall certainly endeavour to profit by your advice, which I *feel* to be most excellent.

There was *one* passage in your notice, which particularly struck me. Ah! Sir, it is *too* true that to any earnest literary man the society of the South *is* uncongenial.

You will not deem me unpatriotic, or false to my people, & section, in making *such* a confession. But often—, how often! I think of the dear friends I have in Boston, & contrasting the society *there*, with the society in Charleston, (I mean of a *literary* kind),—it is impossible for me to feel otherwise than *"sad"*.

Hoping to meet you, in the course of time again,
I remain, *dear* Sir,
Very truly, & cordially *yrs*,

Paul H Hayne

[Aiken, about eighteen miles northeast of Augusta, was a popular summer resort for people from the Carolina coast. Hayne published an article on it in *Appleton's Journal* for December 2, 1871 (VI, 623–6).

Hayne's "Sonnet. Written After a Violent Thunder-storm in the Country" appeared in the *Atlantic Monthly* for October, 1860 (VI, 481). Two earlier poems of his had been published in the *Atlantic*—"Sonnet" (beginning "The brave old Poets sing of nobler themes"), February, 1858 (I, 500), and "Anno Domini, 1860," August, 1860 (VI, 228–9).]

No. 52

PAUL HAMILTON HAYNE to JAMES RUSSELL LOWELL

Aiken (So Ca) Aug. 20th 1860.

Dear Sir;

I write to ask your aid in a matter, which I feel sure will interest you.

I happen, just now, to be Engaged with a friend in the preparation of *materiel* for an essay on "American Sonnets, & Sonnet-writers,"—designed to accompany a most elaborate, & able work on the "Italian, & English Sonnetteers" by the late Mr Leigh Hunt, the *MS* of which is at present, in my possession.

Hunt prepared *his* portion of the work at the instance of a young relative of his, (Mr S. Adams Lee of Washington, Penn), not many months before his decease, leaving the part on our American Sonnetteers, to be composed by an American.

The gentleman to whom the task has fallen, thought proper to associate me with him; I am therefore endeavouring to collect all the material I can, but Heaven knows! it is *so far* scanty enough!——x *Your own Sonnets* will of course, be prominently included in the Collection; only, I should feel deeply indebted, if you would point out to me *those*, which in *your* estimation, are the best. I do not like to rely upon my immature judgment in a matter of this sort. Also, if you can send me the vo*l* of your poems (by mail) in which your Sonnets are published, I should feel still further obligated.

One other request, & I have done. Is it in your power to furnish me with a list of the names of those poets, in Boston *(especially)*, & N. England *(generally)* who have written

Sonnets, Sonnets that are worthy of re-production in the work I have mentioned?

A *list* is before me now, but I wish to do justice to all; hence, my request! Let me hope, *dear Sir,* that you will not deem me presumptuous, or intrusive, in thus asking your assistance;—

I am so situated, that it is *impossible* for me to prosecute the work in question, without soliciting help from those competent to give it.

Confident that you will not misunderstand me,

I remain *Dear Sir,*

Truly & Respectfully Yours,

Paul H Hayne

Direction,

> P H Hayne,
> Care of Jno *R Matthews* Esq
> *Aiken*
> *So Ca*

[The publication of the work in which Hayne was interested was held up until after the war: *The Book of the Sonnet,* ed. by Leigh Hunt and S. Adams Lee, 2 vols., Boston: Roberts Brothers, 1867. (An English edition appeared in the same year.) The essay on "American Sonnets and Sonneteers" is in I, 95–131. Hayne and George Henry Boker of Philadelphia worked on it. See Jay B. Hubbell's statement concerning the matter, *Am. Lit.,* V, 147–8.]

No. 53

PAUL HAMILTON HAYNE to JAMES RUSSELL LOWELL

Augusta, Geo
March 11th (1870.)

Dear Sir;

Will you honor me by accepting a copy of the enclosed "legend"? The story is doubtless familiar to you, as one recorded, first, in "Albion's England," and subsequently, amplified by *Hunt* in his essays.

I hope my own treatment of it may please you.

It is however, with a *sincere* diffidence that I venture to bring such a comparative trifle to the notice of the author of *"Under the Willows,"* & *"The Cathedral"*,.

My excuse is, the belief, that to the *true* Poet *anything poetical*, (no matter how humble, & unambitious the department of poetic Art represented), will be regarded with something of indulgence, if not favor . Under the name of *"The Fair Revenge"*, (see Hunt's *"Indicator"*) this narrative was a special favorite with *Shelley*.

> Believe me, *dear Sir,*
> Most Respectfully,
> & Truly Yours,
>
> *Paul H Hayne*

P O Box 635,
   Augusta Geo

[Hayne's "Daphles. An Argive Story" appears in *Complete Edition,* pp. 89–100. "The Fair Revenge" is found in the *Indicator* for Wednesday, January 12, 1820 (I, No. XIV, 109–112). The opening sentence begins: "The elements of this story are to be found in the old poem called Albion's England. . . . " It tells the story of Daphles, queen of Argos.

Lowell's *Under the Willows and Other Poems* came out in 1869 and *The Cathedral* in 1870. Hayne may have seen the latter in the *Atlantic Monthly* for January, 1870.]

No. 54

PAUL HAMILTON HAYNE to JAMES RUSSELL LOWELL

> *"Copse* Hill," near *Augusta* Geo
> *April. 5th 1875.*

My Dear Sir;

   Twenty years ago, after a dinner party in the old Albion Coffee House, Boston, at which Mr Emerson, Mr Longfellow, Mr Whipple, and other famous men were present, I distinctly remember having had a pleasant half hour's conversation with you upon poetry in general, and some of your *own* poems, *("The Wife of Brittany")* &c, in particular. You kindly informed me *when* [*where?*], and *how* you had composed that noble story; and seemed not ungratified by my boyish, but conspicuously *sincere* admiration of it.

There and then in the dusk of an Autumn afternoon, we parted,—*you* to to [*sic*] conceive, embody, publish, yet more vigorous poetry; to win year by year, a still higher place in the esteem of your Contemporaries; to mingle with the great world abroad, and enjoy the converse of the "marked minds" of our century; in brief, to develope your lofty genius loftily; to live a full, rare, unfettered existence in the brightest sunshine of Art—, whilst I, turning my face homeward, went to encounter—*what?* Why, for some time, the discouragements which always attended the Literary aspirant, residing in the South; and then, a very "blackness of darkness" during the *four years* of that awful sectional war,—with—(in common with all my people), *utter ruin afterwards!* I am merely stating facts, not hinting a complaint. Are *any* of us "stronger than destiny?"—

Thro all changes, and chances, however, I have endeavored to develope whatever small artistic gifts I might possess; and now, I venture to send you the *only* vo*l* which I am not utterly ashamed of, trusting its perusal, (should you honor it so far), may *not*, at least, weary you.

When these *"Legends & Lyrics"* were published, you, I think, were in Italy.

During the summer of 1873, I visited the North for the first time since 1855. I was bitterly disappointed to find *you* still absent from *America;* so, all I could do, was to ride around your Cambridge house, and to exchange a few words with Mr *Aldrich,* under the shadow of your garden trees.

Your works, *(prose & poetry)* have been invaluable to me, and many a lyric & sonnet of yours I know by *heart;*—but among your graven efforts, I know of nothing so thoroughly noble, & suggestive of all manful, elevated sentiment, as the Ode upon the death of *Agassiz.* It stirs one's *innermost* soul!

Some stanzas ring out grandly, like martial music; some bring unconsciously the tears to one's eyes.

As for the *political* portion, (which appears to have offended certain people), well—"the greater the *truth*, the greater the *libel!*"

But I must not detain you longer.

I should like to know that the little book, together with the present note had duly reached their destination.

With sentiments of deep admiration, & respect—

I am Always Faithfully

Paul. H *Hayne*

P. O. Box 635, *Augusta Geo*

[On October 14, 1854, Hayne dined at the Albion with Alcott, Emerson, Lowell, E. P. Whipple, John Sullivan Dwight, and Horatio Woodman. (See George Willis Cooke, *John Sullivan Dwight: Brook-Farmer, Editor, and Critic of Music: A Biography*, Boston: Small, Maynard & Company, 1898, pp. 238–9.) It is probable that this is the dinner party to which Hayne refers. Anyway, Lowell was in Europe in the fall of 1855.

Lowell's poem referred to in the first paragraph is probably "A Legend of Brittany."

Legends and Lyrics came out in 1872. In that year Lowell went to Europe and remained until the middle of 1874, mainly in Paris, Rome, and Florence. Aldrich occupied his house while he was away.

In 1873 Thomas Bailey Aldrich (1836–1907) was editor of *Every Saturday*, of Boston. From 1881 until 1890 he was editor of the *Atlantic Monthly*.

Lowell's "Agassiz" appeared in the *Atlantic Monthly* for May, 1874 (XXXIII, 586–96). The second stanza of the poem begins with a spirited attack upon the scandals and corruptions of Grant's administration, of which attack, of course, Hayne heartily and enthusiastically approved.

Louis John Rudolph Agassiz (1807–1873), Swiss naturalist, had been Lowell's intimate friend and colleague on the Harvard faculty and in the Saturday Club.]

No. 55

PAUL HAMILTON HAYNE to JAMES RUSSELL LOWELL

Augusta Ga,
Sep 30*th* 1875.

Dear Sir;

Some months ago, from *four* to *six mts'*, I suppose—, I wrote you a long letter, accompanied, (if my "memory" serves), by a little vo*l* of verse, which I prayed you to accept.

Now, so doubtful are the mails from this quarter; so often have I had the trouble & disappointment of mailing letters, (some of importance) only to hear of their loss that I fear my communication to you must have *miscarried.*

Could you drop me *a line* upon this topic? & thus oblige

Yours Faithfully

Paul H Hayne. (P O Box 635)

No. 56

PAUL HAMILTON HAYNE to HORACE ELISHA SCUDDER

"Copse Hill"
Near Augusta Ga Dec 11*th* '68

My Dear M*r* Scudder;

I am writing for your magaz a little story which I really think you will like. It is called *"The Life of a Robin Red-breast, As told by himself"*, partly a fairy-tale of course, but by no means extravagant.

Some intelligent literary gentlemen who have seen portions of the tale encourage me to proceed, so, I will finish it.

By the way, did you Ever hear of a *tamed* Robin;, I mean of a *Robin* confined in a Cage? Would a representation to *that* effect contradict the facts & principles of Ornithology? & even if it *did* so contradict them, would not the licence be allowable in a half-fairy tale? Weighty questions, which I know you will kindly answer!

Now, if my little story suits you *perfectly*, will you accept it? And supposing the *MSS* is mailed you about the latter part of Jan or 1st Fe*b*, *when* would it appear?

By the way, when your Ja*n* no is issued, may I venture to ask for 2 or 3 extra copies? The cost of these, you know, can be *deducted* from whatever amount you conclude to pay me for the article on N Orleans.

As the Christmas approaches, how I wish it were in my power to visit "old Boston", & walk its dear, crooked Streets once more.! A rabid Southerner Some would call me, but for all that, I love Boston, & once I had many good friends there. But alas!, there is no travelling, no recreation for me or mine *now:* That thrice-accursed war has ruined us. My little boy—, (a really bright little fellow who loves "The Riverside" better than anything in the world), can't even be sent to school;—I teach him myself. No loaded Christmas tree will adorn our cottage home: *Turkey* is a dream of past ages, & *plum-puddings* visit the children only in the visions of night!

Thankful are we if the *Bacon*, & *homony* [sic] don't give out, & the brown sugar remains to sweeten a scanty jorum of egg-nog, with just a soupçon of *corn whiskey!*

Such is a faint outline of the condition of our Southern homes in general. *One* reason why I stick to the Country is, that Tailors' Bills may be avoided! Why, bless your soul, I've worn *one* pair of *patched breeches* for 3 years *(seasons)*; & like Philip in Thackeray's latest novel, I rather glory in my broken boots.

Excuse all this egotism. I d'ont [sic] know what has tempted me to write thus.

Only *never* suppose we *complain*. A beggar can be merry as any king, & his cares are comparative trifles—while the Bacon & flour lasts!

Please let me hear from you, & Believe me

Always Faithfully,

Paul H Hayne

[Written in the margin:]

P. O. Box 260. Augusta Ga

[Horace Elisha Scudder (1838–1902) was editor of the *Riverside Magazine for Young People* (1867–1870). I have not had access to a file of this magazine. Scudder edited the *Atlantic Monthly* from 1890 until 1898. He was a prolific author and editor.

Hayne's only child, William Hamilton Hayne (1856–1929), was educated mainly at home but went to school for a time in Charleston. He became a poet and critic and contributed frequently to the leading magazines. He did not marry. He spent most of his life at Copse Hill and in Augusta. One small volume of his poems (*Sylvan Lyrics and Other Verses*, New York: Frederick A. Stokes Company) appeared in 1893, but most of his verse remains uncollected.

Thackeray published *The Adventures of Philip* in the *Cornhill Magazine* (in 1861–1862), of which he was editor. This was his last complete novel.]

No. 57

PAUL HAMILTON HAYNE to WILLIAM DEAN HOWELLS

Augusta, March 11*th* 1870.

My Dear Sir;

An author like yourself, is sure to make many friends whom he can never see on earth.

For *myself*, I can truly say, that your books have been to me an ever present delight. They have re-created, (particularly those on "Italy"), the buoyant glory of my youth, and transported me to a land I can never, while life lasts, forget.

Would to Heaven I could impart to you a *hundredth* portion of the pleasure which I have derived from *your* writings;—yet, since *this* is impossible, I must content myself, with the request that you would do me the honor of accepting the enclosed poem,—a legend the treatment of which may possibly interest you. The *elements* of the story are to be found in "*Albion's England*," but I encountered it *first* in Hunt's "*Indicator*."

Pray believe me, *Dear Sir*
Your sincere *Admirer*,
& *friend*,

Paul H Hayne

P O Box 635, Augusta Ga

[William Dean Howells (1837–1920) had been American consul at Venice from 1861 until 1865 and had written *Venetian Life* (1866) and *Italian Journeys* (1867). He was on the staff of the *Atlantic Monthly* from 1866 until 1881, being editor after 1871. Later he was on the staff of *Harper's* for twenty-five years (1886–1891, 1900–1920).

"Daphles" was the poem which Hayne sent with the letter.]

No. 58

PAUL HAMILTON HAYNE to WILLIAM DEAN HOWELLS

Augusta,
Saturday, 14*th* Dec:
1872.

My Dear Mr Howells;

Enclosed, I send you the only photo of myself I can now procure. Everybody pronounces it *bad;* and my wife goes so far as to declare it looks absolutely *"crazy"*.

But the *artists*—one after another—, assuring me that there's "somewhat amiss" in my ugly "mug" which prevents them from taking a satisfactory "presentment,"—why—I'm *forced* to send you the *best* or *worst* they have attempted!

Need I say, *My kind Sir*, that your *own* photo: would be *especially welcome* in our *Cottage?*—Indeed, I cannot but regard our list of likenesses of American *Literati* as wofully incomplete without the face of the author of *"Italian Journeys"* & *"Venetian Life."*

In great haste,
but *Always Faithfully,*

Paul H Hayne

(P O Box 635)

[The friendly regard which Hayne entertained for Howells, as indicated in this letter, was later to undergo a decided alteration. One cause was Howells's cold or silent rejection of poem after poem which Hayne offered him for the *Atlantic Monthly*. He may have heard also of Howells's cavalier treatment of Lanier. Moreover, he was greatly irritated by Howells's frequent praise of the type of fiction being produced by

Henry James in preference to the kind written by Simms, Scott, Thackeray, Dickens, and others whom Hayne admired.

For a Hayne letter to Howells dated May 21, 1873, see J. DeLancey Ferguson, "A New Letter of Paul Hamilton Hayne," *Am. Lit.* for January, 1934 (V, 368–70).]

No. 59

PAUL HAMILTON HAYNE to [?]

Augusta, Dec *4th* 1874.:

My Dear Sir;

Since you have no *unpublished* piece of mine on hand at present, (excepting a very *brief poem* of some 3 or 4 stanzas), I venture to offer the enclosed for your examination.

Perhaps it would appear most appropriately in your column for the *Juveniles;* but of that *you* must judge; if indeed, the verses should suit your paper *at all*, which of course I *hope* they may.

I offer these verses at your *usual* price for such things.

Can you drop me a line ab't their fate?

Always most Respectfully & Truly,

Paul H Hayne.

(P O Box 635):

[The poem enclosed, apparently, was "On the Death of Canon Kingsley."]

No. 60

PAUL HAMILTON HAYNE to JOHN GREENLEAF WHITTIER

"Copse Hill," Georgia Rail Road,
17*th* December 1881

Address:

P. O. Box 275
Augusta, Ga.

Dear Friend,

My *wife* & I wish you to know that you are held in sweet remembrance to-day, & we pray God that his *richest spiritual* gifts may be yours.

The papers say, that you are *again* sick, & I fear there is *some* truth in this report, as I have not heard from you of late.

Please let us hear *directly*, (if you are *able* to write, which I trust you may be), but if *not*, ask one of the ladies to inform us how you are.

By the present mail I send a book for *Phoebe, directed* to you. Do give it to her on *Xmas* morning.

Dr Holmes wrote me, that the journals say, Longfellow had *Vertigo* and *since* I have heard, (about 2 weeks ago) from Miss Annie Longfellow, that tho her father was "decidedly better he was nevertheless, mending *very* slowly; had been confined to his chamber *six weeks*, & was forbidden to *write* anything, or to see any visitors".

—Since my last communication both Dr Holland & Sidney Lanier have passed away. In regard to myself, I am as usual; (i e) *sick* one day & up the *next;* but *always* determined to surrender *only* when—I *can't* help it!—

We are having a keen touch of *Winter;*—a season I'm not fond of.

Our love to the ladies & to little Phoebe, & for yourself believe me

now as ever

Your devoted friend,

Paul H Hayne.

[Hayne's correspondence with John Greenleaf Whittier (1807–1892), New England poet, began in 1870 when Hayne sent to Whittier a copy of "Daphles." Samuel T. Pickard (*Life and Letters of John Greenleaf Whittier*, Boston and New York: Houghton, Mifflin and Company, 1894, II, 502) quotes from a letter from Whittier to a friend: "I was one of the very first to recognize the rare gift of the Carolinian poet Timrod, and I was the intimate friend of the lamented Paul H. Hayne, though both wrote fiery lyrics against the North." Albert Mordell (*Quaker Militant: John Greenleaf Whittier*, Boston and New York: Houghton Mifflin Company, 1933, pp. 281-2) says: "Curiously enough, Whittier established in late life closer relations with Paul Hamilton Hayne, a Southern poet who had upheld slavery and secession, than he did with the New England poets." He adds (pp. 282-3) that both Hayne and his wife visited Whittier in the fall of 1879 and that Hayne visited Whittier a second time in the summer of 1885. Hayne paid tribute to Whittier in several poems. See *Complete Edition*, pp. 290-3 and 339.

Six letters from Hayne to Whittier were published in *Whittier Correspondence from the Oak Knoll Collections 1830–1892*, ed. by John Albree, Salem, Massachusetts: Essex Book and Print Club, 1911. The dates and page references follow: March 23, 1870 (pp. 175–7), April 22, 1870 (pp. 178–9), March 19, 1874 (pp. 187–9), January 10, 1878 (pp. 199–201), February 8, 1878 (pp. 202–5), and October 26, 1880 (pp. 219–23).

The day on which this letter was written was Whittier's seventy-fourth birthday.

The ladies with whom Whittier lived at Danvers, Massachusetts, after 1876 were the three daughters of Colonel Edmund Johnson: the Misses Johnson and Mrs. Abby Woodman. They were his cousins.

The young girl referred to is Phoebe Woodman, the adopted daughter of Mrs. Abby Woodman. She was about 11 when Hayne visited Whittier in 1879. Whittier was very fond of her, and apparently Hayne was too.

Hayne knew personally and corresponded with Oliver Wendell Holmes (1809–1894).

Dr. Josiah Gilbert Holland (1819–1881) died October 12, 1881. He was editor of *Scribner's Monthly* from 1870 until his death. He was a popular author of poetry and fiction. Hayne contributed poetry to the magazine, and many other Southern writers found a welcome there.

Sidney Lanier (1842–1881) died September 7, 1881. He and Hayne were friends and corresponded for years, though they had never met.]

No. 61

PAUL HAMILTON HAYNE to [JOHN GREENLEAF WHITTIER?]

"Copse Hill,"
Georgia Railroad.
June 23*rd* 1882

Address:

P. O. Box 275,
Augusta, Ga.

My Dear Friend;—

I wrote you at some length a few days ago, and hope that my communication did not miscarry?

Now, I wish your artistic advice in reference to a *personification*—(in a "Farm Poem") entitled *"In the Wheat Field"*.

After describing to the best of my ability, the different phases which such a "Field" presents at *dawn, noontide* &c, I come to the *evening effects* . . (E. g.)—

> "And the sky in its mellowed lustre seems
> Like the realm of a master Poet's mind,
> A shifting kingdom of splendid dreams,
> With grander. & fairer *truths* behind:—
> And the changeful colors that blend or part
> Ebb like the tides of a living heart,
> As the splendors melt, & the shadows meet,—

Which?
{ And the tresses (hair) of Twilight trail (trails) over the wheat!
And the dusk of gloaming droops over the wheat!

The idea of *Twilight* descending upon the Earth in the form of a woman veiled in her *own dusky hair* whence a shadowy radiance exhales, I derived from one of *Turner's pictures* a copy of which *used* to hang upon the walls of the *"Boston Athenaeum"*.

Is this *image in my lyric* under the conditions outlined, *too bold?*

With best remembrances from my wife,

I am (in *haste*) but
Ever affectionately

Paul H Hayne.

[This letter has faded so much that a few words are practically illegible. Miss Carolyn E. Jakeman of the Harvard College Library thinks it was sent to Whittier. Although it does not refer to the letter which Whittier wrote to Hayne on June 6 at the Isles of Shoals (see Hayne's next letter), the explanation is probably that the letter had not reached Hayne by June 23. There was no post office on any of the islands (says Ambrose O'Connell, First Assistant Postmaster General, in a letter to me dated December 10, 1941), and mail to and from the islands had to be transported by private means, probably from and to Portsmouth, New Hampshire.

The *American: A National Weekly Journal of Politics, Literature, Science, Art and Finance* for May 27, 1882 (IV, 108) states: *"Home and Farm,* a very prominent rural semi-monthly, published at Louisville. Kentucky, announces that it has arranged for a number of poems from the pen of Paul H. Hayne, 'illustrating the various aspects of life on the

farm.' The first, 'The Farmer's Wife,' appeared in the March issue."
Hayne's "In the Wheat Field" appeared in the issue for August 1, 1882.
I have not seen the issue, but the poem was quoted in the *Southern
Bivouac* for September. 1886 (II. 229–30). In the latter place, the last
two lines in the passage quoted in the letter above are reduced to this
line:

"And the tresses of Twilight trail over the wheat."

"In the Wheat Field" is a good nature poem, but it was composed too
late to appear in *Complete Edition*. which had already gone to press.

Turner was the famous English painter (Joseph Mallord (or Mallad)
William Turner. 1775–1851). Elinor Gregory Metcalf. Librarian at the
Boston Athenæum. writes me (December 24. 1941) that the Athenæum
owns a water-color copy of a Turner. made in 1867 by Ward—probably
William Ward (1829–1908)—under the direction of John Ruskin. Her
description of the picture reads, in part, as follows: "A harbor or river,
boats in the foreground, castle on rocky hillside at left. another castle
or tower in background. sky half light blue. half darker blue—*could* be
twilight." Whether this is the picture which Hayne had in mind I do
not know.]

No. 62

PAUL HAMILTON HAYNE to JOHN GREENLEAF WHITTIER

"Copse Hill", Georgia
July 16*th* 1882

My Dear Friend;

Assuredly our days *do* slip away somehow, with remarkable, & elf-like facility.!! Here, for example, is your last
affectionate & interesting letter from *"Isles of Shoals"*, bearing date the 6*th* ult!!— *More* than a month ago; (!!) I can
hardly believe it. There's a certain buoyant bright atmosphere about this epistle of your's [*sic*], which of itself assures
me, *dear Friend,* of your improved *health.* May the ocean
breezes contribute *still* further to your restoration! The
Island you now sojourn upon, must indeed be a charming
place; and doubtless, Nature's beauty is enhanced by the the
[*sic*] companionship of *such a* woman, & poet as Mrs Thaxter.

She knows *well* what I think of her exquisite genius;—
for some years since, I had a critique upon her last vol, (*but
one)* issued in *"the H Journal,"* in acknowledgement whereof,

she wrote me a very cordial, sweet, womanly letter. xxxxxxx You touch again, (& quite naturally), upon the sadness of the reflection that so many *old friends* have recently left for *"the undiscovered Country"*. And you express the wish that *"some courteous ghost"* might return, to speak definitely of his *"whereabouts"*.

—*Apropos,* I am about to communicate, upon this solemn & momentous topic, a series of facts to you, which I have *never told before* to any human being, *but my wife.*

After a candid perusal of my narrative, *(for the details of which I vouch),* you can form your own opinion, as to the *legitimate deductions,* which *Logic & Reason* are authorized *to draw* (!)—

Here, then, are the circumstances:—

x   x   x

About the autumn of the year 1862–3—the bloody battle of *"Fort Wagner"*, was fought in *Charleston Harbor.* An *old & very intimate College friend* of mine,—a Major in the Confederate Infantry—, participated in that Engagement. His name was *David Ramsay*—a *grandson* of the distinguished *Ramsay,* (whose Christian name also was David), to whom we owe one of the earliest & best of our *"Histories of the U. States".*

At *that* period I chanced to be staying temporarily near Greenville C. H. So Carolina— The news of the fight came (I *think*) upon a Tuesday evng.—

Among the names of the wounded was that of *my friend.* "Major David Ramsay", (the *"Charleston Courier"* said in effect), "had been *painfully but not dangerously* wounded, in the groin".

"In a few *weeks"*, the paper added, "he would doubtless be enabled to *resume* his command".

—Thinking, of course, that this account was correct, I expected to hear *soon* of *R's* convalescence.

There was no *presentiment* of Danger;—no room for the exercise of *imaginative fears.*

xx   Well!—upon the Saturday evng, which followed the reception of the intelligence indicated—I happened to be walk-

ing along the rustic path outside of the the [*sic*] village, which
led to my *temporary* home.

It was after sunset; and the dim rays of *the moon* began
to mingle with the shadows of the oakwood opposite.

Just *then* I saw about 30 *steps* in front of me the figure
of a man slowly sauntering along; & wrapped in what looked
like a brown cloak!!— As I approached him, he crossed the
road toward the wood; then turned, crossed the road again;
and came directly towards me.

The light was quite sufficient for me to see his face;—&
you may fancy my feeling when I at once recognized it as
Ramsay's.— While I hesitated, under the influence of an
absolutely *indescribable* sensation, the figure, apparition,
phantom—(whatever we may term it), *again* crossed the
road, and—*disappeared* among the trees!.

Forty-eight hours after, I *learned* that *Ramsay* had, *(unexpectedly)* died, upon that very Saturday afternoon; his *wound*
having proved far more serious than was at first supposed.

The facts of this case I put literally before you.

My *wife,* (as stated above), has—up *to the present period*—
been the *only recipient* of my confidence; & for obvious reasons, I would ask you not to mention the matter.

But you must see, that I, at least, believe in the possibility
of our dead returning sometimes.

Ever Most Faithfully

Paul H Hayne

Address P O Box 275
          Augusta Geo

[The Isles of Shoals, eight or nine in number, are located ten miles
southeast of Portsmouth, New Hampshire. Appledore, Star, and White
are the names of three of them.

Celia Laighton Thaxter (1835–1894) was a poet and story writer. Her
father was keeper of the lighthouse at the Isles of Shoals. In 1848 he
opened a summer hotel on Appledore Island which became famous as the
resort of artists and writers, including Whittier, Lowell, and Thoreau.
After Celia's marriage and removal to the mainland she often spent
a part of each year at Appledore and died there. Her volume to which
Hayne refers may be *Poems* (1874). Lowell describes the island in
"Pictures from Appledore."

The *Home Journal* was a New York weekly edited, at that time, by Morris Phillips and George Perry.

The siege of Fort Wagner, on Morris Island, at the south side of the entrance to Charleston Harbor, lasted from July 10 till September 6, 1863.

David Ramsay (1830–1863) was the son of Dr. James Ramsay. He and Hayne attended Coates' School and the College of Charleston, but Ramsay left in 1849, before graduating, to study law at Göttingen, Berlin, and Heidelberg (where he graduated *summa cum laude*). He practised law in Charleston and was elected to the legislature in 1858 and 1860. He entered the Confederate service as a captain and was later promoted to the rank of major. He and others put up the flag when it was shot down at Fort Wagner on July 18, 1863. On the evening of the same day, which was Saturday, he was wounded and he died on the night of Tuesday, August 4. The first account of him which I have found in the Charleston *Daily Courier* is in the issue for Monday, July 20 (which may have reached Greenville on Tuesday), but it states specifically that Major Ramsay was "severely" and "dangerously" wounded. The issue for Wednesday, August 5, announces his death on the preceding night. Hence Hayne's memory was somewhat inaccurate.

David Ramsay (1749–1815), physician and historian, produced a number of works, including a history of South Carolina (1809), a history of the American Revolution (1789), a life of George Washington (1807), and *History of the United States, from . . . 1607, to the Year 1808 . . .* (1816).

Of course the "C. H." after "Greenville" stands for "Court House."]

No. 63

PAUL HAMILTON HAYNE to JOHN GREENLEAF WHITTIER

\#   Address (for the present) at
Grovetown, Columbia Co
Georgia.
"Copse Hill" Geo
Oct 1*st* 1884

My Dear Friend;

I feel absolutely *impelled* to write to you, every now & then; for it seems as if the Fates had pretty well determined never to bring us together "in the flesh" *again!*

You cannot travel *South,* & I've no reason to suppose that I shall ever enjoy the opportunity of visiting the North in these, my latter days! The conviction deeply saddens me!

Ah me! *what* a difference in one's innocent enjoyments, & covetted companionships the lack of a little needful money *does* make!

Wealth I *care not* for; but it appears *hard, hard* that the non-possession of so trifling a sum as some men spend on their cigars in the course of a few months, should "cabin and confine" one to prosaic surroundings, and keep forever apart sympathising hearts, & minds!! Let me hope, *my old & honored friend,* that the "sunset of life" is in *your* case, bright, & serene?— You are a *good* no less than a *gifted* man!—& the consolation of knowing that your *Muse* has elevated & consoled *thousands, ought* to bring the most *soothing* peace to your declining days. *Is* it *not* so, indeed?— x x x x x For myself, you'll regret to hear that my health is steadily declining.

In Sep: I almost gave up; so feeble was I, so nervously exhausted.

I'm a trifle *better* at *present,* but my life-term cannot now be long.

Probably I shall precede you to the land of shadows & of mystery. (*All this* is *in confidence,*—for I strive to keep up— concealing from my wife the actual weakness which oppresses me; since if I finally recover, why should she have been made to suffer?— Please *d'ont* [*sic*] allude to *my illness* in replying).

End of miserable egotism.

Won't you tell me in writing something of yourself? Not merely of your health but plans, & prospects? May we expect another vo*l* of Poems from your hand? I *hope* so, *fervently.*

Despite ill health, I have myself, not been idle. Glance over the enclosed, & tell me, frankly, how it strikes you. By the way, please return *printed* copy, which is the *only* one I possess.

Our best remembrances to your kind kinswomen, the *Misses Johnston* [*sic*].

For yourself receive our *united love,* (my *wife's* & mine). Trusting to see soon your familiar handwriting;

Believe me *Ever affectionately yrs*

Paul H Hayne.

How is *Phoebe?* How I would like to meet that child again— hardly a child now, I suppose.

[Hayne died July 6, 1886, less than two years after he wrote this letter. He had had tuberculosis for many years and had complained of "the lung trouble" as early as the 1850's.

Albert Mordell (*op. cit.*, p. 283) says that Hayne visited Whittier again in the summer of 1885. I do not know what the evidence of the visit is.

For information concerning the Misses Johnson and Phoebe see the notes on the Whittier letter, above, dated December 17, 1881 (No. 60).]

V. LIBRARY OF THE UNIVERSITY OF VIRGINIA
(NOS. 64–70)

No. 64

PAUL HAMILTON HAYNE to JOHN REUBEN THOMPSON

Charleston, May 22nd 1860

My Dear John;

I have been expecting to see you for some days past, because I indulged in the hope that possibly, you would pass thro Charleston. But I was disappointed to observe by yesterday's *"Mercury"* that you had stolen a march upon us, & repaired to Augusta, quietly, &, as it were, by night.

Let me say, once for all, that I anticipate the pleasure of seeing you here, at least occasionally, now, that you have taken up your abode in our sister city. I myself, shall be compelled to leave Charleston with my wife, in 3 weeks' time, for Aiken (S C), where we expect to spend the summer. This move altho most inconvenient, so far as *I* am concerned, has been rendered absolutely necessary, by the continued ill-health of Mrs H—. For nearly *a year*, she has not been able to leave the *house*, & for *months*, has been a prisoner in her *chamber*. During this period, I have suffered, God only knows how deeply, from anxiety, & the effects of continual watching.

When we return to our home in autumn, I look forward with pleasure to the chance of having you with me on a visit. Early in Nov, we can go together, to Mr *Simms'*, whose plantation is only 4 hours ride (on the cars) from this place. There, we can enjoy ourselves, hunting.

Yesterday, I sent you No 9 (or rather the first part of it) belonging to a series of Lit papers, I propose continuing for some months, or, at least weeks longer—, provided you accept them.

I am also about preparing for the *"F & F,"* under a *nom de plume*, a far more important series, of articles on the old, & least known of the *British Poets*, detailing the main events of their lives, and offering brief criticisms upon their work. I shall take *especial pains* with these essays.

As for *"the Whittington Club,"* I am forced to compose the
no*s* hastily, & the *MSS* must often seem slovenly. Henceforth,
I will make them *shorter*, if possible, so as not to take up too
much of your valuable space. In order to accomplish this, I
will do as I did yesterday, viz, divide the no*s* into *two parts*
&c &c.

And now, *My dear old friend*, let me wish you the most
abundant success, in your new undertaking. I speak my honest sentiments, when I declare, that I have always regarded
you as—, in *many respects*—, the *best literary* Editor in this
country.

Graceful, honest, vigorous, your criticisms, (altho *I c'ant*
agree with them always), are such as to command every
intelligent man's consideration; and we all look with peculiar
interest to your *debût* in the *"F & F"*—.

Please remember that I am *not flattering* you, but speaking
as an *old friend*, may, (I think) with propriety, be allowed to
speak, sometimes.

If you are not well acquainted with M*r* Gardner, I Can tell
you, that he is one of the most liberal, & gentlemanly persons
it has ever been my good fortune to meet. Your connection
with *him*, *must* prove *agreeable*.

Success & health.

Ever y*rs*,

P H Hayne

Please write soon.

P. S. By the way, I am *now* composing a notice for the
Courier's Editorial columns, referring to the *"F & F,"* and particularly,—to your own connection with it.

You have *materially* aided *me* in my humble literary progress,—and, *so long as God* grants me life—, I shall never forget
your kindness.

[John Reuben Thompson (1823–1873), native of Richmond, law graduate
of the University of Virginia, had been editor of the *Southern Literary
Messenger* since October, 1847. In March, 1860, he agreed to become
editor of the *Southern Field and Fireside* (Augusta weekly), since the
salary was $2,000 a year and he needed the money. The last number of

the *SLM* which he edited was that for May.   On the 15th of the month his friends gave him a farewell dinner.   He arrived in Augusta on May 18.   He edited *Southern Field and Fireside* only until the end of the year.   See the biographical introduction to *Poems of John R. Thompson,* edited by John S. Patton (New York: Charles Scribner's .Sons, 1920).

The *Mercury* and *Courier* were Charleston newspapers.

Aiken is only about eighteen miles from Augusta.

The plantation of William Gilmore Simms was near Midway, South Carolina, about half way between Charleston and Augusta.

In the *Southern Field and Fireside* for March 17, 1860, Hayne began a series of articles, in the form of dialogues (in which James Whittington and Henry Bishop, of Charleston, express their views of books and writers, mainly contemporary), under this title: "The Whittington Club; or, Dialogues upon Literature, with Special Reference to Current Publications." Some of the numbers were signed "P. H. H." and some were unsigned.

James Gardner was the proprietor of *Southern Field and Fireside.*]

No. 65

PAUL HAMILTON HAYNE to JOHN REUBEN THOMPSON

Monday 28th *May* [1860]

My dear John;

—I have recd your note of the 26th, & I will *immediately* see Russell, & arrange about the new books, which you ought certainly to receive.

I think there can be no difficulty whatever.

—On the opposite page you will find a little *Song,* which I fear does not come up to your standard. If it *does* however, publish it;— Of course, *My dear fellow,* I cannot write for *nothing.* Even this trifle (if accepted), it seems to me, I have a right to charge something for. Anything that is worth publishing, is surely worth also a certain degree of remuneration. But please remember that I have the prosperity of your journal deeply at heart;— & that *I really wish you to reject anything of mine not calculated to interest your readers.*

God bless you, my *dear old friend*, & console you under the dreary pressure of your present existence.

Ever affectionately,

P H Hayne

P.S. The 1st no of the *"F & F"* under your auspices, is the *best* no of the paper *ever issued*. Your "Rhymed tribute to *Virginia*," I have just sent down town, in order that it may be re-published in *"the Courier"*. It is a most successful performance.

[The year (1860) is written lengthwise in the margin. I am uncertain whether it is in Hayne's hand, but it is correct, regardless of who wrote it.

John Russell was the Charleston bookseller and friend of literary men who gave his name to *Russell's Magazine* (1857–1860), of which Hayne was editor.

The rhymed tribute to Virginia referred to in the postscript is probably "Virginia, in Our Flowing Bowls," pp. 181–84 in *Poems of John R. Thompson*, edited by John S. Patton. There is a reference to the same poem in the next letter.]

No. 66

PAUL HAMILTON HAYNE to JOHN REUBEN THOMPSON

Sunday June 10th 1860.

My Dear Friend;

—Yours of the 9th inst, has given *me very great pleasure*— because, (apart from the satisfaction, which *your* letters *never* fail to afford me)—, I see *in* it, an evidence of that *outspoken confidence*, & cándour, which, above most other things in this world,—I value in a *friend*.

As for the *rhymes I sent* you,—pray forget at once what I said about payment. To tell you, the *truth*, I am rather *ashamed* that I charged *anything* for these very *médiocre* pieces—, the productions of "years agone!".

Mr *Gardner* has been *liberal*, no less than *prompt* in his pecuniary remuneration, & *henceforth* My *dear John*,—please to regard *every* poetical trifle I may send you as a *"free-will offering"*.

The *2* poems now in your possession—, viz; *"Bessie,"*, & the *Lines* beginning *"He is weary of the too"* &c are entirely at your disposal. Only, d'ont put my *name* to *latter;*—because they are simply juvenile performances *"re-vamped".!!*

—You express yourself as pleased with what I have written in reference to your Editorial management of the *"F & F"*. My *own* self-esteem is not a little excited by this ready appreciation of my hasty, & imperfect commendatory remarks.

Indeed, I feel certain, that under *your* control, the *"F & F"* will prosper beyond all *precedent*, (at *least*, beyond all *literary* precedent in the *South*). &c &c. Your poem contributed to the "O. D Society"—in NY,—is a witty[,] spirited, graceful, effective performance, which, (together with some of your *excellent editorials*), you will soon see re-published in one of our Charleston papers.

Your critique upon Mr *Walt Whitman delighted* me beyond measure!

The *comparative* success of his work demonstrates the lowness both of *morals & taste* among even the better class of readers, & critics at the North. God help this poor country, for—, assuredly it needs help, & enlightenment.

You ask when I expect to visit *Aiken;*— We have already engaged rooms, & consequently, we must leave Charleston about the *20th* of June. You speak of coming to this city on Friday next. Pray stick to this resolution—, I do so long to see, & talk with you once more. I should insist upon your staying with us,—but alas! the entire household, (the *female part*, I mean) is *hors de combat!* x However, in the *Autumn*, I shall *certainly* expect you. x x x To *morrow*, I shall see *Russell*, & endeavor to make the most satisfactory arrangements about the new Publications designed for the *"F & F"*. The next no of the *"Whittington C—b,"* I'll mail on *Tuesday noon.*

Ever Yrs

P H Hayne

[The Thompson poem referred to in this letter is the tribute to Virginia mentioned in the last letter and note thereon: "Virginia, in Our Flowing

Bowls." Patton's note (*op. cit.*, p. 243) on this poem reads: "This tribute to Virginia was read, by N. H. Campbell, at the first anniversary of the Old Dominion Society of New York, at the dinner at the Metropolitan Hotel, May 13, 1860. The author was about to leave Richmond for Augusta, Ga., and could not be present at the banquet."

Of course Thompson's and Hayne's opinion of the poetry of Whitman was the same as that of the great majority of readers and critics at that time.]

No. 67

PAUL HAMILTON HAYNE to JOHN REUBEN THOMPSON

Greenville, May 1*st* 1864.

My Dear John;

Your note of the 25th ult is just at hand. Indeed I feel your kindness to a degree which it is difficult for me to express. Under *ordinary* circumstances, *nothing* could induce me to trouble you again about that wretched medicine; but hard necessity urges me, & so I must claim your kind indulgence. It strikes me that we can manage the affair thus:

Since *Jany* last the "Illu*s* News" has paid me *not one* cent for the Poems of mine which have appeared in its columns. Now these poems are at least *seven* in number.

Here are the names;

Peace (with an engraving)	$ 30—
The Ruined Homestead	$ 30 *(thirty)*
Charleston at the Close of 1863	$ 30
Sonnet—"Stonewall Jackson,"	$ 25
Sonnet To J. R. T.	$ 25
Sonnet, To England	$ 25
Song—"What matters all the care &"	$ 15
Total	$180—

This amount (you perceive) comes within $20 of the needful sum. As the "News" has accepted 3 or 4 other pieces of mine (not yet published), "Ayres & Wade" may not be unwilling to *advance* me so trifling an amount upon them.

You know these gentlemen, &c perhaps, (since I authorize you to do so), you will collect the money, & appropriate it to the purchase of the medicine. *Should they object to my prices, why then, take whatever they may give you.* But, I fancy, there will be no difficulty whatever.

Lastly, (as I said before), empty the morphine into a good stout envelope, or a couple of envelopes, & send it *by Mail.* There is *no Express* from Columbia to Greenville *now.* I cannot fail to receive the package safely:

A thousand pardons, *mon ami* for all this trouble!!. I would do the same for *you*, were our positions *reversed.* (If "Ayres & Wade" *refuse* to pay you, *get the medicine at all events,* & I will see that you are not inconvenienced by your courtesy. This however, I regard as next to impossible.)

Miss Jennie Dickson spent another day with us last week. What a charming lady,—how intelligent, & well read:

She persuaded me to prepare a Lecture for the benefit of the Soldiers here. I am to deliver it on the 20th inst, the Gods permitting. Meanwhile, I have for weeks been laboring upon a Poem, composed somewhat in the style of "Avolio", but much more elaborate. It will be divided into 3 Cantos, & may reach to a considerable length, perhaps *900 lines.* The plot is taken from one of Chaucer's Canterbury Tales. I read aloud a portion of the work to Miss Dickson, who seemed greatly pleased. She says, it is *superior* to *"Avolio,"* & her commendation, sincerely given, I prize far above the plaudits of a hundred ordinary mag*z*s, & newspapers!!

We had an agreeable talk about *you;* Miss D——, was exceedingly delighted with certain of your letters to the "Index"— In fact, they *are* capital. I wish you could give me some of your grace· & facility in prose composition. Heaven knows, how much I need them, especially at the present period:

Observe what paper I am constrained to use!! When your English stationery arrives, (unless it can come thro the P

Office), send whatever you can spare me *by Express to Columbia*, directed as follows;

Paul H Hayne Esq
Care of M. P. O'Connor,
Corner of "Laurel & Barnwell" Streets,
Columbia (S. C)

Mr O'Connor will get the package up to me by some *private* opportunity:

My wife's *best* regards. Willie is now playing bare-footed about the farm, & looks like a dirty plough boy; but his *health* is good, & that's the important point just now:— Hoping to hear from you soon, I am dear friend,

Ever P H Hayne

[The *Southern Illustrated News*, Richmond weekly, ran from September 13, 1862, until March 25, 1865. John R. Thompson was one of the regular contributors and was editor for a time in 1863. All the issues that I have seen name Ayres & Wade as "Editors and Proprietors." The issue dated November 30, 1862, contains an editorial note welcoming Hayne as a regular contributor: "We take pleasure in enrolling this morning among our list of regular contributors the name of Paul H. Hayne, Esq., one of the sweetest poets of our sunny land. The piece which we publish from his pen in this issue of our paper, is a spirited and eloquent tribute to the gallantry of one of Virginia's most chivalric sons.—Long may the gallant Stuart live to wield his sabre in defence of Southern rights, and may he always have a Paul Hayne to extol, in beautiful verse, his dauntless courage and his virtues." The poem is a good ballad entitled "Stuart" and appears in *Complete Edition*, pp. 72–73. I have not seen the issues containing the poems listed in the letter above. "Charleston at the Close of 1863" and "Stonewall Jackson" are found in *Complete Edition*, pp. 78–79 and 82–84. There is also a sonnet entitled "England" on page 263, but it may not be the one mentioned in the letter, for it appears in the section headed "Later Poems." The "Sonnet to J. R. T." was probably to Thompson, who had published a sonnet to Hayne ("To Paul H. Hayne") in the *SLM* in 1857 (see Patton, *Poems of John R. Thompson*, p. 145). In the *Southern Illustrated News* for July 4, 1863, Hayne and Thompson exchange poetic tributes, Hayne in "The Southern Lyre" and Thompson in an editorial note (with poem).

Miss Jennie (or Jeannie) Dickson may have been a relative of Samuel Henry Dickson (1798–1872), prominent physician and occasional poet of Charleston (later of Philadelphia), but this is merely a conjecture. I do not know who she was.

Hayne's long poem (909 lines) which Miss Dickson correctly considered superior to his "Avolio" was "The Wife of Brittany," based on Chaucer's "Franklin's Tale." See *Complete Edition*, pp. 118–137. It is both the longest and the best of Hayne's narrative poems.

"*The Index*, the Confederate organ in London, took a weekly letter from him [Thompson]." (Patton, *op. cit.*, p. xxx.)]

No. 68

PAUL HAMILTON HAYNE to JOHN REUBEN THOMPSON

Sunday 17th March 1867

My Dear Thompson;

I am *exceedingly* annoyed to find that my copy of "Beyond the Potomac", which I mailed you more than 2 weeks since, has *miscarried*.

Just now, I am so sick, weary, & despondent, that it is with an effort I am able even to scribble these few *lines*.

The enclosed *Sonnet* is therefore the only piece I can send. Let me hope it may answer your purpose.

If I live long enough, (which is doubtful), for I have had several severe *hemorrhages* lately),, my design is to publish *two* vol*s*, *one* of "War-Poems", & the *other* of miscellaneous verses, *chiefly ideal*.

The *War-pieces* I shall dedicate to *you*, because you were the first friend, who encouraged me in literary undertakings. As regards the other vol*l*, I will leave the *MSS* with you, if time is not granted me to superintend them myself. I believe, *old friend*, you will not refuse this last *kindness*, will you?

I am really *very ill*, *Thompson*, or I should not write thus.

The room turns round, & round, as I glance up from the *paper*, & sometimes, I can, with great difficulty, *catch* my *breath*. Ah! the *great secret* we all pant to discover, seems very near me now.

Always Faithfully

Paul H Hayne

[Hayne's "Beyond the Potomac" appears in *Complete Edition*, pp. 73–74. From the summer of 1864 until the fall of 1866 Thompson was in London. He was then in Richmond until April, 1867, at which time he moved to New York. He may have been on the staff of some magazine or newspaper at the time of this letter, though very little is known concerning his activities during his first year in New York.

Hayne lived to bring out three volumes (1872, 1875, 1882), but he did not publish a volume of war poems. He lived thirteen years after Thompson's death.]

No. 69

PAUL HAMILTON HAYNE to JOHN REUBEN
THOMPSON

"Copse Hill," (near Augusta, Ga)
Oct 4th 1869:

My Dear Thompson,

I was *vividly* reminded of you, & old times this morning, by the reception of a dainty little pamphlet of a dozen p.p., containing your Poem, "read before the Society of Alumni of the University of Virginia".

I had *previously* made acquaintance with these verses thro the medium of the "New Eclectic", but it gave me much pleasure to peruse them *again*, for they are marked by your invariable grace, feeling, & crisp *finish* of style.—the verses of a scholar, & gentleman!

I like *particularly* the expression you have given to an old thought in stanzas XIII & XIV; the imagery which represents the "mind's *ideal*" flying, forever flying, or mocking endeavors with a cruel "*if*"!!

Did you have a fine *audience* when you delivered the Poem?.

And how, O friend of my youth, from whom Circumstances have always separated me, how does the world use you at this, the 11th hour?

They tell me that you belong to the Editorial staff of the NY "Evening Post," so I make one more effort to reach you, which God grant, may be successful.

Did you translate V. Hugo's novel in "Appleton"? Miss Jeannie Dickson wrote me to that effect, & I suppose she was not mistaken. Indeed, I *hope* not, because the translation is *wonderful*, & *ought* to have brought you a *small fortune*.

As you see, I write sometimes for the Appletons myself. They have hitherto, treated me with *peculiar* courtesy.

For the first time in years I left my forest home during the month of *August*, & went to Montgomery (Ala), whither I had been called to arrange a personal difficulty between my *Brother in Law*, & some other *doctor*. (I allude to a *younger* brother, D*r* R. Fraser Michel). *There*, to my astonishment, & delight, I met *John Bruns*, summoned like myself for purposes of *mediation*.

We had many talks together. He alluded to *you* in very *warm, friendly* terms, as the companion of a *portion* of his sojourn in England.

You must have had some charming times together—you two. *Bruns* is a wonderful fellow—as a *comrade*, & clever *raconteur*, unsurpassed.

Pray answer this note, & tell me *something* of *yourself*, *& fortunes*.

By the way, c'ant you mail me a copy regularly of the *weekly edition* of the "Post."? I would *so* like to read your articles.

In haste, but Ever Yr*s*

Paul H Hayne

P. O. Box, 635 Augusta, G*a*

[Thompson's "Poem Read before the Society of Alumni of the University of Virginia, at Their Annual Meeting, July 1, 1869," appeared in the *New Eclectic Magazine*, V (September, 1869), 328–336. This was a Baltimore monthly.

Thompson was literary editor of the New York *Evening Post* from 1868 until 1873.

The translation of Victor Hugo's *The Man Who Laughs; or, By the King's Command* ran in *Appleton's Journal* from April, 1869, until September 4, 1869. Thompson was rumored to be the translator, but no definite proof has been discovered. Hayne refers to the matter in his letter to Simms dated May 17, 1869 (No. 118).

See the notes following letter No. 116 for information concerning Richard Fraser Michel and John Dickson Bruns. Also see all of Hayne's letters to Simms for passing references to both men. The letter to Simms dated December 28, 1869, mentions Dick's quarrel.]

No. 70

PAUL HAMILTON HAYNE to JOHN REUBEN THOMPSON

Augusta, Jan 7th 1872.

My Dear Thompson;

—As the *oldest—literary* friend I have in the world, *can* it be wrong in me to ask your aid in bringing a vo*l* of Poems, (the *Lippincotts* have just published for me) before your NY public? I hope not!

This latest vo*l*—entitled, *"Legends & Lyrics"* contains, I may say, without affectation or egotism, some carefully wrought verse, and I believe, some genuine thought & sentiment; and so—if I am right—it will not offend your conscience to put forward a few earnest words on its behalf.

If you only knew; if you could *faintly* imagine, how grateful I would feel for *such service*, there could be no hesitation on your part!

I look forward to no gratification of *vanity* in this matter, but to ends at once more practical, and more noble. Please— whether you find it convenient to prepare a critique yourself, or not, *please mail me such reviews of the book* as happen to come under your observation in the *various* ·"exchanges" at your office; the *more savage*, or *contemptuous* these notices, the *better* would I like to read them!

——Eno' of *self!* Tell me how your *health* is at present? what your prospects are,—everything ab't you; & take from me, *beloved old comrade*, and *literary elder brother* my *earnest wishes* for your welfare, prosperity, & peace, &c.

God be with you!
Always Faithfully

Paul H Hayne.

P O Box 635, Augusta Ga

[I have not seen Thompson's review of *Legends and Lyrics*, but I have no doubt that he wrote one. Patton (*op. cit.*, pp. lxi–lxii) points out the fact that Thompson's last literary effort before his death was a review (barely begun and left incomplete) of Hayne's edition of Timrod's poems.]

VI. HENRY E. HUNTINGTON LIBRARY (NO. 71)

PAUL HAMILTON HAYNE to [ONE OF THE EDITORS
OF *SOUTHERN SOCIETY*]

Augusta Sep 15*th*
'67

My Dear Sir;

Your polite note of the 5*th* is before me. Many thanks!xx
I shall do all in my power to advance the interests of the
undertaking, which you have evidently commenced in a liberal & intelligent spirit.

First, thro the columns of the Richmond "So Opinion," of
which I am Li*t* Editor, my design is, to refer tò your enterprise in warm terms;—*then,* I will notice it in Some *prominent* Augusta daily.

These notices I will mail to you.

M*r Jas. R. Randall's* address is, *"Constitutionalist Office,"*
Augusta, (Ga).

In reference to M*r* Gayarré, I regret to say, that I d'ont
know where he resides at present.

By the way, I mailed you a few *trifles* the other day, for
your 1*st* issue—*(poems).* Did you receive them? In addition to these, let me remark, that I have on hand, a *perfectly original piece,* called, *"Fire Pictures"*—with which I
took *great pains,* & which read aloud to several of our most
distinguished Authors,—they have urged me to publish as
soon *as possible.* It embraces however, upwards of *300* lines,
which is a great objection, when the vehicle of publication
happens to be a weekly paper. Still, I offer you the refusal
of this performance—, because, if what my friends say, *is true,*
it may really be of service to you. Hereafter, my contributions to "So Society" will be *chiefly prose.* Few people care
about *verse*— The journals are "drugged" with it—& generally speaking, a clever prose-essay will eclipse *any* but the
ablest rhymes.

Send me your "weekly" from the beginning, & depend
upon my being your faithful ally.

> *In haste*—but Always Truly,
>
> *P H Hayne.*

P. O. Box 260 Augusta, (Ga)

[Written across the top of the first page:]

Please write, & tell me whether I must send you *"Fire-Pictures"*.

[*Southern Society* (1867–1868) was a Baltimore weekly edited by E. L.
Didier, W. J. M'Clellan, and Porter Morse. Eugène Lemoine Didier
(1838–1913) wrote a good sketch of Hayne in the *American* (Philadelphia)
for January 21, 1882, in which he said (III, 232): ". . . in 1867–8, Mr.
Hayne contributed frequently to *Southern Society*, a weekly literary journal
of high character commenced in Baltimore in October, 1867. In this
paper first appeared his 'Fire Pictures,' which was republished after the
great Chicago fire." On December 31, 1867, Hayne sent to Mrs. Margaret
J. Preston, of Virginia, a copy of a poem "just published in the Baltimore
'Southern Society.' " Her reply indicates that the poem was "Fire Pictures." (See Elizabeth Preston Allan, *The Life and Letters of Margaret
Junkin Preston*, Boston and New York, Houghton, Mifflin and Company,
1903.)

Hayne was literary editor of *Southern Opinion* (1867–1869), Richmond
political and literary weekly, during the two years of its existence.

James Ryder Randall (1839–1908), native of Maryland and author of
"Maryland, My Maryland," taught school, just before the war, in Louisiana,
became associate editor of the Augusta (Georgia) *Constitutionalist* just
after the war, and continued to do journalistic work for most of the remainder of his life (mainly in Augusta and Washington, D. C.).

Charles Étienne Arthur Gayarré (1805–1895) was a distinguished his-
torian, author, and statesman of Louisiana. See Hayne's three articles on
Gayarré in the *Southern Bivouac* (New Series) for June, July, and August,
1886 (II, 28–37; 108–113; 172–76). See also Charles R. Anderson's
"Charles Gayarré and Paul Hayne: The Last Literary Cavaliers," in
American Studies in Honor of William Kenneth Boyd (Duke University
Press, 1940).

The Henry E. Huntington Library also has two other Hayne letters
(HM 7178 and HM 23473), "one dated 1873 Mar. 29, addressee unknown,
the other dated 1876 Jan. 29 to A. H. Dooley." (Letter to me dated June
9, 1941, from H. C. Schulz.) But permission to publish the two letters had

already been given to someone else. I have (with the aid of Miss Nannie M. Tilley of the Manuscript Department, Duke University Library) identified the addressee of the letter dated March 29, 1873, as Charles W. Squires of Albany, New York. See the letter in the Yale group dated April 18, 1875 (No. 37). A. H. Dooley was an Indiana bookseller and journalist.]

VII. CRAIGIE HOUSE (NOS. 72–96)

PAUL HAMILTON HAYNE to HENRY WADSWORTH LONGFELLOW

Augusta Geo
Jan *24th* 1872.

My Dear Sir;

I venture to send you, (thro my *Publishers*) a copy of a little vo*l, one* Poem in which, *("Daphles")* met with your kind approval some years ago, when issued in one of the magazines.

Perhaps a few other pieces, as they now appear; will interest you likewise.

At least, allow me to *hope* so.

A political "ode" on the Bravery of So soldiers &c, will be pardoned by you, (I mean in reference to some undue bitterness of expression), when you look at the *date* of its composition. In 1866, we, of the *South*, were *heartbroken*, and *desperate!* A generous foe will remember *that!*

From the obscure lower regions of *Parnassus*, I send greeting to *you*, whom a beneficent *Fate* has placed so near the glorious *summit!*

Long may you continue to live, & delight the world with music as full of *perfect art*, as of a divine *hope*, & a faith in all things good, pure, and noble! *Your* poetry elevates the spirit, and makes strong the heart, instead of merely charming the *fancy*, and then leaving one in the twilight of scepticism, as to the existence even of a *Hereafter!* Recent poetry is the poetry of *Doubt;*— Look at Morris, Rossetti, Swinburne!.

But I must close.

Ever Most Faithfully

Paul H Hayne

P O Box 635
Augusta Geo

[Hayne's little volume was *Legends and Lyrics* (Philadelphia: J. B. Lippincott & Co.), 1872. His poem "Daphles" had appeared in Albert Taylor Bledsoe's the *Southern Review* (Baltimore quarterly) for January, 1870.

The Southern poem referred to is probably the "Ode" composed "in honor of the bravery and sacrifices of the soldiers of the South," for which Hayne won a prize of one hundred dollars, awarded by the *Southern Opinion*, a Richmond weekly, in 1867. It appeared on the first page of the issue of June 22, 1867. It may be found in Hayne's *Complete Edition*, pp. 67–71. It is sometimes referred to as "The Confederates in the Field," though Hayne called it "Ode" and added an explanatory subtitle.]

No. 73

PAUL HAMILTON HAYNE to HENRY WADSWORTH LONGFELLOW

Augusta Fe*b* 13*th* 1872.

My Dear Sir;

I feel *very* sensibly the considerate courtesy which induced you to mail me the critique from the *"Boston Transcript"*. There was a generous forethought & kindness in the act, which be assured is deeply appreciated.

As for the little vo*l* of *Poems*, let me hope that it has now reached you; not because the book is worthy altogether of M*r* Whipple's *most cordial* praise; but because I *do* trust there are a *few* pieces in it, that will appeal to *your noble heart*, if they do not *satisfy* your high *artistic ideal*.

I have written *again* to the *Lippincotts* to be sure and mail you the "Legends".

Should the vo*l* fail, may I *beg* you to let me know?—

Meanwhile, I am,
Most Respectfully &
Gratefully, yours,

Paul H Hayne

P. O. Box, 635, Augusta
(Geo)

[Edwin Percy Whipple (1819–1886), Boston critic, author, and lecturer, was Hayne's personal friend and correspondent for many years. See the letters to him in this collection (Nos. 30–32).]

No. 74

PAUL HAMILTON HAYNE to HENRY WADSWORTH LONGFELLOW (WITH POEM)

Augusta, Jan 6th 1874

My Dear Mr Longfellow;—

Since I saw you last—forgive my egotism; it is necessary to the clearness of certain explanations—; since I saw you last—, I have suffered from illness so *severe*, that *twice* I confidently expected a removal from this ·strange world to the mysterious *Beyond*. *Partially* recovering, I hastened South, and my native air has somewhat restored the strength which seemed gone forever. Believe me, I take the *first* opportunity of thanking you for the generous kindness shown me during the summer; and had I only been able to *work* as usual,— or, had not that terrible autumn "Panic," struck *me* down— pecuniarily—with so many others—I would long since have cancelled my obligation, in a *material sence* [*sic*], tho in far *higher* respects, it never *can* be cancelled, nor would I *desire* it!

As matters *now* stand, I am *forced*, literally forced, to solicit your indulgence & generous construction of my conduct. *"Who of us is stronger than destiny?"*—

Need I observe, that *as soon as* possible, I will refund that most kindly loan?

Great Heaven! what a clinging *curse* is Poverty! It *killed* my friend *Timrod*, long before his time; and many a dark hour, & sleepless night of bitterness & bewildered fear, has it brought upon me!

Pardon such an outburst;— I d'ont mean to complain, or whine against Fate.

One must endure one's own burdens manfully. x x x x
x x x x x x x x x x x x x x x x x x x x x x x x

More than a year ago, the idea occurred to me of composing *three* brief Poems upon our chief American Poets; *namely, yourself, Bryant, & Whittier. Two* of these have been completed; and *now* I venture to enclose for examination, the verses dedicated to your honored *self*. They can claim *one* merit—a profound *sincerity*.

Had you lived in Ancient Greece, Mr Longfellow,—I think they would have called you a favorite of the Gods!

What a splendid career you can now look back upon! And ah! how much better than all splendors of mortal fame must be the conviction that you have penned no line,—no solitary line, which,

"Dying, you could wish to blot!"

Now-a-days, there are many writers, and as many readers, who sneer at what they choose to term *"moral* verse," confounding *such,* wilfully, with a dull didacticism; but for my part, I can perceive no valid reason why a *Poet,* however passionately intense his genius, & and [*sic*] temperament—, should not be a Christian, and a gentleman! In default of the *latter,* Swinburne's sonorous stanzas are likely to become *"vox, et praterea nihil"*, (always excepting his *"Atalanta in Calydon"*), and as for this new "Light", *Miller,* he seems fated to illustrate the common saying of "going up like a *Rocket,* and descending like a *stick!"* x x x You meet Dr Holmes, occasionally, I presume?— Will you courteously give him my *best regards,* and say, I shall write him soon?

Farewell, *my Dear Sir,* and may the year—'74 bring you *many blessings.* And please believe that in this quarter of the World, you have no more earnest Admirer, or truer friend,

than Yours Always Faithfully

Paul Hayne.

P. O. Box 635, Augusta Ga

P. S. I formed the acquaintance, last summer, of your quaint old *Gardener;* and your *former* housekeeper, who despite her affliction, seemed intelligent still. I would like much to be remembered to them, *both.*

To HENRY W LONGFELLOW:

Of darkness born, in darkness fade our lives,—
And few of all these mortal lives complete—,
May lay at last their offerings at God's feet,
With—"lo! thy gifts redoubled!": strong the gyves
Of sin, or fate! and 'gainst our purpose strives,
E'ven [*sic*] at its noblest, some strange Power of Ill;
Yet, once in centuries, Heaven's *Elect* there are,
Who fronting life & doom with God-like will,
Toil but to conquer; from fair height to height
Rising forever, 'till *that* height be won,
Whence they shine on us, splendid as the sun,
Stainless & perfect as the Evening Star!

Yea! such *thy* life, thy victory, thy calm light
Of exaltation O! benignant Soul!—,
O'er whose broad forehead—cast in antique mould—,
The mystical tides of stormy seasons rolled,
Have left their mark in furrows, sown with thought,
And the deep lore of ages! thou hast wrought
With aim unwavering, with consummate skill
Of matchless mastery, & high-tempered might—,
                    guide, and
Truth thy sure leader, spotless fame, thy goal!

And now, thou stand'st—the wings of labor furled—,
Like some lone eagle of the mountain rocks,—
Thine eyes turned heavenward, thy white, reverend locks
Worn halo-wise about thy sovereign brow:—
Thus stand'st thou, scarcely knowing that all men bow
Before thee!—that alike thro palace halls
And humble cottage homes, thy music calls
True hearts to fervent prayer & tender praise;—
That evermore thy pure, beneficent lays
Shall sweetly ring, re echoed round the World!.

Paul Hayne.
"Copse Hill," Geo R. Road
Jan 5th 1874.

[Hayne visited New York and Boston in the summer of 1873. Apparently he became ill while in the North and had to secure a loan both from Longfellow and from the editors of the *Christian Union*. He discharged his obligations to the magazine by poetic contributions, but Longfellow seems to have cancelled the indebtedness to him with the suggestion that when able he might befriend someone else in a similar financial plight.

Henry Timrod (1828–1867), South Carolina's best poet, died at Columbia. He had always been poor but had been in extreme poverty since Sherman burned the city.

Hayne here speaks of Longfellow, Bryant, and Whittier as "our chief American Poets." He also had a high regard for Emerson (see *Complete Edition*, p. 340) as a seer whose inspiration was of divine origin. In his later years he several times referred to Lowell as the best American poet, and he came to think more kindly of Joaquin Miller (1841–1913) than he does here.

The melodious verse in *Atalanta in Calydon* (1865) pleased Hayne. Although he dissented from certain of Swinburne's religious, moral, and critical views, he considered Swinburne a great poet (see *Complete Edition*, p. 269).

For other poetic tributes to Longfellow see *Complete Edition:* "To Henry W. Longfellow" (p. 268), "To Longfellow. (On Hearing He Was Ill.)" (p. 308), "Longfellow Dead" (p. 312), and "The Snow-Messengers" (pp. 290–93). The last is a tribute also to Whittier. In the poem printed here, Hayne has written "guide, and" above the word "leader" in l. 21, apparently as a substitute for the word "leader."]

No. 75

PAUL HAMILTON HAYNE to HENRY WADSWORTH LONGFELLOW

Augusta, Geo Jan 16*th* 1875

My Dear & Honored Friend;

I have heard with *deep solicitude* that you are sick; perhaps *seriously* sick! No doubt this terrible winter, (*unparalleled* even at the South), must have tried your constitution severely. But I hope for the *very best*. I hope that *our poet*— the poet of the *whole* Country *now*—, may *speedily* recover.

Meanwhile, I enclose you a little critique, (cut from the "*NY* [?] *South*", and written by Mrs M. J. Preston of V*a*, a woman of *true genius*), which it may gratify you to peruse, if your Strength admits.

Ah! Sir, *South* & *North, we love you;* and (D V!) you'll not leave us *yet.!*

Always yours

Paul H Hayne

(P O Box 635)

[I am uncertain about the "NY" in "NY *South*," which to me does not make sense. Possibly it is "Sy *South*" for the *Sunny South,* a weekly published in Atlanta from 1875 until 1907. Mrs. Margaret Junkin Preston (1820–1897) was the well-known poet of Lexington, Virginia. She and Hayne never met but corresponded for eighteen years.]

No. 76

PAUL HAMILTON HAYNE to HENRY WADSWORTH LONGFELLOW

P. O. Address:
    P. O. Box 275
        Augusta, Ga.

Copse Hill, Ga.,
April 1*st* 1877

My Dear Mr Longfellow;—

You have lately reached, the newspapers inform me—your 70*th* birth-day! Let me, as one among the *sincerest* of your friends & admirers, offer my congratulations upon the attainment of three score years & ten, distinguished throughout, by your noble achievements as an *artist,* and now crowned in the end by that *Poet-wreath,* which *Time* cannot wither, because the flowers that form, & illumine it are genuine *immortelles!*

My wife begs me to enclose for you some of our earliest woodland flowers in spring;—the yellow Jessamines, with the *earnest* wish that your life so well & nobly spent, may be happily prolonged.

Often, *Dear Sir,* I think of my visit North during the year 1873, and of the pleasant, tho too brief interview I enjoyed with you at Nahant. Ah! in all probability we are not destined to meet again, in this world;—but thank God! there is a *better;* and somehow I believe that I shall recognize your kindly face, and earnest eyes in that mysterious Country.

I write on *Easter morn,* & am vividly reminded of the *"Resurrection & the life to come"!*

Most Faithfully Yr's

Paul H Hayne.

P. S. I enclose a lyric which will explain itself. Your heart is too generous, & your brain too broad, to misunderstand my verses.

I am sure, on the contrary, that you sympathise with the wrongs of my unfortunate Section, which *Grant* tried so hard to ruin, but which Mr Hay[e]s (I *trust*) will redeem.

[Longfellow was 70 on February 27, 1877. He had a summer cottage near the seashore at Nahant. In 1879 Hayne and his wife visited Longfellow again, at Cambridge. The lyric which Hayne enclosed may have been "South Carolina to the States of the North" (*Complete Edition,* pp. 297–99).]

No. 77

PAUL HAMILTON HAYNE to HENRY WADSWORTH LONGFELLOW

"Copse Hill," Georgia Rail Road,

Address:

P. O. Box 275,

Augusta, Ga. 187

My Dear Mr Longfellow

I recd your kind note yesterday, & hasten to reply (I almost feared you had forgotten me, as no answer reached me to the note of congratulation I sent you upon your last birthday; but I know how very busy you always are).

I mail you to day a copy of Timrod's vol;— You have my "Legends & Lyrics" I know; and I *think* I sent you my last book, called *"The Mountain of Lovers"*[.]

In "*Legends & Lyrics*" there is but *one* poem which *might* answer your purpose; and that is called "*by the Autumn Sea*," p 74. Altho as *now* published the circumstance is not mentioned this piece was "*Composed on the Beach of "Sullivan's Island*["] *near Charleston S. C*[.]"

"In the "*Mountain of Lovers*," there are two poems on the Pines. These were suggested by a superb pine forest just opposite my residence "Copse Hill" which is in "Columbia Co" Georgia. The special names of these pieces are

> 1. "*Aspects of the Pines*" p. 65
> 2. "*Voices of the Pines*" page 55

To this group a piece "*Under the Pine*" ('*to the Memory of Henry Timrod*') upon page 37 of "*Legends & Lyrics*" belongs, (tho of course it *need not* be included, as the others are complete without it.)

I leave the *naming* of them, i e, the general *title* to yourself.

A *distinctly local* poem occurs on p 87 of "The *Mountain of the Lovers*" called "*By the Grave of Henry Timrod*". All that is needed here is to amplify the caption thus.

> "*By the Grave of Henry Timrod*"
> *In* "*Trinity Church Yard*" *Columbia S. C.*

Enclosed are a *Group of Sonnets* which may suit you; also a Ballad about Charleston S. C., referring to the *old Revolution*[.]

Most of the Poems of place I see in my *So* collections by *Simms, Davidson,* & others, are "*war Poems*["] (the late *Civil* war).

Would you wish any of these?

I have a ballad upon "*Macdonald's Raid upon Georgetown S. C*", which I'll send you a copy of, when I procure it. 'Twas formerly published in "Harper"—being likewise a poem of the *old* revolution.

I d'ont know of any poem on "*Tallulah Falls*," but shall try & get one upon "*the* Stone Mountain" by Dr F O Ticknor of this State.

I heard from Mr Whittier not long since, & regretted to learn of his feeble health. He said that he would like to so-journ with me, (during the winter), under our Pines.

Let me hope that you, *Dear Sir*, are well & strong?—

Believe me

Ever Faithfully Yr's

Paul. H. Hayne.

[Written on a separate page:]

\#   *Simms'* Poems, I lost; or rather, they were destroyed in the great fire of *Charleston.* His 2 vol*s* published by Redfield NY in 1852—or 3—contain many poems that might suit you.

[Written on another separate page:]

P. S. When I alluded to a *general title* for the *Poems on the Pines*, I meant something like this;—

For example, could you not call the group

*"The Pines of Columbia"** as a *general caption.?* Then the 2 or 3 poems could follow; each entitled as now;

1   "Aspects of the Pines"
2   "Voices of the Pines"

3rd *"Under the* Pine (to the *Memory of H. Timrod)* ["]
if you chose to include the last mentioned verses.

**Note* Columbia Co, Georgia, is noted for the extent & gloomy magnificence of its Pine forests.

The special Pines referred to in my verses, rise opposite *"Copse Hill,"* on *the Ga R Road* &c[.] They form a noble grove thr*u* which H. Timrod loved to wander.

[This letter is undated. The heading is printed. Apparently its place is between the letters dated April 1, 1877, and April 29, 1878. The first volume of Longfellow's series entitled *Poems of Places* had appeared in 1876. Longfellow had requested Hayne to suggest poems for the forth-coming volume dealing with the Southern States.

Hayne had edited *The Poems of Henry Timrod*, with a memoir, in 1873. His own *Legends and Lyrics* and *The Mountain of the Lovers* had appeared, respectively, in 1872 and 1875.

The Revolutionary ballad about Charleston may be "Charleston Retaken" (*Complete Edition*, pp. 280–83).

The collections by Simms and Davidson are these:

William Gilmore Simms, *War Poetry of the South* (New York: Richardson & Company), 1867.

James Wood Davidson, *The Living Writers of the South* (New York: Carleton), 1869.

Hayne's "Macdonald's Raid—A. D. 1780" appeared in *Harper's New Monthly Magazine*, July, 1876 (LIII, 200–203).

At the time of this letter the poems of Francis Orray Ticknor (1822–1874) had not been collected. They were published in Philadelphia by J. B. Lippincott & Co. in 1879, and for the volume Hayne wrote the introductory sketch of the author.

Simms's *Poems Descriptive, Dramatic, Legendary and Contemplative,* two volumes, appeared in 1853 (New York: Redfield).]

No. 78

PAUL HAMILTON HAYNE to HENRY WADSWORTH LONGFELLOW

Address P O Box 275

Augusta Geo
April 29*th* 1878 .˙.

My Dear Mr Longfellow;

I replied to your last letter, & sent you some poems, as you desired.

To day I enclose a poem I have just written *specially* for your book upon "Tallulah Falls"; and another on *"Toccoa"* by Gen Henry R Jackson of Savannah.

Please kindly inform me whether I would have time to publish this poem on *"Tallulah"* in any of the periodicals *before* you *need* it?— If this plan should prove inconvenient to *you*, I am sure you'll candidly tell me.

Just here my wife begs me to say, that she omitted in copying Mrs Preston's *"Goshen Pass,"* to *head* it correctly. Pray have it headed *thus:*

"Goshen Pass Virginia".
("Matthew F Maury's Last Wish")

I hope soon to mail you *other* poems of which I am trying to procure copies.

Among them, is an *Ode on Washington* which I was requested to write for *"the S. School Times"* of Philadelphia. The same request was made of Mr Bryant with which he likewise complied.

I think that this piece *may* possibly come among your introductory poems on America, should you like it sufficiently well to place it there.

I observed that you had *one* upon Wm Tell in the Swiss Poems, & *two* on Homer in the Poems on Greece.

Inform me too, whether you desire any poems of place from the *South* connected with the War.

If you are going to have any pieces on *Australia,* I would like to call your attention to *"Widderin's Race"* in my *"Legends & Lyrics."*

Of Course as remarked before, I merely send you verses in a *suggestive* way; to *choose from.*

> In haste, but Ever Yr's,
>
> *Paul H Hayne*

[Henry Rootes Jackson (1820–1898) was a lawyer, editor, Confederate brigadier general, and United States minister to Austria and Mexico, as well as a poet.

Mrs. Preston's poem appeared in her *Cartoons* (Boston: Roberts Brothers, 1876), pp. 81–2, under the title:

> "Through the Pass.
> (Matthew F. Maury's Last Wish.)"

Longfellow included it in *Poems of Places* (vol. 27) under the title:

> "Goshen Pass, Va.
> Through the Goshen Pass.
> Matthew F. Maury's Last Wish."

For some reason he attributed it to "Anonymous." Maury (1806–1873) was the famous oceanographer.

Hayne's poem on Washington pleased the proprietors and editors of the *Sunday School Times* and Hayne found the payment ($20) "quite satisfactory." See Hayne's letter (in the Boston Public Library group) to F. B. Stanford dated March 14, 1878 (No. 111), and *Complete Edition,* pp. 296–7.

In *Poems of Places*, vol. 27 (*America. Southern States.* Boston: Houghton, Osgood and Company, 1879), Longfellow included these poems by
Hayne: "South Carolina" (pp. 9–10), "The Voice in the Pines" (pp.
11–12), "Aspects of the Pines" (pp. 12–13), "Forest Pictures—Morning"
(pp. 13–14), "Magnolia Garden[s]" (pp. 28–9), "A Group of [Three]
Sonnets" (pp. 42–3), "By the Autumn Sea" (pp. 209–10), "Tallulah"
(pp. 217–9), and "The Bombardment of Vicksburg" (pp. 222–3). In vol.
31 Longfellow included Hayne's "Widderin's Race" (pp. 18–26).]

No. 79

PAUL HAMILTON HAYNE to HENRY WADSWORTH LONGFELLOW

(Address me P O Box 275)—

Augusta Geo.
April 30th 1878

My Dear Mr Longfellow;—

I rec*d* your letter last evening, and am *very glad* that I
have been enabled to help you in any way, as perhaps *some*
return for your former kindness to me,— This kindness you
begged me not to mention again, but to extend a like a [*sic*]
courtesy to any that might need it.

Now I think it right to tell you that I have followed your
suggestion, and aided those more in need than myself. But
this was really your gift to them, not mine.

You are right—pre-eminently right—*me judice*—, in not
inserting any war poems on either side of "*the fiercest* kind";
for it should be the aim of all true Patriots *now* to inaugu-
rate a kindly feeling between the two great sections.

"*Legends & Lyrics*", and "*The Mountain of Lovers*" *were
sent you by the* Publishers—as I remember—at my *special*
request; therefore please accept them from me, with the
warmest regards.

I wrote you yesterday afternoon, Enclosing two poems, one
upon "Toccoa", the other some original verses on "*Tallulah*";
& by to day's mail I send "*Macdonald's Raid upon Georgetown*—S. C."—& the poem (mentioned in my last) upon
Washington.

Hoping that your *health* is good, I remain, *my honored friend*

Most *Faithfully & affectionately*
Yours

Paul. H. Hayne.

\#   Remember again, *all* I send whether of my *own* or *others* is sent by way of *suggestion, only*—

No. 80

PAUL HAMILTON HAYNE to HENRY WADSWORTH
LONGFELLOW

"Copse Hill," Georgia Rail Road,
May 6*th* 1878 ∴

Address:
    P. O. Box 275,
        Augusta, Ga.

My Dear Mr Longfellow;

I send you by to day's mail Mrs Preston's *corrected* poem of Lee's "Mausoleum" at Lexington; & *Several other* poems by her.

Also, I mail you her book, which I know she would be pleased to have you accept as a gift from herself.

The enclosed letter, (which please kindly return when you next write), I thought you would be gratified to see.

I took the liberty of putting in Mrs Preston's vo*l* a "*Prospectus*," which I sent you *simply* to show that I was doing my *best* for *Simms'* Monument, but with no design of taxing your generosity at all. The edition of the Biographies will be 1000 not 500, as erroneously stated in "Prospectus".

By the way, among my nature Poems in the last vo*l* ("Mountain of Lovers") there is one called "*Golden Dell*"; essentially a *poem of place,* since the "dell" is not more than 2 miles from my residence, here, in Columbia Co Georgia. (The piece may be found upon p. 68).

. ... Again, in *"Legends & Lyrics"*, on p 55, there is a *Sonnet* beginning,

"Of all the woodland flowers of earlier spring". &c

which celebrates the beauty of our *Southern Jessamines;* and the wonderful lyric-force of the mocking-bird— It *might* be called, perhaps,

"The Mocking-Bird's Bower,"
"A Picture in the So Woods," or something like that.

. . . . I have been *compelled* to *seem* egotistical in alluding to so many of my own verses; but I thought, perhaps, that your intention was to devote a vo*l*, or part of one to the *South;* and there are so few writers here, I having composed more of nature poems than anybody else. Even where these pieces have not had a "local habitation & a name", you'll find a good many that represent different phases of our So scenery.

. . . To day I will write to Mrs *Annie* C. Ketchum, & see whether *she* has any poems suitable for your purpose.

[In the margin, written vertically:]

I will tell Mrs. Preston your decision touching *War Poems.*

Ever, Most faithfully

Paul Hayne.

[Hayne sent Longfellow Mrs. Preston's *Old Song and New* (Philadelphia: J. B. Lippincott & Co., 1870). Possibly that is why Longfellow attributed her poem on Goshen Pass to "Anonymous": the poem is in her later volume, *Cartoons*, but not in *Old Song and New*.

The biographies referred to are Hayne's lives of Robert Y. Hayne and Hugh Swinton Legaré, published together in a little volume in Charleston in 1878. One thousand copies were printed and offered for sale with the understanding that any profits would be donated to the Simms memorial fund.

Mrs. Annie Chambers Ketchum (1824–1904) was a minor writer of Kentucky and Tennessee.]

No. 81

PAUL HAMILTON HAYNE to HENRY WADSWORTH LONGFELLOW

May 11*th* 1878.

I *can't* say, my *Dear Mr Longfellow*, that two lines in my *"Tallulah"* suit me as they stand. The term *"Elf"* as applied to a flower is rather forced is'nt it?—

Would the passage (towards the close of poem), read better thus?—

"And tranquil hour by hour,
Uplift a crystal glass,
Wherein each lithe Narcissus-flower
May view its slender frame & beauteous face
Mirrored with softly-visionary grace &c"—

I leave the matter to *your* discretion wholly.

Retain the original, or substitute these lines as *you* please.

Let me hope that my last packages reached you;? one with poems by Mr*s* M. J. Preston, in addition to her vo*l* (called *"Old Song & New"*) which she begs you to *accept* as specially from herself;—also, a little book by *James Legaré* of S. C. a nephew of the illustrious *Hugh. S. Legàré*, who died in 1843, you may remember in the house of his friend Ticknor, *Boston*. . . . *Don't allow me* to *annoy* you by these various *notes* & inquiries. My only object is to give all the help I can to a *good work*.

Please pardon the rudeness of my handwriting, which is even *worse* than usual, my *wrist* being *sprained*. And the scantiness of paper, excuse also. I've *misplaced* the key to my desk, and must be contented (for the time), with any small sheet that turns up.

Always Faithfully,

Paul. H. Hayne.

[The passage towards the close of "Tallulah" reads as follows in *Poems of Places* (vol. 27, p. 219):

>"And tranquil hour by hour
>Uplift a crystal glass,
>Wherein each lithe narcissus flower
>May mark its slender frame and beauteous face
>Mirrored in softly visionary grace. . . ."

James Matthews Legaré (1823–1859) was a Charleston lawyer and inventor and the author of *Orta-Undis, and Other Poems* (Boston: W. D. Ticknor & Co., 1848).

Hugh Swinton Legaré (1797–1843) was a Charleston lawyer, editor, statesman, diplomat, and attorney general of the United States.

George Ticknor (1791–1871), of Boston, was an important literary historian, scholar, and Harvard professor.]

No. 82

PAUL HAMILTON HAYNE to HENRY WADSWORTH LONGFELLOW

"Copse Hill," Georgia Rail Road,

Address:

P. O. Box 275,
Augusta, Ga.   June 26*th* 1878

My Dear M*r* Longfellow;—

I *would* have thanked you long ago, for your prompt reply to my inquiries about the latest publication of your *Complete Works;* but have been *ill* from several attacks of hemorrhage. Therefore, you'll excuse my using a pencil, since I am too weak to stand at my desk.

The *Tornado* (of which perhaps you have read an account, & which occurred on the 19*th* of this month) nearly swept us away. The rain pouring in thro the roof deluged the house, & the *wetting* I underwent, *increased* my indisposition.

I hope that you rec*d* a "batch" a [*sic*] poems sent you some days since. I enclose another ("Hatteras") which reached me yesterday—

Mr. Swinburne's *"Ballads"* directed to me by the NY firm, I found upon opening the pck, was *your* copy, sent you by the Publishers *the Worthingtons*. I presume the copy designed for *me* was mailed to you by mistake.

Is it worth while to exchange copies?

Of course if no copy has reached you, let me know, and I'll send the book I have immediately.

With warm regards
Ever Yr's,

Paul H Hayne

[Swinburne's *Poems and Ballads*, second series, 1878, was published in New York by R. Worthington and in London by Chatto and Windus.]

No. 83

PAUL HAMILTON HAYNE to HENRY WADSWORTH LONGFELLOW

\#   *Address me P O Box* 275
Augusta Geo
August 9*th* 1878

My Dear Mr Longfellow;

Enclosed, I send you a *"Sonnet"* which perhaps may suit your book of *"Places"* &c[.]

By the way, did you receive a *"Sonnet"* addressed to *yourself*, & mailed some weeks ago?

I only ask, because our mails *from* & *to* this secluded Country residence, often fail.:

Excuse so hurried a note!

The intense heat has almost *annihilated* me; and I write with difficulty.

With best wishes,
I remain Ever Yr's

Paul. H. Hayne.

No. 84

PAUL HAMILTON HAYNE to HENRY WADSWORTH LONGFELLOW

"Copse Hill," Geo R R.
August 16*th* 1878.

My Dear M*r* Longfellow;—

I rec*d* your kind note of the 13*th* inst, and am glad to hear that the *"Magnolia"* Sonnet seemed to you "beautiful".

Certainly you are correct in saying, that the "proper place for it will be under *Ashley, the River"*. I had forgotten to give that general title.

The missing *"Sonnet"* to *yourself*, I now enclose, or rather I send *two* versions of the same poem from which please choose the *best*. Believe me, every line is *profoundly sincere*. I *love & venerate* you; & you are equally loved & venerated in my household.

Let me consult you in reference to *one* artistic point. You agree with me I am sure, that as a *general* rule, the *Sonnet* ought *not* to end with an *Alexandrine?* Yet—sometimes, *very occasionally*, it appears admissible does it not?

Among your *own* noble *Sonnets*, I have found one, (on *"Parker Cleaveland"*), which concludes thus;

"He sleeps, but wakes elsewhere, for God hath said, Amen!"
—a clear *Alexandrine*, and quite effective.

There is no *typographical* error in this line, is there?— If I could only be assured so far, of course, my question would be answered!

But again, there are *Alexandrines, and* Alexandrines!

Does *mine* run into superfluity, & would it be as well, after all, to clip it down into the ordinary "heroic" line?—*thus?*

"Let golden dreams ascend, and thoughts of fire"?
I would like to publish this *"Sonnet"* in "The Atlantic", but M*r* Howells *for two years* past, has systematically refused *everything* I offered him. (This in *confidence!*)

Always Faithfully

Paul. H. Hayne.

P. S. I am under the impression that a little poem by Henry R Flash was enclosed you in the missing letter; (I mean the one in which I first sent the *Sonnet* to yourself).

I'd like to know whether this piece by Flash miscarried, so that I can procure another copy. It was a graceful lyric on the *"Blue Lick Springs"* (Ky), and might serve your purpose.

[Written at the top of the first page:]

Poetic *inspiration* does *not* always come to illustrate *feeling.* Thus earnest as my "Sonnet" to H W L is, I am (upon a *2nd* perusal of it) *sadly dissatisfied* with its *expression,* its *art generally!*

[The "Magnolia" sonnet concerned Magnolia Gardens, across the Ashley River from Charleston (see *Complete Edition,* p. 263).

The line about which Hayne was so concerned reads thus in *Complete Edition,* p. 268:

"Let golden dreams ascend, and thoughts of fire!"

Henry Lyndon Flash (1835-1914) was born in Ohio but spent most of his life in New Orleans until 1887, after which he lived in Los Angeles. During the war he served for a time in the Confederate Army and later went into business in New Orleans. He published volumes of poems in 1860 and 1906.]

No. 85

PAUL HAMILTON HAYNE to HENRY WADSWORTH LONGFELLOW

"Copse Hill," Georgia Rail Road,
October 12*th* 1878.

Address:
    P. O. Box 275,
        Augusta, Ga.

My Dear Mr Longfellow;—

Your *last* note of some weeks ago, closed our Correspondence in regard to *"Poems of Places",* which really important work, advances regularly towards its conclusion; as I gather from the newspaper notices.

When your *last* batch of *"MSS,"* or printed *Materiél* leaves you, will not your mind be lightened; or will you feel, *au contraire,* a certain melancholy sensation at the completion of a pleasant task?

By the way, this reminds me to ask, whether you can *consistently* request your Publishers, (who send *me their new publications,* very *often,* for review in the *So* journals), to *mail me* an *early copy,*—an *unbound copy,* if they choose—, of the vol on *"American* Places."?

In *that* case, I will notice the work so *promptly* & *conspicuously* in more than *one influential So* paper, that its *sale* at the South may be possibly increased.

Frequently, *Northern* books of value are neglected at the South, merely because the Public have no means of being duly informed of their merit.

Enclosed, I send you a poem which appeared in the *"N Y Sun"* of the 6*th* in*st;* the *feeling* of which, is now *universal* in this most unfortunate section.

The liberality, sympathy, & brotherly kindness of your people have indeed *subdued* us . . . at last!

x x x The *half-wilted* flowers I enclose, are *jessamines;*— *autumn* jessamines; I send them because they are (at this *special* season) *great curiosities. Not more* than *once in a quarter of a Century,* is the jessamine known to bloom in *these latitudes,* at so late a period of the year. They are, indeed, a *March* flower.

Something very unusual in the atmosphere is betokened by the re-appearance of such flowers.

Can it have—think you,—any subtle connection with the heated, unwholesome, noxious air, which is killing thousands upon thousands in the far S. West, and some slight *"waft"* of whose unnatural influence may have visited us; thus stimulating to an unwonted efflorescence?

But *basta!* I must not interrupt you!

Always Most Faithfully

Paul. H. Hayne.

P. S. Do you ever see a monthly published at *Springfield, Mass,* called *"The Sunday Afternoon"*? In the last number, *but one*, of that periodical *"Tallulah"* appeared *correctly* printed.

The Sonnet on *"Magnolia Gardens" Ashley River"*, will soon appear in *"Lippincotts"*, (I *believe!*), & the *"Sonnet"* to yourself, which *circumstances* prevented me from offering to *"the Atlantic"*, has been accepted by the Phila *"S. School Times"*. Will send you a *copy*, of course *when* issued.

[I have not seen the New York *Sun* for October 6, 1878, but I conjecture that the poem referred to is "The Stricken South to the North" (*Complete Edition*, pp. 299–300), which expresses gratitude for relief sent to Southern cities stricken with yellow fever. By "the far S. West" Hayne means Memphis, New Orleans, and other points in the Mississippi Valley.

Sunday Afternoon (called *Good Company* after September, 1879) was a Springfield (Massachusetts) monthly published by E. F. Merriam from 1878 till 1881. F. L. Mott (III, 39n) says it "had an excellent corps of contributors."]

No. 86

PAUL HAMILTON HAYNE to HENRY WADSWORTH
LONGFELLOW

"Copse Hill," Georgia Raid Road,
Dec *9th* 1878.

Address:

P. O. Box 275,
Augusta, Ga.

Dear Mr Longfellow;

Since my letter of this morning, chancing to turn over some papers, &c I found to my surprise, that a notice of *"Keramos &c"*, which I really believed had been mailed you weeks ago, still remained in my desk. *Now*, I enclose it!—

. . . One little *stricture* I have ventured upon, (touching the *Sonnet* to Tennyson), you'll observe is only put in the shape of a *question?— —*

I may be *absurdly* wrong.

\#   *Please* think *seriously about flying from your winter annoyances in the way of visitors*, and coming for *rest & peace, Southward*. I could so manage the *matter*, that no one would *know of your visit*, and oh! what *peace* would come *to your Spirit*; and how many new, quaint experiences I could *promise* you!!

. . . My *wife* would treat you *as tenderly* as if you were *her own father*; and you'd feel just as *truly at home*, as any mortal *could* feel.

Only say the *word!!* and everything can be *prepared* in *a trice!—*

. . . About that poem *"Summer Studies"*, I experience a sensation as *if I might* have composed *it in a Dream*; but *let me repeat*, that if indeed I composed the verses, they have— *in detail*—escaped my memory!—

. . . . I am *dreadfully puzzled*; I *d'ont* know *what* to do concerning them; but *leave the entire matter to you!*

Where on *earth, did you first come* across them? in what *periodical?*

But pray do *not* trouble yourself—. They had better appear *anonymously under* the circumstances,—*d'ont you think* so?—

In haste, but Always,

Paul H Hayne.

{Longfellow's *Kéramos, and Other Poems* (Boston: Houghton, Osgood and Company) appeared in 1878.

"Three Summer Studies" appeared in *Poems of Places* (vol. 27, pp. 83–6) over the name of James Barron Hope (1829–1887), Virginia poet. He served in the Confederate Army, attaining the rank of captain, and after the war wrote and did editorial work at Norfolk and served as superintendent of schools.]

No. 87

PAUL HAMILTON HAYNE to HENRY WADSWORTH
LONGFELLOW

"Copse Hill," Georgia Rail Road,
December 10*th* 1878

Address:
P. O. Box 275,
Augusta, Ga.

My Dear Mr Longfellow;—

Think of *our* having a *snow-storm early this morning,* or
at least a *snow scurry,* lasting about 20 minutes, and driven
furiously before a No West gale! So unusual are these snow
falls in the latitude we inhabit, that *one* is always taken aback
when they *do* come!

Vastly disappointed were all the youngsters, white & black,
at the sudden cessation of the snow! 'Tis now blowing "great
guns" more directly from the frozen Northern lakes, and
something almost as unusual (*considering the hour* 12. M.)
as the snow-flakes has just occurred in the boom & clang
of an immense flock of wild-geese passing over our heads
high in air! *These* geese *generally* pass *about sunset,* & not
unfrequently— so the hunters say—at night, when the moon
shines; a statement I can't vouch for!—

. . . . I suppose you recd my letter of yesterday with
"proof" of *"Three Studies".?* I now enclose the last fragment of "proof", which you kindly transmitted, & which
came *last* evng . . . . I am more & more puzzled concerning
this piece. Has my memory, I ask, myself, been so shaken
by many troubles, and the dreadful incidents which accompanied, and immediately followed the *War,*—that verses composed *before* the great "Deluge" (as I term it)—, "Deluge of
blood"—, have grown shadowy, as it were, & unrecogniz-
able?— *What especially* torments me in this matter, is, what
I communicated yesterday; *viz.* a *species of half-conscious-
ness* that at some time I *did* write a poem like the one mentioned;—but, of course, so *twilight* a remembrance, could not

constitute a *"fee-simple"* to anything on earth, not even a series of *rhymes!*

O! it is *disgusting!* I am tempted to relieve my mind after the fashion of "the *Army* in *Flanders!"* . . . . . .

. . . . . . *Don't allow* the mention of *"snow"* to turn your heart against us! Ten to one, we shall see no more of it for the *entire winter!*

Would it not be a fine thing for you to *cheat* all these precious *"Bores,"* and lay up stores of health besides, by a *sojourn South?*—

. . . . Please reflect *seriously* upon my proposal!

Always Most Faithfully.

Paul. H. Hayne.

[Hayne's reference to the swearing of the army in Flanders is an allusion to Sterne's *Tristram Shandy.*]

No. 88

PAUL HAMILTON HAYNE to HENRY WADSWORTH LONGFELLOW

"Copse Hill," Georgia Rail Road,
December 14*th* 1878 ∴

Address:

P. O. Box 275,
Augusta, Ga.

My Dear Mr Longfellow;—

. . . . Please pardon me for returning your beautiful *"proof sheets"* so defiled!! The truth is, that when I glanced over them, I was struck by the presence of *verbal repetitions* which actually *ruin* the Sonnets; or, at least, mar whatever merit they otherwise possess; which is small; since I composed them nearly a quarter of a century ago, when the *true* meaning of *art in poetry,* had not yet dawned upon me!—

I *do* hope it is not *too late* to have the alterations made.?.

The first material change I have marked, is for line *4th*
1st Sonnet.

Instead of

"With a perpetual benison of rest" &c

a halting line, *per se,* and *not* true to Nature besides, I've
suggested,

"With buoyant radiance, & warm-breathéd rest":

or "hale-hearted rest,"

—if you prefer the *latter.*

In *2nd* Sonnet, I would like the *4th* & *5th* lines, to read
thus;—*viz*—;

"Of morn & evening, glimmering everywhere

From wooded dale to dark-blue mountain mere [''']: —.

—better *one* dubious rhyme, than verbal tautology!!

. . If *too late* for the emendations mentioned, why, I must
suffer from the consequences of my own carelessness! The
other poems I sent you, will need *no* corrections like these;
tho (if *perfectly convenient, not otherwise*—), I would like
to glance over "proof sheets;" &c:

. . . . . . I *had* to mail the *printed "Sonnet"* to yourself,
published in *"Phila S. School Times"* so *hastily,* that perhaps
some *errors, (typographical),* escaped my eye.? But I trust
not!!

Ever Faithfully,

Paul. H. Hayne.

[The sonnets referred to here are the first and third of three sonnets
found in *Complete Edition,* p. 29, under the title "Mountain Sonnets.
[Written on one of the Blue Ridge range of Mountains.]." In *Poems of
Places* (vol. 27, p. 42) the lines quoted above read as follows:

"With a perpetual benison of rest; . . ."

and

"Of morn and evening, glimmering everywhere
From wooded dell to dark blue mountain mere; . . ."]

No. 89

PAUL HAMILTON HAYNE to HENRY WADSWORTH LONGFELLOW

Address P O Box 275 Augusta Ga
"Copse Hill" Geo R R.
December 24*th* 1878.:

My Dear Mr Longfellow;—

. . . I *am glad* that the mystery of the Poem has been cleared up; *doubly, glad,* inasmuch as it proves my memory not so much at fault after *all*! You speak of having given me *"trouble"* in this matter. *Why, my dear old friend,* if I may thus call you,—the *"trouble"* was a *real delight,* & therefore, I wish it had been *multiplied fourfold!*

About your *visit South.* Of course I see how impossible it is for you to leave home, until your present important work is done;—but suppose that you are free by the *beginning of next Spring;*—why *not,* in *that* Case, *come,* & *sojourn with us,* and *rest yourself, body & mind?*—

. . . . . It will be a *"rest,"* I *promise;*— *Nobody,* (unless you desire it), *shall* ever *know* of your presence in the *Country* . . . . And *you*—who have been all over the world—, would'nt you like to catch a *glimpse* of this land, unlike any *other* in certain particulars?

Moreover, we could pass into *Florida* for a while, should you desire to see that "flowery kingdom".

Bref! think over *my proposal; & make up your mind to come.*

. . My wife will take as much care of you, as if you *were her own father.*

With best wishes of the season, I am

Ever *Faithfully & affectionately* Yr's

Paul H Hayne.

P. S. What a sad sad *death B. Taylor's* was!! In *sight* of his *goal; just when* he had *prepared* himself for a *bolder flight* than *ever,* to be thus stricken down!

No. 90

PAUL HAMILTON HAYNE to HENRY WADSWORTH LONGFELLOW

\#   *Address P O Box 275.:*

Augusta Geo
December 28th 1878.:

My Dear Mr Longfellow;—

Your last note (as kind as ever), has been rec*d.*

Indeed, so far from wondering that you should ·"leave out". or forget certain things in your communications, my marvel is, that you remember, *generally,* so well!

"I trust," you observe, "that you were rather *amused* than *offended* at my blunder about Mr Hope's poems, & all the trouble it gave *you?"*— "Offended!" how *could* I *possibly* be *offended* by the most *natural* of errors;—and as for *"trouble",* I wish *that* I really *did* have the chance of taking some *real "trouble"* on *your* behalf. It would, *under* the Circumstances, be transformed into a *pleasure!*

About the corrections in *"Blue Ridge* Sonnets", I am glad that the *emendations* in the 2*nd* Sonnet pleased you. Concerning those in the 1*st* I honestly acknowledge (after a thorough study of the point), that *you* are beyond *doubt correct;* & therefore, I would, as *you suggest,* leave the *"expressions"* as they *originally* stood.

The discovery of the *proof sheets* of *"Widderin's Race",* gratified me much. The piece is so exquisitely printed, that I see nothing to correct, but a *single letter*, in the word *"ravin"!*— . . . By present mail *I return "proof".*

With best wishes of the season from *all here;* I am

Most Faithfully Yours,

Paul. H. Hayne.

P. S. My answer to *your last letter but one,* must have crossed yours *in the mail.*

No. 91

PAUL HAMILTON HAYNE to HENRY WADSWORTH LONGFELLOW

January 20th 1879

My Dear Mr Longfellow;

You have been so uniformly kind & courteous to me, that I am about to tax your kindness still further.

Some months ago, Mr Whittier asked the *Publishers, Houghton Osgood & Co,* if they would issue a vo*l* for me of my *latest poems;* (i e) *those* written *since the appearance* of *"The Mountain of* Lovers".

Mr Houghton, he said "thought the *time not* favorable, as the Book Trade was *so* "much depressed". Mr Whittier added, however, "I *hope* he may see his way clear to do it 'ere long!" Since *that* period, the Book trade seems to have greatly revived; therefore, *would you* kindly exert your influence in this matter, *provided you have no objection.*

Do *not,* thro any motives of *delicacy, hesitate, for one moment,* to be *frank* with me.

(The vo*l* would not be larger than *"Mountain of Lovers")* [.]

x x x And so, our friend *Bayard Taylor* has passed away; and it seems so sad to think, (as I understand by the papers), that the *first* copy of his *"Deükalion"* reached him on *the very* day of his death!! I had *never* met Taylor, but his *letters* to me were so genial, frank, even *affectionate,* that I shall *miss* him, ah! how much!

Your tribute to him, I read with *truest* admiration. It is preeminently characteristic of your best style.

Let me hope that you saw my offering to his memory. It was published in the "N Y Tribune". How universally beloved he was!

I observe verses addressed to him everywhere, good, bad, & indifferent. I hear that *both Stedman & Fawcett* are engaged upon Poems on the same topic. . . With *kindest* wishes of the season; *I am, as Ever,*

Faithfully Yr's,

Paul. H. Hayne.

[The two volumes referred to are these:
The Mountain of the Lovers; with Poems of Nature and Tradition. By Paul H. Hayne. New York: E. J. Hale & Son, 1875.
Prince Deukalion. By Bayard Taylor. Boston: Houghton, Osgood and Company, 1878.
Edgar Fawcett (1847–1904) and Edmund Clarence Stedman (1833–1908) were prolific, versatile writers in New York. The latter was of considerable importance, especially as a critic.]

No. 92

PAUL HAMILTON HAYNE to HENRY WADSWORTH LONGFELLOW

"Copse Hill," Georgia Rail Road,

Wed 19*th* Feb. 1879.

Address:
> P. O. Box 275,
> *Augusta, Ga.*

My Dear Mr Longfellow;—

—When I heard the other day, of the death of Mr Dana,— (a man you loved, I am sure, from pure intellectual & spiritual sympathy, not to speak of the *connection* between your family & his),—my mind at once reverted to a period of youth, when I had the happiness of forming Mr Dana's acquaintance, and spending several days & nights at his house, near the seashore. I *marked* the time of that visit, with the *"whitest of white chalk"*; & among my precious relics, is a long letter from the old man, (he was *comparatively* an old man, even as far back as 1854–5), wherein he alludes kindly to my first trifle in the way of a vo*l* of verses, and gives me some invaluable advice, concerning the *"art Poetical."*

And again, I conjure up his image, as I last beheld it, in Boston, 7 years ago, bowed, and tremulous, yet full still of vital force;—his grand head, deep eyes, and flowing gray hair, all combining to make a striking picture of age, untouched by imbecility!—

And thus it chanced, that I was led *irresistibly* to compose the humble little tribute upon the page opposite; which tho *nothing artistically*, has at all events, the single merit of *sincerity!*—

By the way, may I venture to ask *whom* you refer to, in your last *exquisite* "Atlantic" poem *"The Chamber over the Gate".?— Is* it, perhaps, to *B. Taylor's* father?

But, I must not trespass upon your scant leisure.

Ever *Most Cordially*
and *affectionately* Yr's,

Paul. H. Hayne.

[Longfellow's daughter Annie Allegra married Richard Henry Dana, 3d. the son of the author of *Two Years Before the Mast* (1840), and the grandson of the man to whom Hayne addressed his poem, Richard Henry Dana, Sen. (1787–1879), lawyer, poet, essayist, who devoted most of his time to literature after he was 25. Hayne's poem (with unimportant changes) appears in *Complete Edition*, pp. 321–2. "Dana" appeared in *The Youth's Companion* for March 13, 1879 (LII, 86).

Longfellow's "The Chamber over the Gate" appeared in the *Atlantic Monthly* for March, 1879 (XLIII, 368–9). In his journal Longfellow wrote: "30th. [Oct., 1878.] Wrote 'The Chamber over the Gate.' It was suggested by writing to the Bishop of Mississippi on the death of his son." See *Final Memorials of Henry Wadsworth Longfellow*, ed. by Samuel· Longfellow, Boston: Ticknor and Company, 1887, p. 279.]

No. 93

MARY MIDDLETON MICHEL HAYNE to HENRY WADSWORTH LONGFELLOW

Copse Hill April 24*th* 1879.

Dear Mr Longfellow,

Your very kind letter was both a surprise, & genuine pleasure to me, & would have been acknowledged sooner had I not

been painfully anxious in regard to my husband[']s condition
of health. Several weeks ago we were obliged to summon a
physician from Augusta for him, so entirely had his capacity
for mental labor given way. The Dr pronounced upon the
case more favorably than we expected, but thought Mr Hayne
suffering from an entire prostration of the nervous system,
brought about by constant loss of blood, (for nearly a year)
& unremitting brain work. A change, & perfect rest for a
time was prescribed. Europe was impossible so my husband
has gone to Charleston where he will be under the tender care
of my brother Prof. Middleton Michel—who will likewise be
his medical adviser. Mr Hayne reached Charleston a week
ago—very much fatigued by the journey. On the 22nd he
writes "Middleton thinks more favorably of my condition than
I dared hope— We must thank God for this!" I make no
apology for thus making you a sharer in our domestic troubles,
because I feel very sure of your sympathy. I claim too the
privilige [sic] of being one of your most appreciative readers—
One of the class Miss Mulock says—"every author takes
strangely enough into his heart's depths, as he takes not even
those who sit at his board & drink of his cup"—

Now let me say how very beautiful we all thought your
poem "From My Arm-Chair"— And how considerate it was
of you to send such a garland in exchange for my wild jas-
mines— Something perennial in its bloom, in place of a few
withered flowers, whose perfume has already passed away,
except perhaps, from the memory of our tenderhearted Poet—
I have to thank you also for your beautiful volume on the
Southern "Poems of Places"— You ask me to "judge them
leniently and sympathetically"— Apart from their own merit—
it would be impossible for Mr Hayne's wife to do otherwise.
I thank you for giving my husband so fair a representation—
And we will prize I assure you these Poems *doubly* as a present
from yourself. I feel sure that you will be much relieved
when "the stone" is completely "rolled away from your door"—
for what was no doubt a pleasure (when this small library
of Places was begun) most [must] have become a burden long
ere this. Your work is a most valuable collection—& this
thought should bring compensation. I would like you to look

at "Wide Awake" for April so as to have a glimpse of "Copse
Hill". Our home is very humble, but we would have been so
glad to welcome you under its roof—

With warm regards—
Very sincerely

Mary M. Hayne

P. S.

I am delighted, & so was Mr Hayne, that the poem on Richard
Henry Dana pleased you— Do give me—if you have the
leisure—his son[']s address on the enclosed P. C. I would like
to send it to him.

[Mrs. Hayne had two brothers, Middleton and Richard, prominent
physicians in Charleston and Montgomery, respectively. William Middleton Michel (1822–1894) edited the *Confederate States Medical and
Surgical Journal* in 1863–1864, practiced in Charleston and contributed to
medical journals, and later became professor of physiology and histology
at the South Carolina Medical College, Charleston.

Dinah Maria Mulock (Mrs. Craik) (1826–1887), English author, wrote
John Halifax, Gentleman (1857).

Wide Awake: An Illustrated Magazine for Boys and Girls (1875–1893)
was a Boston monthly published by D. Lothrop & Company (publisher of
Hayne's *Complete Edition*, 1882).]

No. 94

MARY MIDDLETON MICHEL HAYNE to HENRY
WADSWORTH LONGFELLOW

Copse Hill
June *7th* 1879.

Dear Mr Longfellow,

Let me thank you, even at this late date, for your very kind
words of sympathy. They have dwelt in my mind, and
heartily must I *ever appreciate* their thoughtful concern for
Mr Hayne, & remembrance of his wife in her grave anxiety
about him. I have had a weary season of waiting. From time,
to time, my husband['] s physician wrote me of a "slow but
sure recovery"—but some weeks ago—first one abscess, &

then another (the last necessitating two surgical operations), caused great suffering, and considerably reduced Mr Hayne's already enfeebled strength. The last operation was of a serious character; but I am told that all risk from *it* has passed leaving great weakness however in its wake. God willing! our invalid will return to us, so soon as he ca[n] travel; which I trust will be about the middle of this month. I *had hesitated* about sending Mr Hayne's tribute to Mr R. H. Dana— until your letter assured me; "that it would give his son great comfort." Then I wrote at once to the Paris address, enclosing the poem, which Mr Dana no doubt received.

Yours very Sincerely

Mary M. Hayne

Box 275.

[In a letter to Col. John G. James (dated June 18, 1879) Mrs. Hayne wrote: "I received a beautiful letter of thanks from Mr. Richard H. Dana in Paris—for the tribute to his father."]

No. 95

PAUL HAMILTON HAYNE to HENRY WADSWORTH LONGFELLOW

"Copse Hill" Ga R Road.:
Saturday 28th Feb 1880.

My Dear Friend;—

— — Upon this day, (your birthday, as the papers tell us),—my wife begs me to enclose for your acceptance, the *very first Jessamines* of the season, which her observant eyes saw, growing on the vines above our Cottage porch. In their fragrance, & beauty, may they prove a *type* of the years still, (I trust), in store for you on earth!

—————— Need I observe that our visit—, my wife's & mine—to your Cambridge home last summer, is a cherished memory?—

— — — For myself, I have tried to embody, or illustrate my sentiments, in the poem, *"Snow-Messengers"* just published in *"Harper's Magz"* for March. Isn't it a strange coincidence,—& certainly to me most pleasing—, that you too should have a Poem in that number; the characteristic, and striking poem upon *"Peter &c"*?—

M*rs* Hayne desires me to tell you, that she brought on *with great care*, the *Willow Branch*, you gave her, at the same time expressing the wish to have it grow at *"Copse* Hill".

Very tenderly does she care for it; but we *cannot* know until Spring whether it has taken root, & will consequently live!

With our *joint & affectionate remembrances*, believe me

Your attached friend,—

Paul. H. Hayne.

[Longfellow's birthday was February 27.

In *Harper's New Monthly Magazine* for March, 1880 (LX), appeared Longfellow's "The Sifting of Peter" (p. 587) and Hayne's "The Snow-Messengers" (p. 598). The latter contains pen portraits of and tributes to Whittier and Longfellow.]

No. 96

PAUL HAMILTON HAYNE to HENRY WADSWORTH LONGFELLOW

"Copse Hill," Georgia Rail Road,
Oct 19*th* 1881.

Address:

    P. O. Box 275,
      Augusta, Ga.

My Dear M*r* Longfellow;—

It is a long time since I have written you; altho you may be sure that both my wife & I *continually think* of you, & of that delightful visit we were privileged to pay you this autumn two years ago.

Your health (we earnestly trust) is as vigorous as usual; and of course I know that your Scholarly habits continue uninterrupted.

x x x x x x x x Enclosed I send you a poem upon the death of Pres: Garfield, which (in certain verses), expresses the *really profound sentiment of sorrow* this section experienced on account of his decease. Out of this Tragedy a new, (& I hope permanent tie) of good feeling has grown up between the North & South.

And now, dear friend, with Mrs Hayne's best remembrances, I am, as

Always Faithfully & affectionately

Paul. H. Hayne.

[In a correspondence journal of Hayne that I have examined he wrote under date of Friday, April 8, 1881: "To Mr. Longfellow (thanks for "U Thule")." In *The Christian Union* for January 5, 1882, appeared Hayne's "To Longfellow. (On hearing he was ill)."

Hayne's "On the Death of President Garfield" may be found in *Complete Edition*, pp. 312–3. It was published in *Harper's Weekly*, October 1, 1881 (XXV, 670).]

VIII. BOSTON PUBLIC LIBRARY (NOS. 97–112)

PAUL HAMILTON HAYNE to F. B. STANFORD

Near Augusta (Geo)
"Copse Hill," Geo R. R.
Jan: 28th 1876..

Dear Sir;

I have certainly been *most unfortunate* in the *two notes* addressed to you, during the last month. *Both* must have failed; otherwise, I feel assured that the Editor of a Christian paper, & himself,—as I understand, a *Gentleman* & scholar, could *never* have allowed those respectful & courteous communications to remain so long unacknowledged.

Allow me to call your attention *again* to a poem of mine, published *(as I hear),*—for *not even* a *copy* of *your "weekly"* *has been* mailed me—, in the *"Sunday School Times"* of about a month ago, called *"The Shadow of Death,"* the *"MS"* of which was furnished you by my friend Mrs Dodge of Brooklin, with the understanding, of course, that if *accepted,* the verses *should be paid for.*

I took *great pains* with this *special piece,* and I think it *fairly worth* $15.00, (the average price recd by me for all poems of the sort, contributed to No magazines &c), but since no *particular sum* was *originally* mentioned, I leave the *amount* of the *"honorarium"* to your own sense of justice, modified, perhaps, necessarily by Circumstances.

I *have been, and continue* very ill; my means are of the narrowest, most precarious sort; and every dollar, owing me, is important beyond what an ordinary prosperous person could easily imagine.

This being the case, may I not look for a *Check from you at once?* accompanied by the copy of *"S. S Times"* containing my poem.?

+ It pains me to enact thus the *rôle* of *Dun;* but surely you will pardon me, when you come to think of the matter quietly & fairly.

Respectfully,

Col Paul H Hayne.

+ *Address me P O Box 635*
  Augusta Georgia

[The *Sunday School Times* (1859........) of Philadelphia succeeded the *Sunday School Journal* (1831–1858). These letters make clear that F. B. Stanford was on the staff of the magazine, but I have not been able to identify him further. The present Editors wrote me (November 6, 1941): "We do not find him named on the editorial staff of The Sunday School Times but have found that he wrote four stories for our department of 'Children at Home' in the issues of The Sunday School Times of February 26, 1881, June 25, November 5 and December 31, 1881. This seems all that we have been able to find about him." Mr. H. Glenn Brown, Reference Librarian at the Library of the University of Pennsylvania, wrote (October 31, 1941): "We are sorry to report that after considerable search we are not able to find anything about F. B. Stanford." Rev. William Barrow Pugh, Stated Clerk, General Assembly, Presbyterian Church, wrote (July 3, 1942) that the Philadelphia Directory for 1877 listed F. B. Stanford as an editor. Hayne addressed Stanford as follows:

F B Stanford Esq*r*—
(Office *"S. School Times"*)—
No 610, *Chestnut St*
Philadelphia—
Penn—

Hayne's autographed MS. of "The Shadow of Death" is preserved in the Boston Public Library. The poem appears in *Complete Edition,* p. 334.

Mrs. Mary Elizabeth Mapes Dodge (1831–1905) was the author of successful juvenile writings (the most popular being *Hans Brinker; or the Silver Skates,* 1865) and editor of *St. Nicholas,* juvenile monthly (1873–1905). Earlier she had been an associate editor of *Hearth and Home* (New York).]

No. 98

PAUL HAMILTON HAYNE to F. B. STANFORD

Augusta *Ga*
Feb 6*th* 1876.

My Dear Sir;

Your *most courteous, & Christian* letter of the 2*nd* inst, with its *ample* explanation of the delay in writing me, I have this *moment* recd; and really its friendly tone *shames* the somewhat petulant style of my own communication.

Attribute the *latter* I pray you, to the exasperating results of long illness, rather than any wrong doing on your part. More than once in life, I have myself been an *Editor;* and I *should have made* allowances for an Editor's various & often conflicting duties, and embarrassments. However, 'tis *all right* now; and I thank you heartily for the Check, ($15.00), and yet more *cordially* for the gracious manner of its presentation.

Doubtless, the copy you promise of *"the S. S Times"* will arrive by the next mail.

It has never been my good fortune to see your paper yet; and therefore, I anticipate much satisfaction in reading it.

Phil*a* & NYork friends have repeatedly alluded to it, as among the most influential & brilliant religious organs in America.

—. *En Passant,* let me say, that I am connected as *Literary Correspondent* with some of our best So *weeklies & dailies;* & that if you chose to mail me your *"Times"* for 6 months, or a year, I could certainly give you a *quid pro quo* in the way of *judicious notices* from month to month.

Hundreds of new subscribers could thus be added to your List; for the Southern people are *widely religious,* and now that sectional animosities have been allayed, they would be *sure* to patronize a paper like yours. No *selfish purpose* moves me to make this suggestion; as I receive, even now, a larger number of papers & periodicals from all parts of the world, than I can thoroughly peruse; but your letter has won my heart by its *absolute manful frankness;* and I'd do, henceforth, all in my power to advance the interests of your establishment.

x x x x x . I am well acquainted with some of your Phil*a* literary celebrities. For example, Geo Boker, (*Minister to Russia* at this time), is among my *oldest* friends; and I have had a charming correspondence with *Mrs Rebecca Harding Davis,* the author, you know, of that *powerful* novel, *"Dallas Galbraith".* And by the way, may I inquire as to another friend, the venerable Mr*s* Hale, Editress of *"The Lady's Book?."* Is that magz still extant, with its good its good [*sic*] natured Proprietor, Mr Godey, who always reminded me of the *"Brothers Cheerable* [*sic*]"? But I am forgetting myself, as a poor Invalid, confined to his room, is apt to do; or rather, I am becoming troublesome in my questioning.

Excuse this, & Believe me,

Very Respectfully & Truly Yr's

Paul. H. Hayne.

(P S.) I enclose a *dramatic lyric* for your examination; a lyric with an *under current of meaning,* you'll not fail to *appreciate. Is it suited* to your columns? If so, take it at your *own* valuation;—if *not;* there is no *harm done.* You can *return "MS,"* & I'll *at once refund the Postage.*

[Hayne had done editorial work on the *Weekly News and Southern Literary Gazette* (1853–1854), the *Weekly News and Gazette* (1854–1855), and *Russell's Magazine* (1857–1860).

Hayne here received $15 for a poem of twenty-one lines.

George Henry Boker (1823–1890), of Philadelphia, was playwright, poet, and diplomat.

Mrs. Rebecca Blaine Harding Davis (1831–1910), mother of Richard Harding Davis and Charles Belmont Davis, was a novelist and story writer. Her *Dallas Galbraith* appeared in 1868.

Mrs. Sarah Josepha Buell Hale (1788–1879) was a prolific author and one of the best editors of ladies' magazines in her day (the *Ladies' Magazine* of Boston and Godey's *Lady's Book* of Philadelphia).

Louis Antoine Godey (1804–1878) was a publisher in Philadelphia, his best-known publication being his *Lady's Book,* later called *Godey's Lady's Book.*

The brothers Cheeryble are characters notable for benevolence and kindness in Dickens's *Nicholas Nickleby.*

The repetition of "its good," as well as most similar repetitions in these
letters, occurs at the beginning of a new page.]

No. 99

PAUL HAMILTON HAYNE to F. B. STANFORD

Augusta 15*th* Feb 1876.

My Dear Sir;

Your paper has been coming regularly & I can now judge
of it, and the kind of article you would like.

Consequently, I fear that my poem, *("The Accusing Face")*
will hardly answer.

However you must judge of this.

I only wish at present to express my thanks for your great
courtesy.

Ever Faithfully

Paul Hayne.

Can you drop me a line?

No. 100

PAUL HAMILTON HAYNE to F. B. STANFORD

"Copse Hill," Geo R R.
May 26th 1876

My Dear Sir;

Enclosed, please find a *brief descriptive poem*, with the
wording of which I have taken much pains.

At a *first reading*, this may *not* appear; but examine *details
carefully*, & I'm sure that the *labor limae* will then be evident enough.

I offer this piece to your journal on the usual terms (viz) $8.*00*, (i e) if you chance to like it.

If *not*, you'll be as frank with *me*, as I am with *you*.

Pray drop me a line as to the *fate* of my *verses*, & Believe me,

Ever Truly

Paul Hayne

No. 101

PAUL HAMILTON HAYNE to F. B. STANFORD

Copse Hill, Ga.,

June 6*th* 1876

P. O. Address:

   P. O. Box 275

   Augusta, Ga.

My Dear Sir;

I rec*d* your P. C. of the 31*st* ult, & am glad to learn that the verses pleased you.

By the way, as this accepted piece is brief; and as many months must elapse before I can again write for you; perhaps you will take one more poem from me; I mean the poem now enclosed, *wholly religious* in *theme & treatment.*

Ever Truly Yr's

Paul Hayne

P. S. Will you drop me a line *as to the fate* of my contribution?

I send P. C.

Of course, I offer these verses for the usual price (viz) $8.*00*.

No. 102

PAUL HAMILTON HAYNE to F. B. STANFORD

P. O. Address:
   P. O. Box 275 Lock Box
   Augusta, Ga.

Copse Hill, Ga.,
Sept 29*th* 1876

To/ F. B. Stanford;—

Dear Sir;

I rec*d* yours of the 23*rd*, and in reply let me say, that I *will* prepare the article, (the *single* article) on the Mystics referred to, & mail you the "*MSS*" as soon as possible.

But this may not be for a long time yet, because I find myself *deeper* in (literary) business engagements for other periodicals than I had dreamed of, when first I addressed you on this topic.

Since but one brief lyric of mine is now in your hands accepted; I venture to offer you a descriptive *Sonnet* with which I have taken much trouble artistically.

Generally I receive for "Sonnets" from "*Harper's*" monthly, "the *Atlantic* &c", from $10.00 to $15.00; but I am *perfectly willing* to take the $8.*00* from you, *should* the poem be approved.

Indeed $8.*00* for only *14 line*s of verse, would seem to *outsiders* a vast *price* anyhow! But these persons do not know, cannot imagine the trouble involved in composing a *really* good *Sonnet*.

Often I have labored upon *one, for hours every day*, during a *whole week!!*

In haste, but Ever Yr's

Paul H Hayne.

No. 103

PAUL HAMILTON HAYNE to F. B. STANFORD

\#   *Address P O Box 275 Augusta Geo—*

"Copse Hill," Geo R R.
November 29th 1876.:

My Dear Sir;

I have just recd your note, with the rejected "MSS". Why, *of course,* you are *right* in *not* accepting verses which fail to suit your paper; and I can *now readily* see why these last pieces failed to recommend themselves. *Often* an author so busy as I generally am, acts a trifle hastily in the offer of his contributions.

'Tis *always* for the *Editor* to decide; and any *Writer* who *resents* a decision against himself, or his communications, when *courteously* given, must be an *egregious ass!*

Certainly I will continue, (as you kindly suggest), to write for *"the Times"* [.]

Whenever my pieces suit, well, & good! Whenever they do *not,* you'll *frankly* tell me so.

With best wishes,

I remain Ever Yr's

Paul H Hayne

[Undoubtedly Hayne studied the magazines and tried to send editors the sort of thing they might like. For one in his circumstances there was nothing else to do. Yet in some cases it led him to compose pieces below the standard which he would have preferred to maintain. Most editors preferred poetry that was sentimental or moralizing, but Hayne was primarily an artist.]

No. 104

PAUL HAMILTON HAYNE to F. B. STANFORD

Augusta, (Geo) Dec 21st 1876

My Dear Sir;

I purpose writing for the "S. S Times" *four* hymns upon the seasons, the 1*st*. of which is now enclosed. Please tell me frankly how you like it.

I took a *good deal* of pains with this piece, *simple* as it is.

By the way, you won't be offended if I beg you to send me a Check for the *two poems, & one prose article* (on *"The Essenes,"*) lately published in your weekly. My dear sir! we are in awful pecuniary difficulty at the *South;* especially those *(who like myself)* have our property in S. Cà. In haste, but

Ever *Paul. H. Hayne.*

[The Essenes were a brotherhood of ascetics among the Jews of Palestine from the second century before Christ to the second century of the Christian era (*Webster's Collegiate Dictionary*).

The property in South Carolina referred to probably belonged mainly to Hayne's mother (d. December 9, 1879). Taxation in South Carolina was very high during the reconstruction period.]

No. 105

PAUL HAMILTON HAYNE to F. B. STANFORD

\# *My Address is, P O Box 275, Augusta Ga*
Augusta (Geo) Feb 1st 1877.

My Dear Sir;

I have remarked, of late, with pleasure, what *a great improvement* has taken place in your weekly, "The S S Times"!

Always an excellent hebdomadal of its class, it seems to me *now, exceptionally able,* and *suggestive.*

By the way, *can* you mail me a few *extra* copies of the *"Times"* containing my verses, on *"Winter"*?

They shall be followed up, *in due season*, by a poem on Spring; called *"A Vernal Hymn"*.

"The Winter Hymn", I see, has been already copied by several So journals, and very highly commended, your paper receiving the *proper credit*. I am glad of *this*, quite as much for *your* sake as my own.

Meanwhile, I offer the *"S. S Times"*, a *"Sonnet"* of a serious, nay, *solemn* character, carefully elaborated. Tell me frankly whether it *suits*.

[Written vertically in the left margin:]

If it *does*, you can have it on our usual *terms*, (viz) $8.*00* for a single poem.

Ever Truly

Paul. H. Hayne.

["A Vernal Hymn" and "A Winter Hymn" are found in *Complete Edition*, pp. 325–6 and 330, respectively.]

No. 106

PAUL HAMILTON HAYNE to F. B. STANFORD
(Private)

"Copse Hill," Geo R. R. . :
July 20th 1877

My Dear Sir;

I have just recd your "Check" for last verses, and send you my hearty thanks.

Also, I must thank you for the kind words wherewith you have greeted the "notice", & likeness in August *"Eclectic"*.

It is very pleasant to receive such words of cheer.

"The Eclectic's ["] "notice" is flattering indeed; and its *cordial tone* I particularly appreciate, but my "winsome marrow", who chances just now to stand at my elbow, *piteously* Entreats me to say, that the *likeness*, whatever its merit as a work of *art*, is *utterly unlike* her husband!

She did not marry, (she says), a black-browed *brigand*, but a quiet, civil *gentleman.*

How dark, by the way, the present style of engraving is! I can't say that I admire it myself.

Best wishes attend you! & Believe me,

Always Faithfully,

Paul. H. Hayne.

[The notice of Hayne and his portrait appeared in the *Eclectic Magazine of Foreign Literature, Science and Art,* 89 (August, 1877), 247. (Vol. 89 is *New Series,* 26.)]

No. 107

PAUL HAMILTON HAYNE to F. B. STANFORD

Augusta (Geo)

August 22nd 1877

My Dear Sir;

I send you a *brief* poem, which may suit *"the Times."*

It is simply the commemoration of a *real* event, touching the life & death of *one* of the loveliest human creatures I ever knew.

Please drop me a line to say whether it is *accepted.*

x x x By the way, I shall close my series of *season-hymns* with a little poem on *"Autumn".*

With *this* I intend to take great pains.

Believe me Always

Faithfully Yours,

Paul H Hayne.

No. 108

PAUL HAMILTON HAYNE to F. B. STANFORD

"Copse Hill" (near Augusta)
August 22nd 1877

My Dear Sir;

In the note I sent you this morning, (bearing a very brief lyric), I forgot to ask your views upon a certain *metrical* question.

The *3rd* line of *1st stanza* of *"Among the Morning Glories,"* reads thus

"Filled her fair hand by ripples of light o'er run &c"
Now, the *"ripples,"* of course, as a *two* syllabled word makes the line a *foot too long;*—yet I *purposely* introduced it, with that very design, upon the principle of an occasional *"discord"* in music.

If you *don't* like so decided an example of this style, however, why the line can be changed, as follows,

"Filled her fair hand, by *rippling* lights *o'er*-run &c"
x x x How is your *paper* progressing?   It *deserves* to succeed.

Very Truly Yr's

Paul H Hayne.

No. 109

PAUL HAMILTON HAYNE to F. B. STANFORD

Augusta, P O Box 275
Sep 14th '77

My Dear Sir;

Certainly you were right to return the *MSS* of the trifle (*"Among the Morning Glories"*), since it did not suit you. Enclosed, I send the *last* of the series of *Season Hymns,* which perhaps you may like.

The very sudden transition represented in it, from despair to hope & triumph, is natural, because the person who speaks, is supposed to be a *Christian,* visited by a deep, yet *temporary* feeling of gloom.

Please *tell* me of the reception of this communication, & oblige your friend,

P. H. H.

No. 110

PAUL HAMILTON HAYNE to F. B. STANFORD

"Copse Hill," Georgia Rail Road,
January 10th 1878.

Address:

    P. O. Box 275,
        Augusta, Ga.
           (Private!)

My Dear Sir;—

Your very courteous note of the 22*nd* ul*t* gave me *sincere* pleasure.

It is strange, but, do you know I have rec*d several* letters referring in high terms to that very poem, *"Before the Mirror"?* One of these comes from perhaps the most distinguished of the *younger* literary women of Boston; and *she* announces her determination to quote the entire piece in an article contemplated upon certain of the lyrical phases of Chivalry!

How it is to be introduced into *such* a paper I cannot divine.

By the way, I must tell you, *(entre nous),* that *"Before the Mirror",*—like many other of my poems—began with the *worst* possible luck. *Four* periodicals refused it, one after the other.

One Editor thought it had no true *raison d'être;* another did'nt altogether like the style of versification; a third condescended to write that it "was *good* in its way," but that *he (W D Howells), did not "like the way;"* and a *fourth* indignantly repudiated the performance as *"indelicate,"* and smacking of *"Swinburne's morality!"*

During my literary life, I have had many experiences of this sort;—and *often*, I have observed that the *very pieces* which *finally* succeeded most unequivocally, were those rejected even by first-class Editors.

One really remarkable example I *must* mention—of course, in *strict* confidence; & simply because *you* seem to take so kindly an interest in what I have written.

About 2 years ago, I composed a long poem called *"Muscadines"*; a lyric of pure imagination, & picturesque effects.

I almost exhausted myself in making it as perfect a work of *art* as possible.

Having been previously admitted to the columns of *"The Atlantic,"* I offered this production to *Howells*. He never *even* answered my note, enclosed with the *"MS"*; and the said *"MS"* was *never* returned. And yet my *name* was on his *"regular list"* of Contributors.

Then, I gave the poem to *Alden* of *"Harper's Magz,"* who was so delighted with it, that he published the verses in two months' time!

Lastly, this performance (so contemptuously treated by Howells), found its way across the Atlantic ocean; and I have in my desk a letter from *Swinburne*, in which he alludes to it in the *warmest terms of commendation;* and S— is *not* generally lavish of his praise!

But what am I doing? You'll deem me an insufferable egotist.

Remember tho that your kindness led me astray, in the first instance.

x x x While wishing you everything pleasant & happy, during the year to come; let me hope that the *"S S Times"* is flourishing as such a paper *ought* to flourish.

I heard with pleasure, of my old friend Chas Richardson of *"The Independent"*, having entered your office.

Give him please my *best regards;* and believe me, *Dear Sir,*

Faithfully Yr's

Paul. H. Hayne.

P. S. I think that you have *one* poem of mine, on hand, called *"Patience,"* have you *not?*

En passant, Mr Stanford, if ever you have a leisure hour, with nothing better to do, I would be delighted to hear from you in a *friendly way*.

You *can't* imagine how *lonely a life* is *mine*, here, among the vast pine woods; and outside my *(very small) immediate* family, I have scarcely any acquaintances, who can be said to add much to the *liveliness* of existence, or whose *tastes*, in any sense, coincide with *mine*.

["Before the Mirror," "Muscadines," and "Patience" are found in *Complete Edition*, pp. 232, 222–4, and 328–9, respectively. "Muscadines" appeared in *Harper's New Monthly Magazine* for December, 1876 (LIV, 127–8).

W. D. Howells joined the staff of the *Atlantic Monthly* in 1866 and was editor from 1871 until 1881.

Henry Mills Alden (1836–1919) edited *Harper's* from 1869 until his death.

Charles Francis Richardson (1851–1913) was on the staff of the New York *Independent* for five or six years in the 1870's, on that of the *Sunday School Times* from 1878 until 1880, and on that of *Good Literature* (N. Y.) from 1880 until 1882. After that he served as professor of English at Dartmouth until 1911. In his *American Literature 1607–1885* (New York: G. P. Putnam's Sons, 1891), II, 229–232, he ranks Hayne next to Poe among Southern poets—above Timrod and Lanier. He was mistaken, however.]

No. 111

PAUL HAMILTON HAYNE to F. B. STANFORD

Address P O Box 275 Augusta Geo
"Copse Hill" Ga R R ∴
March 14th 1878 ∴

My Dear Sir;

I was rejoiced to hear thro Mr Chas Richardson—, that the Proprietors were so much pleased with my poem upon Washington! I tried my *best*, under *very unfavorable circumstances*—.

Thanks for your Check, (for $20.00,) recd 10 days ago. It is quite satisfactory.

And now, by the way, allow me to ask of you a *particular favor*.

Please look over the *back files* of the *"S.S. Times"*, as far back as the winter, (I think), of 1875, and you'll find the *very first poem* I ever contributed to your columns, called *"The Shadow of Death,"* or some such title.

Do send *me a copy;* if *not* in print *then* in "MSS". I mean have the *piece copied* for me, provided it is impossible to furnish the *printed* verses. I am willing to pay *any Clerk who will copy* it off.

> *In great haste, but as Ever
> Your sincere friend,*
>
> *Paul. H. Hayne.*

[Hayne included his poem "Washington!" in *Complete Edition*, pp. 296–7.]

No. 112

PAUL HAMILTON HAYNE to JOHN SULLIVAN DWIGHT

"Copse Hill," Georgia Rail Road,
January 29*th* 1879

Address:

P. O. Box 275,
Augusta, Ga.

My Dear Mr Dwight;

I rec*d* last ev*ng* your very courteous & considerate note, re-enclosing my *"Song"*. That is all right; only I regret that you should have been troubled by such a veritable trifle!

The melancholy news concerning my old, & honored friend, *Horatio Woodman,* has *shocked me profoundly*. Great God! what a *fate!!*

When in Boston about the year '73, I saw a good deal of *Woodman!* He was *sadly* changed from the blythe, witty, indomitable "good fellow," & Prince of jovial comrades, whom

I had known 15, or 20 years before, in my own "green spring," and there was *something* in this change, which I did not like! His eyes seemed alternately to *glare*, or contract; & upon a certain night during which he slept in my bed, he was restless & continually muttering; in a *"nightmare"* condition indeed!

The *explanation*, however, reached me, to the effect, that he was under a *pecuniary* cloud. At that period he was still a *Bachelor*, tho not less than 48 years old I should fancy.

When & how did he subsequently marry? and above all, *whom?*.—

x x x   You will confer upon me, *My Dear Mr Dwight*, the *greatest of favors*, if you will, *immediately*, give me information on these *points*, sending too his *widow's address*.

. . . . Is it *certain* now that he perished in the way you suggest?—

. . . . . Thus, one by one, our companions leave us! There is something inexpressibly sad in the retrospections of men who have reached *your* age, or *mine!!* More than *two thirds* of those we loved, now sleep the mysterious sleep!—

May I venture to ask what is *your* idea upon this *momentous* topic?— *Do* you believe that with man's *final breath*, everything is, in sooth, *over?*—that he sinks into everlasting annihilation?—

So many wise & *"learned Thebans"* advocate this doctrine, at present, that, upon my soul! one begins to doubt the Spirituality of the *Pulpit* itself; & to rank all mankind as *"Saducees"*.!!

Pardon this digression, & believe me *as*

Ever Faithfully,

Paul. H. Hayne.

P. S. What has become of Miss *Doria?*. Is she still a *Singer*, a *public Performer*, I mean, or has she married, & retired to the *stage of the Nursery?*—

[John Sullivan Dwight (1813–1893), of Boston, was a music critic and editor of *Dwight's Journal of Music: A Paper of Literature and Art* (1852–81). Lowell speaks of him in *A Fable for Critics*. He was an original member of the Saturday Club. I quote the following from George Willis Cooke, *John Sullivan Dwight: Brook-Farmer, Editor, and Critic of Music: a Biography* (Boston: Small, Maynard & Company, 1898), pp. 238–9: "In his diary, under date of October 14, 1854, Alcott made this record: 'Dine at the Albion with Emerson, Lowell, Whipple, Dwight, Hayne (of South Carolina), and Woodman; and we arrange to meet there fortnightly hereafter for conversation.' "

Horatio Woodman (1821–1879), native of Maine, came to Boston to study and practice law. He was fond of the society of intellectual and literary men and founded the Saturday Club. He did not marry until about two years before his death. In his closing years he "became seriously involved in some business transactions, and increasingly depressed. He was lost from a steamboat during a trip to New York in 1879 [January 2]." See Edward Waldo Emerson, *The Early Years of the Saturday Club 1855–1870* (Boston and New York: Houghton Mifflin Company, 1918), pp. 126–7.

In his sermon at Hayne's funeral the Right Reverend John W. Beckwith, the Episcopal Bishop of Georgia, spoke of Hayne's struggle with religious doubts but implied that Hayne had overcome them and added: "Some years ago, when he was too weak to come to church, at his own home in the pines, I administered the rite of confirmation. . . ." See the Augusta (Ga.) *Chronicle* for July 13, 1886.

George Willis Cooke (*op. cit.*, pp. 272–3) says that Dwight (who was a bachelor) enjoyed the friendship and confidence of a good many young people of talent whom he advised and influenced. Possibly the Miss Doria mentioned in the postscript was one of them. Hayne may have met her or heard her sing on one of his trips to Boston. I do not know who she was.]

IX. LIBRARY OF THE UNIVERSITY OF NORTH CAROLINA (NOS. 113–114)

PAUL HAMILTON HAYNE to NATHANIEL RUSSELL MIDDLETON

"Copse Hill," Georgia Rail Road,
March 13th 1881

Address:
P. O. Box 275,
Augusta, Ga.

My Dear Mr Middleton;

I *would* have answered your kind inquiries concerning my health, (in your note of Feb 9th), at an *earlier* date, but I have been as busy as my frail physique would permit, in some imperative literary labors.

I *still* suffer from occasional attacks of Hemorrhage,—a reminder over & over, that *I*, at least, am very near the other world, & may cross the boundary line at any moment—; & yet *(Laus Deo!)* I can still work a little.

Thanks for what you say as to my having "enriched the Literature of my State," a grateful compliment from one whom I so *highly respect as both scholar & author* as I do you.

Just now, I am engaged in *revising* my Collected Poetical *"Works"*, (a *big term*, of which Chas Lamb used to make such fun you remember)—in process of publication by Messrs *D. Lothrop & Co of Boston Mass;*— & with this revision, came the *bitter regret* that it had not been granted me to write more noble [nobly] & suggestively. Oh! heaven! how a man's *Ideal* reproaches him in the presence of its *imperfect embodiment!!*

x x By the present mail, I venture to send you a *Sonnet* on *Carlyle*. We, of the South, *ought* to appreciate this rugged, but sincere Genius,—one who had the justice & manhood to stand up for a persecuted People, when all the world were howling anathemas against them!

I am a lonely man, Mr Middleton, a dweller in silent woodland places, and I would so like, & feel so greatly honored
to hear from you sometimes.

May I sign myself—

Your true friend,

Paul H Hayne.

[Nathaniel Russell Middleton (1810–1890), native of Charleston, South
Carolina, graduated from the College of Charleston in 1828, was a planter
from that time until 1852, served for a few years as treasurer of the
Northeastern Railroad Company and then as treasurer of the city of
Charleston, and was president of the College of Charleston and professor
of philosophy from February, 1857, until October, 1880, when he resigned
as a result of criticism occasioned by the small enrollment of students.
He was noted locally as an orator. His connection with Bristol, Rhode
Island, came through his maternal grandfather (Nathaniel Russell,
Charleston merchant) and his own second wife (Anna Elizabeth de Wolf):
both were natives of Bristol. After 1880 Middleton divided his time
between his winter home in Charleston and his summer residence in
Bristol.

D. Lothrop and Company of Boston published the *Complete Edition*
of Hayne's poems in November, 1882.

Charles Lamb's "Dedication" of the first volume of his *Works* (1818)
to Coleridge begins:

"My Dear Coleridge,
    You will smile to see the slender labors of your friend designated
    by the title of *Works*. . . ."

In other places (both in letters and in essays) Lamb suggests that "Works"
or "Essays" is too pretentious a title for his "poor ramblings," adding (in
"A Character of the Late Elia") that the ponderous ledgers which he
kept while a clerk in the East India House "more properly than his few
printed tracts, might be called his 'Works.' "

Hayne recorded in his correspondence journal that he composed the
sonnet on Carlyle and mailed it to W. R. Balch, editor of the *American*
(Philadelphia), on February 9, 1881. It appeared in the issue for February 19, 1881 (I, 304). It is found in *Complete Edition*, pp. 269–70.

For Carlyle's views on the American Civil War see James Anthony
Froude's *Thomas Carlyle: A History of His Life in London 1834–1881*
(New York: Charles Scribner's Sons, 1884), II, 209.]

No. 114

PAUL HAMILTON HAYNE to NATHANIEL RUSSELL
MIDDLETON

"Copse Hill,"
Georgia Railroad.
July 3rd 1882

Address:
P. O. Box 275,
Augusta, Ga.

My Dear Mr Middleton;

I was deeply *touched,* & *gratified* by the reception of your cordial note of the 25th ult from *Bristol,* R. I.—

The *interest* you express in my forthcoming vo*l;* and the conviction that that interest comes from a generous *Heart,* and a noble *Mind,* could not prove otherwise than *peculiarly pleasing* to me.

In reference to my health, (after which you kindly inquire), it is much as usual; (i e) fluctuating & feeble; at certain seasons, I confess *so trying,* that the *soul longs* for escape; for a passage into some condition of existence where this Eternal load of fleshly trouble, of nervous irritation, or nervous exhaustion, shall be known no more! Under some such *yearning,* I composed the brief lyric, (to which you refer), for *"Harper's".* *Subjective* in *one* sense, I yet strove to make the central idea *un-ëgotistical,* sufficiently so, at all events, to embody (however partially) the feeling of suffering Humanity worn & wasted by long conflict,—but with the goal in view *at last!!—*

— *You* understand *this* I am sure. The *overladen* spirit is relieved by expression; and then a species of re-action arrives; & a *hopeful* Manhood re-asserts itself!

—. Your *kindly interest tempts* me to enclose for your perusal a lyric, (*very* different from *"In Harbor"*), which was primarily inspired by one of *Leigh Hunt's* charming translations from *Theocritus.*

It has had a *wonderful* success, having been copied & re-copied in numberless journals, from Fl*a* to Canada.

After all, the *humbler* themes, when sincerely touched, are most effective.

But *basta!* eno' of myself. Your great cordiality has made me *egotistical.* x x x x I learned *with regret* that you had left the *"College of Charleston,"* & that my old *"Alma Mater"* had passed into other *Presidential* hands!—*So* much the *worse* for the *"College"*—. I cannot *doubt,* (& I say this in *absolute* sincerity), that *your learning, influence, genius & character,* kept up that *Institution for years; & now,* from all I [hear] it is unquestionably declining!—Professors *Gibbes* and *Porcher* are still there, I presume? Able men both!—yet; I cannot but figure them, as moving rather disconsolately among the half deserted Halls, & the *attenuated* classes! For *yourself*—, I *can't* help wishing now & then, that your *great abilities, learning,* & conscientiousness, combined with a rare knowledge of young men, and *sympathy* with their feelings & aspirations,—had been allowed by Providence a larger field of labor. *Arsenius must* succeed even in the *"Laura"* of *Nilotic* Solitudes; but his *real* place was among the amplitudes of *Rome!*

How true is this of many gifted men! x x x x x x x x x x x x x x x I suppose that you are staying in *Bristol* only for the summer? Mrs Middleton, I know, is a *R. Island* lady; and you must find it very agreeable to pass from the sultry Charleston climate to the *pleasanter* climate of R I.—with your friends & connections there!

At *"Peace Dale"* (in that State, a *venerable & honored* friend of mine lives,— I mean the distinguished *Writer,* and Merchant, Mr. *Roland G. Hazard.*

Did *you ever read* his answer to *John Stuart Mill* upon the *"Will"?* His reply *staggered* the *English* Metaphysician [.]

x x I should feel so glad to hear from *you My Dear Mr Middleton*, at *any* time, when you found it convenient to write.

Meanwhile, pray believe
me Most Faithfully Y*rs*

Paul H Hayne.

. . . .

P. S. A few days, perhaps a week *previous* to the reception of your letter, I sent you a *copy of the "Life of Carlyle" by* Freud; & not knowing your address mailed it to the *"Charleston* College." I trust it has reached you by *this time.*

[Hayne's "In Harbor" appeared in *Harper's New Monthly Magazine* for July, 1882 (LXV. 290), and is found in *Complete Edition*, pp. 337–8.

Lewis R. Gibbes was professor of mathematics and natural philosophy at the College of Charleston from 1838 until 1892, and Frederick A. Porcher was professor of history and belles-lettres there from 1848 until 1888. Since Hayne graduated from the College of Charleston in 1850, he probably studied under both of them—both the faculty and the students were few in number.

Arsenius (c.354–c.450), surnamed "the Great," was a famous Egyptian monk who was at one time (383–394) tutor to the sons of the Roman emperor Theodosius the Great and spent forty years (394–434) as a hermit in the monastic wilderness of Scetis in Egypt. He also lived for three years in the island of Canopus and for thirteen years in Troe (near Memphis).

Rowland Gibson Hazard (1801–1888), native of Rhode Island, was a manufacturer of woolen goods and writer on philosophical subjects. He traveled a good deal, engaged in philanthropic work, and served three times in the Rhode Island state legislature. He was a personal friend and correspondent of John Stuart Mill. Two of his publications were *Freedom of Mind in Willing* . . . (New York: Appletons, 1864) and *Two Letters on Causation and Freedom in Willing, Addressed to John Stuart Mill* (Boston: Lee and Shepard, 1869). His mother (Mary Peace Hazard) was a native of Charleston, where his father (Rowland Hazard) had engaged in business for a time. When the elder Hazard returned to Rhode Island (c.1800), he called his home "Peacedale" after his wife's family name.

J. A. Froude's *Thomas Carlyle: A History of the First Forty Years of His Life, 1795–1835* (two volumes) came out in 1882 both in London and in America.]

X. LIBRARY OF COLUMBIA UNIVERSITY
(NOS. 115–161)

No. 115

PAUL HAMILTON HAYNE to WILLIAM HAWKINS FERRIS

"Copse Hill," Ga R. R.
(March 27th 1867)

My Dear Sir:

Last night I recd from my old friend, Mr Simms, a letter enclosing your note of the 18th inst.

It affords me *pleasure* to comply at once, with the request that note contains.

You will consequently find herewith, copies of two brief poems, the *Song*, written— ah! I cannot say how many years ago—, & the descriptive *Sonnet* of a much later date.

I should like to hear whether these trifles had reached you.

Very Respectfully,

Paul H Hayne

W Hawkins Ferris, Esqr   Box 260 Augusta (Ga) P.O.

[For a comment on the relations between William Gilmore Simms and William Hawkins Ferris, of Brooklyn, see William P. Trent, *William Gilmore Simms*, pp. 291, 302, 309, and 310. Simms frequently exchanged letters with Ferris and saw him often in New York. After the war Ferris sent Simms $315 for the poor of Charleston. Ferris was interested in autographs and Simms added a number of important letters to his friend's collection.]

No. 116

PAUL HAMILTON HAYNE to WILLIAM GILMORE SIMMS

"*Copse Hill*," 23rd Feb 1869

My Dear Friend;

I find in glancing over my "Diary", that *more* than 6 months have passed since I had the pleasure of receiving a single word from you.

Twice during that period I have written, but no doubt my letters miscarried, for until recently the Conductors of our Accommodation Train were in no way to be trusted.

One of these gentlemen, a lovely youth of Tipperary took to drinking every blessed morning before breakfast, Continuing his potations at intervals of 30 minutes until 11 o'clock at night, & it is not therefore to be wondered at, that my epistles, & the epistles of others were often mistaken for waste paper, & used as cigar-*lighters!*

But at last the Irish Conductor alluded to, was so evidently bent upon conducting everything, & everybody to a most undesirable place, viz *Hades*, that the magnates of the R. Road decapitated him, & since we have had safer officials, & easier times.

Neither thro the papers, nor thro any other source have I been able to hear *of*, or *from* you, for a "Sair wearifu' time," as the Scotch say. I have *finally* grown very anxious, & must beg you—if possible—, to answer this letter *at once*. Years, *my friend*, misfortunes, sickness—, all the ills to which our So "flesh" has especially fallen "heir," cannot weaken my affection for the "old man eloquent", my literary father, & patron.

With the *brightest* hopes of my youth, no less than the few humble successes of manhood, *you* are *indissolubly* connected, & I c'ant allow *you* to pass thus mournfully, as it were, out of my life.

I want to know what you have been doing—, what have been your plans—what your achievements, & whether the Future offers a prospect of peace & comfort to your declining years.

On all these points I am *absolutely* in the dark.

For myself, I continue my old humdrum existence in this pine-land Solitude, studying, & composing for such periodicals, Northern or Southern, as are able & willing to "pay the piper" moderately.

Recently, I've turned my attention to *Juvenile* Literature, & find that it is a branch of our àrt that promises well.

My family are as usual; perhaps I may say a little better in health than *common*, the noble climate of the pine-barrens,

& breezy hills, having done its salubrious work upon the constitutions of them all.

Willie grows apace—, & altho terribly backward in all branches of *conventional* knowledge—, he is developing the muscles, & nerves of the body, & gathering a queer sort of miscellaneous education from books of every description.

I have pursued Dr Johnson's plan, & let him go wild among my literary "preserves,"—following, so far as study is concerned, the *lead* of the spirit—, a dangerous plan perhaps, but Circumstances left me no choice.

I am on the point of negotiating with *Hurd, & Houghton* of NY. in reference to the publication of poor Timrod's *Poems;* & perhaps, my *own.*

Whether anything will come of these negotiations I know not—but I begin to feel *hopeful.*

Have you settled again at Midway.? So far back as *April* last, Middleton Michel—while on a brief visit to my cottage—, told me that you were preparing to rebuild your house &c.

Let me hope that the Fates have been kind—, that you are once more safe, & comfortable under your own "roof, & figtree".!.

Every now & then, I receive a line from our friend Jno *Bruns.* He does not write in good spirits, however.

I am disposed to think that his *children* are not favourably situated, & that the matter seriously annoys him.

You remember our jolly comrade, Dick Michel.? Is he not associated with *petite soupirs,* which Lucullus would have been an ass to despise?

The savour of those roasted *mullets,* & devilled *Crabs,* is in my nostrils still—, and I never recall his punch, except, as Robinson Crusoe says, "to mine exceeding *great* refreshment!". Alas! for the pleasant times of *Eld!*

Life grows darker, & darker, as we recede from the *golden* gates of *youth!*

Thank God!—, there is balm for all our sorrows in the conviction, that,

"Peace waits us on the shores of Acheron!"

These be gloomy thoughts, but really, who can blame us, poor ex-Confederates, for indulging them?— We have been hurled into the depths of Gehenna, & "hinc illaë lachrymaë!." Love from all. Write *soon*, & believe me

Faithfully

Paul H Hayne

[Written in the margin of the last page:]

Address, P. O. Box 635, Augusta, G*a*.

[William Gilmore Simms (1806–1870), of Charleston, was an amazingly prolific author of great versatility and talent. He edited various magazines and wrote poetry, novels, romances, stories, histories, biographies, dramas, essays, criticism, and political discussions.

Hayne was in the habit of keeping journals in which he recorded letters received and sent and contributions mailed to editors. I have examined one covering certain days in 1880–82. Most of them, I believe, are preserved at the Duke University Library. See the *Georgia Historical Quarterly*, XXVI (September–December, 1942), 249–272.

Willie was William Hamilton Hayne (1856–1929), the poet's only son.

Boswell quotes Dr. Samuel Johnson as saying that a young man should read five hours a day, just as inclination leads him, not adhering to a "particular plan of study."

Hayne's next volume was *Legends and Lyrics* (Philadelphia: J. B. Lippincott & Co., 1872) and was published at his own expense, he says. His edition of Timrod's poems was brought out in New York by E. J. Hale & Son in 1873. The sale of the latter was fairly good. The royalties went to Timrod's widow, I believe.

Midway is a small station on the railroad midway between Charleston and Augusta. Simms's plantation, "Woodlands," was within walking distance. The main part of his house was burned by fire of undetermined origin about April 1, 1862, resulting in a loss of $10,000, but his manuscripts and most of his books were in a wing which did not burn. Friends raised $3,000 to help him rebuild, but his new house, his library, and his outhouses were all burned when Sherman's army came through, though it is not certain that Sherman's army was responsible. He rebuilt his house in 1868, but not on the old ample scale. From the fall of 1868 until the middle of 1869 Simms was engaged in suicidal literary toil in an effort to pay for his house and support his children and grandchildren. As a result, his health broke down.

Richard Fraser Michel was one of the young intellectual men of Charleston who gathered around Simms. He and his brother, William Middleton Michel (1822–1894)—both physicians,—were the brothers of

Hayne's wife. Mary Middleton Michel Hayne. After the war Richard settled in Montgomery. Middleton remained in Charleston and later became a professor in the Medical College of South Carolina. Their father was a distinguished French physician who had served under Napoleon before settling in Charleston.

John Dickson Bruns (1836–1883) contributed prose and verse to magazines and newspapers but by profession was a physician. He graduated at the College of Charleston (1854) and at the Medical College of South Carolina (1857). He was the intimate friend of Simms, Hayne, and Timrod. and was especially fond of Timrod and Timrod's poetry. In 1858 he married the daughter of Dr. Samuel Henry Dickson of Charleston. She died during the war. leaving two children. Bruns was in charge of a Confederate general hospital at Charleston and later at Summerville (twenty-two miles from Charleston). He visited Europe in 1866 and thereafter lived in New Orleans as professor in the Medical School of New Orleans and later as professor in the Charity Hospital Medical College. About 1870 he married Miss Mary Pierce, daughter of Levi Pierce, a lawyer.

Lucius Licinius Lucullus (B. C. ?–57?) was a Roman consul and general.]

No. 117

PAUL HAMILTON HAYNE to WILLIAM GILMORE SIMMS

Address me P O Box 635 Augusta Ga

"Copse Hill," *Ga* R. Road
25*th* April 1869.

My Dear Friend;

It is more than 6 weeks since I rec*d* your last kind letter— a letter especially valued by me, because you took the trouble to write it under the pressure of sickness, & consequent low-spirits. My answer *should have* been more prompt, but really without any humbug, my whole time has been fully Employed.

Tho not associated at present with any *one* periodical, in an editorial capacity, I contribute to nearly *all;* composing a story or essay to day for the full-blown adult monthlies, and to morrow entering the lists of fancy for the benefit of the Juveniles, thro the medium of Burke's "weekly" at Macon, or

Scudder's "Riverside" in Cambridge (Mass). Only by becoming an absolute *free Lance*, or a *Bohemian* of Letters, can a man, of my *light calibre*, make his bread now-a-days. Fame, posthumous renown, & "a' that & a' that," I must leave to my intellectual betters; content if the cupboard is never *wholly* empty, & the demi-john of Rye or Bourbon gives out a sound, not *too* manifestly hollow;—

For *yourself*, I perceive that the "Old Guard" still claims your services. After a long interregnum, Van Horton, & Burr have kindly taken to sending me their periodical again; so, I have enjoyed the opportunity of reading your serial novel, written with the ancient vim, and spirit. You stand now, the *last,*— *ultimus Romanorum*—, of those vigorous *Literati*, who thro much travail, laid the corner-stone of the temple of American art in fiction. May God bless, & preserve you for some gallant efforts still—altho if ever man since the primal curse (or blessing?) of labor—had won the right to rest upon his laurels, *that right* is yours!.

My little boy, Willie, is now in Charleston, with his grandmother, and consequently, Mary & I reside here among the pine-barrens, as utterly alone as Selkirk on *his* desert-island.

But I have imbibed a thorough taste for the existence of the *Solitaire.*

Of course, its disadvantages are patent—, but 'tis not without compensating pleasures, & *uses* too.

The *money-question* could nowhere be solved as readily as it is here. Upon an income of Lilliputian proportions, one can at least be comfortable— One suit of clothes will last for indefinite periods—, & for *half the year*, one's Garden supplies all, or *most*, that we need to support us.

There's no show, or humbug of any kind,—no necessary *social drains* upon one's scanty exchequir. Therefore, I'm settled here, for life—perhaps.

Unless indeed, a certain Claim of my mother's now being urged upon Congress,—her claim to the *pension* of a widow of a U S officer, should at some period be allowed!

Under such a *possible*, but now dubious condition of things, the country bumpkin *might* re-appear once more amongst the gentlemen of the metropolis.

Apropos of Congress, *what* a pitiable spectacle our Rulers are presenting to the world! The race of Statesmen has died out. Those ridiculous "Jacks in boxes," who pop their heads out for blatant debate, & screach upon the floor of the Senate Chambers, ought to be sent to the Circus to enact Harlequin.

The best of them may be described in the pregnant sarcasm of Madame De Staël, directed I believe against La Fayette; whom she compared to a tallow candle, "qui ne brille que pour le *peuple*, et qui *puere en S'éteignant!*."

Well, well, the Country has fairly gone to the Devil, so *words are useless.*

The wisest way, is to *laugh*, (if one *can*), at the stupidity of the muddle-headed *Mobocrats* whom a fantastic Destiny has elevated to power.

There's *Grant* for example! He undertook the duties of *his* office with an *insouciance* which, I presume, he thought marvellously impressive, & in a week thereafter showed that he was ignorant of the A. B. C of the Constitution—but the topic is disgusting— Pardon its introduction. x x x x x Do you stay in Charleston during the summer?— Please let me know particularly.

I must'nt forget, by the way, to inquire whether you have heard recently of, or *from* Jno Bruns.? He has not answered my last 2 letters, but no doubt his business Engagements are pressing.

My *wife* begs me to send her best love, & remembrances, & pray Dear Friend, Believe me

Yours Faithfully,

Paul H Hayne.

P. S.—Tell me about your *health.* You complained much in your last.

[*Burke's Weekly for Boys and Girls* (1867–1871) was edited by T. A. Burke at Macon, Georgia. In its last year it became a monthly. Hayne (and later his son) contributed to it. Another frequent contributor was F. O. Ticknor.

Horace Elisha Scudder (1838–1902) was editor of Hurd & Houghton's *Riverside Magazine for Young People* (1867–1870) in Boston.

The *Old Guard*, New York monthly, was published by Van Evrie, Horton & Co. C. Chauncey Burr was editor until December, 1869, when he was succeeded by Thomas Dunn English. Simms and John Esten Cooke wrote prose for it and Hayne contributed a number of poems. Simms's "The Cub of the Panther; A Mountain Legend" began in the issue for January, 1869 (VII, 11) and was concluded in the December number of the same year.

Defoe's *Robinson Crusoe* was based upon the adventures of Alexander Selkirk (1676–1721), who spent five years on the island of Juan Fernandez.

Mrs. Emily McElhenny Hayne, of Charleston, lived at Copse Hill after the war and died there December 9, 1879, at the age of 74. She was the widow of Lieutenant Paul H. Hayne (1803–1831) of the United States Navy, who died while on duty aboard the U. S. S. *Vincennes* and was buried at Pensacola. His grave is in the Barrancas National Cemetery, Fort Barrancas, at Pensacola. His gravestone, which was erected by his widow, was located for me by Will J. Davis of the Pensacola Chamber of Commerce and Mrs. John H. Black of Fort Barrancas. Lieutenant Hayne was the youngest brother of Robert Young Hayne, United States senator and governor of South Carolina. Mrs. Hayne declined a pension because she did not need it but applied for one a few years after the war, during which she had lost most of her property.]

No. 118

PAUL HAMILTON HAYNE to WILLIAM GILMORE SIMMS

"Copse Hill," Ga R. R. May 17*th* '69

Dear Friend;

I was much relieved in my mind by the reception of your letter of the 13th inst. True, you have been ill, but from the very fact of your ability to sit up, & attend to your correspondence, I argue that your strength has measurably returned.

It made me *shiver* to hear how tremendously you have "overworked" your powers—physical powers I mean—, during the last 6 months. Still, I'm in no way surprised. Ten years ago, you told me of your unalterable determination to "die—if possible—in harness"—, and verily, it is evident you design keeping your word. God knows I think you *right*. Better a thousand times fall over at the desk in a deadly faint, or an apoplexy that smites like a cannon-ball, than linger thro months of torture in one's bed!

Nevertheless, the processes of *labors* you describe, which tend to such a result, affect one very painfully.

O, the "burden, & mystery of this unintelligible world!".
It *does* seem devilish hard that *you*—after the gallant fight of 30 years, with victory almost grasped, should have to renew the wearing struggle. Yet we poor mortals can but "do our best," like Hubert's grandsire at Hastings, and then—"permitte divis caëtera"!—leave the rest to the all-seeing Gods!.

You refer to two Elaborate fictions of yours—one, I presume is "the Cub of the Panther," being issued in "The Old Guard"—but what is the other? I should like to know.

For *myself*, you will be glad to hear, that I progress as favorably as could be expected. Tho Pollard *did cheat* me horribly,—to the tune indeed of about 500 dollars—, still I manage to make eno' for my humble wants.

I write for half a dozen magazines; Lippincott's, "The Galaxy", "the Riverside" (juvenile) &c &c.

Prose in every shape—small sketches, stories, essays, critiques, they all serve to bring some grist to the family mill.

Just now, I'm preparing an article on Hugh S. Legare for Bledsoe's "Quarterly".

My Garden can't compare with yours, of course, but—chiefly owing [to] the indefatigable attention of my *wife*—, it has put on a sufficiently cheerful countenance. Green *peas* we have had in abundance; young Irish Potatoes are about ready, and we have a fine prospect of corn, onions, okra, tomattoes [sic], squashes, beans, egg-plants, cucumbers, melons, beets, peppers, parsley, and &c &c.

Were you here now, you could not recognize this place as the squallid [sic], miserable waste you beheld in 1867. *Everything* has changed for the better. Within doors, my wife's ingenuity has converted ugliness into taste, & beauty. She has papered the walls elegantly, and with little help has made 12 pieces of furniture, such as chairs, tables, minor bookcases, lamp-stands, & benches.

Indeed, I have come to consider my position fortunate. *Leisure* I can command in abundance—many of the new books, and all the best periodicals, (English & American) reach me. I have nothing whatever to do with the wretched turmoil of cities, and as for politics, & tyranny,

"Stultorum regum, et populorum continete[?] aestus!" "the eternal rage of stupid people, & stupid rulers",—it howls afar from this quiet nook, and even its echoes—except as they reach me faintly thro the papers—, are disregarded & unheard!

Yes, had I but *health*, I should be that *rara avis*—a *contented* mortal. An important *desideratum*, truly, yet to be borne— with the exercise of proper patience!. Like yourself, I never hear from John Bruns.

Probably—he is more agreeably engaged than in writing to old friends. Report sayeth, that John is enamoured of a certain fashionable, & handsome woman, & that his faculties are concentrated upon a tremendous love-siege.

In *that* case, we may pardon his silence.

Sam*l* Lord—to whom you refer—has been doing us good service.

He has recovered $2.500 [$2,500] for my *mother*—a small fortune to humble folks like ourselves, living cheaply in the back-woods.

This astonished me, for [I] never *dreamed* that *one* cent could ever be squeezed from the Insurance Company.

My mother, & boy, *Willie* are at present in Charleston, where they have been staying on a visit to relatives, for 6 weeks past.

We expect them back on the 25th inst.

I have just dispatched a long letter to our ancient friend, Jno R Thompson, now settled "for good" in N. York City. He had been very ill during the *winter*, with what resembled a lung-disease, but is at length recovered, & working hard at a translation of V. Hugo's new romance for "Appleton's Jour- nal". The novel *per se* is pedantic, pragmatical, incoherent stuff, but Thompson's *translation* is praised on all sides. People wonder how he could have made sense even out of such a conglomeration of bad images, & confused circumstances, as chiefly make up Hugo's *"Man who Laughs"*.

But I must conclude. Minna joins with me in best regards
to your family, & earnest remembrances to yourself.

Believe me,

Always Faithfully yours,

Paul H Hayne.

[Written at the top of p. 5 of the letter:]

My address now is, P. O. Box 635
Augusta, Ga

[In Scott's *Ivanhoe* the forester Hubert has a set speech to the effect
that "a man can but do his best" and that his grandsire "drew a good
long bow at Hastings." See Chapter XIII. For this reference I am
indebted to my colleague Professor James Hinton Sledd.

In 1869 Simms's "Voltmeier, or the Mountain Men: A Tale of the
Old North State" appeared serially for several months in the *Illuminated
Western World*, a New York weekly. Simms was at work on a third
tale, on which he broke down.

Hayne was literary editor of *Southern Opinion* (1867–1869), Richmond
weekly, edited by H. Rives Pollard (1833–1868). Other magazines
referred to are *Lippincott's Magazine* (1868–1916), Philadelphia monthly;
the *Galaxy* (1866–1878), New York semimonthly until April 15, 1867,
and monthly thereafter; *Riverside Magazine for Young People* (1867–
1870), Boston monthly; and Albert Taylor Bledsoe's *Southern Review*
(1867–1879), Baltimore quarterly.

Hugh Swinton Legaré (1797–1843), of Charleston, was a scholar, critic,
author, editor, lawyer, and diplomat. Hayne's article on Legaré appeared
in the *Southern Review* for January, 1870.

Simms arrived at Copse Hill to visit Hayne in December, 1866.

Hayne's wife papered the walls with carefully chosen pictures cut
from magazines.

Samuel Lord, Jr., was a Charleston lawyer and lifelong friend of
Hayne. He graduated from the College of Charleston a year before
Hayne did. In the late 1850's he was one of the literary men who gathered
with Simms, Hayne, and Timrod at Russell's bookstore.

John Reuben Thompson (1823–1873), editor of the *Southern Literary
Messenger* from 1847 until 1860, became literary editor of Bryant's New
York *Evening Post* in 1868. The translation of Hugo's "The Man Who
Laughs; or, By the King's Command" ran in *Appleton's Journal* from
April, 1869, until September 4, 1869. Mott says (III. 418) ". . . such
success as the new journal [*Appleton's*] had at its beginning came from
its serial publication of Victor Hugo's *The Man Who Laughs.*" It may

not have been by Thompson. At least, John S. Patton (who edited
Thompson's poems in 1920) could find no proof.

Minna is Hayne's wife, Mary Middleton Michel Hayne.]

No. 119

PAUL HAMILTON HAYNE to WILLIAM GILMORE
SIMMS

"Copse Hill," Ga R Road
Dec 19th 1869:

Dear Old Friend;

It is just 3 years, (ye Gods! how the time flies!) since I
enjoyed the pleasure of meeting you here, at my humble
cabin in the woods.

Since, *both* of us have been very busy, in our different literary ways—*you* working your great Guns, and doing tremendous execution with broadsides of something bigger & heavier
than grape or canister,—I popping away with my poor little
pocket pistol, and making by no means a very distinguished
figure in the great literary show, or shall I call it *"row"?*

It amazes me, it would amaze *anybody* to look back, and
see the amount of head work you have managed to accomplish in the course of the years specified. What a constitution! *what* what [sic] energy, and steel-like will!

The *concluding* parts of your tale in the *"Old Guard"* struck
me as vigorous, and dramatic.

I recognized the couplets quoted in a note from your famous
old Ballad of the mountain girl, and could'nt help wishing
that *les Convenances* had permitted the quotation thereof in
its integrity. How funny some of your lady readers would
have looked, when they reached the pathetic refrain,

"What will my Mother say to me,
When I go home with *a big bellie?*"

The *substitute* you were forced to adopt for this last vigorous line, is *comparatively feeble.*

By the way, I saw your name with pleasure on the list of regular Contributors to Scotts' Atlanta Monthly, or rather "The Cosmopolitan," as the new Proprietor terms it.

The said Proprietor, (Mr W H Wylly) has engaged me as assistant *Editor*, but I am doubtful of him,—i. e. I know nothing of the man either good or bad, & I've lost too much to go into affairs of this sort heedlessly.

I am *testing him* however.

Our friend *Bruns* I correspond with regularly. He wrote me a more cheerful letter than usual, (for, strange to say, John who is the merriest of the merry in society, grows always lugubrious on paper) about 4 days ago, wherein he confirms a report I had heard of his *engagement.* Yes, after 6 years & more of widowed grief, he has at last met his fate a second time in the shape of a woman! May he be happy!

He's a noble. fellow— — brave, gallant—, and full of genius, or at all events, brilliant *talent.*

x x I suppose at this season you are living at Midway, or *near* it on your plantation! How I would like to visit you there once more, to revive our mutual memories, sad or pleasant, & to drink a *toast* to friends, (whether still on earth, or in "the land o' th' Leal"), with (in both cases), an equally cheerful, & assured spirit.

But tho I know well you would welcome me, the thing is impossible; I cannot come. x x x Meanwhile, how is your health.? A few words dropped by Jno Bruns in his last letter, on this topic, have made me somewhat uneasy. He (Bruns) speaks of your "increasing feebleness." What! have you been *ill—* — or does he allude to the natural, inevitable infirmities of old age?

I have hoped *always* in *your* case, that Life would lengthen your span much beyond the ordinary limit: your constitution was so magnificent!!

Heaven grant it may be so still!

x x x x I am just now sitting before a roaring fire of imperial pine knots—big enough each to knock down the giant *Despair* at a single clip—, and at my right hand is a table just large eno' to hold a decanter of the queerest *cordial* you ever tasted— — a cordial, *amber*-hued, *oily*, delectable, which was first made— think of it—by the Benedictine Monks in Germany as far back as the year 1576, and the *flavor* whereof is only equalled by the *odour*, both being altogether Paradisaical, and divine; I should rather say, *Olympian, & divine*, all Christian notions of Paradise being of a strictly cold, and watery kind.

(*Milk & honey* is the favorite future drink of the *Orthodox*, which I take to be sickening stuff! Now milk *punch*, or honey and *peach, ah,!* there you have me!) But, as for my *Cordial;* would that you were here to partake!! It came to me *mysteriously*, but is being swallowed in a manner strictly *natural!*

Altho close upon *Xmas*, my little Garden is blooming still.

I send as evidence, a few stray violets, peeping out like fairy eyes amid the mould.

My boy, *Willie*, has gone to school in Charleston, and we don't expect to see him again until next August (D. V.). His grandmother went with him,— so Mary & I, are a trifle *lonely*.

And now, *dear old friend*, accept from me the *best* wishes of the season, & Believe me, *despite* Changes, distance, and the lapse of years, Always Y'r attached & faithful,

Paul H Hayne

P O Box 635 Augusta Ga

[The "couplets quoted in a note" occur in the *Old Guard* for August, 1869 (VII, 581n), in a footnote accompanying a chapter of Simms's *The Cub of the Panther*. The last two lines read thus:

"Oh! what will my mother say to me,
    When she shall see—when she shall see?"

Scott's Monthly Magazine, of Atlanta, was published from December, 1865, until December, 1869. W. J. Scott was founder and editor, and H. T. Phillips, an Atlanta bookseller, was associate editor from April, 1868. W. H. Whylly took over the magazine, changing its name to the *Cosmopolitan*, but only one issue under the new title appeared, that for January, 1870. I have not seen this issue.

Of course "the giant *Despair*" is an allusion to *The Pilgrim's Progress*.

The sketch of William Hamilton Hayne by Willis H. Bocock in *The Library of Southern Literature* states (V, 2317) that he "received his education at home, with the exception of a few months' study at Dr. Porter's academy in Charleston."]

No. 120

PAUL HAMILTON HAYNE to WILLIAM GILMORE SIMMS

"Copse Hill," Dec 28*th* 1869

Dear Friend;

Notwithstanding all the cares, anxieties, troubles, doubts, & misfortunes, physical and mental, which your last letter records, I have read it with a species of exhilaration. Your brave words embodying braver thoughts, your expressions of gallant resolution under circumstances the most trying, affect one's moral sense as with the ring of great spiritual trumpets, the blare of silver clarions from some unseen region far above our heads!

It is impossible for me to express in words my profound admiration of your moral *pluck*, of the true Anglo-Saxon, I ought rather to say, Anglo-*Norman grit*, and steel-like endurance, (which may be made to *bend*, but refuses to *break*,) that characterise your nature, and make you in misfortune simply *great!*

You indulge neither in a whine, nor a *snarl*, but accepting the *Inevitable*, with a mental *"Kismet," "it is written,"* you reserve your forces to battle with enemies whom mortal skill & courage *may* overcome!

I confess to the greatest astonishment at what you tell me of your literary labors during portions of this year, and the preceding. Such uninterrupted work, (*imaginative* toil too, which is the most exhausting of all), was eno', & *more than* eno' to *kill* you, or worse, consign you to that lamentable condition of mental wreck of which the concluding years of Walter Scott's life furnish us with so sad an example. It seems to me that no necessity short of *absolute starvation*, or its direct approach, could have justified you in undertaking such *suicidal* tasks.

But the mischief has been done, & I can only trust 'tis not irremediable.

All the symptoms of ill-health you describe I clearly recognize at once.

Every one of these pains and aches has at some one period or another, been mine own familiar— — fiend! *Dyspepsia!!*, bless your soul!, I've shaken hands with that particular devil ten thousand times at least;—he has taken up his abode in every conceivable corner of my poor brain, and poorer stomach! has twisted my back, clutched savagely at my bowels; cut my breath off as sharply, & neatly as if my Breath had aristocratic pretentions, & must be decapitated by an invisible Guillotine;— has *now*, loosened my *liver*, until I thought my whole being would melt away in liquid abominations, and then, plugged me up so tightly, that (I'm *not* joking!!) every operation became a sort of bastard *accouchement* which caused me to yell like twenty regiments of monkeys afflicted *ad eadem tempore*, with Asiatic cholera!!

And as for *nerves!* I have been, and often *am* one huge bundle thereof!! Fancy a conglomeration of sensitive cords, inextricably tangled together, & each one going off into S*t* Vitus' dance, and *there* you have a *faint* picture of my frequent condition of — the Lord only knows *what* to call it!

Who then, on this broad earth, can comprehend, and sympathise with, your sicknesses more sincerely than myself?

And what in *your* case makes the matter worse, is the fact that all your life until these recent years—, health and strength have been always with you!

After all, a constitution like yours, even *after* 60, may revive, with proper rest, and *regimen!* The resilient powers of the human frame are wonderful.

x x x x Tho when thinking of *you*, I feel like an idle dog, yet I *have* tried to "perform my devoirs" bravely during the year about to close. Almost the entire field of periodical literature, North & South, I have at least *hurried* over! That is to say, I have written for all styles of magazine, weekly paper, and quarterly Review,. Indeed, in Literature, I am little better than a *lanskneight* *[landsknecht?]*, or "free rider," gathering all the plunder I can from North, South, East & West.

Long ago I made up my mind never, (upon *principle*), to write *gratis. Something,*—if only pens, paper, & ink—, I peremptorily demand for my work. When the Blacksmith is paid, & the carpenter, when the very Scavenger, collecting refuse, has his annual salary—, I d'ont see why the Poet—however humble—, should be expected to sing for *love* not *money!!* At all events, *I* invariably refuse to do so!

Some trifling reputation as a verse-monger, has helped me so far, that "Appleton's Journal" (for example) pays me on an average, $15.00 for each poem of 6 or 8 stanzas, and I get the same from *"Hearth & Home"*, Edited by *Donald Mitchell*.

Bledsoe's Review I'm now writing for likewise.

In the Jan issue you will find a long article on H. Legaré. That is mine. And a *story* (in verse) called *"Daphles,"* occupying about 10 pp of the Review, and embracing nearly 600 lines, *that* also is mine.

The *two* contributions will probably bring me from 80 to 100 dollars, but this is an unusual haul!!

x x x x x x Did Jno Bruns, in writing, send you his photograph? I have it on my mantle-piece, as large, or rather *larger* than life;— — you would scarcely recognize our friend in his present condition of superfluous fat. His abdomen sticks out a couple of feet, and shakes like a huge jelly whenever he moves. His cheeks are dew-lappy, and his chin is not a *double*, but a *treble* one! When last summer I went as John's *second* to W. Point (in that desperate quarrel of Dick Michel's), and we expected him to *fight* the very *next* morning, I could not but look on his abdomen with melancholy anticipations. I suggested a *brace* of some kind around it—, but no, the obstinate fellow swore it was *only fat*, and said, that a bullet thro that quarter would do no harm, but could be plugged up with—bread, & cheese!!

Those "old boys" at Montgomery were amazed at Bruns' manners, his hilarity in the most trying circumstances, his *bonhommie*, rich humor, and never failing sources of fun, anecdote, and wit! They regarded him with open eyes, and mouths, as

> "A man in all the world's new fashion planted,
> That had a mint of phrases in his brain,"

without I am sure, completing the couplet even in thought, or fancying that he could under any conditions be one,

> "one whom the music of his own vain tongue
> Doth ravish like enchanting harmony."

x x x I am glad to hear that *Govan*, (whom I recollect as a chubby little chap, with *Dutchified* legs) goes to the same school with my son & heir— — (to *nil!*), Willie. The news that the latter "promises to be a Poet," has seriously *shocked* me.

Mon Dieu! *Can* it be possible that the poor little devil has inherited this dreadful *virus* from his unlucky papa? Let us trust that the report is exaggerated!!

To be in earnest, my boy *is* doubtless, quite intelligent, tho very *backward* in his studies! I kept [him] by me in the Country to the last possible moment, for the purpose of developing his *physique*—naturally feeble—, and I've succeeded so far at least, that I believe *Willie* will grow up into a moderately vigorous man, and never be tormented by the constant ill-health which more than aught else, has dogged his father's progress thro life. *Morally;* he is pure as any youthful Sir Galahad;—and I have never known him *hint a lie,* or outline deliberately or carelessly even the shadow of falsehood!! x x x

[Written in the margin of—and partly across—the last page of the letter:]

The evening shades warn me to close. Mary (my wife) sends her *best love* and wishes for your speedy recovery.

Write soon, if possible, & Believe me

Always Faithfully

Paul H Hayne.

[Written at the top of the first page of the preceding letter:]

Please *return the Poem I enclose.*
'Tis my only copy.

[*Appleton's Journal* (1869–1881) was a New York weekly until June 26, 1876, and a monthly thereafter. *Hearth and Home* (1868–1875), edited by Donald Grant Mitchell, was a New York weekly. I have not seen the latter for 1869, but in that year *Appleton's Journal* contained these poems by Hayne:

"Ma Belle," May 22, 1869 (I, 242)
"The Nest," July 3, 1869 (I, 427)
"Krishna and His Three Handmaidens," July 17, 1869 (I, 497–8)
"Sonnet," August 7, 1869 (I, 601)
"The Bonny Brown Hand," November 20, 1869 (II, 433)
"Sonnet," December 18, 1869 (II, 558)

The *Southern Review* (Baltimore quarterly) for January, 1870, contained Hayne's "Hugh Swinton Legaré" (VII, 123–58) and "Daphles" (VII, 213–25).

The four lines quoted are from *Love's Labour's Lost*, I, i, 163–6.

Govan was Simms's younger son.

Concerning "that desperate quarrel of Dick Michel's" I have no information except that given here and in Hayne's letter to John R. Thompson dated October 4, 1869 (No. 69). There is a town named West Point in the southwest corner of Troup County, Georgia, close to the border of Alabama. Possibly this is the place where the quarrel was settled, though West Point may be the name of a place nearer Montgomery.]

No. 121

PAUL HAMILTON HAYNE to WILLIAM GILMORE SIMMS

"Copse Hill," Jan 2nd
1870

Dear Friend;

I cannot resist the impulse of writing, & thanking you for the mournful pleasure I have just derived from the perusal of your poem "Agläus," which I could not obtain a copy of until yesterday. It is a touching threnody!

By the way, Dr Bledsoe of the "So Review" has asked me, (I say this, *sub rôsa!*), to review *that* portion *of a late book,* by J Wood Davidson, which alludes *impertinently* to yourself, & *especially* your Poems. This book, issued by Carleton (NY), and composed of a number of newspaper squibs, & *critiques!* (God save the mark!) the crude out come of a very sufficient ass,—you have possibly seen under the title of "Living Writers of the South." Davidson is one of that Caldwell clique, who, I presume, by lustily "blowing his own trumpet," & emphasizing the handle of *Prof:* which he has placed to his name upon the strength of having once been a teacher in some little provincial up-Country Academy,—managed to *humbug the Yankee* Publisher, and to get his ridiculous vo*l* put upon the market.

T'will ['Twill] probably prove an *abortion* in every respect.

For myself, I will give M*r* D———— well!— what he *deserves,* no *more,* no *less!*

The evil, mean, bitter *animus* of his articles is even more apparent than their *stupidity.*

Such a scribbler would have deserved no sort of notice, if he had not committed the folly of trying to perpetuate his pestilent nonsense in *book-form.* Now,—he must receive no quarter. One c'ant always be amiably sparing—*vermin!!*

If I forgot the *violets* in my *two* other letters, you perceive, they are present here. What a *hardy* little flower the violet is! Tho our weather is bitter-cold, and all the winds seem let out at once from the caves of "old AËolus,"—still they, (the flowers), refuse to succomb. So, I send you in Mid winter a *whiff* from some fairy Spring.

Besides your *elegy,* I've been reading with great interest your sketches of the ancient celebrities of Charleston. How infinitely superior *these* reminiscences are to the crude, Egotistical, weakly arranged, & unsatisfactory biographies, or *ana* of So great men by *Perry!.* Why, P—— gossips like an old woman! omits almost everything one would like to know, and retains all sorts of shreds of wretched gossip.

Have you rec*d* the "So *Review*" yet? At your leisure, glance over my Greek tale of "*Daphles,*" & the essay on *Legaré.*

And now, wishing you a *peaceful* if not a *happy* New Year—
(who of us can look for *happiness* here, and now?), I am,

Always Faithfully,

Paul H Hayne.

P O Box, 635, Augusta Geo

[Simms's "Aglaus," a poem written in memory of Henry Timrod,
appeared in the *XIX Century* (Charleston monthly) for July, 1869.

James Wood Davidson (1829–1905), miscellaneous writer, taught
Greek in various institutions in South Carolina before the war, served
under Stonewall Jackson in Virginia, and entered journalism after the
war. He was in Washington for two years and in New York for ten
years (on the staff of the *Evening Post*). Later he lived in Florida,
Washington again, and elsewhere. In the *Crescent Monthly* for March,
1867 (II, 203–6), he had published a critique on Hayne's verse, which
contained both praise and faultfinding. He did not like Hayne's long
narratives or his discussion of the sonnet, and he said that though Hayne
was a good student of English literature he was no classical scholar.
Later Hayne came to think better of Davidson as a man at least, if
not as a critic. (See Davidson in the index of Jay B. Hubbell's *The Last
Years of Henry Timrod 1864–1867*, Duke University Press, 1941.) Davidson's *The Living Writers of the South* (New York: Carleton, 1869) was
reviewed in 1870 in the *Southern Review* for April (VII, 499–502) and
for July (VIII, 222–28). The notices (probably by Albert Taylor Bledsoe,
the editor) are exceedingly harsh and charge Davidson with many gross
blunders as to facts. Neither notice mentions Simms, but the second one
praises Hayne's nature poetry by way of reply to Davidson's comment
on it. Evidently Hayne did not write any part of either notice. Davidson
ranked Simms as one of the very best American writers of prose fiction,
but he seemed to find malicious delight in ridiculing his poetry.

Howard Hayne Caldwell (1831–1858), South Carolina poet and journalist, had been offended by a review of his poetry which Simms wrote for
Russell's Magazine (April, 1858: III, 36–47).

In 1869 and 1870 Simms published in the *XIX Century* (Charleston
monthly) a series of sketches of early writers of South Carolina. The
titles of the series varied. The title in the issue for January, 1870 (II,
631–37) was "Early Literary Progress in South Carolina."

Benjamin Franklin Perry (1805–1886) was a South Carolina lawyer
and journalist who had been governor of the state. In 1869 and 1870 he
published a series of sketches of eminent men in the *XIX Century*,
Charleston monthly (1869–1872). In the *Southern Review* Hayne referred
to Perry's series as "loose, egotistical, and unsatisfactory" (October, 1870:
VIII, 277n). Apparently Hayne was offended by what Perry had said
concerning Robert Young Hayne.]

No. 122

PAUL HAMILTON HAYNE to WILLIAM GILMORE SIMMS

"Copse Hill," Geo R Road,
March 31st 1870

Dear Friend;

You were right in making excuses for what *seemed* my "shortcoming" in leaving town without seeing you.

Indeed, it was no fault of mine, but rather the fault of *circumstances*. I was *forced* to depart unexpectedly, and some days *before* I had previously intended. My wife's *position* in the Country was becoming disagreeable, if not *dangerous*, and Willie's health imperatively demanded an *instant* change.

Nevertheless, I had set apart some hours to be with you, when one of these horrible *bores*, who refuse to leave one until all the patience is sucked out of one's soul, caught hold of me, & prevented my visit.

I *deeply regret* to hear of your continued weakness. Can't you manage to rest this spring & summer; to go from Charleston, & *recreate* among your Northern acquaintances?

About "the Cosmopolitan," the report of its decease is correct. Wylly—the Editor—turned out a complete, & very dirty scoundrel! He has mulcted *me* to the amount of some 50 or 60 dollars, & I have not even been enabled to get back all my *MSS*.

You ask me to recover Your story from this wretch, if possible. I've *already* written him on the subject, claiming authority from you to do so, & demanding that your "copy" be sent to me, (with the remainder of my *own*), by Express. As for the *Magazine*, only a *single number* (the January no) appeared, and that I mail you along with the present letter. *Apropos* of—Mr Wylly, Phillips, the former Proprietor of "Scott's Monthly," says, that his failure was wholly unnecessary, & proceeded from the man's laziness, imbecility, & conceit! "He tried to play the *gentleman* Editor," writes Phillips, "shirked all needful work, plunged into *debt*, wherever he

could, and finally borrowed, and ran off with, my beloved
German flute, an instrument worth some *hundreds* of *dollars!*
"I suppose," P——— adds, with philosophy, "that he took a
special fancy to the *flute,* and wanted to *keep* it as a *memento*
of the pleasant days he had spent in Atlanta!"

The fellow's place of retreat from his *creditors,* &c, is at
present, *Brunswick* Geo.

Thanks for your courtesy in reference to the package I had
enclosed for M*rs* Chapin. M. Michel writes me, that she is
on the point of publishing a book, & that the Publishers promise her *"liberal* remuneration!" A "vigorous woman!.," as you
observe, but do you know, I was much more favorably impressed by the manners of her husband? He appeared a
genuinely kind, natural, considerate, and courteous *gentleman,*
whereas about M*rs* C———, there was a certain overstrained
aplomb, a desire, too evident, to "show off", as the children say!
An absence of that cold,

      "repose which stamps the cast of Vere de Vere,"

is *not* certainly to be regretted in any woman; yet there's a
"golden mean" in these matters, which I d'ont think this lady
has attained! A slight touch of the *parvenu* is apparent in her
tone & bearing. So at least, it seemed to me. I may be *wrong.*

My boy is now quite well—almost. But the old lady, my
mother is in a sad way. Her strength has deserted her. A
dreadful cough racks her slight frame, day & night. Still, I
trust in the renovating effect of the genial Spring weather.

Have you heard aught of Bruns (John) lately?— He is
doubtless profoundly in love, and unwilling to break the charm
of his present Elysium by the *bother* of letter writing!

Dick Michel gets on swimmingly in Al*a.* He is a born *Electioneerer,* & *Caterer.* So, 'tis not to be wondered at, that thro
his strenuous exertions, he succeeded in assembling at Montgomery on the 17*th* inst, the *largest* body of Medical men that
have met anywhere in the South since the war, (excepting
indeed the *National* meeting of these "Leeches" at N. Orleans
in May '69),.

As Pres: of the Ala State Med: Society, Dick seems to have
really distinguished himself.! He sends me a *Bill* of *Fare,*

printed on Satin, whereupon, the various dishes that charmed the *souls*, & filled the *bellies* of his brother *Medicoes*, are duly mentioned! Such an *appetizing menu* coming under the eyes of a poor back-woodsman, stirred within me certain feelings of envy, and discontent! What the devil have I to do with Canvass-back ducks, wild turkeys, snipe on *toast*,—*patés* of every description & style of "serving up," *Mushroom, Sheeps' head*, & Heaven knows what beside? It was a sheer *cruelty*— the obtrusion of these delicacies upon one starving in "Lapper-Land."

But I must close. My literary duties are quite heavy at present. In addition to an elaborate article (for the "So Review"), on Gen*l* Hayne, which I am to have ready by the 1*st* of May,—I am preparing a vo*l* for Hurd & Houghton, (a *simplified Froissart* for Children), which the Publishers must get the *MSS* of in *June*.

Let me hear from you, when your *health* permits.

With best remembrances from my household, I am,

Always Faithfully,

Paul H Hayne.

P. O. Box, 635, Augusta Geo

P. S. That fellow, *J. Wood Davidson*, is *at last* receiving his *dues!!* Everywhere—North & South, his book has been rec*d* with *hoots* of derision! In the April *"So Review,"* Bledsoe gives him the *very devil;* and promises to repeat the dose in *July*. This sort of thing does me good, for *D*——— is a *malignant*. One can pardon anything but deliberate malignity.

[Mrs. Sallie F. Chapin of South Carolina wrote *Fitz-Hugh St. Clair, the South Carolina Rebel Boy; or, It Is No Crime To Be Born a Gentleman* (Philadelphia: Claxton, 1872).

Hayne's "Lapper-Land" is related, I suppose, to the expression "Sand-lapper," which was sometimes applied to poor whites, or clay-eaters, but which South Carolinians now apply to any native of their state.

Hayne's article "Robert Young Hayne" appeared in the *Southern Review* for October, 1870 (VIII, 275–317).

In *Burke's Magazine for Boys and Girls* for March, 1871 (p. 125), there began a series of prose sketches by Hayne entitled "Pictures from Froissart." A footnote explained that the series had begun in *Riverside*

Magazine for Young People before it was discontinued, and that in *Burke's* the series would begin from the first. sketch, repeating what had already appeared in the *Riverside*. The latter had been published by Hurd & Houghton. The series did not appear in book form.]

No. 123

PAUL HAMILTON HAYNE to WILLIAM GILMORE SIMMS

"Copse Hill," April 30*th* 1870.

Dear Friend;

I answered your *last letter* at some length, but have heard nothing of late, which makes me somewhat uneasy, since your health, I know, is very precarious now. And for *myself*, I've had a hard, weary, and anxious time, on account of my mother's continued *illness*, which not many weeks ago, promised almost hourly, to terminate in a *fatal* manner. And even at present, despite a certain improvement, we are kept day & night on the *qui vive*, in a style pre-eminently calculated to excite & harrass the nerves.

God Allmighty [*sic*] save *me* from a protracted illness, when Fate has decreed that my time in this queer world is "up"!

I recd *10* or *12* days ago a very *courteous* note from your friend Mr*s* Chapin, who speaks of a Poem I had sent her, (*"Daphles"*) in warm terms of approval.

She refers to you, & your visits to her house in a way which plainly shows that they all deem your presence there both an *honor & a pleasure*. I am *sincerely* glad to think that you have such kindly & unselfish friends so near you!! Do you know that throughout life one circumstance has peculiarly struck me; the fact, namely, that one is much more apt to receive *real, substantial* favors, and courtesies, and appreciation from (comparative) strangers, or at least those who belong neither to one's *own blood*, or *household*, than from persons nearly connected with us? Never was there a *profounder* truth than *that* Embodied in the saying, "a prophet is not without *honor* &c &c"; and whether one be a *"prophet"* or not, the same truth holds good!! x x x You recd—let me trust—the *Magazine*,

("*The Cosmopolitan*"), which I mailed to you with my last communication?— 'Twas slightly mutilated, but I had no *other* copy. That fellow, *W H Wylly*—has finally disappeared to parts unknown. He retains, for some purpose of his own, my best & most *available manuscripts*. A shabbier scoundrel never existed.

Years since, you urged me to compose & publish a Biography of my Uncle Genl Robert Y. Hayne. I had collected a large mass of *material* for this purpose, which unluckily was *destroyed* at Columbia, (with other invaluable matter), when Sherman & his freebooters harried So Ca. . Nevertheless, I succeeded in procuring such *facts*, &c, as enabled me to write, (*not* a voluminous biography,) but an elaborate review article, the "copy" whereof has just been despatched to *Baltimore*, with the hope that the article may appear in the July issue of Bledsoe's "*Quarterly*". x x x x Unexpectedly, & to my great relief & joy, I heard last week from a mutual lady friend of ours, *Mrs Fanny Downing*, who asks after *you especially*. She has been desperately *ill*, but is now *recovered*. Her present residence is in No Ca, & her address reads, Shufordsville, Henderson Co (N. C). What I have heard convinces me that she has separated *finally* from her husband, (who must be a worthless fellow), and intends to remain with her *bachelor Brother*, an ex-Confederate Naval Officer, & a man of some *means*. Mrs D——— is a most *intelligent* woman, an enthusiastic friend, and possessed of energies & a will which we seldom encounter now-a-days among her sex; assuredly *never* among the "grecian-benders," and the enormous "chignon"-wearers!

By the way, I've just recd a copy of the Translation of the "Iliad" by your ancient associate, *Wm W* [*sic*] *Cullen Bryant*. Typographically, the vol is magnificent. In reference to the translation,—after spending a whole night over the 1*st* book, it seems to me very literal, marvellously correct, but somewhat lacking fire, and poetic *nerve* [*verve?*]. The blank-verse also, here and there, is *exceedingly blank*, tho I'm bound to acknowledge that *occasionally* one meets with noble passages. Scholars everywhere *approve* of it.

But doubtless, the book has reached *you*, and my criticism is superfluous.

If you ever go out, & *happen to see John Russell, w'ont you oblige me* by telling him that my *mother's illness* has prevented my writing him on *business;*—that soon he will hear from me. (I've a *special* reason for asking *this!*).

Write soon, *old friend*, if you *can*. A *single line* as to your present condition of health will greatly relieve,

Yours Always *affectionately*,

Paul H Hayne—

[Mrs. Fanny Murdaugh Downing (1835–1894), native of Virginia, wrote novels and poetry. In 1851 she married Charles W. Downing, then secretary of state of Florida.

Bryant's translation of the *Iliad* was published in Boston by Fields, Osgood & Co., 1870.

John Russell was the Charleston bookseller who had assisted Hayne in editing and managing *Russell's Magazine* (1857–60). In 1873 Hayne talked with Russell at his bookstore for the last time. Russell died a few months later.

Simms died on June 11, 1870.]

No. 124

PAUL HAMILTON HAYNE to [THE EDITORS OF
WIDE AWAKE]

Address me P O Box 275,
Augusta Geo
Oct 17th 1877.

Gentlemen;—

I have asked my friend, Dr Wm Hayes Ward of *"the NY Independent,"* (with which, they tell me, your magz clubs), to forward the enclosed versified story to your address.

I offer it as a contribution to *"Wide Awake"*. Should you *accept* the poem, we can *easily come to pecuniary terms*.

If 'tis *refused, please return* me the *"MS"* at once, since I can *readily* dispose of it to advantage elsewhere.

En passant, let me remark, that if you feel disposed to send me a copy of your periodical for the next *6 months* &c &c,—I will (as *"Literary Editor"* of several *prominent* So journals), frequently notice it, & thus contribute towards the increase of your circulation in the Southern country.

—Hoping to hear from you at your *convenience*, I am

Most Respectfully

Col Paul. H. Hayne.
Augusta Georgia
P O Box 275.

Should you have *to return* my *poem*, I will, (*of course*), transmit, *afterwards*, the *am't of Postage*—, whatever that may be.

[William Hayes Ward (1835–1916), native of Massachusetts, archaeologist and classical scholar, had an editorial connection with the *Independent*, New York weekly, from 1868 until his death. He was superintending editor at the time of this letter.

Wide Awake: An Illustrated Magazine for Boys and Girls (1875–93), Boston monthly, was published by D. Lothrop & Co. and edited by Ella Farman (who became Mrs. Charles Stuart Pratt).]

No. 125

PAUL HAMILTON HAYNE to EDMUND CLARENCE
STEDMAN

[From a copy in what looks like the handwriting of
William Hamilton Hayne.]

Copse Hill, G*a* R Road
Jan. 8, 1875.

My dear Sir:

I have long *long* desired to write you, to make your epistolary acquaintance, even if Fate wills it that I should never make your *personal* acquaintance[.]

And yet how narrowly I missed the *latter* pleasure! When the news came that you had passed thro Augusta, on your way from *Florida,* I am afraid that my imprecations upon the damnable luck which prevented our meeting, were neither few nor carefully chosen. However, "none of us are stronger than destiny."

The *immediate* occasion of my writing is this: I have just finished a very *particular study* of your papers upon the *Poets* of the Victorian epoch, &c. *Browning,* Tennyson &c.

The *rare* instruction, the *keen* delight your pages have afforded me, I *dare* not, just now, put into detailed expression; because you would think me extravagant, & a flatterer.

But *one* thing I *must* say.

These critiques are *unrivalled* in philosophic insight, and a genuine appreciation of every light & shade of the higher imagination. Only a *Poet* could have written them, endowed with *that* faculty some poets lack, I mean, the acutest analytical perception.

Such critiques *must* live. They must take their place in the permanent literature of the language. Many of your poems too, have greatly charmed me. *Chief* among them I place as no doubt as [*sic*] you do yourself, the narrative poem of *"The Blameless Prince.*["]

I *never* read certain portions of that sad and truly dramatic story without a moisture of the eyes, and a "sweet pain" at heart.

I wish to Heaven you would compose other narrative poems like it. Your genius is *so pronounced* in that department of *Art.*

And then *how* I have relished some of your translations from the Greek!

Excepting Leigh Hunt (and *your* translations are far *closer* than his, I know of no scholar who seems so thoroughly to have entered into the *spirit,* the essential mind & being of *Theocritus!*

My admiration, *Dear Sir,* is a free-will offering; as sincere as *Sincerity itself.* Why should not artists occasionally communicate with each other[,] exchange views, encourage and uphold each other? For *myself,* I occupy but a humble position; yet I *can* appreciate *others,* (thank God!) with my whole heart and soul.

Have you any new work in contemplation? If so, please inform me. I should be proud to do all I can (as the Lit. correspondent of several So. journals) to advance your literary interests in this section of the Land.

Our people are almost dead to *Art*, I fear; still something might be accomplished. Believe me

most Faithfully yours,

Paul H. Hayne

(P. O. Box 635,
    Augusta, Ga.)

[The body of this letter was published (possibly from the original) in *The Life and Letters of Edmund Clarence Stedman*, by Laura Stedman and George M. Gould (New York: Moffat, Yard and Company, 1910), I, 505–6.

Edmund Clarence Stedman (1833–1908), native of Connecticut, spent most of his life in New York as journalist, poet, critic, editor, and Wall Street broker. His best work was as a critic of poetry.

Stedman visited Florida in 1874. On his way north he called upon James R. Randall in Augusta.

Stedman's *Victorian Poets* was published in Boston by James R. Osgood and Company in 1875. The various critiques in the volume had been appearing for several years in the magazines, mainly *Scribner's Monthly*, where Hayne first read them.

Stedman's *The Blameless Prince, and Other Poems* was published in Boston by Fields, Osgood, & Co. in 1869. It contains "Translations from Theocritus," pp. 181–92.]

No. 126

PAUL HAMILTON HAYNE to EDMUND CLARENCE STEDMAN

[From a typed copy.]

"Copse Hill" *Ga.* R Road .˙.
June *7th* 1875

My dear Mr. Stedman,

I just learned the *other* day of your *return* from your So. American voyage; and it gave me *heartfelt pleasure & satisfaction* to be informed that your health was so *much improved!*

Now, allow me to acknowledge your letter,—the letter, I mean, which you sent me, previous to your departure from N. Y. some months ago. It was a generous, and *noble* communication, and it touched my *very heart*.

And here, let me congratulate you upon the re-publication of your articles on *"The Poets of the "Victorian epoch"*, in England. Conway will edit the book, I am told; and it thus goes before the public of G. Britain, under fair auspices.

If that work *does not* bring you a *peculiar, & permanent fame*, I (for one) am vastly mistaken.

By the way, I have asked my *Publishers—E J Hale & Son of N York*—to send you a copy of a new vol. of my own, (Poems), which I do trust, may in some respects, please you.

If, dear friend, (may I thus call you?) if you can *conscientiously* help on this vol, *I am sure* you will. My position—as a literary man, is *very peculiar, & unfortunate*, or I would never, *never* venture upon *such* a *hint*.

Being sick, I can write no more, but do write me a line, & Believe you have no *warmer sincere admirer, & better friend*,

Than Yr's Always

Paul H. Hayne

P. O. Box 635

Augusta Ga

[On February 27, 1875, Stedman and his wife sailed from New York for the West Indies and on April 24, 1875, set sail for the return voyage. So far as I know, he did not visit South America on the trip, though he visited Panama on business in December of the same year.

An English edition of *Victorian Poets* was published in London in 1875 by Chatto & Windus.

Hayne's *The Mountain of the Lovers* was published in New York by E. J. Hale & Son in 1875]

No. 127

PAUL HAMILTON HAYNE to EDMUND CLARENCE STEDMAN

[From a typed copy.]

Augusta, June 18th 1875

My Dear Mr. Stedman,

Since my last letter (of 2 days ago,) I have recd. a really charming communication from a woman of genius,. whom *you know personally;* & whose unstudied & sincere expressions, touching your *"Victorian Poets"* I can't deny myself the delight of quoting:—

Hear her:

"You speak," she observes, "of *Stedman's critiques.* "Indeed they *are superb! I have seen nothing approaching them anywhere, in any language, in all my life. I cannot express what impression they made upon me. How delicate, how Strong!"* Then follow certain *reminiscences* of a dinner party at your house in N York, last autumn; which I would quote, likewise, only I wish to spare your *modesty.*

Now, guess *who* this lady is! No common, (*so-called*) "brilliant" writer, I assure you; but one with *genuine gifts, poetical,* and *constructive.*

And believe me, *her* opinion of your forthcoming book, is, with *little* if *any* qualification, the opinion of *all* thinking, & unprejudiced persons. So, *my dear Sir,* do *not "falter in the furrow,"* but learn to know your *own* great powers, & *continue* to exercise them *aright. To do this,* however, be *chary of your health. Rest from literary toil,*—if necessary, *for years!! Per Hercle!* if you do not compose another line in this life, you have done eno', for *"The Victorian Poets"* are destined to become "classics", and the best of your poems *must endure.* I write *deliberately,* with the *head,* no less than the *heart!*

With some hesitation, under the fear that I may seem obtrusive, I venture to ask *what (physically)* is the matter? *Liver,* or *Lungs?* If the latter, you *ought,* by all means, to come South *next winter!*

And in passing Florida-ward, why should you not pass *thro Augusta,* and give me *the chance* of *meeting* you, & *bringing you up here* to *"Copse Hill"* (not *"corps hill"* as a *Correspond-ent* once spelt it!) How *honestly glad we would all* be to see you!! I'd carry you, for a ride, among the pine-berries [bar-rens?], and, (should a young *pointer* of the *"bluest blood,"* the real *sangre azzura* I'm now training), be in condition, *what* partridge hunts we would enjoy! As for *smoking,* bless your soul! we could smoke *all day* & *all night;* meerchaum, or cigar, or cigarette; for I confess myself a *human chimney.*

Of Champagne, & Madeira & Port, & Claret, I am, alack! destitute; but *old Rye,* or unadulterated *Bourbon,* or genuine *"Mountain Dew",* *each* & all, will be within *easy reach.* The ugliest country in the world (except the Saharan desert), is the Country surrounding my cottage; but secluded beauties can be found, "bits" of woodland scenery, nooks, rocky, se-cluded dells, a few rivulets brawling over the hill sides, and some curious stone formations, which resemble rude fortifica-tions erected by the aboriginal inhabitants.

At all events, I can make you comfortable *within* doors, if not enthusiastic *without!*

x x x x My poor little book is getting on *slowly, slowly.* What can one expect *at the South,* when even one's friendly acquaintances of the same (literary) "guild" deliberately *ignore* one?

Here is Randall, a good fellow as I've always deemed him, whose *genius, in public & private,* I *never* missed the chance of honoring, who receives my poems, and (practically) hurls them aside, probably into the coal-scuttle, or waste paper basket!

This, of course, I mention *confidentially;* Upon no earthly consideration would I complain!)

Please give my *best love* to *Stoddard,* when you see him, & to *B. Taylor,*— Write *only* when you can without undue *fatigue.*

& Believe me, *Always Faithfully*

Paul H. Hayne
(P. O. Box 635)
Augusta
Ga

[Hayne was quoting from a letter to him from Constance Fenimore
Woolson, written from Charleston, South Carolina (where she was visiting), and dated June 15, 1875. Much of it is quoted in "Some New
Letters of Constance Fenimore Woolson," edited by Jay B. Hubbell, in the
New England Quarterly, XIV (No. 4, 1941), 719–20. Hayne does not
quote quite accurately but does not materially change the sense of the
original.

See letter No. 178 for a more attractive and more accurate picture of the
country surrounding Copse Hill.

James Ryder Randall (1839–1908), author of "Maryland, My Maryland," was editing a newspaper in Augusta. He was generous in his
references to Hayne just before and after Hayne's death, but it seems
that he was one of the last to recognize Hayne's worth. See Hayne's
letters to Richard Henry Stoddard (1825–1903) at the beginning of this
collection and letter No. 210. Hayne also corresponded with Bayard
Taylor (1825–1878). Selections from Taylor's letters to Hayne may be
found in vol. 2 of *Life and Letters of Bayard Taylor*, by Marie Hansen
Taylor and Horace E. Scudder (Boston: Houghton, Mifflin and Company,
1884). See the index.]

No. 128

PAUL HAMILTON HAYNE to EDMUND CLARENCE
STEDMAN

Augusta Geo
Feb 28th 1876.

My Dear Mr Stedman;

Occasionally I have seen your name mentioned among those
who attended certain evening Receptions in NY City; and
therefore, my hope is strong that you have recovered your
health;—or at all events, that you are *measurably* better than
you were some months ago.

Supposing that it would interest you to see all notices of
"*The Victorian Poets*" which bore marks of cleverness, or culture in their preparation,— I venture to enclose a rather
elaborate review taken from "the *Balt Gazette*," & written,
(I conjecture), by *Mr Edward Spencer of Randallstown, (Md)*,
a person of scholarly attainments, and marked natural ability.

Personally I *disagree* with the Critic on various points; but
his remarks are perhaps not unworthy of perusal.

It is impossible for me to express adequately my disgust at the Supercilious, patronizing, *minutely carping* article on your great work, which appeared in a recent no of the *"NY Nation"*.

Godkin, (or whatever the writer's name), ought to "go to *Jericho*, and *abide therein*, until his (intellectual) *beard* be grown!".

The *devil take* Godkin's *impudence!*—

I have been *very very* ill myself; and can hardly do any work at present; unless indeed, with great effort.

Always Faithfully
Y'r friend.

Paul Hayne

Lock Box 275,
Augusta (Geo)

[Edward Spencer (1834–1883) was a critic and versatile writer of Maryland.

Edwin Lawrence Godkin (1831–1902) edited the *Nation*, New York weekly, from 1865 until 1881. Stedman's *Victorian Poets* is reviewed in the *Nation* for February 17, 1876 (XXII, 117–8). The review contains a good deal of praise but finds fault with Stedman's qualifications as a philosophic critic, with his broad generalizations, and with his lack of clearness in various passages. The criticism seemed rather harsh at that time but agrees pretty well with what critics say of Stedman today.]

No. 129

PAUL HAMILTON HAYNE to EDMUND CLARENCE
STEDMAN

Copse Hill, Ga.,
May 15*th* 1877

P. O. Address:
  P. O. Box 275,
    Augusta, Ga.

My Dear Mr Stedman;

I write to ask if you can aid me by advice & influence in procuring a place for my only son as *Librarian*, or in some newspaper office.

He is now just 21, an intelligent youth, but without any taste for the Professions.

However, he is passionately fond of *books*, and from *childhood*, has always taken *great delight* in making Catalogues, and keeping me posted as to the various Publishing Houses, and their issues.

At *first*, he thought of entering Some Publishing Firm, if possible; and I applied to *Harper*, who said he had no vacancy, but would put his name on file!

M*r* Bunce of "Appleton's" I then applied to, for advice, and also M*r* Alden of *"Harper's Monthly"*[.]

M*r* B— dissuaded me, on the ground that the Publisher's *Employeés* were "mere [?] machines, with little chance of rising,"—and that *no* one should attempt the Publishing business, (which fact I knew well enow), without an adequate *Capital*, and we, alas! *since* the *war*, have been *poor*!

M*r* Alden *Endorsed* his views, advising me to apply to *yourself*, & M*r* *Bayard Taylor*, for the exercise of an influence which he himself does not possess, as "he leads the life of a *hermit!*"

My son, (Willie) would *prefer* being in N. York.

I would have applied for some position for my son before, but his *health* was very precarious.

Now,—owing to an out-door "*Country* life," he is *much stronger*; & *he* believes that a Northern climate would quite build him up!

I would feel *inexpressibly* grateful for *any* aid you can give me in this matter. You know there are no Publishing firms, *South*, and no newspapers which would furnish a Support.

I shall send a duplicate of this letter to M*r* Taylor; and I'm *sure* you will answer me *as soon as convenient*. Have I taken too *great* a liberty.? Let me trust *not*[.]

Ever Truly

Paul H Hayne.

[William Hamilton Hayne (1856–1929) became a poet and critic and spent most of his life at Copse Hill and in Augusta.

Fletcher Harper (1806–1877) was head of the Harper firm. He died May 29.

Oliver Bell Bunce (1828–1890) was one of the two chief editors of *Appleton's Journal* from 1872 until its end in 1881 (he had been an assistant editor before 1872).

Henry Mills Alden (1836–1919) was editor of *Harper's* for a half century beginning in 1869.]

No. 130

PAUL HAMILTON HAYNE to EDMUND CLARENCE STEDMAN

[From a typed copy.]

Address P. O. Box 275 Augusta Ga

"Copse Hill", Ga. R. R.

December 6th, 1877.

My dear Mr. Stedman;—

I am shocked in glancing over my note-book, to perceive how many weeks have elapsed since, I recd. (from your own hand by mail,), "Hawthorne and Other Pieces." Please excuse my apparent neglect.

I have been tremendously overworked, for one thing; and much troubled *(entre nous)*, by pecuniary anxieties for *another* thing; the poverty of the South, or at least this section thereof,—despite all reports to the contrary—, being fearful.

Yet, be sure that I have made the time, not only to read, but to study your little vol. from title page to "finis."

It proved a very agreeable study, I need hardly say.

Your *"Hawthorne"* Ode is worthy of its subject; in saying which, have I not said all?

Still, I can't help going a little into detail; and remarking upon the marvellous subtlety of insight displayed; the same analytical keenness imaginatively and rhythmically rendered, which must secure for your prose Criticism (in *"the Victorian Poets"*), a permanent value, and acceptance. Some lines of your "Ode" in sooth, are pregnant with suggestive sweetness, or power; e. g.:

"An eremite whose life the desert knew,
Who gained companionship in dreams alone!" etc.

— . . "One who in his heart's wilderness deep
Shrunk darkling etc."

"But sleepless even in sleep, must gather toll,
Of dreams, which pass like barks upon the river etc."

. . . . . . "one that can predict
"The whole flight from the flutter of the wing!"
(superb!!)

. . . "The beautiful from his eyes
"Looked outward with a steadfast purple gleam!"

"Deaf Chance and blind, that like the mountain-slide,
Puts out youth's heart of fire, and all is dark!"

"He saw the strong divinity of will
Bringing to halt the stolid tramp of Fate!" (fine!!)

"The Robin's voice; the humble bee's wise drone."—

"Sees beyond the shade,
"The Naiad Nymph of every rippling rill,
And hears quick Fancy wind her wilful horn etc."

. . . .

"Sister Beatrice" among the narrative pieces, is very pathetic; tho frankly, it does not seem to me, as a whole, quite so deftly and carefully versified as your "Blameless Prince," for instance.

But the sad story is feelingly told.

Of course "News from Olympia" charmed me; and "The Skull in the Gold Drift" struck me forcibly from its first appearance in "The Atlantic" years ago. "The Lord's Day Gale" is a noble ballad; and I like your "Songs" and "Madrigals" for their absolute simplicity; but I must cease this bald "cataloguing" which expresses next to nothing!

You are, in fine, a true Poet, no less than a profound Critic. The Fairies dealt liberally with you at your birth; and 'tis evident that their generous endowments have been most conscientiously cultivated, strengthened, and improved.

May still further success attend you!!

x x x By the way, I have myself just completed a lyric poem of about 250 lines, written for a certain "Memorial Association" in Charleston S. C. which desires to erect a monument to Wm. Gilmore Simms, the So. novelist, etc.

I presume that you knew nothing of Simms? He was not so much a "romancer," and poet, as a really powerful essayist, and controversial author; a man however all of whose faculties (marvellous by nature), were allowed unluckily to remain "in the rough"; he lacked aesthetic culture to a lamentable extent; and left the world finally with more than half his intellectual force wasted, or untried.

Yet, he did noble service in his special sphere; and deserves to be *honored and remembered!*

You are acquainted with Edgar Fawcett?

Do you know that he appears to my judgment, *the coming* Poet of the No. younger generation; if indeed, he may not be said to have "come" already; [.]

I look forward to his forthcoming vol. of verses with great eagerness.

How, My Dear Mr. Stedman, is your health now? Drop me a line, when you are able; the sooner the better; and Believe me as Ever

Faithfully and Cordially,

Paul H. Hayne

P. O. Box 275,

Augusta, Ga.

P. S. Look into "Scribner's" for Jan. (when it appears) and tell me whether the Poem called "Unveiled", which you will see therein, pleases you?

[A little more than half of this letter is quoted (possibly from the original) in *Life and Letters of Edmund Clarence Stedman*, by Laura Stedman and George M. Gould (New York: Moffat, Yard and Company, 1910), II, 291–3.

Stedman's *Hawthorne and Other Poems* was published in Boston by James R. Osgood and Company in 1877. "Hawthorne" is found on pp. 11–25. The lines quoted occur on pp. 15, 16, 18, 22, 24, and 21. They are not quoted with entire accuracy. Other poems in the volume which Hayne mentions are "Sister Beatrice," pp. 31–45; "News from Olympia," pp. 50–54; "The Skull in the Gold Drift," pp. 80–85; "The Lord's-Day Gale," pp. 97–108; "Song from a Drama," pp. 86–7; and "Madrigal," pp. 90–2. "The Skull in the Gold Drift" had appeared in the *Atlantic Monthly* for February, 1875 (XXXV, 200).

For Hayne's poem entitled "W. Gilmore Simms" see *Complete Edition*, pp. 315–20. The headnote reads: "Delivered on the night of the 13th of December, 1877, 'at the Charlestown Academy of Music,' as prologue to the 'Dramatic Entertainment' in aid of the 'Simms Memorial Fund.' "

Edgar Fawcett (1847–1904), of New York, poured out such a flood of novels, plays, and poems that R. H. Stoddard called for someone to turn off the "Fawcett." His forthcoming volume was probably *Fantasy and Passion* (1878).

Hayne's "Unveiled," dedicated to Bryant, appeared in *Scribner's Monthly* for January, 1878 (XV, 383–6).]

No. 131

PAUL HAMILTON HAYNE to EDMUND CLARENCE STEDMAN

"Copse Hill," Georgia Rail Road,
February 10*th* 1878

Address:

P. O. Box 275,

Augusta, Ga.

Your letter, *My Dear Mr Stedman*, of the 31*st* ult, from the *"Coleman House"*, reached me a few days ago; and it is hardly needful to Say, afforded me the *sincerest pride & satisfaction.* Honestly, without the shadow, even, of anything resembling an *arrière pensée*, I have previously told you in what *exalted* estimation I hold your Critical powers;—especially when brought to the elucidation of *Poetry*—, & therefore, it is but natural that your praise of *"Unveiled,"* and the *"Simms Monody"*, Should be esteemed by me a bright & lofty feather in my literary cap!

Far above this commendation; however, invaluable & precious as it is, do I prize the *genial & generous Spirit* of your letter. O! if all literary men were only like *you*, in breadth of views, and Catholicity of temperament! If they would only cultivate *your* noble *esprit de corps,* which urges one to recognize a brother or sister in *Art,* everywhere, & at all seasons!

But such appreciative cordiality can never, I fear, become universal, until the dawn of some Aesthetic Millenium, far removed from us in the realm of an ideal, indefinite Future! On that *very* account, its manifestations, here & there, the occasional ring of the true heart metal, preluding a worthier, & more harmonious Time, must possess for us an exceptional & lovely significance.

At all events, it is *thus* with *me!*

. . . . I am *deeply* pained to learn of your pecuniary misfortune; rendered doubly disgusting by the *manner* in which it was produced.

What a hypocritical scamp & humbug, *that* fellow Bonner must be! For *such* rogues (were I a lawgiver, or law-*inflictor*), I would have but little mercy & consideration! They are a *million* times worse than the vast majority of Burglars, & professional Thieves, many of whom have been absolutely driven to crime, by *want!*

It seems, indeed, a cruel blow—this destruction suddenly, & unexpectedly—, of all the hard-earned proceeds of years of toil; above all, this ruin of your project of English travel, the results of which *might,* probably *would* have been, so intellectually opulent. But often I have found, under my own misfortunes, a certain species of consolation in reflecting upon the trials of people even *more* unlucky than myself. Thus, let me suggest, *my kind, and genial friend;* that bad as they unquestionably are, *your* pecuniary position or fortunes may be, sooner or later, *retrieved.*

Now, to *some* of us—and I count myself among the number—, *Fate* (the abominable jade!) has so arranged matters, that any *real retrieval* of position, is—to all *human* seeming, impossible.

Once, I too, had my bright hopes of foreign travel; of mingling with the good & great of other lands, & beholding all that is venerable, beautiful, romantic in the old world! These hopes have not been merely "scotched" but "killed," *murdered,* I feel certain, outright, & forever! Their destruction

has left my heart sore, sad, & full of bitter, melancholy yearn-
ings. Yet I fight manfully against such feelings, as I rejoice
to perceive, that *you* are fighting against your disappointment.

Let me venture upon a prediction! Long after *my* head shall
be laid low,—*you* will be travelling in the "far, fair foreign
lands," your fortune recovered, and your Spirits buoyant, and
happy. "Take heart of grace!" My presentiments seldom
deceive me!

By the way, you think that I "have too much time, & too
little friction with the outer world; while you are tormented
to a shadow by the cares of city life!" . . . Well! I doubt
whether I *do* after all, "have too much time["]; for every
moment seems occupied; and often the days are too short for
the days' duties & employments. . . . Touching the *"friction
of the outer world,"* there are moments, perhaps, when I
would like to mingle more freely with my fellow men, or
rather fellow *artists;* yet, the desire is but fleeting, since (omitting exceptional cases), I have, in the Past,—when I saw eno'
of *such* society—, observed how narrow, egotistical, & selfish
even literary workmen can be!.

Upon the whole, Solitude "next the vast heart of Nature",
suits one of my temperament far better than any Society!
And I say this, despite the assertion of both M. Arnold, &
Robert Browning who agree, as some Critic has remarked, in
regarding the need of re-actionary escape from Solitude to
Society, as among the subtlest, surest proofs of genuine poetic
power! Says Arnold, you remember,

> "Ah! *two* desires toss about
> The Poet's feverish blood—;
> *One* drives him to the world without,
> And *one* to Solitude!"—

And there is Browning's *"Parting at Dawn,"*—

> "Round the Cape of a sudden, came the sea,
> And the sun looked over the mountain's rim;
> And *straight was a path of gold for him;*
> And *the need of a world of men for me!"*

Less and less as life advances, do *I* feel this "need of a world
of men"; but *"straighter"* and *brighter* grows that "path of gold"

which leads thro the tranquil heart of Nature, approximating
her haunts by indefinite & lovely gradations, to the region of
Eternal Beauty, the *Dawn* that can never fade!

Yes! *Stedman!* in defiance of all the tremendous agencies of
materialism, more vigorously, & insidiously urged *now*, than
ever before. *I believe* in that immortal Country, having faith
eno',—(as L. Hunt wrote in his last epistle to *Keats*), "having
faith eno' in the high things that *Nature* herself, (apart from
all Revelations), puts into our heads, to think that *all* who
are of one accord in mind & heart, are journeying to *one &
the same place; &* shall unite *somehow, or other, again, face to
face, mutually conscious, mutually delighted!"*— . . . . To
turn to a different topic, let me thank you for your hint about
song-writing.

I *must* try my hand at a *nocturne,* love lyric or something
of that kind; and should success crown my effort, may I not
send you the *"Mss"* to present to some Composer? (or rather
a copy of the piece after its publication, in some periodical,
according to the latter part of your suggestion?

. . You refer to a *"lunch",* recently, with *Aldrich,* &
Fawcett. *Aldrich* I've met, personally, once or twice in Boston; but in a very brief, casual way; occasionally we correspond; and of course, I greatly admire his delicate & beautiful
genius; & his conscientious *art-study.*

Some of his minor lyrics strike me as *perfect* . . . *Fawcett*
is the *most regular* of all my Northern Correspondents. For
4 or 5 years, we have kept up a constant epistolary connection;
and I have learned *not* merely to *admire* the *Poet,* but heartily
to *love* the *man.* I feel convinced that a kinder hearted gentleman never existed. And as for his *poetical genius;*—I *may*
possibly be mistaken, but—*me judice*—, it is *equally vigorous,
and versatile.* Some of his pieces affect me *strangely.* One
called *"Fidelitas"* is *almost* divine in its mournful beauty. I
cannot read it without a touch of the *hysteria passio* wherewith
poor old Lear exclaims,

> *"Cordelia! Cordelia! Stay a little!"*

. . . . Very anxiously I await the issue of Fawcett's *"Fantasy
& Passion".*

. . . . How I wish that Circumstances *would* allow you to carry out your admirable idea of composing a *"book of Tropical verse."*!

A N Englander by *birth*, you nevertheless own a vast deal of genuine *Southern* blood, which manifests itself in the warmth & cordiality of your letters, no less than in the lyric glow of your poetry.

. . . I have been re-perusing, by the way, your *"Blameless Prince,"* & like it more & more, the more closely I examine it. . . 'Tis a marvellously *subtle* poem, and of certain passages, one can scarcely speak too highly.

Please write me whenever you conveniently can. I *prize your letters so* truly!

By correspondence *alone* am I enabled to keep *en rapport* with the esteemed members of my own "Guild".

Always Faithfully,

Paul. H. Hayne.

P S. You ask, "Are *there* no more Southern Poets except yourself?"

Have you never read Mrs Margaret J Preston's *"Old Song & New,"* (issued 6 years since by the *Lippincotts*), and her later vol. *"Cartoons,"* (pub: by *Roberts & Bros*), *now* in its *2nd* Edition?. To *my* mind, she ranks *very* high among the female Poets of this Country; & Longfellow & Whittier esteem her genius as highly as I do. Still, she cannot get a *single piece* accepted by *"Atlantic,"* & even finds some difficulty with the other magazines. (I only mention *this* to show how we Southerners are often treated by Northern Edt's) . . . As to *myself*, I may Say to you, (*in strict confidence*) for I *d'ont admire* the *rôle* of *whining Poet!*), that after having been *asked & encouraged* by *Howells* to write regularly for his monthly, after having, for a *certain period*, been admitted as an acknowledged regular Contributor to its pages,—suddenly, unaccountably, 2 years ago, he (Howells) began to *reject everything I sent him.*

One *piece*, according to him, had no *"raison d' être,"*— another his Lordship liked *parts* of, but not the whole; &

still, a *third* "was [Here Hayne ends the page and apparently
the rest of the sentence has been lost—at least it does not
appear on the microfilm.]

As to other *So Poets*, you know Randall, of course, whose
lyric force is *unquestionable;* and then, there is *Dr Frank
O Ticknor* of Columbus Geo, *(alack he's dead)* whom I shall
endeavor to introduce to the Northern Public soon, thro the
columns of *"The Independent,"*—a fiery, terse, imaginative
writer, whose Songs thrill one like the *"sound of a trumpet!"*

. . Then, Mrs *Annie Chambers Ketchum* is certainly possessed of a sweet, idyllic power; and of genuine fancy &
feeling. *Her* "Benny" has touched all hearts, and the poem
called, *"Dolores"* seems to me finely imaginative.

. . . . My wife begs me to say to you, with her kind
regards, that she *"especially* prizes *your criticism* of her husband's poems, thinking *so very highly of your "Victorian
Poets,"* the reading of which gave her deep delight,—"! (*I
should say so* since *absolutely,* I could'nt, for *4 nights,* induce
her to take her natural rest, after she had possessed herself
of that fascinating vol!*).

And now adieu: *P H. H.*

[Written across the top of the last page:]

You must pardon what I have *confidentially* said of
Howells; if he chances to be a friend of yours. Perhaps, I
may wrong him; but the circumstances are literally as detailed. *Put yourself in my place,* and say what you would
think of such treatment. 'Tis not wounded *amour propre,*
under which I suffer; but something far *sterner & deeper.*

[A portion of this letter was published by Laura Stedman and George
M. Gould, *op. cit.,* II, 320–1.

The Charleston *News and Courier* for January 1, 1878, contains an item
about the failure of John Bonner & Co., 32 Broad Street, New York.
Stedman wrote in his diary that he had lost $5,500 in "Bonner's great
failure and fraud." (Laura Stedman and George M. Gould, *op. cit.,*
I, 574.)

Hayne's prediction concerning Stedman's fortunes proved correct.
Stedman spent the summer of 1879 in England, Scotland, and France,
returning to New York in October. By November he had bought a home.

He went to Europe again in May, 1882, stopping in London for a few days and then going to Italy, but he was recalled to New York on business the day after he settled in Venice (early in June). He was still to experience many financial "ups and downs." He remained in Wall Street from 1864 until 1900. When he retired and paid all debts, he probably had between fifteen and twenty thousand dollars left.

The quotation from Arnold is from "Stanzas in Memory of the Author of 'Obermann' " (November, 1849), lines 93–6.

The title of Browning's poem is "Parting at Morning" (1845).

The passage quoted (inaccurately) from Leigh Hunt (1784–1859) is from Hunt's letter to Severn in Rome, written on March 8, 1821, containing a message to Keats, who he thought was still living. See Barnette Miller, *Leigh Hunt's Relations with Byron, Shelley and Keats* (Columbia University Press, 1910), pp. 47–8.

In the summer of 1873 Hayne visited Boston, at which time Thomas Bailey Aldrich (1836–1907) was living in Lowell's home at Cambridge (Lowell being in Europe) and editing *Every Saturday* in Boston. Hayne called upon Aldrich at Lowell's home and may have seen him in Boston also.

Edgar Fawcett's *Fantasy and Passion* was published in Boston by Roberts Brothers in 1878. "Fidelitas" may be found on pp. 57–8.

For a discussion of the poems inspired by Stedman's travels in the West Indies see Laura Stedman and George M. Gould, *op. cit.*, I, 532–55.

Mrs. Margaret Junkin Preston (1820–1897), of Lexington, Virginia, had written (as Hayne says) *Old Song and New* (Philadelphia: J. B. Lippincott & Co., 1870) and *Cartoons* (Boston: Roberts Brothers, 1875).

Lowell had accepted three of Hayne's poems during his editorship of the *Atlantic Monthly*. James T. Fields had rejected those submitted to him in the 1860's. William Dean Howells (1837–1920) was editor from 1871 until 1881. He had accepted the following:

"Aspects of the Pines," September, 1872 (XXX, 351)
"Forest Pictures," December, 1872 (XXX, 662)
"The Voice in the Pines," January, 1873 (XXXI, 53)
"The Wood Lake," April, 1873 (XXXI, 405–6)
"Golden Dell," October, 1873 (XXXII, 425–6)
"The Woodland," October, 1874 (XXXIV, 474)
"Visit of the Wrens," December, 1874 (XXXIV, 717–19)
"After the Tornado," March, 1875 (XXXV, 322)
"Sonnet," June, 1876 (XXXVII, 650)

No other verse by Hayne appeared in the *Atlantic* until 1884.

Francis Orray Ticknor (1822–1874), of Georgia, was a physician and poet. (His friends called him Frank, though his name was Francis.) Hayne wrote the introductory sketch for the edition of his poems published in 1879 by J. B. Lippincott & Co. of Philadelphia. A larger collection was edited by his granddaughter, Michelle Cutliff Ticknor, in 1911 (New York and Washington: The Neale Publishing Company).

Mrs. Annie Chambers Ketchum (1824–1904) was a minor poet of Tennessee and Kentucky. Her *Christmas Carillons* (New York: D. Appleton and Company, 1877) contains "Benny: A Southern Christmas Ballad," pp. 103–8, and "Dolores," pp. 9–15.

Stedman and Howells were good friends and Howells frequently urged Stedman to write for his magazine, though occasionally he took the liberty of making unauthorized changes of which Stedman did not approve.]

No. 132

PAUL HAMILTON HAYNE to EDMUND CLARENCE STEDMAN

[The Library of Columbia University has only a typed copy of the first page of this letter.]

(Pardon this informal use of the pencil. I am in bad physical trim, suffering from a species of neuralgia in the wrist, among other things; and so, I find a pencil easier than a pen.)

"Copse Hill" Geo. R. R.
Feb. 14th, 1878.

You recd., I presume, My Dear Mr. Stedman, my last long letter, in which I acknowledged your great kindness, and expressed the profound pleasure which your criticism of "Unveiled" gave me.

Now, as a curious illustration of the different light in which the same production is apt to strike Critics of ability, allow me to quote (in strict confidence), certain words addressed to me upon the subject of this Poem by our friend, B. Taylor.

(I say *in confidence*, because, if he knew that I had thus quoted them, perhaps [he])

[The remainder of the letter, beginning "might fancy that I was hurt," is from the microfilm of the original.]

might fancy that I was hurt, or offended by his strictures, which is *very, very* far from the truth)—

Here is what T—— writes.

"I have in view the general Public, in the following estimate of *"Unveiled"*.

"The poem may *not* be *vague* to me, or any other *Poet*,—but the truth is, that we do *not* write merely for one another, if we hope to be recognized by the world.

"Excuse me, if I say that I knew this phase of your poetic genius, thro my own experience. The Greek Tragedians, and Goethe, *led me out of it*. I learned to see the *absolute need* of distinct, *sculpturesque conceptions in poetry*—; to rise from Dim delightful moods into *positive, symmetrical* form. Take Wordsworths "*Intimations of Immortality*," & notice how distinct & palpable are his thoughts.

"Few minds can receive & retain poetry which does not possess *this distinctness*.

"Imagination is a faculty which cannot be cultivated by *indulging* it. But it becomes broader & grander thro the study of the very Element which might seem to hamper it—; *viz.* clear, positive, form in ideas, and proportion of *parts* to a *whole*.

. . . "Now, your "*Unveiled*" *ends* nearly as it begun; (so far as the average mind will discern),—when there *should* have been a sudden expansion, illumination, revelation, at the close! There is the *Substance* of a noble poem in it; but the Key-stone of an arch is lacking!"—

x x These be striking words, & 'tis needless to say, how truly I thank *Taylor* for his sincere criticism;—but what *does* puzzle me *(entre nous)*, is—as hinted before—, the utterly different impression which the Poem appears to have made upon *your* mind, & *his*. *Can* he be right in affirming that, it "ends very much as it begun"; and lacks "an *arch*," i e, a coherent principle, binding the separate parts together?—

Excuse *all* this egotism; but I am *thoroughly bewildered;* and do'nt perceive the clue by which to reconcile your verdict with T's—. . Indeed, they seem utterly irreconcileable. x x x x x x x x x x x But to quit this subject, let me tell you something just brought to my knowledge, which has annoyed & troubled me much. Of course, you know *Stoddard*, well. He is one of my oldest *Northern* acquaintances; and I owe him the most affectionate allegiance, because of many *personal* favors & kindnesses. Therefore, it pains me to be told that he has been making enemies, lately, on all sides, by the bitter tone of his reviews in the *"NY Express"*. (I *think* that's the title of the journal)—. What is the matter with *R. H. S?* *What* can he hope to gain by this sort of thing? . . . Sometimes, do you know, that I congratulate myself, upon the *Fate* which has placed me among the "Pine-Barrens,"—*far* from the hatreds, envy, and ceaseless literary bickerings of a great Metropolis.?

Why cannot men live *at peace* with one another? Life is really to[o] *short* for *squabbling!* x x x

Did I ever tell you, that I enjoy the great honor & pleasure of a correspondence with Swinburne.?.

I have found him affable, generous, & considerate, to an extraordinary degree;— But, doub[t]less, you know him even better than I do. In one of his letters to me, he alludes to your Criticism in *"The Victorian Poets,"* with exalted commendation, as indeed, he well *might.*

Your analysis of his poetry is *simply superb.*

Write to a poor Devil of an Exile, & Invalid, whenever you *(conveniently),* can; & believe me, *my Dear Mr Stedman,*

Your *obliged & affectionate Friend,*

Paul. H. Hayne.

P S I hope that my outburst against *Howells,* in the last letter, did not annoy you?— Perhaps, I was wrong in writing so bitterly;— but ah! the sense of injustice cuts *deep!* And when palpable *mockery* is added to injustice, what *can* one do, but, (in our *sandlapper"* patois), *"cuss like blazes,"* to relieve one's mind?—

[R. H. Stoddard was literary editor of the New York *Mail and Express* from 1880 until his death in 1903. No doubt he wrote reviews for the *Evening Express* before it united with the *Evening Mail* to form the *Mail and Express.*

Stedman and Swinburne had been corresponding for several years. Stedman visited Swinburne in England in the summer of 1879. See index to Laura Stedman and George M. Gould, *op. cit.* A limited edition of *Letters from Algernon Charles Swinburne to Edmund Clarence Stedman* was printed in London in 1912.]

No. 133

PAUL HAMILTON HAYNE to EDMUND CLARENCE STEDMAN

[From a typed copy.]

In Wall Street:

Copse Hill, Geo. R. Road
March 28, 1878

My Dear Stedman:

Have just received your Card!

Be *assured* that I *perfectly comprehend* your position, which for you own sake (since I have learned not only to admire and respect, but to feel *true friendship* for you), I *deeply regret;* this incessant activity both of *brain and body* being of absolutely suicidal consequences!

I would to God that you could abandon such habits of *over toil,* but should this prove impossible— and I fear you may find it so—, why then I regard you as a gallant soldier whose *duty* compels him to encounter certain risks, and can only exclaim, 'Heaven guard your course! and give you a safe deliverance!!'

I hardly *think* that in your noble modesty, you understand the great value I place upon your friendship, (I would fain believe, you see, that my own sentiment is returned?) and that I am really unconventional, and unselfish in this matter shall be proved by the resolution I have just formed, a resolution to write you *every now and then, with the distinct understanding that no answer whatever is expected on your part.*

The truth is, that I am vain enough to think that I can occasionally *entertain* you by such communications, raise your spirits, and send you certain *healthful whiffs* of fragrance from these remote regions of the South. *Do not forbid me!* I am heartily in *earnest!*

Just now, I must take care how I write at length. Beyond doubt, *the very sight* of a letter, before its contents have been mastered, must annoy and embarrass you.

So, let the enclosed flowers speak for me!

Always Faithfully yours,

Paul H. Hayne

No. 134

PAUL HAMILTON HAYNE to EDMUND CLARENCE STEDMAN

[From a typed copy.]

Copse Hill, Geo. R. Road
December 17th 1878.

My dear Mr. Stedman,—

I hope that you rec'd my *last letter*, which (if I mistake *not*), was in reply to a very courteous communication of yours, in which you told me why the Musician Bach, had not been able to provide a certain lyric with an appropriate air.

Now I desire to say how delighted I have been by a careful perusal of your Bryant "In Memoriam" which appeared in the *"Dec. Atlantic"!*

Excepting always the noble Hawthorne "Ode", this appears to me the subtlest, sweetest, most delicately imaginative of all your (comparatively) brief productions,—brief, I mean as compared with "The Blameless Prince", "Alice of Monmouth" etc.

Apropos, to this day, *I have never seen*, nor (thro some infernal fatality) have I been able to procure the last named work.

Please inform me of the *Publisher's name*, so that I may obtain it.

To return to your Bryant piece, what I particularly like, is the idea of the personified forces of Nature, the various Seasons etc welcoming the emancipated Poet's "return" to the Spirit-land, and the Shelley-like manner which pervades the entire performance, as it were an omnipresent, and most ethereal atmosphere!

Taylor & Stoddard, I understand, have written upon this same theme. Of course I long to see how they have treated it. . . About the former, a paragraph has just met my eye, (taken from The St. Louis "*Staatz Zeitung*["]), which has caused me great uneasiness. Said passage occurs in the letter of a "Dresden Correspondent" of this German "weekly["] and is positive to the effect, that B. Taylor's case is "*utterly hopeless*",—that he is "*dying of dropsy*"; indeed, probably that he is now *dead!!*" With difficulty I endeavor to realize such an announcement as this;— — I say, it is exaggerated, grossly magnified, a mere rumor, founded upon T's late well-known sickness (whereupon the news of his recovery was so positive, so circumstantial, that I wrote him a *fervent* note of congratulation), and yet, do, argue, reflect, as I may, somehow the "Dresden" letter writer troubles, and indeed fills my mind with gloomy presentiments! Heaven grant that they may prove as idle as the vagrant wind! Only to picture our friend, going abroad in the very zenith of his fame and usefullness, to perish from the face of the earth!!

I can't bear to credit it!

Yet how often is the "irony of Fate" exemplified thus!! . . . Have you seen Prof. M. Coit Tyler's new work upon "*American Literature*", i. e., the first 2 vols, just issued by the Putnams and quite complete in themselves. *Me judice*, they are delightful reading, besides possessing a rare philosophical value. . . . Such a work has long been a *desideratum*.

By the way, I may remark that Prof. Tyler (whom I am proud to call friend) will be in N. Y. about the 21st of the present month, and he intends I know, to consult you, touching certain verses I want to bring out, if possible, in the Spring, if not earlier. He will explain *everything*; and assured I am that you will help me in the mode he may indicate, by your advice, and experience!

Drop me a line, when you *can*, my *honored Friend*, & believe me,

> *Always faithfully,*
>
> *Paul H. Hayne.*

[Stedman's "The Death of Bryant" appeared in the *Atlantic Monthly* for December. 1878 (XLII, 747).

Stedman's *Alice of Monmouth An Idyl of the Great War with Other Poems* was published in New York by Carleton in 1864.

Taylor's wife wrote: "The last verses which he wrote were those of his 'Epicedium,' written in September [1878] to be read at the Century Memorial to William Cullen Bryant." (*Life and Letters of Bayard Taylor*, by Marie Hansen Taylor and Horace E. Scudder. Boston: Houghton, Mifflin and Company, 1884, II, 763.) Stoddard's *William C. Bryant* was published in 1879.

The "Dresden Correspondent" was correct. Taylor was dying of dropsy in Germany, where he was United States minister. He died two days after Hayne wrote this letter (d. December 19, 1878).

Moses Coit Tyler's two-volume work was *A History of American Literature during the Colonial Period, 1607–1765*, Putnam, November, 1878.]

No. 135

PAUL HAMILTON HAYNE to EDMUND CLARENCE STEDMAN

[From a typed copy.]

"Copse Hill," Georgia Rail Road,
February 19th, 1879.

Address:

P. O. Box 275,
Augusta, Ga.

My Dear Friend;

I briefly acknowledged your kind letter of last month; but had no leisure, just then, to tell you about your book; indeed, I had not then, been able to read it.

But, *my dear Poet*, the little vol. has been carefully perused since; and (let me assure you, in no *conventional* phrase) *truly* enjoyed.

You did your *"Alice of Monmouth"* far *less* than justice by the deprecating manner in which you mentioned the poem. There are some very spirited scenes in it; and certain "Songs" which have the genuine ring of the Cavalry bit and bridle, and the true flash of the Cavalry sabre! Bless your soul! I wasn't always the poor devil of an invalid I am now; and your lyrics bring back the remembrance,—of how many a glorious rush, thro autumn, or winter air; with a gallant horse bearing me onward, winged almost, like an eagle! Eheu!!. Shall I ever "boot, saddle, to horse, and away, again!"—in the innocent sports of peaceful fields?— Still, I don't think your "Alice" equal, in any respect, to "The Blameless Prince"; a work, I am going to review for a So. Maga. (with which I have just formed an Editorial connection), as soon as possible; (D. V.!)!— The latter is a gem, in its way, and nobody— *me judice*—North or South, has begun to appreciate it yet. You composed that most suggestive and pathetic narrative in a high spring-tide of real inspiration.

I have been amazed at the comparatively cool, and indifferent fashion with which the Critics recd. it. But the majority are pretentious Donkeys!! That is the simple explanation.

x x x Of the miscellaneous pieces in the "Alice of Monmouth" vol., I like "Alectryôn" (of course) best, among the serious, and "Jean Prouvaire's Song", among the semi-humorous ones; altho "Edged Tools,"—a trifle à-la-Tennyson, is capital also.

In fine, many thanks for the pleasure which your Book has afforded in more ways than one!

And now, to intrude upon your courtesy, or rather to enlist your *esprit-de-corps*, so far as to solicit your *candid*, unbiased opinion of the enclosed *Sonnets*.

If they are worthless, do, I entrust [entreat?], say so, without mercy, and without compromise. Never mind if you do draw blood!

x x x I am interrupted by an intolerable Bore, and can write no more at present, nor even glance over what I have already penned.

Drop me a line in pity,—

And believe me Always yours
most Cordially,

Paul H. Hayne.

[The Southern magazine with which Hayne had just formed an editorial connection may have been the *South-Atlantic: A Monthly Magazine of*

Literature, Science and Art (1879–1882), begun at Wilmington (N. C.)
and then moved to Baltimore, edited by Mrs. Cicero W. Harris. Many
issues carry Hayne's name as "Editorial Contributor," and for it Hayne
wrote poetry, criticism, and reviews.
The page references in the *Alice of Monmouth* volume are as follows:
"Alice of Monmouth," pp. 11–91.
"Alectryôn," pp. 95–105.
"Jean Prouvaire's Song at the Barricade," pp. 147–51.
"Edged Tools," pp. 119–21.]

No. 136

MARY MIDDLETON MICHEL HAYNE to EDMUND
CLARENCE STEDMAN

Copse Hill
May 8*th* 1880

My dear M*r* Stedman,

It has long been in my heart to write & thank you for
your very kind & thoughtful attention to my husband during his illness in N. Y. Believe me, we both appreciated your
unselfishness, yours & M*rs* Stedman's, in going yourselves for
the D*r.* at a time when you were wearied, & had not (I heard
you remark to M*r* Morford), "enjoyed a night[']s rest since
your return from Europe".

Mrs Stedman's sympathy for myself expressed in such a
simple homely fashion— "M*rs* Hayne I am so sorry for
you"—touched me truly because I *felt* that it came from the
heart. Your beautiful gift of flowers we took with us to
Philadelphia; & after they had faded, as all lovely things will,
I brought the basket home[,] colored, varnished & filled it
with moss; & it now stands upon a little bookcase which I
made to contain Osgood's edition of of [*sic*] Hawthorne's
works, & "Poems of Places[.]" M*r* Hayne often regrets that
he was too sick to talk with you, & to have you tell him of
your European trip: to ask if you had seen Tennyson, Swinburne, Miss Ingelow, & others, & what impression they made
upon you? About six weeks after we reached Copse Hill M*r*
Hayne lost his Mother, & this shock has resulted in great
nervous prostration of his system already weakened by many

hemorrhages— Since[,] he has had other hemorrhages; & for four Months past my gentle, patient husband, has suffered daily from a distressing shortness of breath, which almost incapacitates him for Mental labor. And yet, he keeps up bravely. If only a trifle better, for a day or so, he is cheerful & hopeful— & again at work. Please accept our congratulations on the marriage of your son— Mention of which I saw made in the "Home Journal". I send an editorial cut from yesterday[']s Augusta paper which I thought would gratify you. I will not expect a reply from you knowing that your physician has advised against general correspondence; but I could not bear to have you think us unmindful of your substantial kindness. With warm regards from Mr Hayne & I [sic], to Mrs Stedman & yourself—

Believe me,

Gratefully yours

Mary M. Hayne

[In 1879 Hayne and his wife visited New York and New England in August, September, and October. In October Stedman and his wife returned to New York from England, where they had spent the summer. The Haynes returned to Copse Hill early in November. Hayne's mother, Emily McElhenny Hayne, died at Copse Hill on December 9, 1879. She was 74.

Mr. Morford was probably Henry Morford (1823–1881), journalist, poet, novelist, and guidebook writer, who had a bookstore and travel office at 52 Broadway. At any rate, Henry Morford and Stedman were good friends.

James R. Osgood & Co., Boston publishers (who became Houghton, Osgood & Co.), had issued two editions of Hawthorne in twenty-three volumes and one in eleven volumes.

Poems of Places, 31 vols., was edited by Longfellow (Boston: Houghton, Osgood and Company, 1876–1879).

Stedman had two sons. I believe the marriage was that of Frederick Stuart Stedman (1856–1906), but I have not seen the reference in the *Home Journal*. For a time Frederick was his father's business associate.

In the Augusta *Chronicle and Constitutionalist* for May 7, 1880, there is an editorial entitled "Tragic Stock Brokerage." Only the first sentence refers to Stedman: "If Mr. Edmund C. Stedman, who is perhaps the only first-class poet and literary man engaged in stock brokerage, would write a book, in his own inimitable way, detailing the romance of Wall street.

it would have a great sale and add to his reputation." Many years later Stedman did attempt some such account. See Laura Stedman and George M. Gould, *op. cit.*, I, 591–601.]

No. 137

MARY MIDDLETON MICHEL HAYNE to EDMUND CLARENCE STEDMAN

"Copse Hill," Georgia Rail Road,
April 29*th* 1881

Address:

P. O. Box 275,
Augusta, Ga.

My dear Mr Stedmen [*sic*],

I am glad you found Dr Ticknor's poems of "positive interest" to you— We felt sure that this would be the case. Mr Whittier wrote me that Dr T— "would have been one of the foremost men of his time, had he written more". Judging by Dr T——' [s] letters to Mr Hayne—and the love of his wife— which is so reverent & lasting— I am sure that his life was pure, & Christian, to a very high degree. Mrs Ticknor writes us that her sons "are Noble boys, & a great comfort to her"— She has five of them, if I remember correctly. Dr Ticknor was an unequal writer, for he was dependent upon his profession for the support of his family, & found that "pills paid better than poetry—".

And now let me tell you what a surprise, that was anything but agreeable, the latter part of your letter conveyed to us. Who could have been personating my husband— And for what purpose? We tremble to think in what connection! For if the resemblance is so great that you who have seen Mr Hayne were deceived by it; to what extent may not this Man impose upon the public thus ruining my husband[']s character for honestly [*sic*] & uprightness. Mr Hayne has *never* left Copse Hill since we reached home in November of 1879, except for *three* days, with intervals of Months between, with the purpose of Consulting certain physicians of Augusta as to his health. "Please at your leisure", Mr Hayne asks, "will you let him know particulars of the man's visit to you"? Not many weeks ago Mr James R. Randall mentioned, in the "Chronicle & Constitutionalist" of Augusta, that some man had been personating him in N. Y. & borrowing Money from several gentleman [sic] of your City, & I recall your Name in the connection but cannot now remember if money or a letter of introduction was asked of you. Mr Randall spoke of his Double as a "small, dark Man"—adding that he would have to visit N. Y. in order to prove his identity, & establish the fact of his being a man of weight—any thing but a "small dark Man". "Do expose the man in some of the prominent N. Y. papers, if he has been using Mr Hayne's name for the purpose of getting money," my husband asks— And when he hears from you Mr Hayne will call attention to the Matter in the Southern papers. My Husband would write you, instead of myself, this Morning if he were not busy with Mss. to be sent to Lothrop & Co. today. I suppose you have seen the Notice in the May Number of "Wide Awake" "Publishers Department" of the complete edition of Mr Hayne's poems to be brought out by Lothrop & Co.? Until the announcement reached us we did not know the "get up" of the work would be so satisfactory; as the risk is all assumed by the Publishers— There you will see Mr Hayne at his best before his health failed him, nearly four years ago—the likeness was perfect— I could not have him taken now, looking so thin & unlike his real self, after disease laid so heavy a hand upon my gentle-hearted, tender Singer— No! I could not so have him attached to his life work. Should I be left behind I could not bear it! If God in Mercy take me first then it would not Matter! Mr Hayne sends warm regards to your kind wife, & love to yourself— He has had no return of hemorrhage for a Month but suffers much from an almost constant shortness of breath & oppression on the chest.

Do give my love to your wife, and accept the true regards of your friend

Mary M. Hayne

P. S.

Please excuse haste, for my brother[']s children are with us—
sent from Charleston to escape Scarlet— and I hardly know
what I have written.

[Francis Orray Ticknor married Rosalie Nelson of Virginia and was
survived by five sons: Douglas Cairns, George William, Thomas Michelle,
Francis Orray, and William Nelson.
   Wide Awake was a juvenile monthly published by D. Lothrop & Co.,
Boston. Lothrop brought out Hayne's *Complete Edition* in the fall of
1882.
   William Middleton Michel (1822–1894), Charleston physician, married in
1866 and four children survived him.]

No. 138

PAUL HAMILTON HAYNE to EDMUND CLARENCE STEDMAN

May 6*th* . . 1881.

My Dear Stedman;—

They have done me the honor to appoint me the Lyrist
for a grand occasion;— (viz) the Yorktown Centennial Celebration in Oct next.

Now, I believe that you are an accomplished *Musician,* no
less than a Poet, & — (bear in mind, please, that my lyric
is to be set to *music,*) I venture to ask of you a favor.

Recommend to me the *metre* which in your judgment— I
had *best* select for this effort.

A *single line,* (of course) of *any* poem, you may recall, &
quote as a *specimen* of the right metre, would sufficiently
guide, & enlighten my choice.

x x x x x x Did my *wife's* note of two days' ago reach
you, concerning the person who has been personating me in
NY?—

With best wishes, & special remembrance to Mrs Stedman,

Always Cordially & Gratefully

Paul. H. Hayne.

[For Hayne's "Yorktown Centennial Lyric" see *Complete Edition*, pp. 304–5. The norm is like that of Scott's "Lochinvar" (amphibraic tetrameter, catalectic), but nearly half of the lines are anapestic tetrameter. All but two of the sixty-six lines rime in pairs. They are grouped into five stanzas, four containing fourteen lines each and one having only ten.]

No. 139

PAUL HAMILTON HAYNE to EDMUND CLARENCE STEDMAN

"Copse Hill," Georgia Rail Road,
May 13*th* 1881

Address:

P. O. Box 275,
Augusta, Ga.

My Dear Stedman;

Your very considerate letter to my wife, of the 2*nd* ins*t*, was not only duly rec*d*, but, you will perceive by the enclosed "*Card*", that I have made practical use of it.

Despite your graphic description of the individual who visited you upon the 19*th* of Ja*n*, I find it *impossible* to form even a faint conjecture as to his identity. *What* a cool, clever, indomitable rogue he must be! And you say, that he is "*perfectly* familiar" with my concerns, knows "all my plans" &c (!!). Singular indeed!

If I ever "*spot*" this fellow, there is assuredly a little *account to settle between* us.

Apropos, not long after the war, I was amazed, one day, to receive from the *Editor* of "*The Home Journal*" (of *NY*) a note, enclosing the "Mss" of a poem called "*The White Slave*", *signed by my name. This* piece was fairly written; but contained sentiments *utterly foreign* to my *own;* & once published as a genuine production of mine, would have fatally injured me among my compatriots of the South. Luckily M*r* Morris Phillips, or M*r* Geo Perry *Scented* a *fraud;* and thus, *consulted* me in due season!

The whole affair demonstrated the existence of *deep malignity* on the writer's part;— and yet, I *can't* remember having ever offended any *man,* (or *woman*), in such a way as
to justify so mean a revenge!

. . . Thanks! for your kind, sympathetic inquiries in
regard to my health. Alack! it is still *most* precarious. Often
& often during the past winter I have had to endure a species
of nervous agony from repeated attacks of *shortness of
breath!*— a complaint which the Doctors tell me is owing,
not to lung disease, but rather to the irritability of that *bunch
of nerves,* which connects the organs of the throat & stomach.

All I know is, that anything more trying to one's fortitude
it would be hard to conceive.

Fancy a man gasping (like a fish out of water), every
minute or two, for hours together;—Sometimes indeed, so completely abandoned by the *Breath* which is *Life,* that the involuntary question arises, "Shall I ever *ever* catch my breath
again?"—

Occasionally, the *moral effect,* is deep *despondency,* verging
on *despair;* but again, a sort of nervous *fury* possesses me,
and I stamp about the room like a Madman; or a Member of
Congress elocutionizing for "Buncomb" (!!).

x x x Did you receive a paper which our friend *John
James Piatt,* asked me to mail to you, (after signing it), in
reference to his appointment as U. S. Minister at *Frankfort
on the Main?*

His direction on the envelope, by the way, was no *8, Pine
Street NYork;*— your *business address,* I presume?.

. . — Do you ever correspond with *Swinburne* now? *He*
sent me copies of his two last vols of Poems; which, of course,
are full of noble verse; yet — *entre nous* —, *don't* you think
he is beginning to *repeat himself,* both as to *thought & metre?*.

x x x I must not omit to *cordially* thank you for so kindly
& characteristically offering to "do all you can for Lothrop's
plucky venture with the "complete Edition"." I *well* know
what *your* influence is in literary matters; & would be so

glad if you *could* introduce my book to *English* readers especially.

x x x x *Dear Stedman,* I appreciate, (*how* profoundly) the *affectionate* manner in which you speak of me, in your letters to my wife; *and above all,* I appreciate your *kindly* allusions to *her; "my loyal wife"* She has indeed been *always,* &c *aye! and more!!*

We both *earnestly* wish that we could have seen *more* of Mrs *Stedman* & yourself— while in NYork; but we hold you in the warmest, most genial remembrance.

Above *even* your *literary fame, O! my friend!* & *intellectual brother,* (*brother,* whose flight upward, has been *far far* higher than mine), I recognize & love your *knightly, noble unselfish Heart!* — as pure & true a *Heart,* I verily believe, as ever pulsed in a human bosom!—

God be with you & yours!

Ever affectionately

Paul H Hayne.

Never bother yourself to answer my letters until a convenient moment[.]

[Written in the margin:]

Fields is dead! Well! his career was over;— he had *worked nobly, enjoyed much,* & *how* quietly & suddenly Death released him from physical suffering!! *"O! sè* [?] *sic omnia!* &c [."]

[I have not seen the card which Hayne enclosed. Possibly it was a printed denial that he had visited New York recently.

Morris Phillips became chief editor of the *Home Journal,* New York weekly, upon the death of Nathaniel Parker Willis in 1867. He had been an associate editor since 1864 and remained an editor until 1900. In 1867 he took George Perry into partnership, and Perry was one of the editors until 1890.

John James Piatt (1835–1917), journalist and poet, was United States consul at Cork, Ireland, from 1882 until 1893.

Swinburne's *Songs of the Springtides* and *Studies in Song* were published in New York in 1880 by R. Worthington,

Hayne's estimate of Stedman's character was correct.

James Thomas Fields (1816–1881), famous Boston publisher and editor, had died on April 24. Hayne had known him personally before the war, and his firm had brought out Hayne's first and third volumes (at Hayne's expense). Later Hayne had been hurt by his rejection of his offerings to the *Atlantic*.]

No. 140

PAUL HAMILTON HAYNE to EDMUND CLARENCE STEDMAN

"Copse Hill," Georgia Rail Road,
May 15*th* 1881.

Address:

P. O. Box 275,
Augusta, Ga.

Dear Stedman;

Your very considerate P. C. about the *"Yorkville"* ballad, or "Ode", has arrived; & *heartily* I thank you for your kind suggestion. Yes! *"The Battle of the Baltic"* *is* a superb lyric; and I may be enabled to do something by taking it in (a *general* way), as my *model*.

Apropos of verses, I am *particularly anxious* that *Mrs Stedman* should read a ballad of mine, in *"The June Harper,"* called *"The Dead Child, & the Mocking Bird."*

Ah! your large-hearted, tender, affectionate, motherly wife!! Shall I ever forget the kindly light in her eyes, when she so sweetly, accompanied you, upon your visit to my sick chamber?—

—*She* is the *"Laura"* of your youth, the heroine, of course, of that wonderfully Musical Song,—the words of which *literally* seem to *sing themselves*—

"Laura! my darling! the roses have blushed &c" . .

How *exceptionally* blessed is the *Poet*, who has a helpmeet to sympathise with him in *all things;*—in his *loftiest* ideal toils & aspirations, no less than in the responsibilities, & joys of home (!!). *Such a woman* the Fates gave to *you* (!!) *Such a woman* also, they gave to me!!

— . . Let us daily thank Heaven *therefor!*—

. . . . . . A newspaper paragraph sent me yesterday, by my friend *Mrs F. S. Saltus,*—(cut from *"the Ev: Post"*), refers to your visitor of the 19*th* Jan:, and unhesitatingly pronounces him to be the *same* individual, who, with our friend *Stoddard,* passed himself off as *James. R. Randall.* Probably, you had this piece published yourself; and I am *glad* that you did so.

. . — — — — We are having unexampled *heat* here,— considering the fact that *Spring* has *not—technically*—passed. In my shaded library the Thermometer points at this moment, to 86° (!!). —

> In haste, *but Always Most*
> *Faithfully & affectionately Yr's,*
>
> *Paul. H. Hayne.*

["Battle of the Baltic" (published 1809) is by Thomas Campbell (1777–1844), Scottish poet. Hayne did not use its metre in "Yorktown Centennial Lyric."

"The Dead Child and the Mocking-bird" appeared in *Harper's New Monthly Magazine* for June, 1881 (LXIII, 23). In November, 1880, Hayne recorded in his correspondence journal: "Harper $30 (for the Poem 'Dead Child & Mock. Bird')." Most of the magazines paid Hayne upon publication rather than upon acceptance. This payment was at the rate of fifty cents a line.

Laura was the name of Stedman's wife. His "Laura, My Darling" had appeared in the *Galaxy* for August 15, 1866 (I, 707), and was first collected in *The Blameless Prince, and Other Poems* (1869).

The Mrs. Saltus referred to was probably the wife of Francis Saltus Saltus (1849–1889), New York poet, prose writer, and linguist. Hayne's diary indicates that he frequently corresponded with "F. S. Saltus, 23 Waverly Place, New York."]

No. 141

PAUL HAMILTON HAYNE to EDMUND CLARENCE STEDMAN

"Copse Hill," Georgia Rail Road,
June 25*th* June [*sic*] 1881

Address:

P. O. Box 275,
Augusta, Ga.

Dear Friend;

Mr Mosenthal has, 'ere this, shown you my Song for the Yorktown *affair*, (a *deuced poor* thing, which I composed under almost *insuperable* difficulties),—but calculated nevertheless to be popular, if we can only arrange a *"Chorus"*.

For Heaven's sake, *Stedman!* help *me in this!!*

You'll recognize *at once*, the difficulty about the *"lilies"!*

I am really too ill to re-compose the "Chorus,"—so *wont* you "fix it up" for me, as the N England Housekeepers [?] say?—

Anything you suggest, I'll subscribe to!!—

Ever Faithfully

Paul H Hayne.

Of course, my *kind & noble Friend*, I would not dream of thus troubling you;—but the changes needed in "Chorus" are merely *verbal*, & would'nt take you .a quarter of an hour, *probably*, if indeed *it is absolutely necessary* to leave out *"the lilies of France"* in the concluding lines. *Ought this to be done, after all?*— The French Flag at Yorktown *was* the old imperial Flag; the "tri-Color" not having been even *born* or dreamed of at the time. *But I abide* by *your judgement implicitly;*— and all I want, if this judgement is *against the retention* of the lilies; is, that you'll substitute such terms in the "Chorus" as may avoid *repetition*, & awkward *tautology.*

[Joseph Mosenthal (1834–1896) was an organist, violinist, and composer, and after 1867 conducted the Mendelssohn Glee Club, New York. Four of the five stanzas of "Yorktown Centennial Lyric" end with these lines:

"And type of all chivalry, glory, romance,
The lilies, the luminous lilies of France."]

No. 142

PAUL HAMILTON HAYNE to EDMUND CLARENCE STEDMAN

"Copse Hill," Georgia Rail Road,
July 2nd 1881.

Address:
P. O. Box 275,
Augusta, Ga.

My Dear & Kind Friend;—

Believe me! I *appreciate*, & by no means *slightly*, your kindness concerning the *Yorktown* lyric.

It is a matter of pride to me that (in a *general* sense) you think it "very fine".

Regarding the 5*th* verse, let me observe, that I had a *mere popular* liking in view, when I wrote it;— not reflecting that the *Song*, (*after* it had been sung) would be *published* finally, and judged then by its literary merits alone!

Of course, you are *right*, touching its *artistic* incongruity; and equally, of course, I follow your advice, & *entirely omit it.*

About the *"Lilies"*, how glad am I that we agree in opinion!

Moreover, by their retention, the *last* line of *"Chorus"* acquires a certain *ring & resonance;*— the effect of *"artful* alliteration"!

My wife sends to Mrs Stedman & yourself, the *warmes!* remembrances! She can *never* forget you, nor your kindness to her husband.

With *all my* soul, I trust that your country trip may prove beneficial.

Tho not a "man of muscle", you have still immense *vitality* I should suppose. Cherish it, *mon ami!*—

How did *Mosenthal* strike you personally?— I've never seen him; but he tells me that he can boast of *200* pounds of "solid flesh". *Ye Gods!!*

> *Ever Faithfully*
>
> *Paul H Hayne.*

No. 143

PAUL HAMILTON HAYNE to EDMUND CLARENCE STEDMAN

> "Copse Hill," Georgia Rail Road,
> *October 11th* 1881

Address:

    P. O. Box 275,
    Augusta, Ga.

My Dear Friend;—

I rec*d* the enclosed letter from a Physician of your City, which I thought might interest you.

Can it be possible that it was the veritable *Moses,* (*that* renegade Scoundrel from *So Ca*) who so *cleverly* affected aristocratic airs, you *naturally* assumed "him to be a *perfect Gentleman*"?

I can hardly realize the fact!! From *my* recollection of him, as Gov: Pickens' *Secretary,* (he was *made Secretary* thro the influence of *his father,* a *political* adherent of *P's*)—, his appearance was *distinctly Jewish;*— He had a Hebrew physiognomy of the *worst type;*— with rather small, black eyes, placed too near together, on Either side of a somewhat hooked nose; full, *red, sensual lips,* and a chin even *more sensual* perhaps than his mouth!—

I remember distinctly that the *first & only* time my *wife* ever saw him,— (in 1861) she Said to me; "if *I am any Judge of* physiognomy, *that is a very bad man!*["]

Not only is the fellow a *political* renegade, & Traitor to his State & People, but he is an *adept* in *immorality;*— (so *much so,* that his life has long been *forfeited,* & *(entre nous),* I myself would like to *shoot him down like a dog)*—: thus surely a.., punishment he receives will be *richly merited.*
x x x x   But to pleasanter topics!—
I have read your critical papers, (in *"Scribner"*) upon *"Poetry in America";* and the *first* of *these* I have not only *read,* but *studied.*

Assuredly, *mon ami,* you are a *born Critic,* a *God-gifted Analyzer* of the higher aësthetic *nature,* & its capabilities.

Among your numerous critical papers, in the *"Victorian Poets,"* & elsewhere, there is *absolutely* but *one review,* the arguments, & conclusions of which I cannot *honestly respond* to!—

Your subtle logical power has sometimes resolved itself into *aphorisms,* as (E. g.) in the *August "Scribner,"* I find the following sentence;— (page 542):

"America has absorbed the traits of many lands & peoples. x x x Our modern intercourse with the world at large, is unintermitting; so that the raw ingredients of our national admixture, are supplied as rapidly as the stir of the popular system, can commingle them!

"It is too much, then, to expect that our art, or song, from whatever section these may come, will *exhibit a quality specifically American, in the sense that the product of Italy is Italian, or that of France is French!"*

— Here, *(me judice),* you furnish a luminous, logical, & unanswerable response to those who are forever demanding what they call, a *distinctive American utterance in song;* (of course *under the conditions implied).* x x x x x x x

While upon this topic of *American* Poets &c, I see you mention Mrs *M. J Preston* among a group of *Female Singers.*

If you have not seen her *"Old Song & New,"* (published by *Lippincott* in 1870,) and *"Cartoons"* (by Messrs *Roberts*

& *Bros*), which has just gone into a *3rd* Edition,— I shall ask her to send them to you.

In my estimation, she ranks *first* among the *women-singers* of this Country in what may be called the *lyrical-dramatic style;* tho She has had to write *under* great disadvantages.

I recollect for *one thing,* she mentioned to me, in one of her letters, (for we have *never met*), *that* for *7 years* (!) she was *confined* to a *darkened room;* & forbidden to *look at a book, on account* of the *pain in her Eyes.* Moreover, her *general health* is *very frail.* x x x x x x x x x x x x x x x x x xxxxxxxxxxx I remember how kindly you spoke of *"The Vengeance of the Goddess Diana",* when I mailed you my last vo*l* of Poems;— but my *best narrative verse* (beyond all comparison), is contained in my previous vo*l,* *"Legends & Lyrics"*—

When Howells reviewed this vo*l* in *"The Atlantic",* he accused me of having (in *"The Wife of Brittany"* & *"Daphles")* ·imitated *Morris.!!* While the *facts* of the case are *that the* *"W. O. B."* was composed between the years 1863–4, *before Morris was even known in America;* & *"Daphles"* I was correcting the proof of, *when I first saw Morris' "Jason".* (!!) Pardon this *egotism;* but one *hates* to be unjustly accused of *plagiarism.* x x x x

Mrs Hayne joins me *in* cordial remembrances to Mrs *Stedman & yourself—* *Ah!* shall I Ever forget the *kindly face* of your *noble, good, tender* wife, when she *stopped for a moment,* by *my sick bed?*

[Written in the margin of the last page:]

Always affectionately Yrs'

Paul H Hayne.

[Written in the left margin of the first page:]

\#   Your *"Concord Ode"* is a singularly *subtle, & suggestive* poem. It grows upon one with each *additional* reading.

[Written in the right margin of the first page:]

Do glance over my humble tribute to *Garfield* in "Harpers Weekly" for Oct 1*st*.

[Francis Wilkinson Pickens (1805–1869) was one of South Carolina's most active leaders from the 1830's until his death. He served as United States minister to Russia (1858–1860) and was governor at the outbreak of the Civil War (1860–1862). He was the nephew of Hayne's mother.

Franklin J. Moses (1838–1906) was a native of Sumter County, South Carolina. His father held a number of public offices. The Republicans made him chief justice of the state from 1868 until his death in 1877. In December, 1860, the son became private secretary of Governor F. W. Pickens. He entered the army and raised the flag over Ft. Sumter when the Federals surrendered it. Later he was made enrolling officer with the rank of colonel under the Confederate conscription act. He had great gifts of personality and eloquence but great underlying moral weaknesses. Becoming a renegade to all his previous conduct in 1867, he assumed the leadership of the black majority which had gained political mastery in the state. In 1872 he was elected governor and served for two years, with thorough unscrupulousness: he issued fraudulent pay certificates, accepted bribes, misappropriated funds, and in general proved a perfect scalawag. Moreover, his private immorality caused public scandal. His wife divorced him and some relatives changed their family name. After 1878 he was a fugitive and exile from the state, was several times convicted of petty fraud and theft, and served short terms in various prisons. These details are taken from the sketch of Moses in *D. A. B.*

Stedman's "Poetry in America, Part I" appeared in *Scribner's Monthly* for August, 1881 (XXII, 540–50). "Poetry in America, Part II" appeared in the issue for October, 1881 (XXII, 817–28).

Hayne's "last vol of Poems" was *The Mountain of the Lovers* (New York: E. J. Hale & Son, 1875). *Legends and Lyrics* had appeared in 1872.

Hayne's *Legends and Lyrics* was reviewed in the *Atlantic Monthly* for April, 1872 (XXIX, 501–2). The reviewer says Hayne is an imitator of William Morris, especially in "Daphles" and "The Wife of Brittany." In other respects the review is favorable.

Mrs. Stedman had stopped by Hayne's sick bed in New York in October, 1879.

Stedman's "Corda Concordia" appeared in the *Atlantic Monthly* for August, 1881 (XLVIII, 179). Stedman had read it at the opening session of the Summer School of Philosophy at Concord, July 11, 1881.

Hayne's "On the Death of President Garfield" appeared in *Harper's Weekly*, October 1, 1881 (XXV, 670).]

No. 144

MARY MIDDLETON MICHEL HAYNE to [ARTHUR GRIFFIN STEDMAN?]

"Copse Hill," Georgia Rail Road,
November 1*st* 1881

Address:

- P. O. Box 275,
  Augusta, Ga.

Dear Mr Stedman,

My husband, who is suffering from the effects of a large blister upon the left side, begs me to thank you for the papers you kindly mailed him relating to Yorktown. He received your father[']s letter, & was Much cheered by his warm praise of the Yorktown Lyric[.] Your good father is possessed of a tender heart, & is always *generous* in his appreciation of his brother singers. His tender thought for Mr Hayne, when he was ill in N. Y., will never pass out of my Mind. Do give your Mother & himself our very warm regards; tell the former to keep all visitors away from her Poet while he is engaged upon his critical papers, requiring as they do, so much concentration of thought. I send her the last of our Copse Hill flowers; until next May we shall Miss them sadly, for they are company of whose Society we never weary. Say to your father that, very enjoyable as his letters always are, Mr Hayne would not, on any consideration, have him turn aside from his more important work to write him.

With remembrances from Mr Hayne—
Believe me truly Yours

Mary M. Hayne

P. S.

There are Mistakes in the Exposition Ode which my husband failed to correct *fully* in the Copy sent Mr Stedman. Mr Hayne was suffering Much the day he sent the Ode, & therefore Corrected hastily.

[Stedman had two sons: Frederick Stuart (1856–1906) and Arthur Griffin (1859–1908). The former was his father's business associate at the time of this letter and the latter became a kind of literary assistant to his father. My conjecture is that this letter was written to Arthur, but I have not seen the letter to which it is a reply.

The "Exposition Ode" to which Mrs. Hayne refers in the postscript may have been "The Return of Peace" (see *Complete Edition*, pp. 300–304). This poem was written by request "for the opening ceremonies of the International Cotton Exposition, in Atlanta, Georgia, Oct. 5, 1881." (Quoted from Hayne's headnote in *Complete Edition*.)]

No. 145

PAUL HAMILTON HAYNE to EDMUND CLARENCE STEDMAN

[Postal card]

Nov: 11*th* 1881

Dear Stedman;

I *hear* that you have published "in Critic", a review of S. Lanier's poetry.

Can you have a copy mailed me?. Thanks! for your kind appreciation of *Yorktown* lyric; Hope your son rec*d* my *wife's* reply to his letter.?.

Don't trouble yourself to write now that you are so especially busy upon a great work.

By the way, I sent a very brief poetical tribute to *Lanier* to the present Ed: of *"Scribner's,"* but it was *immediately returned*, with words to the effect, that their *poetical* contributions were so numerous, they had to make *"selections"* &c &c! *Comforting!* that?—

Ever Cordially

Paul H Hayne.

[Stedman's "The Late Sidney Lanier" appeared in the *Critic* (New York) for November 5, 1881 (I, 298).

Josiah Gilbert Holland was editor of *Scribner's Monthly* from 1870 until his death on October 12, 1881. Richard Watson Gilder was then editor until his death in 1909. (In 1881 the ownership of the magazine was changed and its title became *Century Illustrated Monthly Magazine*.)

Lanier died September 7, 1881.

Hayne's "The Pole of Death," a poem written in memory of Lanier, appeared in *Harper's New Monthly Magazine*, LXV (June, 1882), 98.]

No. 146

PAUL HAMILTON HAYNE to EDMUND CLARENCE STEDMAN

[Postal card]

\#   *Address, P O Box 275 Augusta Ga*

Nov: 21st 1881

Dear Friend;

I write to tell you that I recd the copy of *"Critic"* containing your notice of S. Lanier. It is *simply a perfect article, &* I am so glad to have seen it!

Don't dream of replying.

Ever affectionately &c [?]

Paul H Hayne

[At the top of this card someone other than Hayne has written: "The inevitable [.]" It was probably written by someone other than Stedman also—some later reader who thought Hayne's comments on Stedman's criticism were flattering. If Stedman believed that, he probably would not have kept up the correspondence, nor would he have spoken so well of Hayne as he did in print. As a matter of fact, Stedman was the finest critic of poetry then writing in America and deserved Hayne's good opinion.]

No. 147

PAUL HAMILTON HAYNE to EDMUND CLARENCE STEDMAN

[From a typed copy.]

"Copse Hill" Georgia Rail Road

(Private!)

March 4th, 1882.

Address:

P. O. Box 275,

Augusta, Ga.

My Dear Stedman;—

Thoughts of you came over me so strongly a night or two ago, as I reflected upon your tender care for me, during my illness in N. York, that I felt absolutely impelled to compose the enclosed Sonnet which I hope may please you. It seems to me fitting, perhaps, that it should appear in *"The Century"*; but I am somewhat reluctant to send it there, because after Dr. Holland's death, I offered some memorial verses, (carefully written) upon poor Lanier, addressed to the Editor, (I knew not at the time who was Editor), and the reply was, that they recd. "so many contributions etc. they must make selections etc.";— "Only that; and nothing more!"

You might, however, prefer to see this Sonnet, in *"The Atlantic,"* but here again, I am reluctant to offer it; because Mr. Aldrich has never given me the ghost of an invitation to write for his maga, altho he had occasion to return some verses sent him by my son, which he did courteously eno', so far as my boy was concerned.

But you can send it to either of them you prefer. I'd like it to appear, as soon as convenient, since I wish this heart-felt tribute included in my "Complete Edition." When precisely the book is to be published I cannot tell. Lothrop told me some months back, that it had been "vexatiously delayed", thro the "long illness of Mr. Allen, the person who had the preparation of the work in hand, but who has now left the Firm." Mr. Lothrop remarked, that he "hoped to get Mr. Arthur Gilman to edit it, but that would defer the publication to another season." (meaning next Xmas I suppose, though I don't positively know). So I have to exercise patience, despite ill health.

My wife encloses a few Jessamines, (first of the season) from our Porch; and sends her warmest regards to Mrs. Stedman, in which I join cordially,

Always Faithfully yrs,

Paul H. Hayne

[For Hayne's "To the Author of 'The Victorian Poets' " see *Complete Edition*, p. 283. Hayne wrote Stedman (March 11, 1882) that he would send it to the *Critic*, but it appeared in the *Christian Union* for March 23, 1882 (XXV, 273).

Thomas Bailey Aldrich (1836–1907) edited the *Atlantic* from 1881 until 1890.

On January 21, 1881, Hayne noted in his correspondence journal that
he had just received a postal card from F. H. Allen of the Lothrop firm
informing him that all was going well with the typesetting of his *Complete
Edition*.

Arthur Gilman (1837–1909), author, editor, and literary adviser to
publishers, was a native of Illinois, but in 1872 he settled in Cambridge.
He was also actively interested in the education of girls and women.]

No. 148

PAUL HAMILTON HAYNE to EDMUND CLARENCE STEDMAN

"Copse Hill" March 11th 1882

My Dear Stedman;

I am *heartily* glad that the little poem should have "gratified & touched you";— but pray let *me explain* at *once*, what
I wrote to you about *you yourself* offering this "Sonnet" to
either the Editor of *"The Century"* or the Editor of *"The
Atlantic"*.

x x x My firm conviction was, that you were *personally
intimate* with *both* these *Gentlemen;* so *very* intimate indeed,
that you could *properly* have gone to either and said, "you
know me too well to suspect me of foolish vanity, or egotism;
here is a *Sonnet* which if suitable artistically, you can
publish!"

But I find that my idea was *erroneous; & need* I remark
that under the circumstances really existing; I not merely
comprehend your refusal to present the *Sonnet* as suggested;
but that situated as you are, I *would have myself* acted *precisely* as *you have done*. How can a Gentleman be *too* careful upon the score of *delicacy?*

x x I feel *sure* after this honest & frank explanation, *my
dear friend*, that you will acquit me of having asked you to
be "guilty of a 'forward,' 'immodest,' or 'indelicate' proceed-
ing".!!— Had I *known* how you actually stood with those
Editors, *nothing could* have *"induced* me" to make the suggestion I did,—for I feel as keenly as you do, the claims of personal dignity, & that delicate reserve of feeling, which above
all is the characteristic *par excellence* of the Gentleman.

x x x I will now offer *"this Sonnet"* to the *"Critic,"* as perhaps I thought you might like, *third best* to see it *therein.* It *sincerely* grieves me to find you so troubled about *monied affairs;* & Heavens! how *profoundly* I can sympathise, having suffered in the *same* way since the war.

Indeed, I would be *rejoiced* to to [*sic*] have you *come here,* & rest from labors and anxiety, while you wrote at leisure, were it possible for you to put up with the discomforts of my poor home among the Pines.

Yet, *after a fashion,* we could make you comfortable; & as for the *welcome,* well!! you would find it *warm* be assured.

Our *best* regards to your dear & good wife.

When at *you are* at *perfect leisure,* I would like to know that this letter had reached you.

Ever Most Cordially
Your friend,

Paul H Hayne.

P O Box 275 Augusta Geo.

No. 149

PAUL HAMILTON HAYNE to EDMUND CLARENCE STEDMAN

[The MS. of this letter is defective; the words in brackets were supplied by a typed copy made earlier.]

"Copse Hill," Geo. *April 17th 1882*
(*late at night*) &c.

My Dear Stedman;—

— Your note, with the newspaper paragraphs, & likeness (*of ex-Governor* Moses), has just arrived, & pray accept my thanks for your considerate kindness.

Judging from *this particular* portrait, I should say that our ingenious Hebrew friend had somewhat improved in appearance with the lapse of years. "Scoundrelism seems to agree with him," as *Vid*[*o*]*cq* said of one of his "lambs."

I have been much amused by the brief semi-biography of him which the NYork paper furnishes. To judge from *this*, one would think that Monsieur *Franklin J. Moses* originally belonged to a very *important*, (if not highly reputable—S. C. family), & had descended from a vast Social height. (!!) The fact is, that his Father was a shrewd Israelitish Lawyer, of *Sumter County (S. C.)*—, a fellow of no *antecedents* whatever,—unless probably connected with *"old Clo' "*—, but tolerably wealthy, a local Judge, & possessed of a certain degree of political influence in his neighborhood. When the War came on, he helped my kinsman, *the Hon.* F W *Pickens*—in his canvass for the Governorship of the State;—in recognition of which service, Pickens, when elected, appointed *Moses' son* to his *staff.* Thus it was that *I* made *M's* personal acquaintance. He was then a young man of 25— or 26, of pronounced Jewish features, belonging to the most unprepossessing type;— raw, boyish manners,—and habits [of lavish] expendit[ure.] He *wormed* himself somehow in his Excellency's confidence, & writing a famous hand, became for a few months, his private Secretary.

In 1862, however, his services being no longer needed, Moses with the commission of *Con: Lieutenant*, went to Fort Moultrie. The officers there were chiefly "blue blooded," Carolinians,—gentlemen of family & breeding; and could'nt stomach ·his peculiarities,—. At all events, he soon left that fortress; and obtained the position of Conscript Officer in *Edgefield village, (S C).*

There, he made himself especially obnoxious to decent folk;— but still contrived to hold his post, until the end of the Confederate Struggle. He *never beheld a battle field;* the *only* occasion of his *even smelling* powder, at a distance, having been when, (*after* the Conflict of *April* 1861), he pushed himself forward at Sumter, & drew down the Federal flag. (His worthy Parents kept likewise, studiously out of harm's way during all the four years of revolution)—[From first to] *last*, both were *parvenus*,— and in the reconstruction [times] proved themselves *villains* & Traitors.

Of marvellously acute mind, no doubt *Franklin J—* *acquired, subsequently*, good manners; *aped* his superiors, and even succeeded in playing the *rôle* of *Aristocrat*, (in mere *outward seeming*)—

But the fellow is really as low in *birth & blood*, as *morale*. Certain *social infamies* which he perpetrated, (during the war), *ought* to have subjected him to "a *short* shrift & a *long* cord."

But his *cunning* saved him. *Physically* he is the most consummate of Cowards; and such a *Liar* as *this* world has seldom known. (*Entre nous*, I may [as well] inform you that Gov. Pickens was *warned against* against [*sic*] employing him, but neglected good counsel)—

Let us hope that Moses will be in retirement for some years!—

He has richly earned the right to be supported by the *State!* x x *Basta* x x x x x x x x x x

I know how grieved you must have been by the news of *Rossetti's* death. About 6 or 7 weeks ago, I heard from *him*. He wrote me a *very* kind & pleasant letter, tho complaining of his health at the time. Little did I dream how Serious his condition really was!!

Ah me! my *friend*,— the Poets, (our brothers), are leaving us. Longfellow gone! Dennis McCarthy, & now Dante Gabriel Rossetti!— How the London *set* of *Poets*, *Swinburne*, *Gosse*—Thompson, Dobson— and beyond all, *Philip Marston* will miss him!!—

x x Do you ever hear from *Swinburne* now?

He writes me by "fits & starts", but always *most* [genially].

I understand that you are to have in *next "Century"* a critical paper upon *Lowell.?* This is good news. L—— deserves your deep analysis.

Upon *some* points I have always considered him a stronger & more original writer than *Longfellow*.

(*Entre nous*), what ails *Stoddard?*— Everybody almost in NY seems disposed to dislike him!!— For myself, (while I view him as one of the *subtlest*, & sweetest *Poets* of our land), I am also *personally* attached to him. Yet he is represented as the author of a very *mean* paragraph against me, in a recent no of the *"Ev Mail"*— I wrote him concerning it; and stated my utter disbelief in the charge!— S— is not the man to stab a friend behind his back. Don't you *think* so?

The newspapers *exaggerated* as to my health. But still I'm a chronic Invalid; and *may die at any moment.*

x x x x Please give my most respectful remembrances to your *dear, good wife,* in which my own *"winsome marrow"* joins.

Always Cordial[ly and affec]tionately

Pau[l H. Hayne]

PS

In your last letter you spoke of being willing to live *"upon hominy", "for a month,"* if freed "from your daily contact (in NY) *with things you loathe"* [.]

Remember, that you have *always* a warm *(the very warmest)* welcome awaiting you *here,* from my wife & self; and at all events, a plenty of *"Hominy";*— if at any period you feel that you need rest & *quiet.*

x x I *profoundly* regret to understand from you, that your trouble is "chronic congestion" *of the Brain,* which must greatly affect your *nerves,* as the *constant hemorrhages* do mine.

Faithfully

P H H

[Written at the top of the first page of the letter:]

Private & Confidential.

Pardon my using a Pencil (!!)

[Written in the margin of the last page of the letter:]

The *Lothrops* write that my *"complete Edition"* will be out in time for the *"Fall Trade".*

[For information on Pickens and Moses see the notes following Hayne's letter to Stedman dated October 11, 1881 (No. 143).

François Eugène Vidocq (1775–1857) was a French detective and adventurer who had earlier been a thief. He was reputed to be the author of *Mémoires* and other works.

Rossetti died April 10, 1882. Longfellow died March 24, 1882.

Denis Florence McCarthy (1817–1882), Irish poet, editor, and translator, died April 7.

The other poets referred to are Algernon Charles Swinburne (1837–1909), Edmund Gosse (1849–1928), Henry Austin Dobson (1840–1921), Philip Bourke Marston (1850–1887)—and by "Thompson" Hayne probably meant James Thomson (1834–1882). Thomson died June 3, 1882.

Stedman's "James Russell Lowell" appeared in the *Century Magazine* for May, 1882 (XXIV, 97–111).

R. H. Stoddard was literary editor ●f the New York *Mail and Express* from 1880 until his death (1903).]

No. 150

PAUL HAMILTON HAYNE to EDMUND CLARENCE STEDMAN

"Copse Hill,"
Georgia Railroad.
April 22nd 1882

Address:

P. O. Box 275,
Augusta, Ga.

My Dear Stedman;—

What an article is that of yours in *"Harper"* upon the "London Poets (!!)"

My dear & honored friend;— God has indeed gifted you with one of the *subtlest* minds, the most discriminating spirits ever vouchsafed to mortal! Your *entire* paper is perfect, & delightful reading of course. I speak *my heart* in this.

I am *rejoiced* that you wrote so genially & tenderly of poor Marston; And, by the way, — *we*, (my wife & I), were *specially* struck by your reply to *Swinburne*, touching *"Thanatopsis"* & Lowell's "Ode".

Therein, you penetrated the *gist* of the matter; & controverted *S's* one-sided logic completely. *(Entre nous)*, how can a man of Swinburne's genius talk such *stuff*, about the lack of music in *American* poetry. &c.? x x

x x x

You rec*d* I hope my letter concerning *Moses;* and also a communication to R H Stoddard (directed to *your* care)?.

Stoddard is the *oldest* of my Northern lit. friends.

I have a genuine regard for him; & a great admiration for his genius:

What a piece [? price?] *"Irreparable"* [?] is!!

x x Well *(entre nous)* you may imagine my surprise, when some little time ago, a printed slip cut from the *"NY Mail"* reached me, which the Correspondent who enclosed it, attributed to Stoddard;— a *snarling paragraph* the substance of which was, that *I* furnished a fair illustration of the feeble & pretentious So *"Versifyer"*, who *fancied* himself a *Poet!—* &c &c

Of *course,* I knew that *R H S* never *could* have penned this from malice; & I wrote him to say so, & to *re*-assert my good feeling towards *him.* He has not yet *replied.*

— — *Do* glance over the *last "NY Independent,"* & read my *Sonnet* to Marston. Odd to say, a *Sonnet* of his *own* appears in *same* issue; and *the last lines, (On Longfellow)* contain *precisely* the idea about a *"spring*[?] *of love,"* which *completes my* verses to the blind Poet. . (!!). x x x x

Never trouble to answer my *"screeds" until convenient.*

Most Cordially & affectionately

Paul H Hayne.

[At the top of the first page of the letter:]

Excuse *once more* the Pencil & *its informality.*

[In the margin of the same page:]

Address me next *Grovetown Columbia Co Geo & not Augusta.*

[Stedman's "Some London Poets" appeared in *Harper's New Monthly Magazine* for May, 1882 (LXIV, 874–92). Among the poets discussed are Marston (pp. 881–3) and Swinburne (pp. 888–92).

For a comment on Stoddard's type and theory of criticism see Richard Croom Beatty, *Bayard Taylor: Laureate of the Gilded Age* (University of Oklahoma Press, 1936), pp. 249 ff. As a man and a critic Stoddard was often morbid and bitter, but as least he was courageous, and certainly he was honest. There is no doubt, however, that Hayne was a better poet than he.]

No. 151

PAUL HAMILTON HAYNE to EDMUND CLARENCE STEDMAN

Address P O Box 275 Augusta Geo.
"Copse Hill" Geo
Dec 10th 1882

My Dear Friend;

As you so *generously* wrote my wife—*many months* ago—, that you were going to send my *"complete Edition"* of Poems to *Marston, Mr Dobson* & *Mr Gosse*, I take the liberty of enclosing *four* copies of *"Errata,"* which I have had struck off for my *own* use in Augusta; with a request that you will send one to each of these Gentlemen (with the vol*s*,) retaining *one* for yourself.

Certainly the *Lothropes* have brought out a *beautiful Book*, for which I am *most grateful*,— but I regret, (as they *could not* mail me *"proof sheets"*) that I did not see the vo*l before* it was *stitched:*—

You'll remark that they have omitted the "Prelude" to "Daphles," & have placed my two last vol*s* under *one* heading, (viz) *"Legends & Lyrics"*.

Then too, they should have *closed* (at my request) the *adult* portion of Book with *"In Harbor,"* preceded by *"The Pole of Death"*, & the *"Children's Poems"* with one of my best juvenile pieces, which I *see* they have retained for the Jan *"W Awake"*. x x x x *The Lothropes* are "hopeful of many editions," (I *quote from them*), "and promise to make full corrections in next edition—["]

But *please do not mention* these *mistakes*, as it might *interfere with the sale* &c.

Judge *kindly*, oh! *my Friend*, these *children of my brain*; remembering that *it is* a *"complete Edition,"* & consequently *some* pieces have been retained, which in a *single vol* (of later verses) I would not have introduced. x x I am *sincerely* sorry to learn that you

[The remainder of the letter is written in the margins and at the top.]

were summoned from *Venice* so abruptly to *NYork*. It must have been exceedingly trying. Let me hope that your health *is better? With love from all* my Household to dear Mrs Stedman & yourself.

Ever Cordially & affectionately

Paul H Hayne.

[The two volumes placed under the heading "Legends and Lyrics" in *Complete Edition* were *Legends and Lyrics* (1872) and *The Mountain of the Lovers* (1875).

When reading Hayne's "In Harbor" (*Complete Edition*, pp. 337-8), one naturally thinks of Tennyson's "Crossing the Bar" because of certain similarities between the two. The *Complete Edition* appeared seven years before "Crossing the Bar" was published. Otherwise certain of the critics —Howells, for instance—might have accused Hayne of imitation. It is interesting to note also that Hayne had requested that the adult portion of his volume end with "In Harbor," whereas Tennyson, a few days before his death, requested that all editions of his poetry end with "Crossing the Bar."

Early in June, 1882, the day after Stedman and his son Arthur had settled in Venice with the expectation of spending several months, they were recalled to New York on business.]

No. 152

PAUL HAMILTON HAYNE to EDMUND CLARENCE STEDMAN

[From a typed copy.]

"Copse Hill", Georgia
Dec. 26th, 1882.

My Dear Stedman;

For your letter of the 20th, I thank you with all my heart! This communication shall go straightway, among my most

cherished epistolary archives; and I please myself with fancying that those who come after me, (perhaps my son's children, if he ever marries) will take up this letter with pride.
and remark, "See here! What the greatest of American Art-
Critics once wrote of our grandfather's verses!"

Indeed, dear Friend, you are very generous in your comments upon my Book; and knowing these comments to be
those of an author equally capable and sincere, (of one whose
insight into the subtlest realms of poetry seems like intui-
tion), how could I fail to value them beyond measure?

x x x Yes! the list of "Errata" does look formidable!, yet,
after all, the errors (tho important .to the critic and the
author) are such as the general reader would hardly notice!

But I do regret (most) the omission of that Proem or Prelude to "Daphles" which was a particular favorite, by the
way, of Longfellow's.

How very kind and generous of you to procure so many
copies of my Poems!

Rest assured that this is deeply appreciated by my wife
and self!

Touching the portrait, it *was* a perfect likeness when taken
about six years ago,— but the work being delaid, it (the
likeness) makes me younger-looking and healthier-looking
than I now am; for sickness has by no means left me
unscathed.

x x x We were greatly pleased by your Ballad on old
"Stuyvesant" in "Harper's" recently (illustrated) pamphlet.

I don't see how you could have managed the subject better;
or more picturesquely.

In reference to the "poems which are in your still," and
which you naturally yearn for "time" wherein to compose
and develop,—let me propose most seriously and earnestly that
you come to us in our solitude here, where you will have
ample leisure; at least, if you can put up with monotonous
environments, plain fare, and a wholly unconventional life.
Your welcome would be of the warmest, and you could remain
just as long as you deemed fit.

I dare not— literally dare not— invite Mrs. Stedman to
accompany you; because she would sadly miss her own home
comforts; Ours is little more than a "shanty" in the woods!

But for yourself, my friend, I pray you think very maturely and seriously of my invitation. You would have the most perfect freedom, relief from all bores and annoyances; (daily) opportunities of visiting a large, prosperous Town, when the quiet became oppressive,—and of course, I'm not such a Barbarian as not to have decent Cigars for a friend, fond of the "weed," and some other "creature comforts," of the stimulating sort!! Come! by all means!! 'Twould give you a new lease of life!

Last night (Xmas night), while sitting all alone by the wood fire; (for my "winsome marrow" tired by multifarious household duties, had retired, and was courting the "sleep of the weary"), I re-perused your "Blameless Prince", very nearly from beginning to end!

Never before perhaps had the beauty, picturesqueness, beyond all, the real dramatic powers, and subtlety of this narrative so struck and moved me.

The concluding portions are especially fine,— worthy— *me judice*— of any narrative poet, even the greatest of our Century. (I know what this means and I say it deliberately.)

The whole of that interview (e. g.) between the betrayed Queen, and the Prince's Mistress, is superb and powerful; showing not merely a high dramatic art, but a profound psychological knowledge. One stanza on page 83, beginning "The air seemed full of lies etc" displays a remarkable species of compressed force; while the condition of the unfortunate Queen's mind is fully revealed to us, as by a lightning flash, in these lines of blended pathos, and power;

> ———————— "From the Kingdom's heir
> Shuddering, she turned her face; his features took
> A shivering horror from his father's look!"

En passant on p. 49 (same poem), is not the 2nd line of the 1*st* stanza a misprint? "himself" has no rhyme in the verse. I thought, perhaps, you had written,

> "But not without a summoning of his will
> To judgment, did the Prince forever part
> From truth and fealty; As he pondered, still
> With stronger voice etc. etc. etc."

(i. e.) he summons *his will*, to discover whether it is strong enough to resist temptation, and finds it too feeble, etc.

Am I right here?

With warmest regards and best wishes of the season from my wife to yours, and also to yourself, regards in which I heartily join, Believe me

Faithfully and affectionately yrs.

Paul H. Hayne

[Stedman's "The Dutch Patrol" (*Harper's Christmas*, 1882) is a poem about Stuyvesant.

The first passage which Hayne quotes (inaccurately) from *The Blameless Prince* occurs on p. 83 of the edition of 1869. The revision which Hayne suggests in the passage quoted from p. 49 involves the substitution of "his will" for "himself." The change would have corrected the rime scheme, but "himself" was probably not a misprint, as later collected editions indicate.]

No. 153

PAUL HAMILTON HAYNE to EDMUND CLARENCE STEDMAN

[From a typed copy.]

"Copse Hill" Geo.
16th March 1883.

My Dear Stedman;

Thanks! many thanks for your kindness in forwarding those copies to Marston[,] Gosse & Dobson. It was wonderfully kind and considerate!

x x x x I eagerly look forward to your Emerson article in next "Century."

I well know that it will be exhaustive, analytical, and superb.

You are King of Poetical Critics!

And also I shall read with special pleasure your "Preface["] to Doré's Illustrations of Poe's Raven.

By the way, Mr. Henry James, I perceive, and his devoted friend Mr. Fawcett, regard Poe's verses, especially his "Raven" with supreme contempt!!

A liking for Poe (says the former) proves a man uncultured, and little better than an ass. Unfortunate Tennyson! infatuated Swinburne!! not to mention a few others!! Why can't people be moderate? Now, if they had remarked that Poe's style is artificial, often; but *cui bono?* 'tis useless to attack prejudice.

x x x I did not answer your very kind note of Dec. 21st, and thank you for your cordial invitation to visit you in the summer at your cottage in N. Hampshire; (i. e.) if you succeeded in procuring such a retreat.

While it is impossible alas! to accept your affectionate invitation, because of a previous engagement, none the less, do I appreciate it.

But to return to my reason for not answering your previous communication, I was just in the midst of my "Sesqui Centennial Ode", and had to put aside all letter writing.

I mailed you a copy of this Poem from Savannah, while attending the Celebration, but since you make no allusion to having recd. it, I am sure it failed to reach you.

So, I enclose a copy, (which please return at your convenience).

Remember now you are not to write me in reply to this, but only to return the "ode" at your leisure.

I'll comprehend your silence.

We are sorry to hear that you have been such a sufferer; truly I can well sympathise with physical and nervous suffering.

Wiggin's Gale has not yet visited us, thank Heaven!

Our united love to yourself, and dear wife, and believe me,

Always Faithfully,
and affectionately,

Paul H. Hayne

[Stedman's "Emerson" appeared in the *Century Magazine* for April, 1883 (XXV, 872–86).

Doré illustrated and Stedman wrote an introduction for an edition of Poe's *The Raven* in 1883 (New York: Harper & Brothers).

In *French Poets and Novelists* (London, 1878, p. 76) Henry James called Poe's poetry "valueless" and added that "an enthusiasm for Poe is the mark of a decidedly primitive stage of reflection." (For this reference I am indebted to Killis Campbell's edition of Poe's poems.)

In *Fantasy and Passion* (Boston, 1878, pp. 182–3) Edgar Fawcett (1847–1904) grouped two poems, on Poe and Whittier, under the title "Antipodes" for the purpose of showing his dislike of the themes and moods of Poe and his preference for those of Whittier.

In the spring of 1883 Stedman bought a piece of land at New Castle, New Hampshire, and in that year built a summer home which he called "Kelp Rock."

Hayne wrote an ode for the sesquicentennial of the founding of Georgia, held at Savannah in February, 1883. See Hayne's letter to Tyler dated January 31, 1886 (No. 204).

The Charleston *News and Courier* for February and March, 1883, contains several items concerning a Professor Wiggins of Ottawa, Canada, who had been predicting severe storms and gales over Europe and America for the week of March 9–16.]

No. 154

PAUL HAMILTON HAYNE to EDMUND CLARENCE STEDMAN

[A part of the heading of this letter has been cut or torn off.]

Geo
15*th* Dec 1884.

My Dear Friend;

It is So long since I have heard from you, that I really feel as if we inhabited different worlds. But I have studiously followed your literary career; & every now & then Something turns up to prove that your genius is bright as ever.

For example those *two* little poems of yours in the last *"Harper"* upon the sweet witch of the 16*th*, & the *perhaps* sweeter witch of *the 19th Century*.

Something, a peculiarly delicate atmosphere, nearly indefinable, makes both pieces (me judice—) exceedingly charming.

Drop me *a line* when you can,— to say how you are now progressing in health, fortune, and literary prospects.

I see you have the English Poet, Mr *Edmund Gosse,* among you. My beloved friend, *Marstòn,* whose private letters *are marvels* of interest, & brilliant epistolary force, has often mentioned Gosse in a very Cordial way. I trust his visit to America may prove both profitable & pleasant.

The purpose of this little "screed" is to discover how you are in every [?] particular concerning your welfare, & to remind you that I have not forgotten nor ever *can* forget your kindness to me, when I was ill in NY, some years ago.

With my wife's & son's best remembrances; & particular regards to Mrs Stedman,

Ever Faithfully

Paul H Hayne

[Written in the margin and at the top of the last page of the letter:]

Do you ever hear from Swinburne? I rec*d* a long letter recently, in which he informs me *(entre nous)* that *Byron* was the most execrable *versifier* on the face of the earth—, did'nt know how to *scan;* in fact, that thousands of his lines are *unscannable.* A little overdrawn, this.

[Stedman's "Witchcraft, 1692–1884" appeared in *Harper's New Monthly Magazine* for December, 1884 (LXX, 102).

Stedman and Edmund Gosse (1849–1928) were mutual admirers and had been in correspondence as early as 1875. At the time of this letter Gosse had completed a lecture tour in the United States and had been offered and had declined a professorship at Harvard.]

No. 155

PAUL HAMILTON HAYNE to EDMUND CLARENCE STEDMAN

"Copse Hill," Feb 6th 1885

My Dear Stedman;

I was *truly* pleased to receive your cordial letter of the 24*th* ult. It is the *best* literary news I have heard for some time, the intelligence you give me of your *great* work, (I *know* it will be a great work), upon *"The Poetry of America"* being ready for the printing at least, next fall!—

Of course I comprehend how *profoundly* your every mental energy must be concentrated upon a performance demanding *such* conscientious care.

How you manage, with your *daily* business duties, involving "work on your feet down town" for many hours, to stick to your desk at night until 1 or 2 o'clock P. M. is more than I can understand. All I know is, it is *very* wrong; *suicidal* in fact! You may feel well enough under the tremendous pressure for a certain time; but *continue* it, and as sure as *Fate*, your friends one morning will be shocked by some such paragraph as this; — "Was taken suddenly ill in his office (at such or such an hour), Mr E. C. Stedman. Removed home. Effusion of blood upon the brain &c", and need I tell the rest.?

If I did not entertain a *real affection* for you, Should I dare to obtrude this warning?—

For myself, I am verily, a chronic Invalid, & I have had, moreover, "many illnesses," as you say, but I take care of my health to this extent; (*viz*) I never fail to Secure from *8 to 10 hours of sleep;* It is *Sleep* that *builds us* up; aye! more completely than any conceivable simulant[*sic*], &c!.

But you restless, active, indomitable *Northern* men, *will* *ignore* the necessity of healthful rest. See, the consequences in death rates & . . alas! . . lunatic asylums! x x x Yes, I have remarked the enthusiastic & lavish welcome accorded to Mr *Edmund Gosse*. He is an author of whom I know little; but *that little* in prose & verse has interested & pleased me. His own account of the attention paid him in this Country is certainly *manly & modest*.

x x x I was *prepared* to hear you say, that you disagreed with Swinburne's estimate of Byron's genius, *"toto cäelo"!* How *could* it have been otherwise?— Swinburne goes *entirely* too far. To comment upon *palpable faults* is *one* thing; to deny B—, *on the other* hand all *imagination, & all music*, is— —well!— Superlative *nonsense!*

Did I tell you that in his last letter to me, *Swinburne*
actually defied me, or any body else to *scan* this line of one
among Byron's loveliest lyrics,

> *"In the wild waste there still is a tree!"*

—I scanned it, but have heard nothing since!

You are *staying*, it seems, in a part of Mrs B. Taylor's
house. Please tell me, has Mrs Taylor come back from
Europe?. She was recruiting, I know, at *Gotha*, during the
latter summer, & autumn. Should she have returned, do give
our love, & *best* wishes, (my wife's, & mine), to that dear,
good lady.

I met her but *once* personally, yet she made a *powerful*
impression upon my mind;— as a woman of singular dignity,
self-restraint,— and depth of nature.

Her biography of her husband is a *model* of its kind. x x x
When you have emancipated yourself from the thralldom of
"prose-work," & have Some "golden leisures", I presume you
will allow the Muses to woo you once more?—

Ah! *what consolation* on this sad, weary, Earth *can* equal
the consolatory Sweetness which comes with the pure immortal tenderness of *one's* faithful *Muse?*

Without *her* help, I would *long long* ago have gone to *"join
the majority"!*

— x x   Pending the Inauguration of *Cleveland*, what a hurly-
burly of politics we are having! . . . You will deem me
an exceedingly heterodox individual., no doubt, but *Stedman*,
the longer I live the *less* do I believe in (so-called) Republican Institutions.

Vox Populi Vox Dei.

> *Once*, on a donkey heaven's miraculous choice
> Wise speech bestowed beyond the brute-born masses;
> *Now, is* it *heaven* that gives *such* potent voice
> Not to *one* Balaam's ass, but . . *countless asses?*

———. .———

— The world is in a lovely condition is'nt it?— as regards
nationalities?— What with Russian *Nihilists*, and Irish Dynamiters, *who* can guess what a day may bring forth?—

Perhaps, the trouble & pother of it all,— the fuss & fury of our miserable little planet, (a mere *speck* in the immensities of Space), may be summarily disposed of, sooner than we *could expect!!*

Newton's planet of *1682*, which *almost* fell into the sun, *two* centuries ago, is to re-appear *astronomers* Say, *Soon;* and *this* time, we may *all indeed* be *done* for!—

After *coquetting* with innumerable Male Planets, from Neptune to Sirius, and far beyond the constellation, *Hercules*, this Madame with the fiery tale, this lawless Messalina of the partially revealed *"Cosmos,"* has only to drop into the *arms of the Sun*, raise his heat by a few thousand degrees, and *presto!*— how suddenly & completely we shall vanish!

x x My wife begs to be cordially remembered to Mrs Stedman & yourself. We both *remember gratefully* your consideration for us, when I was ill in N. York, & Mrs Hayne *still* preserves the little basket you sent her with flowers on the morning of our *departure.*

With reference to my address, I don't wonder you failed to *decipher* it. 'Twas penned in great haste, at a way-Station;— My *Safe* address is always,

P O Box 275, Augusta
Georgia.

Write *only when perfectly convenient.* I shall hold no ceremony with you; nor expect ceremony on *your part.*

Always Faithfully & Cordially

Paul H Hayne.

[On another page but apparently in the letter above:]

Is this trifle *too extravagant?*
An aged *wind* sighed up the desolate hill,
A pauper *wind*, disowned of all its kin;
Shook the closed door, and moaned outside the Sill,
"Open kind Hearts! ah, let me *die within!*"

[Stedman's *Poets of America* was published in Boston and New York in 1885 by Houghton, Mifflin and Company.

The quotation from Byron is line 46 of "Stanzas to Augusta" (1816). The word "wild" should be "wide."

Bayard Taylor's second wife was Marie Hansen, of 'Gotha, Germany, daughter of Peter Andreas Hansen, a distinguished astronomer. She and Taylor were married in 1857. Hayne must have met her during his trip to the North in 1879, for she and Taylor were abroad when Hayne visited the North in 1873. In 1884 she and Horace E. Scudder brought out *Life and Letters of Bayard Taylor*, 2 vols. (Boston: Houghton-Mifflin).

Hayne's references to Russian Nihilists, Irish dynamiters, and Newton's planet are echoes of his reading in newspapers and magazines. For instance, the Charleston *News and Courier* for January 1, 1885, had a long article entitled "The Nihilists of Russia" and another item appeared in the issue for January 27. The same paper had numerous items (*e. g.*, in the issues for January 26, 27, 28, 29, and 31 and February 3 and 4, 1885) on the dynamiters. Professor Richard A. Proctor, English astronomer, was making a lecture tour in the United States, and at the time of this letter had been delivering a series of lectures in Charleston. In one lecture he dealt with the sun and in another he discussed "Comets and Falling Stars." Of course in Hayne's day people were more excited than they are today about the possibility of a collision between the earth and some shooting star.

Messalina, which appellation Hayne applies to the flirtatious planet, was the name of the notorious third wife of Claudius I (B. C. 10–A. D. 54), Roman emperor.]

No. 156

PAUL HAMILTON HAYNE to [ARTHUR GRIFFIN STEDMAN?]

"Copse Hill" June 16*th*
1885

My Dear Mr Stedman;

Your note of the 12*th* reached me last *evng*. It affords me pleasure to give your Father the desired information about Ticknor. His middle name was a rather odd one, *viz*, *Orrery*. (Francis *Orrery* Ticknor).

'Tis pleasant news you give me of your Father's progress in his great work. Simple justice declares that no man in America could perform *such* a task (and a most difficult, delicate task it is), with so consummate a tact, and such thoughtful power.

Of course he cannot satisfy everybody. Far from it. An angel from highest heaven, writing with the *subtlety* of celestial intelligence, could not do *this*.

— I respond heartily to your expressions of good will, and with sincere remembrances to your household, believe me

Faithfully

Paul H Hayne.

[I believe this letter was written to Stedman's younger son, Arthur Griffin (1859–1908), because Laura Stedman and George M. Gould (*op. cit.*) imply that Stedman and his elder son, Frederick Stuart, were estranged from 1883 until about 1901. (The estrangement seems to have been connected with Fred's mismanagement of his father's brokerage business in 1883.)

I do not know what authority Hayne had for his spelling of Ticknor's second name. Ticknor's granddaughter spelled it *Orray* (*The Poems of Francis Orray Ticknor*, ed. by Michelle Cutliff Ticknor, New York and Washington: The Neale Publishing Company, 1911).]

No. 157

WILLIAM HAMILTON HAYNE to ARTHUR GRIFFIN STEDMAN

Grovetown, Columbia Co. Ga.

Nov. 14*th* 1888.

Dear Mr Stedman: —

I have just received your courteous note of the 10*th* inst. and hasten to comply with the request contained in it.

I send you, by to-day's mail, the last photograph taken of my father, (Dec. 1885) which please keep carefully, and return promptly, according to promise, when the wood-cut has been made for "A Library of American Literature".

Please acknowledge the arrival of the photograph, and believe me, with kind regards for your father,

Very Sincerely Yours

William H. Hayne

[*A Library of American Literature, from the Earliest Settlement to the Present Time*, compiled and edited by Edmund Clarence Stedman and Ellen Mackay Hutchinson, with biographical sketches of the authors included by Arthur Stedman, 11 vols., was published in New York by C. L. Webster & Company, 1889–90. Vol. VIII contains a full-page portrait of Hayne (opposite p. 462) and these poems of his (pp. 461–66): "Vicksburg," "A Dream of the South Winds," "Love's Autumn," "Fate, or God?" "A Little While I Fain Would Linger Yet," and "In Harbor."]

No. 158

WILLIAM HAMILTON HAYNE to EDMUND CLARENCE STEDMAN

[Postal Card]

Copse Hill, Ga. Jan. 17*th*
1889.

Dear Mr Stedman:—

I thank you sincerely for the several proofs from the photograph of father, accompanying its return. I am sorry, however, that neither mother nor myself think the reproduction of the photo. a good likeness, and we cannot but regret that it will go into so fine a work as yours.

With regards for your wife, son, and self, and best wishes, I am

Very Sincerely Yours

W. H. Hayne

No. 159

WILLIAM HAMILTON HAYNE to ARTHUR GRIFFIN STEDMAN

Grovetown, Columbia Co. Ga.
Jan. 18*th* 1889.

Dear Mr Stedman:—

I had just written a message of thanks to your father, and mailed it, when your letter arrived: it came too late, of course, for me to allude to it on my card, but I hasten to answer it promptly.

I am very much obliged to your father and yourself for attending to the incorrectly printed lines in my father's poems; and I appreciate your father's thoughtfulness in changing the punctuation referred to.

I wish I could reply to your question concerning the copyright of Henry Timrod's poems satisfactorily, but I cannot: I will, however, tell you all I know on the subject. Father had no share in the copyright, and only edited the poems, and wrote the memoir, as "a labor of love."

I don't think Mrs Timrod controlled the copyright, although I am sure she received something from the sale of the book. In 1873— when I was a lad— father and myself saw Mrs Timrod in Washington, where she had a position in the Treasury Department; but not very long afterwards father lost sight of her, and his subsequent inquiries did not reveal her whereabouts. Mr Timrod's sister is dead, and if either of his nieces are [sic] living I do not know what has become of them; so I think your best plan, under the circumstances, is to search for the successors of E. J. Hale & Son.

I sincerely hope the result of such a search will prove satisfactory, and regret very much that I can't give you the needed information.

With kind regards for your father, mother, and self, believe me

Very Sincerely Yours

William H. Hayne

[The 1873 edition of Timrod's poems, for which Hayne wrote a memoir of his friend, was "entered" by E. J. Hale & Son, who published the volume.

On February 16, 1864, in Columbia, South Carolina, Timrod married Katie Goodwin, an English girl, whose brother, George Goodwin, had married Timrod's sister, Emily. George died on September 6, 1864, and Timrod, who was too otherworldly to take care of himself properly, found himself responsible for the support of two families, under circumstances which might have crushed almost any man. Timrod died October 7, 1867. In the late 1860's the poet's widow and widowed sister were taking in boarders. In the early 1870's they were in Washington, where Emily died of cancer and Katie worked in the Treasury Department. Nothing much is known of her thereafter except that later she married a man named Lloyd and died in 1913. (For these and other details see Jay B. Hubbell, *The Last Years of Henry Timrod 1864–1867*, Duke University Press, 1941.)

Written on the back of the preceding letter, probably by Arthur Stedman:

"Write him that it was re-photographed from the photo *directly* on the *block*—thus it *must* be a faithful reproduction—that we saw it was different from the previous Engravings (in Dibble's[?] book, in the "Poems" &c) but thought it equally characteristic in *its own way*."]

No. 160

WILLIAM HAMILTON HAYNE to EDMUND CLARENCE STEDMAN

Summerville,
Augusta, Ga.
July 22*nd* 1899

My dear Mr Stedman:—

I greatly appreciate your son's cordial letter, and the great compliment you pay me, through him, in inviting me to a place in "An American Anthology." A collection of poetry edited by you has Unique Value (this is not flattery, but an honest tribute to your critical genius) and I shall be more than glad to fill a small space in the book. I enclose a number of poems of more recent date than my volume of "Sylvan Lyrics," and my object in sending so many is simply to give you full freedom of selection, and not to embarrass you by *quantity versus quality*. If you are pleased with a poem, here and there, I shall be more than satisfied. With regard to the more important work of my father, I shall, of course, be delighted for you to use any of the poems in his book. Would you like to see two or three of his lyrics (in my judgment, among his best) published since the edition of 1882?

I sincerely hope that your illness will soon pass away, and you have my very best wishes for a full renewal of health and spirits. Pardon this hurried letter, and believe me, with regards for your wife and son,

Cordially yours,

W. H. Hayne

[*An American Anthology 1787–1900*, edited by Edmund Clarence Stedman, was published in Boston and New York by Houghton, Mifflin and Company in 1900. It contains these poems by Paul Hayne (pp. 317–20): "Aspects of the Pines," "Vicksburg," "Between the Sunken Sun and the New Moon," "A Storm in the Distance," "The Rose and Thorn," "A Little While I Fain Would Linger Yet," and "In Harbor." It also contains these poems by William Hamilton Hayne (pp. 612–3): "The Southern Snow-Bird," "To a Cherokee Rose," "Quatrains" (four of them), "A Cyclone at Sea," "'Sleep and His Brother Death,'" and "The Yule Log."

William H. Hayne's *Sylvan Lyrics and Other Verses* was published in New York by Frederick A. Stokes Company in 1893.]

No: 161

WILLIAM HAMILTON HAYNE to MARIE HOWLAND

Private

Summerville,
Augusta, Ga.
Feb. 16*th* 1897

Mr*s* Marie Howland.
Dear Madam:—

After an absence of nearly two months from Augusta, I returned to find your letter of Feb. 2*nd* awaiting me. I feel some embarassment [*sic*] in replying to it, while I deeply appreciate the tenderness you feel for the memory of my unfortunate relative, who was known and loved by you, under the name of Ada Clare. She was my grandmother Hayne's niece, and her real name was Ada McElhenney. Before I was born, she left her family and friends in Charleston S. C; under the spell of an infatuation for a distinguished musician; and I have always heard that her after life was, in many respects, sad and deplorable. My father saw her in New York in 1873;

and urged her to return south, and share our home; but she would not be persuaded. We afterwards heard of her death (rumor said it was due to the bite of her pet dog, who had become mad) in 1874. Since that time, I have passed through a triple sorrow in the deaths of my grandmother and my parents; and am "the last left" of my immediate family. Poor cousin Ada, while talented, was always eccentric and self-willed; and her erratic Conduct was a great grief to my grandmother and father. Cousin Ada's parents and brother are dead; and I do not know her married sister's address,— or even if she is living. She formerly lived in New York; but I think she ceased corresponding with my grandmother. I am very glad to know of your connection by marriage to cousin Ada; and of your kind guardianship of her grave. Of course I never knew her; but I thank you warmly for the love and regard you entertain for my relative, who has passed— let us hope— "to where beyond these voices there is peace." In view, however, of your real affection for her, do you think a memoir would be the service to her memory that you wish? Her Bohemian life in New York was well known to many, and I fear a full biography of her would only awaken criticism and comment, without accomplishing any lasting good. Pardon my frankness, which arises from the worthiest of motives. Of course the final decision in this matter must rest with you; but it seems best for all parties concerned that the facts of Cousin Ada's life (some of the facts, I mean) should be kept apart from public comment. Do not misunderstand me: I would be untrue to my family and my heart, if I did not feel tender pity for poor Cousin Ada's memory, although I had no opportunity to share your personal affection for her.

With earnest thanks for your letter, and best wishes for your welfare, believe me

Cordially yours,

William H. Hayne

[Mrs. Marie Howland, writer and reformer, was the widow of the socialist Edward Howland (1832–1890). He was born in Charleston, South Carolina, and died in Mexico.

For information about Ada Clare see the notes following Hayne's first letter to R. H. Stoddard (No. 1).

I do not know what the family connection between Ada Clare and Mrs. Howland was. Ada Clare and Edward Howland were natives of Charleston, and it may be that they were related. On the other hand, Ada Clare was married to J. F. Noyes, an actor, at the time of her death. It might be that he was related to Mrs. Howland.

Mary Middleton Michel Hayne was born January 11, 1831, and died January 28, 1892. She was buried in Augusta by the side of her poet husband. The large monument at the graves was erected by the Hayne Circle of Augusta. This information was sent to me (in a letter dated February 4, 1944) by Mrs. Cecilia B. Barrett of Augusta, Mrs. Hayne's niece.]

XI. LIBRARY OF CORNELL UNIVERSITY
(NOS. 162–205)

PAUL HAMILTON HAYNE to MOSES COIT TYLER

My *address* is Col *Paul H. Hayne, P O Box 635, Augusta Ga*

Augusta, Georgia,
April 8th 1873:

D'r Sir;

I had *just* despatched a note to Mr H., W Beecher, (the chief Ed: I believe, of your paper?) asking him — if convenient — to have some copies of *"The Christian Union"* — containing the *Timrod* notice — sent me —, when yours of the *4th* inst: was placed in my hands.

Many thanks for your kind attention!

Of course, I shall read with *peculiar interest* your critique on my *friend's* poems, when it arrives. The little book has been strangely successful; thanks to a sad, simple tale, sadly & simply told, and to the unquestionable beauty of the verses now first presented to the Public at large— —xxx In regard to myself, I shall gladly contribute now & then, to *"The Christian Union"*, since my *poverty* is *great* — (*not* many *shades lighter* in fact at certain *unlucky* seasons, than the poverty of poor Timrod himself!)—, and on the pen I rely for bread. The *war* it was that ruined me! Why should I feel ashamed to acknowledge the whole truth?

Such misfortunes bring no *disgrace!* however keen the suffering, & privation.

I enclose a poem for your examination, called *"Midsummer in the South"*; which may suit your columns, for aught I know!

It is a *true* picture I am assured, and with the artistic management of the *verse* &c, I took much pains. For poems of this class, and length, I receive usually between *25*, & — *30 dollars;* but the remuneration, (*should* the price [piece?] prove acceptable), I leave to the *'Edt's judgement* —

If you henceforth send me a copy of your *"Christian Union"* regularly, I can often notice the paper in the various

Southern journals for which I write and thus increase its circulation.

Most Respectfully

Paul H. Hayne

(P O Box 635

Augusta

Geo)

(P. S) The 4*th line* of my Poem I'm doubtful about[;] whether *"half-articulated* thought", or, "unimaginable *thought"* be the better I can't tell. Let the Ed judge!

[The originals of all the letters in this group are preserved in the Moses Coit Tyler Collection in the Library of Cornell University. In reply to my letter of inquiry, Professor Frederick C. Prescott wrote me concerning the letters in October, 1940. At his suggestion, I then applied to Dr. Otto Kinkeldey, Librarian at Cornell University, for permission to secure copies for publication. Dr. Kinkeldey not only secured for me permission to publish the letters but he employed for me a typist (Miss J. Fern Corp), supervised the copying, and carefully checked the copies with the original letters. It is a pleasure to express my gratitude for his generosity and courtesy.

Moses Coit Tyler (1835–1900), historian, critic, college professor, was professor of rhetoric and English literature at the University of Michigan (1867–1873, 1874–1881), literary editor of the *Christian Union* (1873–1874), and professor of American history at Cornell University (1881–1900). Among his numerous writings the best are *A History of American Literature during the Colonial Time, 1607–1765* (2 vols., 1878); *Patrick Henry* (1887); *The Literary History of the American Revolution 1763–1783* (2 vols., 1897); and *Three Men of Letters* (1895). See Howard Mumford Jones's sketch of Tyler in *D. A. B.* and his *The Life of Moses Coit Tyler*, Ann Arbor: The University of Michigan Press, 1933.

The correspondence between Hayne and Tyler began in 1873 as a result of Tyler's review of♦Hayne's edition of Timrod's poems and continued until 1886, the year of Hayne's death.

The *Christian Union*, New York weekly, began in 1870. Tyler was literary editor from February, 1873, until September, 1874. Henry Ward Beecher (1813–1887), pulpit orator, lecturer, author, was editor-in-chief. Oliver Johnson was office editor. Tyler's position was uncomfortable because subordinate to those of Beecher and Johnson. His name was not signed to any of his articles or reviews. These annoyances and the scandals of Beecher (referred to later in these letters) drove Tyler back to his professorial chair after a year and a half.

The Poems of Henry Timrod, edited, with a sketch of Timrod's life, by Hayne, was published in New York by E. J. Hale & Son in 1873. Hayne dated the preface to a "second edition" March, 1873.

Tyler's review of the book appeared in the *Christian Union* for March 19, 1873. In the issue of May 7, 1873, he reviewed the second edition, which contained additional poems.

I find these poems by Hayne in the *Christian Union* for 1873 and 1874:

"Midsummer in the South," May 14, 1873 (VII, 382)

"Love's Caprice. A Dramatic Fragment," June 25, 1873 (VII, 499)

"Le Petite Duchesse," August 6, 1873 (VIII, 113)

"Grief—Its Universality. A Dramatic Fragment," December 31, 1873 (VIII, 536)

"Eternal Separation," January 7, 1874 (IX, 3)

"The Dryad in the Laurel," January 21, 1874 (IX, 43)

"Calm Under Tumult," March 4, 1874 (IX, 161)

"Sonnet. [Written on a stormy Christmas night (1873)]," March 11, 1874 (IX, 182)

"William Cullen Bryant," April 8, 1874 (IX, 261)

"Sonnet. Inscribed to the author of 'Snow-Bound' . . .," May 13, 1874 (IX, 365)

"By the Grave of Henry Timrod," June 10, 1874 (IX, 452)

"Disenchanted," July 1, 1874 (IX, 509)

"A New Version of Why the Robin's Breast Is Red," July 29, 1874 (X, 67)

"Development in Repose," November 4, 1874 (X, 344)

"The South-East Rain (In Autumn)," November 25, 1874 (X, 409)

"The Imprisoned Sea-Winds," December 16, 1874 (X, 485)

The poem for which Hayne hoped to receive from twenty-five to thirty dollars contained eighty-five lines. Later he revised it (*Complete Edition*, pp. 192–3) and cut it down to seventy-three lines.

Of the two wordings mentioned in the postscript, the editor chose "unimaginable thought," which Hayne retained in *Complete Edition*.]

No. 163

PAUL HAMILTON HAYNE to MOSES COIT TYLER

"Copse Hill", Central Geo R Road:
(16 *miles from Augusta*)
Wed: morning, April 9th
(1873)

My Dear Sir;

— Just after despatching my note of yesterday, together with *"Mss"* of a poem I have offered to *"The Christian*

Union",— I recd a copy of your paper containing the *Timrod* criticism.

Its perusal has afforded me *real*, & *profound* pleasure. In the first place, I appreciate keenly the *generous spirit* which dictated, and which breathes all through this review,— while respecting the artistic insight & discernment that are no less conspicuous!

None of the scores of notices which *T*s little vo*l* (to our great *delight*, & surprise)—, has called forth all over the the [*sic*] Country, surpass, if indeed any of them *equal* your beautiful critique.

In saying this, believe me I am not writing *conventionally!* — In regard to my life of the *Poet* — who was dearer to me than a *brother*—, allow me to observe, that no "*forethought* of *fine writing*" ever for an instant, passed thro my brain, as I — *painfully*, *laboriously*, suffering from a sick *heart*, and a sick *body*—, composed the pages of that sad biography. The *Past*, with all its bitterness, its sorrows, its despair—, *too vividly* pressed upon me — to admit of any attention being paid to the special graces of *style*.

If *one* or *two* paragraphs therefore, should read as if *purposely* decked with needless imagery &c&c, they were after all, but the *natural* expression of emotions, or sentiments aroused by some exceptional incident, or by peculiar & exciting surroundings.

But when you say, "*that I have* "really helped the reader to see what manner of man Timrod was", you say enough to satisfy me; for, it was my main purpose to do, just what, it is here affirmed, I have succeeded in *accomplishing*.

I must not longer detain you.

With renewed thanks for your kindness,

I am Faithfully yr's

Paul H Hayne.
P O. *Box 635*
Augusta (Geo)

P. S. Could you have a *few extra* copies of the paper with your critique mailed to my Augusta address? Of course, I would *pay for* them!

[Tyler's review of Hayne's edition of Timrod's poems is entitled "The Poems of Henry Timrod," *Christian Union*, VII (March 19, 1873), 228. I quote from it as follows:

"He had genius and a life of sorrow—this Southland poet . . .; here, in reality, was one of nature's singers, and this dainty little book . . . is an addition. by no means despicable, to the beauty and the wisdom of our national literature. . .

"This is the bald outline of his story. It is full of heroism, tenderness, and heart-break. . . . What horizons of vision he would have had, what reaches of art and of power he would have attained, had his outward life been liberal—like that of Longfellow or of Tennyson, for example— we can but sadly dream.

"The first seventy pages of this book are taken up by Mr. Paul H. Hayne's sketch of the poet's life, and we do not begrudge that use of them. Mr. Hayne might have improved his sketch, we think, by studiously recasting it. Moreover, some of his sentences, perhaps, intimate a little too frankly the forethought of fine writing. Nevertheless, he really helps us to see what manner of man the poet was. In fact, he helps us to like the poet, and himself, too. . . . It may be said of Henry Timrod that there were two currents of intense feeling which flowed through his life; the one, being his love for the lady who became his wife; and the other, his love for the South. . . .

"But every reader of this book will see, we think, that its author's power is at its highest when awakened by the energy of his patriotism. . . . It is fortunate for Henry Timrod's Northern recognition, that the publication of his poems has been delayed until now, when our deliverance from the perils and the furies of the terrific strife enables us to read these war-lyrics for their poetry, . . . and it is touching, as well as instructive, now to read these tremendous outbursts of enthusiasm, hope, exultation and despair. . . . We trust that we have said enough of this noble-hearted and sorrow-smitten man . . . to convince our readers that here is a poet whom they cannot afford to overlook. In life and in politics he was our enemy; but in death and in poetry we have no controversy with him, and for his memory only love and grief and praise."]

No. 164

PAUL HAMILTON HAYNE to MOSES COIT TYLER

(Private)
Augusta, Georgia,
Wed: April 30th, 1873.

D'r Sir;

Please don't suppose, for *one* moment—, that I wish to *annoy*, or trouble you—: but can you drop me a line to say, whether a *poem*, entitled, *"Midsummer in the South"*, which I offered to your paper, (& mailed ab't a *month* ago), has reached its *destination?*

If so, what is its fate, (i. e.) have the Edt's *accepted*, or *rejected* it?

In the *latter* case, I would beg you to *return* the *"Mss"* by *mail*.

Of course, I'll *remit* the amount of postage *money*, as soon as I know what it *is*. x x x If you kindly *continue* to send me copies of the *"C. Union"*, I'll do my *best* to serve the interests of the *"weekly"* by discriminating *"notices"* in the various *journals*, for which I have éngaged to *write*.

Should *"Midsummer in the South"* please y'r Edt's, I have left the am't of the *"honorarium"* wholly to *their* judgment.

> In haste,
> but Most Truly and Respectfully,
>
> > *Paul H Hayne*
> > *P O Box 635, Augusta Ga*

No. 165

PAUL HAMILTON HAYNE to MOSES COIT TYLER

> *"Copse Hill"*,
> *"Central Geo R. Road"*
> *Friday 9th May 1873:*

My Dear Sir;

I rec*d* your very courteous note yesterday.

Of course I am glad and *honored* too, at the good news ab't my poem. Only, I fear that the corrections I enclosed will reach you *too late!*

In regard to the publication of the poem, allow me *to withdraw the request contained in my last communication*.

If not issued already, why, you can print the verses when you choose, at your own convenience.

T'will be unlucky should the *alterations* not arrive in due season,— for by some odd mistake on my part, a whole line (existing in the first rude copy of the piece)— has been *omitted*, between the picture of the "huge white clouds", some represented as

> "Dumb Babels, with Ethereal stairs,
> Scaling the vast height, *unawares*
> What spirit &c"—

Now between the 1*st* & 2*nd* of these lines which *seem* to flow into each other, *another line came* in, which being lost, I had to re-compose the passage, as you'll perceive, when the corrections come.

As the lines *now* stand, I am made to invest inanimate objects, like the *tower-tall* Clouds, with *vitality*, & perception, expressed in the term *"unawares &c"*

Pardon my dwelling on a comparative trifle. But as you liked the poem, generally, I wanted you to comprehend how this mistake *occurred!*

Thanks for *"The Christian Union"*, copies of which now reach me regularly. I am sincerely pleased with the paper—; *especially* with your *critical department*. As an example of wise critical insight, most happily expressed, I would mention your review of *"Lars"*. That fine story of *Taylor's*, you have understood more fully than *most*, and with every line of your notice I agree — cordially agree.

Thanks too, for your 2*nd* and *truly generous* allusion to Timrod and his vo*l*. I cannot forget *such kindness;*— nor can *Mrs* Timrod, or any of the dead *Poet's* friends—

Believe me your faithful & Obliged
Servant

Paul H Hayne

P O Box 635, *Augusta*, Ga

P. S. When published, would you kindly mail me *some* extra *nos* of the *"C Union"* containing *"Midsummer in the South"?*

And, by the way, — as you courteously ask me to contribute again to your journal, in *prose*, or, verse; do allow me to make some inquiries.?

Do you object to articles, *half* biographical, half philosophical, with a *soupçon* of historic fact (or conjecture)— as, for instance, a paper on *"Cornelius Agrippa, & his Times"*, written briefly, but with care, & force?

Some rather *rare material* has come into my hands, touching this remarkable genius, still misunderstood, and I had thought of using it in the manner indicated.

Is the subject you think, *"caviare* to the general", as Hamlet says?—

P. H. H.

[Written lengthwise in the margin on the first page of the letter:]

— It is *not* pleasant to me to be *forced* to *sell* my verses, but *dear* sir — in *confidence* — I must confess that the war has *ruined!*— me;— I find it hard — almost *impossible* at times —, to *get on at* all!

At my doors, as at poor *Timrod's* the wolf often growls *terribly* &c!!

[Hayne's reference to corrections and a request in his last communication suggests the possibility either that he wrote a letter between April 30 and May 9 or that a separate slip of paper was enclosed in the letter of April 30.

The quoted passage reads thus in the *Christian Union* and in *Complete Edition* (p. 192):

> "Dumb Babels, with ethereal stairs
> Scaling the vast height—unawares
> What mocking spirit. . . ."

H. M. Jones says (*The Life of Moses Coit Tyler*, p. 147): "Besides writing occasional editorials, he [Tyler] originated two regular departments, 'The Outlook' . . . and 'Books and Authors' . . . ."

Bayard Taylor's *Lars* is reviewed in the *Christian Union* for May 7, 1873 (VII, 367–8).

In the same issue appeared Tyler's second "truly generous" allusion to Timrod (VII, 368), from which I quote:

"It is pleasant to learn that the first edition of *The Poems of Henry Timrod* has had a rapid sale; and that, in the preparation of a second edition, which is just published, the editor, Col. Paul H. Hayne, has been encouraged to insert some 'Additional Poems.' These consist of Timrod's Ode sung at the decoration of the graves of the Confederate dead at Magnolia Cemetery, Charleston, in 1867, together with several fine poems. . . .

"We think that Col. Hayne is not mistaken in believing that by the 'Additional Poems' he has 'increased the interest of the volume.' Not only because it confers benefit upon the widow of the poet, but likewise for the good token it implies of kindly and magnanimous thoughts between brethren lately at strife, do we rejoice in the swift success of these poems of the dead Laureate of the Confederacy."

Henricus Cornelius Agrippa (1486–1535), of Nettesheim, was a German scholar and physician who wrote on the occult sciences. For a discussion of Cornelius Agrippa by way of an extended review of Henry Morley's *The Life of Henry Cornelius Agrippa Von Netteisheim, Doctor and Knight, commonly known as a Magician* (London: Chapman & Hall, 1859) see *Russell's Magazine*, V, 161 ff. The article is probably Hayne's.]

No. 166

PAUL HAMILTON HAYNE to MOSES COIT TYLER

Address me always at P. O Box 635, *Augusta Geo*

*"Copse Hill", "Central Geo
R Rôad":
(16 miles from Augusta)
Friday morning, May 16th 1873*

My Dear Sir;

Your very *cordial* note of the 11*th*, I recd yesterday. Let me thank you for the warm, encouraging terms in which you write.

At the South, *literary* men — especially the *very very few* who dare make *Literature* a *profession*—, are strangely, and *painfully* isolated. For *years past*, this has been the case, and for years *to come*, I suppose, the same condition of things will prevail.

Every So Scholar or *writer* of any note has had reason to complain of it.

If we go back to the time of that *magnificent genius*, and profound scholar, *Hugh .S. Légare*—, (believe me! these words *are not* extravagant!)—, we find that despite *Légare's practical vim & tact*, which *aided* by his information & native talents, carried him from a high position at the Charleston Bar, up to the *Attorney Generalship* of the *U. States* —,— he nevertheless, complained of the *drawback* to advancement, and *local recognition*, which his *literary fame*, in *earlier* life—, proved to be—; and so it was with Gilmore Simms, with Kennedy, with Pendleton Cooke, with Poe, and lastly, with our poor friend *Timrod!*—

These *So* communities, intelligent in other *respects*, actually look down upon the *Litteratéur*, with a *species of scorn*, as a half crazed enthusiast, having no firm, wholesome root in the soil of social existence —;— and *therefore* is it a *particularly* grateful thing when a man of *your repute* Stretches — as it were — a kind hand thro the darkness, and greets a brother author struggling here in the bitter "*Slough of Despond*".

You say that my poem on "*Midsummer*" is "*exquisite*". Such a verdict is more encouraging than, perhaps, you dream of.

But please allow me to ask your *critical* opinion—, your *perfectly frank critical* opinion, in reference to the *corrections* which came too late. *Are* they in your judgment, *improvements*, or *not?*—

They refer — you perceive, *firstly*, to the term "*unawares*" as applied to an *inanimate* object —; and *secondly*, to the concluding lines of the Poem, which (as *printed*) embody an idea, or rather, *Personification*, of perhaps, too *bold* a nature. *Some* in fact, would call it in the highest degree, *fantastic, strained, unnatural!!*—

But, I want *your opinion!!*—

The mention of *Hugh Légaré's* name suggests to me this question;— would you not like for "*the Christian Union*", a sketch of the life, character, genius, and works of *that* remarkable man, so little — comparatively — known at the *North*, and yet so *deserving* appreciation?—

Years ago I published a somewhat Elaborate *biography* of him in the pages of a "*So Quarterly*", (which had *little circulation*)—, and from that "*Life*" I could gather the *material* of *another article* to be composed in a *different*, and far more *popular style*.

I could divide this article into *two*, or even *three* numbers, to appear at *different* times;— or I could condense the facts and criticisms into a *single paper* of *no immoderate* length.

— *What* say you?—

Upon my honor, *Dear Sir*, I think such a paper might prove of considerable *interest*.—

And now, thanking you *again*, for your cordiality and kind feeling.

pray believe me

Yours Most Sincerely,

Paul H. Hayne.

P. . S. Could I venture to ask you for some *extra copies* of *"the Union"* containing my verses?—

By the way, I expect to visit N York in *June*. Of course, I shall make it a point to come to your office.

[It is possible that Lowell unintentionally did Hayne a disservice in his review of *Avolio* by suggesting that Southern authors had to work in an uncongenial atmosphere, though the thought was not a new one to Hayne. At any rate, Hayne seems to have brooded over the idea more than was good for him. In discussing "Literature in the South" *in Russell's Magazine* for August, 1859 (V, 385 ff.), Timrod had assigned two main reasons for the difficulties of Southern authors: "It is the settled conviction of the North that genius is indigenous there, and flourishes only in a Northern atmosphere. It is the equally firm conviction of the South that genius—literary genius, at least—is an exotic that will not flower on a Southern soil."

Hugh Swinton Legaré (1797–1843), William Gilmore Simms (1806–1870), Henry Timrod (1828–1867), and Hayne himself were leading writers of Charleston. Legaré, a distinguished lawyer, had served in the legislature, in Congress, as chargé d'affaires at Brussels, and as attorney general of South Carolina before President Tyler appointed him attorney general of the United States in 1841. John Pendleton Kennedy (1795–1870), the author of *Swallow Barn* and friend of Edgar Allan Poe (1809–1849), was a native of Maryland. Philip Pendleton Cooke (1816–1850), the elder brother of John Esten Cooke, was a Virginian.

Hayne's "Elaborate *biography*" of Legaré had appeared in Albert Taylor Bledsoe's *Southern Review* (Baltimore quarterly), January, 1870 (VII, 123–58). Cf. Hayne's *Lives of Robert Young Hayne and Hugh Swinton Legaré*, Charleston: Walker, Evans & Cogswell, 1878, and his sketches of the same two in the *Southern Bivouac*, New Series, I (September, 1885), 193–202.

Hayne and his son made the trip to New York and also visited Boston. He saw Tyler about six times and developed a warm personal friendship with him. He stopped in Baltimore in July, where he found Poe's grave still neglected, and he saw Timrod's widow in Washington. On his way home he passed through Charleston, where he visited John Russell at his famous bookstore, but found its glory departed (*Southern Bivouac*, I (November. 1885), 335).]

No. 167

PAUL HAMILTON HAYNE to MOSES COIT TYLER

Augusta, Feb: 8th 1874

My Dear Friend;

— That word so deeply *underscored*, is no conventional phrase. I c'ant help saying for the *2nd* or *3rd* time that I turn to *nobody* either *South or North*, with the confidence I feel towards *yourself*.

— Your candid eyes, your generous, courteous manner are (as it were), before me still; and I *will*, & *must* believe there is far *more* than *ordinary* sympathy between us!

Thanks for your note of the *4th* inst: Of course I comprehend how closely you *have* been, and *are* engaged; & *that* only makes me appreciate your communication the more keenly.

'Tis all right ab't the rejected "*Mss*". My *only* regret — touching the H. Coleridge essay, is, that .it did not seem to pay, in *part*, my debt to y'r journal. But "better luck next time!", — Meanwhile, if the chance offers, won't you try & *sell* it for me, to *any* paper or mag*e*, you may think of — together with the *two brief poems enclosed?* I am *awfully* "hard up", or I could'nt *dream* of thus troubling you. It is *the last time!*

Ab't the envelopes, a *thousand thanks!*

Some days ago, I *completed* the long poem, to which you allude. When properly *corrected*, I *do* think it may please you.

— In the "*Dryad*" (owing to *my own hasty cal[l]igraph*), there was some odd errors; but *none very bad*.

In haste, but Alway's yr's

Paul H. Hayne
(P O Box 635)

[Hayne underscored the word "Friend" three times.

A two-part article by Hayne entitled "Coleridge's Eldest Son" appeared in the *South-Atlantic* (Baltimore monthly) for March and July, 1880 (V. 208–17; VI. 2–11). He had dealt with the same subject at least twice before: see his "David Hartley Coleridge" in *Russell's Magazine* for February, 1859 (IV. 433–42) and "Hartley Coleridge" in *Scott's Monthly Magazine* (of Atlanta) for February, 1866 (I, 154–61).

Apparently the *Christian Union* had advanced Hayne one hundred dollars—possibly while he was in New York in 1873—with the understanding that it was to be paid in contributions. See the next letter.

"The Dryad in the Laurel" had appeared in the *Christian Union*, January 21, 1874 (IX, 43).]

No. 168

PAUL HAMILTON HAYNE to MOSES COIT TYLER

"Copse Hill", Ga. R Road:—
Thursday 26th Feb:
(1874)

My Dear Friend;

Five minutes ago, I had the great pleasure of receiving the p'c'k of envelopes, & paper which your generous nature induced you to send me as a present.

I value this gift *inexpressibly;* not merely because the "Stationery" was *needed,* but as a remembrance from one I *liked* especially when I first met him; and have learned to *love* since.

Of course the *knife* came also. 'Tis — to empl[o]y a ladie's phrase — a "perfect love" of a knife! the very thing I required to cut pencils, mend pens, (*sometimes* I use the quill pen), and to separate the pages of periodicals, not to mention many other good offices.

Thanks too, for the trouble you've taken to ascertain the precise pecuniary position in which I stand towards the "*C U*". It is as favorable as I could have expected.

You observe that the last *two* "Sonnets" I mailed you, you wd' like "*your Edt's to take*".

Do you mean a "*Sonnet*" (*written* on *Xmas night*), and a complimentary piece to Bryant? If so, by all means accept them. They'll go very near abolishing my debt, for if thus far I've paid $65.00 in *contributions*, why the *Sonnet* now in your hands —(accepted)— added to these two last poems, worth $10.00 a piece will amount to just $95.00, leaving a balance of $5.00 only for me to pay!

A good look out — that! Once freed from the forest of *debt*, you'll perceive how much *better* I shall write — Frankly (and *entré nous*), I have been by no means satisfied with the general literary character of the pieces hitherto sent you —;— but *wait* — have *patience!*— and — *nous Verrons!!*

Many a hearty laugh have I enjoyed over your employment of my random suggestion anent clerical quarrels, and the right way of settling them.

But your *own suggestion* of a *water-syringe* is the richest of *all!!*. *Apropos* of this, I am reminded of the strange duello which occurred between the famous dwarf, Henry Hudson, (celebrated by *Scott* in *"Peveril of the Peak"*), and and a young guardsman of Charles 1*st*! household. The latter (in ridicule of his tiny opponent), came to the ground with a long *syringe*:— but the furious Hudson, being really a person of birth and position—, stung him so severely with taunts, and sarcasms, that *Master Guardsman* had to take to his pistol, & was shot dead by the *Dwarf* at the very first pop!! The moral whereof, is plain. Let us not *despise the "day of small things!"*—

While upon this subject, I am tempted to relate an adventure of my *own;* which but *one human* being now living, *knows anything about. (I do it in the strictest confidence)*

In the year 1855,— *two* years after my marriage — I went with my wife, to spend the summer in *Marietta* (*Ga*).

A *military* school existed at that period in the town, well attended, and remarkably prosperous. Every *Saturday*, the Students, (having holiday), would frequent the village, and especially the *one* Billiard room, of which it could boast. *Two* tables only were arranged in the establishment.

Well! I had engaged the best of these tables for a few hour's [*sic*] play with a friend, upon a certain August morning; and we had just begun our game, when a couple of Students (from the Military Academy), the *eldest* 20, or 21,— came boisterously in, and stopped opposite our table. The elder, a son of the wealthiest Planter in No East Georgia, and a most conceited, overbearing intolerable puppy—, said in a hectoring tone, that the table we were playing on, had always been given to *him*, and that he wished we would be quick with our game.. Being myself hardly *twenty four*, and of an impetuous temper, — I replied that I had engaged the table for 3 hours from the Proprietor, and most assuredly intended to keep it.

This led to further words; and altho I had never kept my temper under better control in all my life—, yet the fellow bent upon a quarrel — used such language, that I shivered a *Cue* over his head; and might have been killed by him; (he was *twice* my size & strength), if the Proprietor had not effectually interfered.

The next day I recd a peremptory *Challenge* from Mr ——; which I was ass eno' to accept.

The affair was conducted with special secrecy; as Mr —— happened to be near graduation; and they hoped,— unless something serious happened—, to keep the fight from the knowledge of Professors, & the Public.

Tyler! I remember the morning of that duel, as clearly as if it were yesterday. My second — a gallant, but inexperienced young fellow, was so agitated, that I had to take the general management of things on my own shoulders—; I had to explain to him *what* to do, and *how* to do it.

Arrived upon the ground, & our positions taken; I charged my friend to hand me before the word, the *lighter-triggered* pistol of the pair we had brought; as a hard - triggered pistol I could never shoot accurately.

He did the *precise contrary* in his confusion—, (a circumstance I've been thankful for, ever since) because it saved me from the remorse of homicide.

I was *intensely enraged,* but as steady as possible, & would have shot my Opponent through the body, if the Pistol I chose had been given me. As it was, the hardness of the trigger caused my hand to fall *two feet* at least, and I shot the fellow thro the fleshy portion — of — his leg instead of the *heart* or *lungs*.

As for him, he was nervous, & shot *miles* above my head.

Pardon this little reminiscence. So strongly did it come back to memory, that I could'nt help relating it.

Upon what *trifles* the most serious consequences turn!!

A *hair-trigger*, or not a *hair-trigger*!! human life being the stake!?

But I must close here.

Again, I thank you for your generous kindness. Drop me a line whenever you can; & Believe me,

Always Faithfully

Paul H Hayne
P O Box 635
Augusta
G*a*

[Concerning the two poems named, see the notes following the first of these letters to Tyler (No. 162).

Tyler wrote this paragraph in his column entitled "The Outlook" in the *Christian Union* for February 18, 1874 (IX, 121):

"A brilliant literary man of the South, who both in himself and in his ancestors is an honorable example of genuine chivalric feeling, has written to suggest an ingenious method of preventing personal disputes among Christian brethren, or of composing them after they have arisen. 'What a pity it is,' he exclaims, 'that certain modified forms of the duello do not exist in so-called religious circles!' He then goes on to explain what he means by this. Thus, if one church member indulges in slander against one of his brethren, our Southern friend would have 'the parties placed opposite each other and vent their indignation, not by firing pistols or rifles, but by launching against each other, let us say, cloth-yard shafts, shot from something like the English bow. . . . Say what we choose, the habit of dueling . . . had a rather good side. It prevented that awful social roughness, that disregard of giving and receiving insults, which characterize our present high civilization. In the most important legislative bodies of the land, such sugar-plums of speech as "liar," "black-guard," "coward," now fly about as thickly as *confetti* at the Carnival, disregarded and unchecked.' We give our friend's suggestion the benefit of a public airing, and would venture to add, that in case of its general adoption in our churches, the weapon might be varied according to the heat of the hostile parties; and in cases where there was very great warmth of anger, the weapons might be certain familiar aquiferous machines. with which the enraged Christian duelists should mutually pour cold water upon each other."

Sir Geoffrey (or Jeffery) Hudson (1619–1682), Queen Henrietta Maria's dwarf, appears in Scott's *Peveril of the Peak* (1822).

Cf. the letter to R. H. Stoddard dated August 24. 1855 (No. 3). for another account of Hayne's duel.]

No. 169

PAUL HAMILTON HAYNE to MOSES COIT TYLER

Augusta 16th M'c'h 1874

Methinks, I hear thee exclaim, *O! my Friend*, "ye Gods of retribution!, *am* I to be *buried* under mountains of mine own paper; or at least, the paper mine own hands did mail to the most unreasonable, and *Showery* of Bards?—

"Will the varlet ne'er be done with his outpourings of 'wishy washy' rhymes? and are his *damp sheets* destined to prove but a sorry *winding sheet* for me, — *me miserable?*—["]

Patience! and a't thou strikest, hear me! I merely send these, and the pre-ceding verses to thy care, that such poems as thou likest, may be retained for the "*C U*", while of the others, thou wilt perchance, make *the best disposal practicable.*

To drop this jargon, let me say that being " '*in th' vein*" just now, I have determined to scribble until my muse or Muses choose to desert me; for I *must* make these fickle ladies *pay*, while they vouchsafe to sojourn in my spirit;— otherwise, you'll hear of me next ('tis no joke alas!) in the hands of the *Augusta* Sheriff, to be thence haled off to the *Augusta* jail, there to die of dirt, stench, and starvation!!

Eheu! Eheu! — *Aï! Aï! Aï! Aï!* — Give me (in *that event*) 2 or 3 lines of kindly mention, & remembrance in thy columns; or by all the spirits of Heaven, Hades, and the middle air, I'll haunt thy slumbers, and make thy nights, and eke thy days *hideous!*—

Why, *per Hercle!* should'nt I compose mine own "*In Memoriam?*"

> *"Here* lies a Bard, whose name was H— e;
> His life was woe; — experience — pain;
> For *twice* a score of years, or more —,
> The Wolf that howled before his door —,
> He fought with gallant mien, & high —;—
> But at the last, foul *D*estiny
> *Forced* him within the S[h]eriff's grip —,
> Whence to the odorous fellowship
> Of rusty jail-birds, he did go —;—
> Till Fate relenting, at *one* blow
> Cut the tight knot of life, *and* woe —;—
> Stranger! at length, he rests — below!"—

Many an *"ower true"* word hath been said, or *sung* — in *jest!*—

Mean while, I perceive that the *"C U"* flourishes, *whoever*, or *what*ever may—*not!*

Long may it wave!

Drop me a line, in my solitude, and perplexity, & Believe me, Always *y'r affectionate* &

Grateful friend,

Paul H Hayne
P. O. Box 635
Augusta Ga

(P S) When I am *incarcerated*, I'll tell you *how* to address me.—

No. 170

PAUL HAMILTON HAYNE to MOSES COIT TYLER

Augusta Ga
M'c'h 18*th* '74

No joke this time!

Tis *positively* Hayne's *last* appearance, for an *indefinate* [*sic*] period. Sing *"Hallelujah"*, or *"Alley loyer"* (as Miss Miggs hath it in *"Barnaby Rudge"*), in the "deep places your heart"!

If, my *Di Friend*, the *"C U"* wants the enclosed to *fill up* small spaces — all well! If not — why — keep them for the nonce,

And Oblige yr's
Ever

P. H. H.

[Miss Miggs is a servant in Dickens's *Barnaby Rudge* (1841).]

No. 171

PAUL HAMILTON HAYNE to MOSES COIT TYLER

"Copse Hill" Ga R Road:
Augusta, March 21st 1874.

My Dear Friend;

— I have been thinking of late, that Accident, or rather a very natural combination of Circumstances —, has placed in my hands, the *materials* for certain biographic sketches, and pictures of the "old Time" in S. Carolina, and other Southern States, which ought *not* to be permitted to lie idle.

— For example, I *have already* prepared an article on the stirring period of *"Nullification"*, with the central figure of Gov: Hayne, to illustrate its events.

This paper published, years ago, (in an obscure So *"Quarterly"*), I propose *entirely re-writing*, taking the *facts* merely, enforced by new *matériel*, and making of them such a *series of word-pictures*, as (my life upon it!) will & *must* interest all intelligent readers.

No individual *political*, or *social* opinions will be obtruded; nothing said to wound the feelings, or shock the convictions of any living person. A *straightforward*, graphic narrative of facts, set in *their own* powerful *dramatic* light — is all I contemplate.

The paper too, will be made *as brief* as possible.

Surely, the period it is designed to cover, ought not to be allowed to rest dryly outlined in our mere school histories!

Now, what think you? Would Mr Johnson *not* object to such a composition?

It could in no degree compromise the principles of *"the C. U"*.

I would entitle it

"One of the Chiefs of Nullification".

Drop me a line.

It haste, but Always
Affectionately yr's

Paul H Hayne.

[Robert Young Hayne (1791–1839), United States senator and governor of South Carolina, was Hayne's uncle and had assisted Hayne's mother in supervising his upbringing. Hayne's sketch of him had appeared in October, 1870, in Bledsoe's *Southern Review* (VIII, 275–317) of Baltimore. In an earlier note I mentioned Hayne's life of him (Charleston, 1878) and another sketch of him in the *Southern Bivouac*, I, 193–202.

Oliver Johnson was office editor of the *Christian Union*. Hayne might have supposed that he would object to an article on a Southerner because the editorial department of the magazine had revealed itself from time to time as anti-Southern. A case in point is the editorial (VIII, 540–1) concerning James S. Pike's *The Prostrate State: South Carolina Under Negro Government* (Appleton, 1873). But it revealed a more friendly and understanding attitude later on.]

No. 172

PAUL HAMILTON HAYNE to MOSES COIT TYLER

Address me, P. O. Box, 635.
Augusta Ga
Augusta April 10th 1874

Dear Friend;—

It seems *very long* since I heard from you last; but I can well understand how *especially busy* you must be.

The considerable batch of verses which I mailed to your address, with the request that you would *keep such pieces* as happened to suit you, (for the "C. U"), and—at your *leisure*—, *dispose* of the *others* for me —, came safely to hand, I trust.

It was a *great liberty* on my part — this burdening you with so many poems; but I have the *most thorough confidence* in the reality & unselfishness of your friendship. & alas! I am otherwise, *so alone* in this world;— the friends of my youth being either *dead*, or in exile.

You will not, therefore, fancy that I have *imposed* upon your good will, and courtesy. The *bare thought* makes me shiver!

And now, I desire to bring to your notice a Poem, which is particularly fitted (I think) for your *weekly*.

Among the innumerable notices of poor Henry Timrod's *Life*, and *works* which appeared both in this Country & England,— I recall *none*, (no! not one!) so pleasing to me, as *your* review in the "*C U*"; and so in the "*C. U*" I would fain see the enclosed elegy published. It is of all my recent poems, the poem upon which I have bestowed most care & pains. Then, it is written not so much with ink, as with *heart's blood*. God grant that you may like it! God grant that it may prove worthy the fame & memory of a most gifted, and unfortunate man!

You will, of course, be perfectly frank in stating your opinion of the merits or demerits of this Elegy.

An author often deceives himself; and yet — I can hardly think I have done so, in the present case. *Nous Verrons!!*

Drop me a line, when you can, telling me something of *yourself*, and *fortunes*. Would to Heaven you were here, with me now, in the Southern woods, as the Spring developes day by day, her beauties! Often & often I think of you—always tenderly, always warmly, as of one among the most chivalric, and noble gentlemen I have ever encountered. *Deus Vobiscum!*

Ever yr's   Paul H Hayne.

P. S. Among the verses sent you, there was a piece, called "*Lucifer's Deputy*".

If *you have not disposed* of it, will you kindly *return* me the "*Mss*"?—

'T'would scarcely suit the "C U", I presume.

P. H. H.

x   I confess that I feel very *anxious* as to the fate of the *Poem on Timrod's Grave.*

There are circumstances' connected with it, which make me extremely desirous to see the piece prominently brought to the public attention of the *North.* Do help me, friend, on this point.

And inform me of your *opinion* of the verses, as soon as practicable, or rather, convenient. — If unfavorable, be *perfectly frank*[.] Don't mind ab't hurting *me.*

["By the Grave of Henry Timrod" appeared in the *Christian Union* for June 10, 1874 (IX, 452).

For "Lucifer's Deputy" see *Complete Edition,* pp. 352–4.]

No. 173

PAUL HAMILTON HAYNE to MOSES COIT TYLER

Augusta Ga, April 21st 1874:

My Dear Friend;—

It was a sincere joy to *me*—, the reception of your kindly & affectionate letter of the 16*th*, recd yesterday.

Words fail me when I think of all your courtesy, your gentle forethought, your unselfish consideration. Well! some day — somewhere — , I may be enabled *practically* to show *how* I appreciate all this!

Meanwhile, understand that *one* heart exists in the world, which you have *completely gained;* that there is *one* man ready to stand by you *thro* thick and thin.

These words *sound* like bathos; they are really expressive of a *simple truth.*

And so, all my *"Ms"*-Poems reached you in safety:? *Laus Deo!!* — It gives me fresh energy, & *much needed* encouragement, when I peruse your sentences of praise. You *overrate* my power; but for all that, such commendation is delightful.

I feel somewhat ashamed at the number of pieces I dared send you, in the brief period between the *7th March,* and the 15*th* or 20*th* of that month; but don't forget that I *merely*

entrusted them to your judgment; — such poems as. seemed
to you *suitable* for the "*C. U*", to be offered to *your Literary
Editor, (Mr Johnson)* and the *others* to be offered to *whatever periodicals* might seem likely to take them, when *leisure
& opportunity combining,* you thought proper to present them,
in my name.

Of course if you believe that *all* these poems are worthy
the "*C U*", or at least, a large portion of them, I'd *rather*
see them published in *your* columns than anywhere else.

And here, to prevent mistakes, and to help you in finding
the different poems, I give their names;

1 Sonnet to Jno G. Whittier
2. "Sentenced"
3. "Disenchanted"
4. "The Rich Optimist, & the Needy Pessimist".
5. "Why the Robin's Breast is Red"— (New Version)—
6. "Critics"
7. "The Ibisses of the Nile"
8. "The Rahât"—
9. *"Grave of H. Timrod".*

You call the last mentioned poem, *"noble".* I am *so* thankful it pleases you!

Those verses were really penned with heart's blood, &
artistically, my endeavor was, to make them worthy a sad,
but most *impressive theme.*

+ You are right ab't *"Lucifer's Deputy".* T'was' sent
elsewhere. As for article on *"H. Coleridge",* you might as
well throw it in the fire. *Nobody* wants it. The article on
"Plantation Life", do keep till I write for it.

Please don't allow *Mr Johnson* to suppose that I complained *querulously,* or, complained at *all,* concerning the
typographical errors. My *own* cal[l]igraphy is to blame.

Besides, such mistakes *will* occur in the best regulated
journals!

I am forced to *conclude* in haste. Believe me, *dear friend,*

Always Most Faithfully

Paul H Hayne.
(P. O. Box 635)

P. S. The two Poems I am most anxious about, are that on poor *Timrod*, & the one called *"Sentenced"*.

If accepted, you will place such a price on these, as you think they deserve; or rather, such a price as *circumstances* allow you to place upon them, *without* seeming unfair, or *exhorbitant*[?].—

[For a list of four of these poems that appeared in the *Christian Union* before the end of the year see the notes following the first letter to Tyler (No. 162).

For information concerning the *"H. Coleridge"* article see the notes following the letter to Tyler dated February 8, 1874 (No. 167).]

No. 174

PAUL HAMILTON HAYNE to MOSES COIT TYLER

Augusta Ga
April 28th 1874

My Dear Friend;

I was wrong in thinking that I had sent you a piece, called *"Lucifer's Deputy"*.

But I send it now. T'will afford you a few minute's [*sic*] amusement, possibly, whether, you think it fit for the *"C. U"*, or *not*.

— By the way, (being merely a good natured sarcasm upon mediaëval credulity), you may deem it not unacceptable after all.

But if too light for the paper, do return *"Mss"*,

& Oblige yr's Ever

Paul H Hayne
(P O Box 635)

[*"Lucifer's Deputy"* is a humorous poem about a poet's going to Hades, his being promised a roasted monk as a tidbit if he guards the place while Satan is out, and his being ejected for losing many souls to Saint Peter in a dice game.]

No. 175

PAUL HAMILTON HAYNE to MOSES COIT TYLER

Augusta, Ga, May 12th '74

Dear Friend; / I write somewhat in haste, to beg that you'll have the following Correction made in the 2*nd* verse of my poem on *"Timrod's Grave"*, provided the piece has met with favor.

Do let the 2*nd* stanza run as follows; (after the 6*th* line).— viz:—

Careless & tranquil as that treacherous morn,
Nor dreamed how soon the blight
Of long implanted seeds of care would throw
Their night-shade flowers above the springing corn:—

When you have leisure, on some night of rest, and ease, by your own fireside, read aloud my poem to your wife and friends, & tell me candidly if it be worthy the subject.

Should the ."*C U*". accept & publish it, won't you get your Clerk to mail me a few *extra copies* of the no in which it appears?

As for the *price* of these *verses*, estimate their value by your *own* sense of justice wholly.

I am *ever satisfied* with *your decisions*. God bless you, *mon ami:*

Ever yr's *P H Hayne*
(P O Box 635)

[In the *Christian Union* (IX, 452) the lines read:

". . . Careless, and tranquil as that treacherous morn;
Nor dreamed how soon the blight
Of long-implanted seeds of care would throw
Their night-shade flowers above the springing corn."

They read the same in *Complete Edition* (pp. 198–9) except that "night-shade" has no hyphen.]

No. 176

PAUL HAMILTON HAYNE to MOSES COIT TYLER

(Private)
Augusta, May 18*th*
'74

Dear Friend;

Thanks for *yours* of the 13*th* inst: (enclosing the "declined" verses). I can well understand why *Mr Johnson* (who is a devout member of the Presbyterian Church, *is'nt* he?)— should regard the *"Ibyes [Ibises] on the Nile"* as theologically inadmissable [*sic*], even were the piece finer than it can at all claim to be *artistically.*

And, *enpassant,* I've dropped Mr J—, an explanatory line referring to the extraordinary *no* of poems I sent him, at the same time. The note is left open for *your* perusal; so that *you* too, may not, *mon ami,* fail to comprehend me.

I dread to appear *obtrusive;* especially among those who have treated me ever, with distinguished consideration.

'Touching the poem on *"Timrod's Grave"*, I may calculate upon *that* having been *accepted?* — *may'nt* I?

And if so, what think you is it *(pecuniarily), worth?*— I took *immense* pains with the finishing of [it]. Don't omit that 3 *line* correction, *please!*

Alack! that I must mingle *poetry* with *pence;* a sincere, profound, life-long *grief* with the economics of material existence; — *heart-break* with sordid purse-strings! The Lord forgive us our trespasses!!

— Yes! I receive *"the C. U"* regularly now. It is perused with *real* satisfaction; *Your* department in especial.

x x x As for *"Lucifer's Deputy"*, it was only meant for *your eyes!* Glad you liked it!—God bless you, & Believe me

Ever y*rs*   *P H Hayne*

[Written lengthwise in the margin on the first page of the letter:]

+ Such of the poems as you think M*r* J— will dislike, don't — *submit* to him —

["The Ibises on the Nile" appeared in the *South-Atlantic* (Baltimore monthly) for November, 1880 (VI, 297–8).

As pointed out in an earlier note, Tyler originated two departments entitled "The Outlook" and "Books and Authors."]

No. 177

PAUL HAMILTON HAYNE to MOSES COIT TYLER

Augusta, May 24*th* 1874

Dear Friend;

Accept the little tribute enclosed, as *wholly your own.*

I was thinking last night of our *first* meeting; of the impression you made upon me then, which Time only has deepened; and my feelings embodied themselves in this Sonnet, a poor thing perhaps, but *sincere.*

Ever Faithfully

Paul H Hayne.

(P. S.) When the piece on *"Timrod's Grave"* is put into the Printer's hand, don't forget to substitute the following lines in stanza 2*nd* for these now in *"Ms"*—

After the line, *"Careless & tranquil as that treacherous* morn,["] let the concluding lines run thus:

"Nor deemed how soon the blight
Of long-implanted seeds of Care would throw
Their night-shade flowers above the springing corn."

No. 178

PAUL HAMILTON HAYNE to MOSES COIT TYLER

*Augusta, June 1st 1874.*ˑ

Dear Friend;

I rec*d* on *Sat: last*, a note from Mr Oliver Johnson, which gave me *very great*, and *unusual satisfaction*. Mr Johnson has written me touching my contributions to *"the C. Union"* in the *frankest*, most *cordial* temper; and really, with such friends as Mr J—, and yourself in the office, I *ought to be*, and I *am more* than *satisfied!* I feel *proud!*

Such courtesy can only stimulate me to compose in the *best* manner of which I am capable, whenever henceforth I assume the pen to indite anything for *you*. Please *ruthlessly* strike out from among the pieces already in your hands, *any* and *all* the poems you do *not* perfectly approve. And may I — without indelicacy, beg that you will look after the "proof" of *"Timrod's Grave"*, whenever 'tis "set up?"

I am exceedingly nervous about that *special* performance. You'll comprehend the reason why!

Apropos of these verses, (which I'll never allude to any more), don't you think the 1*st* stanza might be improved? For example, the lines of the 2nd part of the 1*st* quatrain, now stand thus.`.

> "And moved by fragrant airs, the hill-side Pine
> Stirred in the mellow sunshine pleasantly;" &c

I thought of substituting[:]

> "And moved by fragrant airs, the hill-side Pine
> Thrilled in the mellow sunshine blissfully &c"

yet I don't like "blissfully" either!! Confound it! Perhaps 'tis better to allow the words to remain as in the *original "Ms"*. What say you? *choose for me!*

Be *not* disgusted at all this *ëgoism*. Who have I, (poor devil!), to consult on any art. difficulty, in these heathen— wilds?— Yet, in other respects, the "heathen wilds" are dear to me, *very* dear!! A mingled grandeur & sweetnes[s] characterizes the scenery, to those, at least, who can look far eno' beneath the mere *surfaces* of things.

The forest about us is now one grand *singing hall;* an exquisite Temple of music. As I write, *two* mock birds are vying with each other; all but splitting their tiny throats in the effort to triumph, to conquer!

And round & round the window sill, laden with *vines*, the humming bird darts, glances, flashes like an embodied sunbeam; sucking the cores of blossoms, and filling the air with

his strange, monotonous whizz, his spinning-wheel boom —
boom boom!

Semi-Tropical are all the sights & sounds of the Nature
before me. But, the atmosphere does not blight, and oppress.
On the contrary, one seldom fails to be refreshed by a wind
which after traversing hundreds of leagues of healthful, aro-
matic Pine - wood, wafts coolness and fragrance about one's
brow. Would that *you, my friend*, were with me!

You'd really enjoy the *strangeness* of the climate & *locale*,
if you could enjoy nothing else.

By the way, I rejoice that you speak so *emphatically* in
your *"Outlook"* of the merit of Lowell's *"Agassiz"*. A *grand*
Ode; full of *pith*, and intellectual *vim;* every line a poem
per se. But to[o] fine to be *popular*. One of the *cleverest
women-poets* of this Country writes me *disparagingly* concerning it — (one of yr' NY *lionesses!*) "It can add *nothing"*, she says, "to the fame of the author *of Sir Launfall*[*sic*]."
— Ye Gods!! what blindness! But, when a Poet really becomes *masculine,* disdaining those "mincing airs", of which
you have spoken, few now-a-days appreciate him.

To my mind *Lowell* is *the* Poet of America. He possesses
a *compactness* of creative imagination, a breadth of view, &
a wealth of expressive phraseology *none* of the others can
begin to rival.

But a truce to all this.

Did you receive a brief letter of mine, last week, (enclosing a little poem to yourself, a *Sonnet?*) I hope so.

Must stop here.

In haste, but Ever yr's

Paul H Hayne
P. O. Box 635,
Augusta Ga

(P. S.) Return when you can, the *"Ms"* by my mother on
"Plantation Life &c" a child's sketch, or rather a sketch *for
children.*—

[In the *Christian Union* (IX, 452) the lines read:
". . . And, moved by fragrant airs, the hill-side pine
Stirred in the mellow sunshine pleasantly. . . ."

In *Complete Edition* (p. 198) they read:
". . . And touched by fragrant airs, the hill-side pine
Thrilled in the mellow sunshine tenderly. . . ."

Lowell's "Agassiz" appeared in the *Atlantic Monthly* for May, 1874 (XXXIII, 586–96). Though mainly a tribute to Agassiz (d. 1873), it contains an attack upon the corrupt administration of Grant—"public scandal, private fraud, Crime flaunting scot-free . . . And all the un-wholesome mess . . ." (ll. 35–9). Though Whitman was more aware than most of the corruptions and scandals of the Gilded Age—in and out of office—they did not shake his unbounded faith in democracy. They did, however, affect the beliefs both of Lowell and of Hayne.

Tyler's praise of the poem occurs in the *Christian Union* for May 20, 1874 (IX, 384). He says that it "may not become a popular one, but it can hardly fail to attain celebrity. He wrote it in the spirit of the virile poets of the Elizabethan era, . . . and since it . . . does not in any way suit the lisping and mincing manner too much admired in contemporary verse, this majestic threnody must content itself with the fit audience though few which the present can give, and with an abiding fame and an ever widening reception in the future."

Hayne's mother, Emily McElhenny Hayne, wife of Lieutenant Paul Hayne of the United States Navy, had been a widow since 1831. After the war she lived with Hayne and his wife and son at Copse Hill, where she died on December 9, 1879, at the age of 74. See the *South-Atlantic* for January, 1880 (V, 177).]

No. 179

PAUL HAMILTON HAYNE to MOSES COIT TYLER

"Copse Hill", (near Augusta)
June 7th 1874:

Dear Friend;

I have *recd* your kind note of the 1*st* inst: & I assure you that the few warm words of acknowledgment you write touching my poor *Sonnet* are as *deeply* appreciated, as if you had penned a vo*l!* Well do I understand how busy you must always be; and if *I* write long letters to *you*, 'tis *with no expectation* of *similar* replies.

Confound *ceremony*, say I! Between real friends, men who
comprehend, & believe in, each other,— all this technical
society humbug about a "balance of correspondence" which
means sometimes, that *A* who resides in the Country, & *can*
command more or has [less] *leisure* for friendly *correspondence*,
has the right of anticipating from *B* (whose every moment is
consumed by hard (city) office work), a regular answer to all
his epistles,— is revolting to me in its egoism, and selfishness.

No! write when you are *able*, and *feel* like it! But *otherwise*, don't write at all! *I* am not the person to miscomprehend you.

By the way, do you know any of the Edt's or Proprietors
of *the "NY Nation"?*

+ Desiring to renew my subscription to that paper, I venture to ask your co-operation. As *thus;*—

The "C Union" (I believe) owes me a trifle for the *"Sonnet"* to *Whittier;* $10.*00* is'nt it?   Well! would you from this
sum pay my subscription to *"Nation"* (if *perfectly convenient*)?   Any little *balance* can be added to whatever the *"C U"*
may pay me for the next poem it publishes; *"Timrod's Grave"*,
or any other.

+ As for the pecuniary value of this poem *("By the Grave")*,
you'll remember I placed no *special price* upon it. *That* with
perfect confidence I leave to the Edt's of *"Union"*.

Of course, you'll perceive that my *"In Memoriam"*, (if I
may so term it) was composed with no common care.

I trust you'll not think me disposed to "harry" your good
natures?

Ever, *My friend* Yours

P H Hayne

(P O Box 635)

[Edwin Lawrence Godkin was editor of the *Nation* (New York weekly),
which was published by E. L. Godkin & Company.   The subscription
price was $5—pretty high for Hayne to pay.   Perhaps he had a high
opinion of the magazine, though he often disagreed with its critical views.
Most of the leading magazines were sent to Hayne either in part payment
for contributions or in return for notices of them in Southern magazines
and newspapers.

"Sonnet. Inscribed to the author of 'Snow-Bound' . . ." appeared in the *Christian Union* for May 13, 1874 (IX, 365).

This paragraph occurs in Tyler's "The Outlook" in the *Christian Union* for June 17, 1874 (IX, 469):

"A gentleman whom we may unhesitatingly call the greatest poet now living in the Southern States, and in all respects one of their most brilliant literary men, writes these words in a private letter in response to some words of ours upon the new era of peace and good will between North and South. 'Yes: a new epoch is dawning upon this long distracted land. At all events, in the pure, serene, beautiful realm of Art, there must soon be no division between North and South. The few scholars, writers, thinkers, of which my own unfortunate section can boast, are being drawn daily more closely towards their Northern brethren,—brethren now in reality and not in name alone. May God bless you all for your unstinted kindness!' "

Undoubtedly the reference is to Hayne.]

No. 180

PAUL HAMILTON HAYNE to MOSES COIT TYLER

(Private)

Near Augusta, Aug: 11th 1874

Dear Friend;—

Thanks for your's of the *6th* inst: I am glad that the *"Sonnet"* upon *Poe* pleased you! Will take your kindly hint in regard to the disposition of contributions!

As for the *"dark time"* which has come upon your *Chief;* remember, that *nothing* can overthrow a true integrity;—all slanders must, in the end, defeat themselves. Nevertheless, it is unlucky that H. W. B. ever encountered T. T.

Some *warning Sprite* ought to have whispered in his ear, the moment he first caught sight of that man; "avoid *T. T;* rather than cultivate such an acquaintance, follow the advice which *Heinsius* gave to *Primicrus; viz,* "proximum est ut esurias; *2nd* ut moram temporis opponas; *3rd,* et locum mutes; *4th* ut de laqueo cogites!!"—

But, "none of us are stronger than Destiny!"
When leisure offers, please drop me a line or two.
I am always *delighted* to hear from you.

Ever, *mon ami,*
Yours faithfully,
Paul H Hayne.
P. O. Box 635,
Augusta Geo

[Tyler's *"Chief"* was Henry Ward Beecher, editor of the *Christian Union.* From 1861 until 1863 he had edited the *Independent* (New York weekly), assisted by Theodore Tilton, who succeeded Beecher as editor in 1863. As early as 1866 the two had quarreled over politics and Beecher's contributions to the *Independent.* (See Mott, II, 367 ff.) A few years later a scandal arose concerning the relations between Beecher and Mrs. Tilton, and later Tilton brought suit against Beecher accusing him of adultery with Mrs. Tilton. At the time of this letter, the newspapers and some magazines had been referring to the scandal for over a year. (See Mott, III, 447 ff.) The Augusta (Ga.) *Daily Chronicle & Sentinel* for June 3, 1873, says the charges were that Beecher had "had criminal connection with Tilton's wife and other female members of Plymouth Church." At first Hayne thought that Beecher was innocent, but finally became convinced that he was guilty. Apparently Tyler came to the same conclusion, and that was one reason why he left the *Christian Union.*

I am not acquainted with Primicrus or with the works of Heinsius, but, according to reference books, there were two famous Dutch classical scholars by that name, father and son: Daniel Heinsius (1580–1655) and Nikolaas Heinsius (1620–1681). Apparently the son was the more important writer of the two, though the father was the better scholar. My friend Professor Maurice McLaughlin of Charleston suggests that the "et" before "locum" in the Latin quotation may have been intended for "ut" since this change would make a balance in the subjunctive clauses—though it is difficult to be certain about such a passage divorced from its context.]

No. 181

PAUL HAMILTON HAYNE to [OLIVER JOHNSON]

Augusta Aug: 11th 1874

My Dear Sir;
Mr Tyler writes me that he handed over to you a *"Sonnet"* upon Poe,— or rather, upon the *contemplated monument* to

be raised over Poe's grave —,— which I had composed, and offered to *"The C. Union"*.

Let me hope it may satisfy you; altho I know it does *not* reach the height of the subject.

With all his faults, *Edgar Poe* possessed *genuine original genius*; & it is a shame he has remained so long neglected[.]

+ When I stood by his grave *last July*, in Balt, I beheld a perfectly barren mound of earth, the rank, weeds growing all over, and around it; and not a sign to tell what passionate heart, & fertile brain mouldered underneath!

Mr Geo Childs, however, has taken the matter in hand; and soon a proper stone will mark the spot.

+ Can I, without an appearance of *indelicacy*, express the hope that the *cloud* which now rests over one of your Chiefs, may soon be dispersed?

When the good man is persecuted, his enemies would fain have him chaunt the refrain of *"Spes, et fortuna valete!"*; but neither hope, nor good fortune, (at least in its high spiritual sense), can ever desert the pure hearted, and the upright Christian.

In haste, but ever yours,

Paul H Hayne

(P. O. Box 635)

[Evidently this letter was sent to Oliver Johnson, office editor of the *Christian Union*.

George William Childs (1829–1894), publisher and philanthropist, was born in Baltimore but lived in Philadelphia after he was 14 or 15. From time to time he was connected with various publishing houses (including J. B. Lippincott & Company). His greatest success came as proprietor and editor of the Philadelphia *Public Ledger*, which he bought in December, 1864. In his later years he was known for his philanthropy, especially in the way of memorials to poets, in England and America.]

No. 182

PAUL HAMILTON HAYNE to MOSES COIT TYLER

Augusta, *Ga*. 17*th* Aug: 1874

Dear Friend;

I have rec'*d* the *re*jected *"Ms"* of the Poe Sonnet.

Entre nous, I *can't* understand the *reason* for its rejection.

Mr J—, surely does not deny to Poe all *literary merit; such* an idea is *preposterous;* therefore, he means, that P—'s *character* was so *morally infirm* that he deserves no monument, not even a "modest stone" to mark his last place, & perchance, his *first* place of *rest!*

Is this right? Is it *generous?* However, there's no use in argument.

By the way, may I beg you to take out something from the next payment for any poem of mine, issued in *"The C. Union"*, and purchase a p'c'k of *large envelopes, a bundle* of *good lead pencils, a sharp pen knife,* and *one* box of *superfine steel pens,* which you can send me per *"Express"?*

I *know* you won't deem such a commission an impertinence; for are we not *true friends?*

God bless you!

Ever yrs'

P. H. H.

P. S. That *H. W. B.* affair is truly puzzling & horrible! Great God! to think of the most celebrated preacher in the land —— but I must *not* write on *this* theme. Pardon me!

[*American Authors 1600–1900: A Biographical Dictionary of American Literature*, ed. by Stanley J. Kunitz and Howard Haycraft, New York: The H. W. Wilson Company, 1938, p. 65, says: "The situation was a complicated one, and though the jury disagreed and was dismissed, and Beecher had been previously cleared by his church, the only verdict today can be the Scotch one of 'not proven.' If he was not guilty of adultery, he was at least guilty of incredible carelessness and foolishness."]

No. 183

PAUL HAMILTON HAYNE to MOSES COIT TYLER

Private!

Augusta, 3rd Sep: 1874.˙.

My Dear Friend;

It is some weeks, since *you* wrote *me* a *private* note, in regard to the B. T. affair; observing at the same time, that in a month, or *two* months from that date, you would, *probably*, leave the *"C U"* office. Looking upon you —, *brief* as our *mere personal communication* has been —, — in the light of a *very dear friend* — , I now venture, in all frankness & sincerity, (knowing you can't misunderstand me — ,) to ask you a *direct question. What do you think of this Beecher embroglio*[*sic*]*? Are the Committee right in pronouncing B — , guiltless, or are they merely a packed Jury, aiming at an acquittal, and not at the truth?* I wish an honest answer to this question from one (like yourself), whom I can — *implicitly* trust; and the answer, if given, shall in *any* event, be *immediately consigned* to the *flames.*

Take some chance to tell me how *you* are, & what are your future prospects & designs; —

I take the *sincerest interest* in your welfare, or, never would I have *dared* to propound these questions.

Always, *mon ami,*

Most Faithfully.

Paul H Hayne.

[Tyler gave up his position on the staff of the *Christian Union* on September 12, 1874, and went back to the University of Michigan as professor of rhetoric and English literature at $2,500, one thousand a year less than his salary on the staff of the magazine. See H. M. Jones, *The Life of Moses Coit Tyler,* pp. 142, 159.]

No. 184

PAUL HAMILTON HAYNE to MOSES COIT TYLER

Augusta Geo. —
Sep: 14th 1874:

Dear Friend;

I have *just* learned, from a sufficiently *trustworthy* source, that your design, hinted to me some weeks ago, — has been *practically carried out!* You have left the *"C. U"* *Office:* and, perhaps, already, you are on your way to *Michigan?*

Well! this conduct of *yours,* is *just what* I would have expected from you, under the Circumstances.

The atmosphere of the *"C. U"* office is not *morally health-ful,* eh?

Mon ami! I take your hand, & with all my soul, I *congratulate you* upon being so *independent, brave,* and pure-hearted a gentleman!

Whatever *material interests may* suffer, you have done the *right thing.*

Of *that* I *feel assured!*

+ *Do* write to me, as *soon as* possible, (or at *least convenient*); and tell me of your *future plans;* and your *future address.*

Wherever you go. *whatever happens, count* me, as

Always y'r affectionate
friend,

Paul H. Hayne,
P. O. Box 635
Augusta *Ga*

No. 185

PAUL HAMILTON HAYNE to MOSES COIT TYLER

Address me P. O. Box 635,
Augusta Geo
Augusta, Geo Oct 30th 1874

My Dear Friend;

Because you have left New York, and left the *Editorship* of the "*C. Union*" — a step for which I profoundly *respect* you, — don't imagine that I intend to forget all your kindness, or to drop our correspondence. On the contrary, unless — *you* are tired of *me* — , I shall write you every now & then, ever hoping perhaps that you may have more leisure than formerly to reply.

Don't you feel, (in the warm embraces of your old Professional chair), as if you had escaped from a very unwholesome atmosphere; and from dubious environments? Depend upon it, *W. B.* has got himself into a horrible muddle; and whatever the *Courts* may decree, a powerful, & ever growing public opinion condemns him.

Then, the man shows in his *personal* bearing, under these circumstances, so little common sense! Lecturing everywhere, *obtruding* himself upon the Public, *jesting*, and *philosophising*, may seem to *him* like manly defiance, or, an honest indifference to foul charges; but evidently the *majority* regard his course as simply — "*brassy*", and indicative of the *worst* possible game he could play — a game of *brag*, and *bluff!* Great God! what a fall! ! And yet, (if the *adultery* charge holds good), I — for one — , could have *forgiven* H. W. B. his lapses from virtue a thousand times more readily, (are not ministers human?) —, than I could forgive his duplicity since; and his contempt for the unfortunate creature who shared his guilt. That *was* base!

But *mon ami!* I beg your pardon.

For the instant I forget how painful this topic must be to you. It shall never be again mentioned between us.

x x x x x   We are having *hereabout* the *strangest,* most fluctuating Autumn! One day will be *cold* and *crisp,* with the *"feel"* of coming snow; but *presto!,* in a single hour, back veers the wind due South, and a languid, voluptuous, mist-girded vernal atmosphere is the inevitable consequence!

Tremendous excitement prevails throughout this section, of course, because of the recent; unexpected, Democratic victories. The sounds of triumph, however, reach *my* ears, like noises half muffled in fog.

Never can my soul be stirred again by any *political* trumpet; for I can't honestly say that my confidence in our *Institutions* amounts to much. (*Rash heresy,* no doubt, but *"heterodoxy"* — political, or religious —, is sometimes "the beginning of wisdom") — x x x x

x x x x x x x   Do, my friend! *write* me about the circumstances of your removal *West,* and say how you are, at present, situated; whether the old College welcomed y'r return as warmly as it *ought* to have done.

Tell me *everything;* and believe that I am Ever Faithfully yours

Paul H Hayne

["It shall never be again mentioned between us": but Hayne found the subject fascinating and returned to it.

In the elections of 1874 the Democratic Party gained control of the lower house of Congress.

An article entitled "A Time of Depressed Hope" in the *Christian Union* for July 15, 1874 (X, 38) quotes a part of a speech by Tyler delivered before the "Alpha Delta Phi." It begins: "This seems to be a time of depressed hope in popular government. It is obvious that among thoughtful people there is now more than in any recent time a sad solicitude concerning the final result of our great experiment." Tyler then mentions certain pronouncements of Lowell and of President Woolsey of Yale and adds that educated men of fine character must not leave government and politics to ignorant, unprincipled men.]

No. 186

PAUL HAMILTON HAYNE to MOSES COIT TYLER

"Copse Hill", Geo R. Road
Sat: 26th Dec: *1874.·.*

Dear Friend;—

Most comforting to mine eyes, and refreshing to my Spirit,
was the sight of your well - known cal[l]igraphy, and the subsequent eager perusal of your letter of the 18*th* inst: There
is an atmosphere of unaffected peace, and homely content-
ment, pervading that communication, which conveys to my
mind the *pleasantest* idea possible, of your present position,
and all its surroundings! Ah, well may you "pat yourself",
(metaphorically), "on the back", and offer *mental* oblations
to the beneficent Deity of Fortune, who taking you by the
hand, led you out of the feculence of *Sodom*, (or *Gotham*, 'tis
all one!) into those smiling pastures, by that still river of
purity, and happiness, which have been now given you as a
perpetual possession! While I can imagine nothing more disgusting to a man of your temperament & character, than the
daily association with hard, restless, *frantic* money - Grab-
bers, (their narrow, yet *intense* vision fixed forever on the
"Main Chance", the *"demnition* gold & silver", which *Man-
tallini* describes as "strewing *Tom Tiddler's ground"*)—, on
the other hand, I can imagine nothing more agreeable than
the duties of your present Professional Chair; with unnum-
bered opportunities of quiet study, and a thorough self-culture. I look now to nothing *less* than your re-entering the
domain of authorship, and giving to the World the results of
much intellectual labor, and of philosophic thought carefully
digested. You have it *in* you O, my Friend! , — this *Divine*
powers[?] of instructing and benefitting the Race, by a presentation of the mortal, and moral outgrowths of your own thoughtful, cultivated spirit; and that you will endeavor so to do, I
cannot for a moment, doubt.

It affords me a species of bitter, yet *wholesome* satisfaction
to read your honestly indignant repudiation of *H. W. B.* and

all his damnable devices!! clearer and clearer every day, his guilt becomes, to the eyes of the unprejudiced, & dispassionate public! "Against *what* light!" (as you well exclaim), "against *what* sanctions &c" — has this man sinned!!!

The history of the Christian world, & the Christian Pulpit can furnish no parallel to *his* case. Arthur Dimm[e]sdale in Hawthorne's *"Scarlet Letter"*, has been dragged out of the realm of fiction, and compared, or contrasted with him. *A contrast* it surely *ought to be;* for the Puritan Clergyman gives one the idea of a soul, not merely *troubled,* but *absolutely eaten into* (*Cancer*-like), by an ever-present, torturing *Remorse,* the intense agony of which *forces* him, at last, to grovel down in dust and ashes, at the moment of his *supreme worldly* triumph; to abandon *everything,* at the very instant when *everything* (in the *worldly* sense) had been gained! And then *what* was *his* sin, by the side of *B'—s?*

The *passionate lapse* of an hour, or a *minute;* while in the case of the *other,* we behold systematic duplicity; long continued, & carefully concocted plans for the ruin of a feeble, infatuated woman, and she the *wife of a friend—;* hypocrisy so profound, we have no moral plummet wherewith to sound its dark, abhorrent depths; and as a background to the whole series of damnable transactions, such brazen effrontery, such immeasurable assurance as never before, under similar circumstances, has mortal man exhibited!! But the topic is preeminently *unsavory!* I beg pardon for touching it again.

By the way, *what* think you, *(entre nous!)* of Mr *Oliver Johnson;* I mean, as an *art* — or *literary Critic?*

I enquire, *chiefly* because he rather surprised me sometime ago, by rejecting the *very best* (short) *poem* of mine, composed I think, for years. True! his rejection was founded, *ostensibly,* upon the over crowded condition of his columns; but for all *that,* I *did* feel a *little* surprised, and of course disappointed!

Upon my sending the *same* piece to another paper, it was *not* merely accepted; but accepted in a wonderfully flattering manner.

And while on this subject, let me tell you, that we poor — devil — Authors of the *South* have a "hard road to travel".

Why, *Tyler!* after 25 years (!(of sincere, intense, rarely intermitted work, I am *just beginning* to occupy such a position in our *general American Literature*, as, (with an *equal* amount of labor, & earnestness), a *Northern* man would have occupied after the lapse of a single *lustrum!!* Understand me! I am *not* so foolish, or unjust as to blame the *Northern People* for this condition of things. *Au contraire, nine tenths* of the blame, at least, must remain with our own, the *So section* of the Country! Anything more narrow & bigotted than the temper of our people; more *radically* opposed to the free development of *Art*, cannot be conceived.

And thus, the *So* author, especially the *So Poet*, may be pictured as standing up between *two fires!*

The great *practical* hardship, *I* experience, is the difficulty, nay! the seeming *impossibility* of finding a *Publisher* for my *Poems*, now ready to appear in book - form. All my *previous* vols I had to *pay for myself*; but really I *had* hoped that some of the great No firms would accept *this* —my latest collection of verses! Not so! They refuse the risk of publication with a marvellous unanimity! In consequence, (as I am more impecunious than ever), the mature, carefully executed Works of my ripe manhood, must go down into darkness & oblivion. Pardon such egotism! To few, *very few*, would I open my heart, and expose, so plainly, a deep wound; the source of bitter disappointment & mortification.

¶Your letter shows that you suffer much anxiety on account of *Mrs* Tyler's health. *Thoroughly* I can sympathize with you, here; for my *own* wife — during a period of between 6 & 8 *years* —was a habitual Invalid, and unless we had, per force, removed from the Carolina lowlands into the more bracing atmosphere of the Geo hills, I'm sure she would never have survived.

But may this cloud, like every other, pass away from your household; & leave you all the peace possible, in this strange, phantasmal, transitory world.

Write soon! & Believe me,
Ever y'r affectionate friend,

Paul H Hayne
P. O. Box 635
Augusta Geo

[Mantalini, a character in Dickens's *Nicholas Nickleby* (1838–1839), is a selfish, affected fop who lives on the earnings of his wife, a dressmaker. The speech from which Hayne quotes occurs in Chapter 34 (about two pages from the beginning): "I am here, my soul's delight, upon Tom Tiddler's ground, picking up the demnition gold and silver."

Arthur Dimmesdale was the father of Hester Prynne's illegitimate child in Hawthorne's *The Scarlet Letter*.

The volumes which Hayne says he had to pay for were these:

Poems, Boston: Ticknor & Fields, 1855
Sonnets and Other Poems, Charleston: Harper & Calvo, 1857
Avolio; A Legend of the Island of Cos, Boston: Ticknor & Fields, 1860
Legends and Lyrics, Philadelphia: J. B. Lippincott & Co., 1872
Three later volumes were these:
The Mountain of the Lovers, New York: E. J. Hale & Son, 1875
Lives of Robert Young Hayne and Hugh Swinton Legaré, Charleston: Walker, Evans and Cogswell, 1878
Poems of Paul Hamilton Hayne: Complete Edition, Boston: D. Lothrop and Company, 1882
The book of biographical studies was with Hayne "a labor of love." I judge from an advertisement I have seen in a Charleston newspaper that he neither paid for it nor benefited (financially) from it, that the edition was limited to a thousand copies, that all were sold, and that the profits went to the Simms Memorial fund. The *Complete Edition* was partly a subscription volume. I do not believe Hayne received any money from it, but at least it did not cost him anything. One of the letters in this collection (No. 37) implies that the publishers had taken the risk in bringing out *The Mountain of the Lovers*. The sale of the volume was disappointing (see the letters to E. C. Stedman).

The "two fires" were probably Northern prejudice and Southern indifference. It might not be out of place here to point out that although the sale of Hayne's first two volumes was very small, the majority of the copies that were sold were bought by Charlestonians; that E. J. Hale and his son had moved to New York from North Carolina; and that the *Complete Edition* was made possible largely through the efforts of Colonel John G. James, President of the State Agricultural and

Mechanical College of Texas. Of course Hayne's struggle was terrific and his position after the war was pathetic, but the position of the whole South was pathetic too, and I doubt whether, *in his own lifetime,* any other Southern poet was so widely beloved as was Hayne. Moreover, the majority of Northern poets could not have earned a living by writing poetry alone any more successfully than Hayne did.

Hayne's letters to Stoddard and others written before the war frequently refer to his wife's illness. Her health improved at Copse Hill, and it was Hayne who became a semi-invalid.]

No. 187

PAUL HAMILTON HAYNE to MOSES COIT TYLER

Address me "P O Lock Box 275"
Aûgûsta
Geo
"Copse Hill", Geo R Road:
September 30th 1876.

My Dear Professor;—

Don't suppose that I have, *in any degree,* forgotten you, or ceased to take an interest in your affairs. Not so!

Au contraire, Willie, (my son), and I, continually revert to our New York acquaintances; and *foremost* among these, is *Moses Coit Tyler.*

By the way, you have never sent the *Photograph* of *yourself* I asked for; *do do* send it as soon as convenient.

I shall never regard my *"Photo: Album"* as complete, *until you,* my *valued friend,* shall appear therein. I am *very slow* to make new friendships, but I *know a true man* when I meet him; and therefore, it is, that altho 'we have been with each other "in the flesh" not more than half a dozen times, I nevertheless feel as if we have been friends *for a life time!*

The *only* remembrance recd from *"Ann Arbor"* during the past year, was a *Pamphlet* containing the names of Professors, Students, &c; a book which interested me much; as showing what a superb *"Institution"* your *University of Michigan* must be!

Meanwhile, how have you progressed, & how are your wife & family?

For *myself,* I think that I have written more — especially in *poetry*—during the year or two just passed, than I ever accomplished within the same period before. Of course there has been much indifferent stuff among these rhymes &c Ah me! how *can* a person forced *to write for money,* do justice to himself always?

Nevertheless, I have ready enough good matter on hand to furnish *another* volume. If this 3rd vo*l should* appear, it will consist chiefly of *briefer* lyrics &c. I am more & more convinced that *long poems* violate the artistic spirit of our Time.

Please tell me something of a M*r Newell Lovejoy,* a young gentleman who has just written me a letter from *"Ann Arbor",* wherein he speaks of himself as an earnest lover of Poetry, and a worker in "the Muse's vineyard".

Tell me, *(confidentially),* your opinion of him, both as a man, and author. It will materially help me to answer him aright.

I receive the *"C. Union"* still;—but don't you think it has wofully *deteriorated?* They accept very few pieces of mine now, or indeed of *anybody else's,* being, I take it, unable to pay.

Beecher's recent *"Prospectus",* in which he pronounces his *"weekly"* prosperous; — *more* prosperous than *ever before* —, makes me think it is on the verge of ruin. What an *enigma* the *Rev.* B — is!! There are periods when I feel assured that the man has all along acted a special *rôle* in life; the *rôle* of one who *believing nothing;* regarding the present *mortal existence as the end of all things;*—has deliberately accommodated himself to such conditions, — choosing the Priesthood as the easiest & most influential of professions; — and *practising "on the sly",* every iniquity conceivable!

Assuredly, the evidence against him in the Tilton case, was overwhelming! *Could* any other man in this Country have stood successfully against it? He reminds me of "Assarac High Priest of Baal" in Mellville's powerful novel of *"Semiramis":* a person capable of casting such *"glamours"* over all who approached him, that his ambition, his cunning, his ineffable wickedness, were never ever [even?] suspected, save by a *few* of the *"Initiated"!!*

In *one respect* however, *Assarac could not sin.* He was a *Eunuch!!*

Apropos of Mr *B* —, I am reminded of his friend, and enthusiastic ally *Dr* Holland. The *letter* [latter] having been especially courteous to me, I would not wrong him, even in *thought;* but does it not seem *"passing strange"* to you that an individual of H's shrewdness, & talent, should have gone so far as to denounce *any man* who *even suspected Beecher* of being guilty towards *Mrs* Tilton, as a *malignant or an ass?*

Entre noas [*nous*], I acknowledge it with pain; but this declaration shook somewhat my confidence in the Editor of *"Scribner's"*.

Yet, I would so like to have *that* confidence reinstated.

Do you know *Dr* Holland personally? What think you of him?

Alack! I have wandered into Disagreeable themes. Forgive me!

x x x   I presume that you visited the "Centennial Exposition" in Phil*a*?

From all accounts, it must be richly worth seeing. But we poor *Southerners,* have, most of us, been debarred from this enjoyment.

The major portion of my small Capital — saved from the war —, is invested in S. Carolina; and the *Taxes there* amount to *confiscation!*

From $400 income (E.g) $200 have *often* gone in this manner; and a *third* of one's *Income* has *invariably* to be paid up to these hungry Officials.

How then, could *I* go to the *"Centennial"?*

One must be grateful *here,* if the base [bare?] means of subsistence can be obtained.

Doubtless, you read the Periodicals. ? Did you come across my *Revolutionary Ballads,* one published in *"Harper's Monthly"*;— the *other* in *"Appleton's Journal"*.

The *first* was called *"Macdonald's Raid* (1780)"*, the second *"Charleston Re - Taken,* 1782".

The *style* of *both* is too *antiquated* to suit the present *fantastic taste,* which *denies* poetic merit to Macaulay's *"Lays"*;

& sneers at *Walter Scott's Homeric* narratives in verse, as mere rhymed *novels* or *romances!*

But, I must bring this letter to a *close.* Please *reply very soon;* and *don't forget* about young *Lovejoy;* and *above all, above all, send me your Photograph.*

God be with you!
Believe me,
Ever Faithfully yours

Paul H. Hayne.

P. S. You are fond of *the delicately fanciful & imaginative,* in Poetry. Would that I could mail you a poem of mine just completed in that vein; But 'tis too long to *copy.*

["If this 3rd vo*l should* appear": by third volume' Hayne means third since the war.

George Newell Lovejoy (1844–1915), musician and author, considered music his profession but contributed both verse and prose to leading newspapers and magazines. He was a native of New York State and spent his last twelve years in Rochester, but lived longer in Ann Arbor than anywhere else. He graduated in law at the University of Michigan in 1864 but did not practice law. (For these facts about Lovejoy I am indebted to Lunette Hadley, Director of the Alumni Catalog Office at the University of Michigan.)

Hayne was right about the condition of the *Christian Union.* It had been having trouble since 1873: the panic of 1873, the ill health of the publisher, a fire which damaged the plant, and especially the Beecher scandal combined to lose for the magazine three-fourths of its circulation within two years, and in 1875 the publishers (J. B. Ford & Company) were forced into bankruptcy. After the reorganization which followed, it did somewhat better, but it never regained even one half the circulation it had enjoyed on the eve of the Beecher scandal, and the "array of contributors was not quite so brilliant." (See Mott, III, 425 ff.)

Hayne continued to contribute to the *Christian Union* for years, however. I have not had access to a complete file, but I have seen these poems in it for the early 1880's:

"The Upward Beckoning," XXII (October 13, 1880), 297
"Christ on Earth," XXII (December 29, 1880), 578
"The Three Urns. An Arab Parable," XXIII (March 30, 1881) 300
"The Unseen Host," XXIV (August 10, 1881), 124
"To Longfellow. (On hearing he was ill)," XXV (January 5, 1882)
"To the Author of 'The Victorian Poets,' " XXV (March 23, 1882), 273
"April," XXV (April 20, 1882), 368

"Hera," XXVI (August 31, 1882), 172

"Four Score! To R. G. H.," XXVI (October, 1882), 336

Sarchedon: A Tale of the Great Queen (1871), by George John Whyte-Melville (1821–1878), English novelist, is a historical novel of Semiramis (the famous Assyrian queen) in which the worship of Baal figures.

Josiah Gilbert Holland (1819–1881) was editor of *Scribner's Monthly* of New York from 1870 until his death. He was a popular poet, novelist, essayist, and lecturer, as well as "the most successful editor of his era" (Mott, III, 23).

Hayne's investment in South Carolina was, I think, inherited from his mother—or rather, in 1876, was *her* investment; she died in 1879. It was managed by Samuel Lord, Jr., a Charleston lawyer.

The Prostrate State, under Reconstruction, had to pay five times as much money in taxes as in 1860, although the taxable values of South Carolina were only a little over a third of what they had been in 1860.

"Macdonald's Raid. 1780" appeared in *Harper's New Monthly Magazine* for July, 1876 (LIII, 200–3) and "Charlestown Retaken, December 14, 1782" appeared in *Appleton's Journal* for September, 1876 (New Series, I, 223–4).

Hayne refers to Macaulay's *Lays of Ancient Rome* (1842, 1848) and Scott's *The Lay of the Last Minstrel* (1805), *Marmion* (1808), *The Lady of the Lake* (1810), *Rokeby* (1813), *The Bridal of Triermain* (1813), *The Lord of the Isles* (1815), and *Harold the Dauntless* (1817).]

No. 188

PAUL HAMILTON HAYNE to MOSES COIT TYLER

Address me P O Box 275.
Augûstâ Geo
October 17th 1876..

Dear Friend;

I hope you rec*d*, my *long letter* of about *a week*, or *ten days* ago? *That* letter will explain *Everything!*

Meanwhile let me *repeat* my *earnest* request: *Send me, at once*, a *photograph of yourself!*

I'll give you *no peace*, (take warning!!), until my humble *"Sifflication"*, as *Mister* Richie Meniples, *(vide "Nigel Olifaunt")*, used to express it—hath been amply *satisfied*.

(*over*)

In haste, but Ever

Paul. H. Hayne.

(P S) In the Dec: *no* of *"Harper's Monthly"*, I shall have
a poem, called *"Muscadines"*, which *do read attentively*. I
want your *candid* opinion *thereof!!*

[Richie Moniplies is a servant in Scott's *The Fortunes of Nigel* (1822).
The titular hero is Nigel Olifaunt (or Oliphaunt), Lord Glenvarloch.
"Muscadines" appeared in *Harper's New Monthly Magazine* for December, 1876 (LIV, 127–8). Hayne says the poem was silently rejected
by Howells when it was submitted to the *Atlantic*, whereas H. M. Alden
of *Harper's* liked it so well that he used it within two months. See the
letter to F. B. Stanford dated January 10, 1878 (No. 110).]

No. 189

PAUL HAMILTON HAYNE to MOSES COIT TYLER

"Copse Hill" Geo R R.
Oct 26*th* 1876.

My Dear Friend;

Yours of the 21*th* reached me yesterday. Need I say, that
its contents *deeply interested* me? Above all things, I rejoice
at the prospect of receiving so soon, "your counterfeit presentment".!

Perhaps —(God knows!—) we may never meet on *earth
again;* and in that case *what* a comfort your Photograph will
prove!

Friendship, by the way, cannot be estimated by the number of times persons have met, and conversed with, each other;
but rather by a certain indefinable, subtle sympathy which
attaches one man to another in 3 or 4 brief interviews more
powerfully, than, under *common* circumstances, people are
attached to each other in the course of a *life-time!* This view
is *signally illustrated* in your case & mine. I believe that you
like me thoroughly; and I *know, (without* a particle of *gam-
mon*, or false sentimentality), that I *love you!*

And yet, how many times have we *"foregathered"*, as the
Scotch say?

About *half a dozen times*, at the most!

Tell your *wife* twas an instance, *(so far as I am* concerned) of *"love at first sight"*. What psychological depths are opened by such a confession?

Mr*s* Tyler — you tell me —, is a So Carolinian!

Alas! then, she cannot but *grieve* with her compatriots, in regard to the miserable condition of a State, which has been well called *"prostrate"*. No *human tongue* could fully reveal the tortures thro which So Carolinians have gone under Grant's administration.! Meanwhile, let me *entreat* you, & all my Northern friends, *to put* no *confidence* in *newspaper* reports of insubordination in S. C. So far from being turbulent, murderous rioters, the inhabitants of that hardly - tried section are displaying, at the present hour, a spectacle of *self-abnegation*, of patience under *almost intolerable wrong*, which is — *sublime!* I am no *Politician;*— no *party* - hack;— but an *impartial* Observer, who has studied the condition of affairs, & can *prove the truth of every assertion* he *advances.* In addition, I *engage to have my statements "backed"* by the ablest, & *most intelligent* of the *US army officers, now amongst us!*

x x x x x I am glad that you have gone to live under your "own vine & fig tree!" No *boarding house* can be otherwise than *detestable.* Everybody knows your business, and everybody "puts" a *dirty finger"* into your own *particular* pie!

Ah! *how gladly* I would visit you, were the opportunity granted; and indeed, it *may be granted,* if certain things come to pass, which are surely not *impossible.*

x x I wrote to M*r* Lovejoy some days since, & trust that my letter has not miscarried.

Accept *affectionate* remembrances from my son, *Willie,* & Believe me *Always Faithfully;*—

Paul. H. Hayne.

P. S. Of course you are right about *Beecher!* Apropos of *Holland,* he has been *very kind* to me, and so (like yourself), I can't *analyse his character;* but, *I did not like his unqualified praise* of the *grandest rascal* of *this or any other age!!*

\# To *you* I may mention — *without* the *appearance of egotism*—, that I have ready another vo*l* of poetry for the Press. The verses are wholly *miscellaneous,* & lyrical.

The fact is, experience has taught me *this;*— long narrative or dramatic productions won't *"do"* now-a-days. *High* art, finish *ad urgeum* [*unguem?*], these are what the *Public,* (who *read* poetry at all), imperatively demand. *Of course, feeling, sentiment, passion,* must *"inform"* the *figure,* the mere *outside* so to speak—, [of] one's verses.

[See James S. Pike, *The Prostrate State: South Carolina Under Negro Government* (New York: D. Appleton and Company, 1873) for proof that Hayne does not exaggerate (either here or in other letters) the sad condition of affairs in his native state.]

No. 190

PAUL HAMILTON HAYNE to MOSES COIT TYLER

"Copse Hill" Geo R. R.
November 20th 1876.

My Dear Friend;

I thank you for yours of the 4*th* November, and *above all,* I thank you for the *Photograph.* It is the *reverse* of a flattering likeness, doing you no sort of justice; and still *what* a *noble face* & *head* are presented! With memory to supply the deficiencies, I shall greatly value it.

By the way, I must have expressed myself awkwardly in my last communication.

I didn't mean to say that I had another book of verse actually in press, but that I had enough *poetical material on hand,* to *constitute a volume!*

Poetry however is about the last thing occupying my mind, or the minds of *other* Southerners just now!

Ah! *mon ami!* we approach a terrible *Crisis!* Altho no *Politician,* no party *man,* I am yet *forced* to feel some interest in the result of the singular & most unlucky conflict which has arisen concerning the President[i]al election.

Republican & democratic friends in *both* Lou[i]siana & Fla write me to the effect, that the returning Boards in those States *are wholly* untrustworthy. In L*a* indeed the "Board" is infamous! If therefore, some 6 or 8000 majority of votes for Tilden are "thrown out", God knows what *the end* may be! Think of having a President inaugurated by open, unblushing, palpable *Fraud!!* I know not your own political proclivities, but were I twenty times over a Republican, I should shrink from "cheering" my Candidate thro the power of *false votes* backed by the *bayonet!*

And of course I know you will feel as I do, provided the *facts*, (in their *naked* atrocity), have come to *your* view, as they have come to *mine.*

Meanwhile, poor S. C*a* has been partially redeemed. By a miracle almost *Wade Hampton* wins; and some of the highest offices in the State pass from the hands of negro [,] yankee, and mulatto *aliens*, into those of the true children of the soil!! *Oh! if you could* only *appreciate what this means!* But *none* save those who have lived *in*, or *near* C*a* during the last decade; could fully comprehend the *status* of affairs. Why, even *now*, *now* that the result of the elections is revealed, the *City of Charleston* resembles a Dahomey Town, or *Camp*, rather than a Christian city in a Christian land! Ladies *dare not* leave their homes after nightfall, (and hardly in the *day time*), for fear of being maltreated by negro ruffians in the *Street*;— the very school-girls going to, & coming from School are liable to the *grossest personal insult*;— while (negro) *Policemen* have *not* hesitated to shoot down quiet Citizens, walking towards their offices of business, upon the first indications of a "row" precipitated by roughs & villains of their own color! (Ask your wife, a So C*a* lady), *what she thinks of all this?*)

Henceforth, such violations of law, order, decency, and civilization, are going to be *stopped*. It *may*, probably *will*, need *one terrible* example to bring the negroes & carpet-baggers to their senses; but *after that*, a new *régime* must succeed.

And yet, *oh my friend!* altho an interregnum of peace, & *comparative prosperity* is possible, I entertain but little *ultimate* hope of the *American Republic!* "Revolutions *never* go backward", and when *Grant*, (who combines the *worst qualities* of *Nero*, and *Heliogabalus*), was *allowed* to send his Troops to overawe the electors of *So* States, the *"Revolution"*, whose *end* is *ruin*, was fairly begun;—and *nothing, nothing* can change the inevitable *denouément!* Our *grandchildren*, perchance our *children*, will behold the wreck, *moral & political* of this vast fabric of Government; and, *I do trust*—, that the thoughtful men of the future, disposed to experiment in matters of political rule, will consider all forms of pure republicanism as exploded! *"Vox Populi vox Dei"*, *used* to sound grandly in mine Ears, but I would *now* change it into the *Dog Latin* of *"Vox Populi vox assini"* (*"the voice* of *the People is the brag* [*bray?*] *of jackasses!"*)

+   +   +   +   +   +   +   +   +   +

From the dust, filth & turmoil of *Democratic* & Republican politics, I go to other pleasanter topics.

Do you take *"Harper's* Monthly"? If so, please read over my poem *("Muscadines")*, in the Dec issue of that magazine.

I feel *especially anxious* to have your *candid opinion* of the piece. Is it *too* vague in either *outline*, or *detail?* Does it appear *forced?*

By the way, have you seen Mr *Lovejoy* recently? I answered his letter to me many weeks ago, but have had no acknowledgment from him as to the receipt of my communication. *One only poem* by this young man have I read, (a poem which he must himself have mailed me, published in a religious journal of *Jan* last).

The verses were *melodious*, and displayed *true feeling;* but *(entre nous)*, I did not find in them that indescribable *aroma* of poetic thought, that subtle *"something"* which constitutes the genuine poetical inspiration.

Nothing, however, would be more unfair than to judge of the gentleman's powers by a brief & fugitive performance. + + + + + *Enclosed*, I send you the *very last Photograph* of myself, I had taken *10 days* ago in Augusta. People here pronounce it excellent. *Don't* think me an affected ass, because of the Student's *dressing-gown & Slippers*. I had tried to be taken in *ordinary costume* a dozen *times & failed;*—

therefore, *as a mere forlorn hope,* I adopted the uniform of my *"guild".*

You are fond of art I'm, sure.

Well! let me recommend you to inquire at the book stores for a Xmas book just issued by the Harpers. called *"The Rime of the Ancient Mariner; Illustrated by Doré"*. It is the noblest illustrated vo*l* ever published in this Country. As for the *weird suggestiveness* of Doré's pictures, no language can *adequately describe it!*

Think of the Harpers being so generous as to make me a present of this magnificent book, (worth $50.*00*).!!

Here, I am forced to pause.

Forgive anything like *egotism* in my letter, or political *heat.*

And believe me

Always Faithfully

Paul Hayne.

POBox 275, Augusta Ga

P. S. Do write me soon, & at length.

[According to Professor John Holladay Latané (*A History of the United States,* New York: Allyn and Bacon, 1921, pp. 444–7), it is true, as Hayne suggests, that Tilden was defrauded of the presidency, to which he had been elected both by electoral votes and by a popular majority. Hayes, however, placated the Democrats by withdrawing from the South the Federal army of occupation, whereupon the Republican governors of South Carolina and Louisiana fled, leaving the state governments in the hands of the Democrats.

The South Carolina gubernatorial election of 1876 was exciting and to some extent violent. The results were still in dispute when the Federal troops vacated the State House on April 10, 1877, whereupon Governor Chamberlain fled and Wade Hampton (1818–1902) assumed office April 11. Hampton was also famous as a Confederate lieutenant general and United States senator, but as "liberator" of his people he was best remembered.

Dahomey is a colony, French West Africa.

Nero and Heliogabalus (or Elagabalus) were Roman emperors (54–68 and 218–222, respectively).

"From the dust, filth & turmoil of *Democratic* & Republican politics": Hayne inserted *"Democratic &"* above the line, as if by afterthought.

Possibly he would not have done so had his correspondent been a South-erner.

Paul Gustave Doré (1833–1883) was a French illustrator, painter, and sculptor.]

No. 191

PAUL HAMILTON HAYNE to MOSES COIT TYLER

P. O. Address:

P. O. Box 275.˙.

Augusta, Ga.

Copse Hill, Ga.,
June 25*th* 1877

My Dear Friend;—

Your letter has touched, & delighted me! It is so warm, so frank, so affectionate!! Why may I not cast aside all conventionality, & say, that you are the *only man* I ever met in life, whose transparent honesty, outspoken candor, exquisite courtesy; in a word, whose *genuineness & nobility* of nature, con-quered me at once & forever; making me realize, after two or three interviews only, that in *you* Providence had sent me a *genuine* friend?

And you have never failed me; you never *will!*

It is *very* encouraging to know, that my Poem *("Muscadines")*, struck you so favorably.

Let me acknowledge that the success of that particular piece, amazed me!

I took immense pains with its composition; heart, soul, imagination, feeling, were all enlisted to render it as perfect as possible; but, upon reading the completed poem over, I felt sure that, it would prove not only "caviare to the general",—but that very few persons outside a small circle of classical scholars — would, or *could* admire it.

Well! a pleasant disappointment awaited me. It proved one of the most *popular* poems I had ever published; and it satisfied the scholars too!

I'm certain you'll feel gratified to hear that among numerous letters of congratulation, *apropos* of *"Muscadines"*, which have reached me, there is one from *Swinbourne* [Swinburne], alluding in the warmest terms to my verses which he pronounces, "charming", "so full of the color & fragrance & health of the beauty they describe, that they make one long to enjoy *these also in person!!*"

Isn't that glorious, as coming from the first Lyrist of the present, or perhaps of any other age?

You will not consider me *egotistical* in quoting such commendation.? I could *not* resist the temptation, relying upon your kind indulgence. Ah! well! I needed some encouragement, for my health is, & has been wretched for months past. The mind only keeps me up! Nevertheless, picture me not as a whining hypochondriac!

I'll never *rust* out, but die knightlike in harness; *tho* just now, under the stimulant of your letter, & certain other epistles in the same tone, I am disposed to bid *Death*, and all gloomy thoughts "avaunt!" *Basta! basta!* eno' of oneself!!

x x x The papers inform me to my great delight, (if it only proves true), that you are engaged upon an elaborate work in reference to "English Literature". Pray tell me all about it; how far you have already progressed; what your general plan is; & at what period you anticipate completing this very important undertaking? Perhaps — if the needful information be granted me—, I can do your work "yeoman's service" here in the South.

Something connected with this enterprise, I suppose, has carried you to NYork City during the dog-days; for I can't imagine any human being seeking that Purgatorial metropolis, in summer, unless compelled to do so, by business imperative, and absolute! Talk of So heat! Why, bless your innocent soul! I *never* experienced, even among the semi - Tropical islands, and the *malarial* districts of our section any heat that *could* be compared to the sweltering, infernal atmosphere of the Gotham side-walks, and even the Gotham hotels.

Once in 1855–6, I staid with my *then* youthful wife, at the *"Clarendon"* Broadway, for 2 weeks; and despite every luxury & convenience, ice *ad libitum*, cold baths in marble tubs, Sherry Coblers [cobblers], half frozen sherbet, & mint juleps, — we both of us nearly succumbed [succumbed]! It was awful!! (I don't mean that my "winsome marrow" partook of the "juleps", "cobblers" &c; the Lord forbid!)

Doubtless, in the course of your visit, you'll see many of my NY friends, and literary acquaintances. Remember me cordially to all of them; particularly *Miss Booth*, whose kindness to me, has been *very great*. Alas! I cannot join you there!, altho to meet you once more, I would defy the temperature of an *African* jungle! —

x x Yes! *Politics* are "easier" than they were! and I devoutly thank heaven that my native State, (Carolina), has been at last (comparatively) freed from the Jackalls, & Hyenas who preyed upon her very vitals!

Hayes' course has been markedly conservative, and distinguished by great good sense, and a statesmanlike discretion.

Thus far I honor him; but *oh! mon ami!* his accepting the Presidency at all, under the peculiar circumstances, it is *utterly impossible* (for me) to comprehend.

But I am old fashioned in these matters; and may be considered a mere *"Impracticable"*.

Yet, no *party* prejudice influences me, since I am *neither a Dem!* or *Republican;* believing in *neither* of these great political divisions, & entertaining — to speak plain truth —, but little hope of the *ultimate* success of the U States, and the *"every man free & equal* theory" whereon the Constitution seems founded!

Self government by the masses I believe to be the grossest of humbugs, and any government less powerful than a "limited monarchy", is—*me judice!*—bound, *sooner or later,* to fall to pieces! *Nous verrons!*

Meanwhile, pardon these atrocious sentiments. I can't help entertaining them!

  x   x   x   x   x   x   x   x   x   x

x — Do write me *as soon as possible!!* Your letters are benefactions!

> Ever my dear friend,
> Faithfully yr's
>
> *Paul H Hayne*

P S. I wrote a letter to B. Taylor the other day, (but have not yet rec*d* a reply) in reference to my son *Willie;* asking whether there was any chance in NY of getting a *Librarianship* for him.

What would be the prospect in your *"University"?*, and what is the climate in Mich?

Willie has never been strong eno' for a Collegiate education, & evidently has no fancy for the Professions. I think he would make a capital *Librarian,* for from early youth, he took delight in making catalogues of Books, & really, I depend upon him to find out where my book[s] are, and to keep the library in order.

The reason I ask about the Mich: climate is, that my son believes a cold, bracing climate would do him good.

He is very intelligent, high principled, & exceedingly anxious to find something to do.

Poor boy! with all the natural impetuosity of youth, it irks him to remain here, among the pine - woods, day after day, & month after month, without the prospect of a definate [*sic*] career.

I have tried, & tried, & tried again, to procure him employment; always rairly [vainly?]!

The times are "out of joint"—

If you hear of anything, *anywhere,* that might suit the lad, won't you inform me? 'Twould be a charity!

x x   By the way, I enclose for your perusal, a partly political poem of mine, published *when Carolina seemed* hopelessly *lost.* Make allowance for the apparently savage sentiments. In a word, *"put yourself* in my place!"*— God bless you!!! —*

[In the first of two sonnets "To Algernon Charles Swinburne" (*Complete Edition,* p. 269) Hayne writes:

"Not since proud Marlowe poured his potent song
    Through fadeless meadows to a marvellous main,
    Has England harkened to so sweet a strain—
    So sweet as thine, and ah! so subtly strong!"

Mary Louise Booth (1831–1889) was editor of *Harper's Bazar* (weekly) from 1867 until 1889. Hayne contributed poems to *Harper's Bazar, Harper's Weekly,* and *Harper's New Monthly Magazine.*

Bayard Taylor (1825–1878), poet, journalist, diplomat, was greatly admired by Hayne. See Hayne's memorial poems to him (*Complete Edition*, pp. 320–1). Cf. Hayne's letter to Stedman dated May 15, 1877 (No. 129), in which he says that he will send a duplicate to Taylor. It requests aid in securing a librarianship for Willie (1856–1929). (Willie remained at Copse Hill and in Augusta the rest of his life, except for visits elsewhere, I believe.)

Hayne's political poem was probably "South Carolina to the States of the North. Especially to Those That Formed a Part of the Original Thirteen" (*Complete Edition*, pp. 297–9).]

No. 192

PAUL HAMILTON HAYNE to MOSES COIT TYLER

Address me P O Box 275
Augusta Geo

My Dear Friend;

The advertisement, lately, of your *two vols* of *"Colonial Literary History"* by *Putnam*, has made me think again of you, and of your *noble* literary enterprise, which has been thus auspiciously begun.

May it progress to a *glorious conclusion!!* *Of course* I need hardly say, that if I can an [in] *any manner, advance* the interests of your *great* Work, I will *gladly, proudly do so.*

Would you like me to notice the *vols just out,* in several prominent *So* journals?—

x x x x x By the way, *do* you know, that our *two* long-divided sections of Country; *divided first,* by grave political & moral questions, & then, by the results of War, are *nearer each other this day,* than they ever *have been* since the surrender at *Appomattox?*—

+ The *boundless sympathy of your* People for our Yellow-Fever Sufferers has accomplished what *Cannon* & *"Re-Con-struction"* could *never never* have done! *I am so thankful!!*—

x x x x x *Apropos* of this important topic, please read the enclosed Poem which came from my heart, & the success of which seems to have been *great.*

. . . *Another matter* calculated to unite the North & South just now, is the *Superb* heroism of *Lieut Hiram Benner.*

———— *Actually*, the *whole territory south of* the *Potomac*, from Virginia to L*a*, is in a blaze of excited gratitude, & enthusiastic admiration, touching the conduct of this noble young man. *Again*, I have *endeavored* to give the popular voice & feeling *embodiment;*— I have composed a 7 stanza poem, entitled merely *"Hiram Benner"*, & *dedicated* to his *Wife*, which I mailed to *S. S. Conant* of *"Harper's Weekly"*—. some days since. *Despite* the *popularity of* the subject, and the good likely to result from its sincere treatment, I would *not* be astonished if Conant *declined* my *verses*.

Conant is the *only* man connected with the *Harper's Establishment*, from whom I have *failed* to receive either recognition, or kindness.

He refused to publish from *"The Stricken South to the North"*, upon some miserable, flimsy plea that he had already printed a piece, about as much like mine, as a *"locust is like a lobster"!*—, *(sweet comparison!).*, but if he *does not* wish it, it shall appear *elsewhere*.

My friend! (I *can* be Egotistical with you), I am thinking of collecting my Poems, composed *since* my last vo*l* was published —, if I can get *some Publisher* to take them *free of charge*. I am *too old* a *Writer now*, to *pay for publication;* and *too poor besides!* — . . . I remember your asking me in your *last* letter, whether I had ever tried the *Putnams;* & saying, that you thought my *"Muscadines"* alone, *ought* to ensure their acceptance of my *Mss*. — *Enpassant*, did I ever tell *you, that in* a *private letter* to myself, Swinburne expressed *great admiration of that piece?* I don't mention this, *conceitedly;* but as a *preface* to a request I have to make of you. — As you may have influence with the *Putnams*, & recalling the many kind things you have said of my verses,— would you drop them a *line*, mentioning that I has [had?] written to you of my intention to apply to them as the Publishers of my *next* vol —, *if they would publish* at *their own risk*.— (The vo*l* would be a *very small one*, from 100, to *130* pages do).

Perhaps, you could tell them what you *thought* of my work; stating also, that *my reputation had greatly increased* since the appearance of my last book — (This *latter fact* is stated from a business point of view only).

. . . If you decide to extend to me this kindness, please inform me; because I would not write *Publishers*, until *I hear from* you!—x x x x x x x The *number of I's* in this communication is revolting; but you excuse them;— especially when I tell you of my melancholy state *of health*. Yes! at any *moment, death* may summon my soul away but *what then?* There are *better lives* beyond this "shoal of Time", I do *firmly believe.*

Old Friend! Write me. Always Truly &c

Paul H. Hayne

[This letter is undated. I conjecture that it was written about November 1, 1878: H. M. Jones (*The Life of Moses Coit Tyler*, p. 187) says that Tyler's *A History of American Literature During the Colonial Time, 1607–1765*, 2 vols., appeared in November, 1878; Hayne refers to the volumes as *"just out"*; the next letter refers to a communication from Tyler dated November 6 which was apparently a prompt reply to this one.

The "enclosed Poem" was "The Stricken South to the North" (*Complete Edition*, pp. 299–300). It was published in the Charleston *News and Courier* for October 28, 1878. It says that love has subdued souls which hate could only wound, and expresses the South's gratitude for the relief sent to her fever-stricken cities.

The Charleston *News and Courier* (see issues in August, September, and October, 1878) indicates that the yellow fever epidemic raged through August, September, and October. The region hardest hit was the Mississippi Valley, especially New Orleans, Memphis, and Vicksburg. By October 28 (says the *News and Courier*) 3,864 had died in New Orleans alone.

"Hiram H. Benner" appeared in the Charleston *News and Courier* on November 21, 1878. Several news items and editorials concerning Lieutenant Hiram H. Benner had appeared in October issues. Relief supplies for fever sufferers were sent to St. Louis, whence they were to be taken down the river in the steamer *Chambers*. Lieutenant Benner and Lieutenant Hall volunteered to take charge of the expedition. The *Chambers* left St. Louis early in October. A short time later Benner took the fever and was reported ill aboard the supply ship at Vicksburg. He died on October 17. Editorials and Hayne's poem praised him as a martyr. During the war he had served in an Illinois regiment and had been promoted from the ranks for gallantry in action. After the war he was stationed for several years at Columbia, South Carolina, as a member of the Eighteenth Infantry.

Samuel Stillman Conant (1831–1885?) was managing editor of *Harper's Weekly* from 1869 until 1885, when he mysteriously disappeared.]

No. 193

PAUL HAMILTON HAYNE to MOSES COIT TYLER

"Copse Hill," Georgia Rail Road,
November 16*th* 1878.

Address:

    P. O. Box 275,

       Augusta, Ga.

Dear Friend:

Your characteristically prompt & affectionate letter of the 6*th* inst, reached me in due season. *Heartily* I thank you for the *practical interest* displayed in my Poems.

Whether Putnam says *"yes"*, or *"no"!* (and I am in little doubt as to the *negative response*), of course I shall be *equally obliged* to *you!*— *equally sensible* of your *considerate* courtesy.

When *P*— has definitely answered your proposal *do inform me*.

Concerning your *great Work* upon American Literature,— for *a great work*, I know it is!—, be sure that the 2 initial vol*s*, shall be *properly* noticed, *when they arrive*.

I shall review them *con amore! Copies* of *notices* encountered in the pages of the various journals, & periodicals —, their *"name is legion"*, which litter my library table *nightly —, shall* be cut out, and carefully mailed to your address.

This agreeable task I leave confidently to my "winsome *Marrow"*, who searches the papers &c with an *eagle eye;* thus saving me a *vast deal* of trouble, while at the same time, she gratifies her natural female instinct for *omniverous* [sic] . . news!!

(Wife happened to be leaning over my shoulder, & caught a glimpse of above sentence. Consequence . . . a black &

blue *contusion* upon my skull — *outside*, and *temporary* confusion . . . *inside!!*)— . . *Don't* mention it, however! *"Tis'* of
no consequence!"— *vide* — the *immortal Toots!*— . . . . . .

   . . . I can't tell you how really glad I am. that a student, and man of noble imaginative talent like yourself,
(*above* all, a man of *judicious impartiality*), should have
undertaken this labor, & carefully prepared a work, so long
a *desideratum!*

I *accentuate* the phrase, *"judicious impartiality"*, since how
much excellent literary performance has been weakened or
vitiated by *prejudice, partisanship,* & *one-sidedness!!*

Par example, read our friend Whipple's article on *Rufus
Choate* in last *"Harper"*. Observe, how bitter he becomes, the
moment it is necessary to touch upon So Politics, & So Con-
gressional leaders.!! On several *former occasions,* he had depreciated *Calhoun;*— and now, he must needs refer to *Geo
McDuffie in effect* as a *blatant bully;* a *black* guard, and
"notorious *duellist* with" his *body literally scarred by* the
wounds received in his innumerable *affairs d'honneur!!*

   . . . . He goes even further, *almost insinuating* that Mc
D — was a Coward, *au fond,* & that he *wilted* under Choate's
"merciless invectives, torrent of *sarcasms* &c!"

Now, this sort of thing is to be regretted, coming from a
responsible, eloquent, and far-famed Essayist, like *Whipple!*—
At all events, he should have been *quite certain as to* his
deliberate statements. So far from Mr [Mc]Duffie's being the
bully, and *scarred* Duellist portrayed; he *fought* but *one man
in the whole course of his life;* & *that man was Cumming* of
Ga; who *provoked him, many* think, to the *field!*

  . . Thus much for *prejudice!*

   . . . . . In my last letter, I referred *cheerfully* to the
harmonious relations seemingly about to be established between *North & South.* But *alack!* things have gone towards
the old *disastrous grove* again.

Those Nov! elections played the deuce with the spirit of
Concord. And here *comes W. Phillips,* putting *his* poisonous
finger in our political *Pie* again! *Why* d'ont *somebody* consign *that* disgusting old *Marplot* & *"mawworm"* to a *"Straight*

Jacket",? 'Twould benefit the *Nation;* & benefit *Truth,* Decency, and general *Civilization!*

— The idea of *Phillips* alluding to *Wade Hampton* as a
"vagabond", a *parvenu* Political Scamp, and a *"liar!!"*

However, let us hope that the broadest - souled People *North
& South* will refuse to be guided by such "false lights". *You
& I,* could *"fix* up *matters" in a* day *couldn't* we?, were you
North, & I *South.* . . . I've just recd a note from Mr Whittier.
He says "your *noble* poem (mine) from "*South to* North", has
just reached me. My *whole heart* responds! All thro the long
agony of the Past, I was among the N. H. mountains; & more
than once contributed to the aid of sufferers. *God knows* that
our People felt only that you needed aid; & that you were
our fellow Countrymen! The sad *Past* was thrown so far
back, that it was *not* remembered. *None* gave more readily
than the *"soldiers of the North!"* [*"*]— Dr Holmes seemed too,
to appreciate highly the dedication of these lines, & wrote me
most sympathetically. And indeed, *numberless* other letters
about *them,* have come from other sources, expressing *great
feeling* on the subject!—

My wife insists upon telling you that she contemplates a
Divorce, because of what *she* styles my *slander* touching her
love of news, or Gossip; when she is so quiet a *little body*
that she has not left "Copse Hill" *once* in 12(!) years; &
seldom looks even at a *Fashion Plate!!*

x x x x x I *strive* to write *cheerily,* and to look at the
bright side of things,— *but* to *you* (my *true friend!*) I may
acknowledge that *this world & life* seem "closing in" upon me.

— I am conscious of *growing feebleness;*— my hair has
turned as gray as *Henry Stanley's* since his last African *raid;*
and . . and . . . well! my *summons* to depart may come at
any moment!! *I feel this!*

> God be with you!
> Ever faithfully,
>
> *Paul H. Hayne.*

[Toots is an innocent, humble admirer of Florence, the daughter of
Mr. Dombey, in Dickens's *Dombey and Son* (1847–1848).

E. P. Whipple's "Some Recollections of Rufus Choate" appeared in *Harper's New Monthly Magazine* for November, 1878 (LVII, 875–89). The reference to the debate between Choate and McDuffie (over the tariff) is on page 883. Whipple calls McDuffie "the great fire-eater," "a duellist debater, whose body was riddled with bullets received in many a quarrel which his effrontery had provoked." Rufus Choate (1799–1859) was a famous Massachusetts lawyer and United States senator. George McDuffie (1790–1851), of South Carolina, was governor and United States senator. Every schoolboy knows John C. Calhoun.

William Cumming (1790–1863) of Georgia quarreled with McDuffie over the Calhoun-Crawford rivalry for the presidency and the nullification issue. Cumming sent McDuffie several challenges to a duel. Both men were noisy about their intention to fight. When they met, McDuffie was wounded in the hip and lamed for life.

Wendell Phillips (1811–1884), of Boston, was an orator and reformer. Wade Hampton (1818–1902) was governor of South Carolina at the time and later was United States senator.

The next year (1879) Hayne's wife went with him to New York and New England.

Sir Henry Morton Stanley (1841–1904) told of his "last African *raid*" in *Through the Dark Continent* (1878). Earlier he had gone to Africa to find David Livingstone.]

No. 194

PAUL HAMILTON HAYNE to MOSES COIT TYLER

Address me P O Box 275 Augusta Geo
December 10th 1878

My Dear & True Friend:

I am so *delighted* to see by the Northern papers, that your *Work* has gone into the *2nd* edition!

I *heartily congratulate* you upon this success, &c! —

Now, allow me to thank you in *advance* for your *gift* of these volumes, (which, when rec*d*, will occupy a *prominent place in my library*) & also, for your generous *interest* in my *own* verses.

I shall "express" the *Poems (my Poems)* to you (D V!) "*Care of Putnam & Sons*) ["], on next Monday, 16*th Dec.*, *pre-paid.*

My belief is that *Stedman will undoubtedly* interest himself in my *behalf;*— because his *private* criticisms, (written to myself), were most enthusiastic, in reference to several of my pieces; and he seems to be a truly warm-hearted friend. . . . *But, (entre nous), I would* I would [*sic*] *infinitely* rather you *should not appeal* to *Stoddard;*— because, altho I have ever been genuinely appreciative, (and have so expressed myself), of *his artistic work,*— he gave scant praise, & *scant notice* of my "*Legends & Lyrics*", when he was Editor of "*The Aldine*";— never *noticed* the "*Mountain of Lovers*" at all; and even *after* I had written a *most loving* reply to his piece—"*When All is Done & Said*", (you'll see it in my last vo*l*), he *neither* noticed the verses, nor *answered my letter* containing a *copy thereof!!*

The *fact* is, I understand, that the poor fellow (for whom I *still entertain the kindest sentiments*), has become *embittered* thro poverty, disappointment, and *chronic ill-health!!* *Au fond*, he is *both kind & considerate!* x x x x

x x x   You speak of "loafing" *in NYork*—! *Do* you mean to run up to *Boston?*—

Perhaps your influence, & Stedman's *might* induce a Boston Publisher to *undertake the work;* but I know that you will do what is kindest & best for *my reputation;* & *'tis all* the same to me whether the Poems appear in *NY.* or Boston.

My wife says, that if she encounters any notices of your work in papers she'll be *sure* to mail them.   I receive *most new* Publications (from the various *No* firms) "*by Express*". . . .

There is *one* of my Poems, I desire to include in the collection, but the *only copy* I had, was sent to *Longfellow*, for his "*Poems of Places*". So, I enclose 25cts, begging you to buy the no of "*Harper's Mage*", containing this lyric, called "*Macdonald's Raid*"; to *cut* it out, & place it among the poems I'll soon send to you *care of Putnams!* "*Macdonald's Raid*" occurs in the "*July no of Harper's Monthly*" for for [*sic*] the year *1876.*, and I think *it will please you*, as a spirited Ballad.   The old Fellow who is supposed to tell this story really lived; and as a *lad* I knew him *well!!*—I've a *little* idealized old *Seargent* [*sic*] *Saunders,*—for, from certain *hints* reaching me from other quarters, I'm afraid the old chap rather belonged to the

"Dalgetty" *order* of warriors!   But *brave!! per Hercle!*—He feared *not* the *Devil & all his grips!!*

"*Muscadines*" shall occupy the *first place in* the *Book,* & oh! *mon ami!* I do hope the *contents generally* may meet with your *approval.*

Affectionately yr's *Paul H Hayne.*

[With this reference to Stedman compare the letters of the same period to him.

R. H. Stoddard was editor of the *Aldine* (New York art journal) for four or five years beginning in 1871.   He had been Hayne's earliest intimate correspondent among the Northern poets (see the first letters in this collection).   For Hayne's poem addressed to him see *Complete Edition,* p. 208.   See Hayne's references to him in the letters to Stedman.

"Macdonald's Raid. 1780" appeared in *Harper's New Monthly Magazine* for July, 1876 (LIII, 200–3).

Captain Dugald Dalgetty was a loquacious soldier of fortune in Scott's *A Legend of Montrose* (1819).]

No. 195

PAUL HAMILTON HAYNE to MOSES COIT TYLER

Address me at P O Box 275. —
Augustâ Georgia.˙.
December 16th 1878.˙.

My Dear Friend;

Today, my Poems go per "Express", according to your directions—, addressed to *you,* Care of *G. P. Putnam's Sons,* NYork.

. . . I have had to arrange them so *hastily,* that, I am sure the best order has not been adopted.   Now, let me say that to *your hands, & Stedman's,* I *commit these verses, with authority to change the order of pieces,* and to *omit any poems, you may for any reason dislike,** *before* the *"Mss"* are presented to a *Publisher for consideration.*

I implicitly *rely upon you two;* your judgment no less than *friendship.*

Entre nous, I *don't* think *that R. H. Stoddard*, (tho I have known him for *years*, and have rec*d* some *noble courtesies* from him) *especially* likes my poetry; which was *one* reason, among others, *why* I did *not* "take" to the idea of consulting him on this matter. Don't suppose, however, that *any coldness* exists between us. *Far* from it!

And please consult *your own* reason; and if *S——*, can be useful, forget what I have written; and advise with him also.

As for *Stedman*, a worthier *ally* could *not* be imagined! I consider him, *honestly*, as *a God - made Critic of Poetry*, the *subtlest*, profoundest *analyst of imaginative art, and sentiment & passion, now living!*

And now, *what* am I to say of *your unexampled generosity* & kindness?

Only *this Dear Friend!*, that whether you *succeed* or *fail*, I can *never* cease to recall with pride & gratitude your spontaneous interest and noble appreciation.

I *have a few more Poems* to add to those, *already sent.* If the vo*l* threatens to be too bulky; (as hinted previously), you are authorized to cut down, & curtail; retaining the *crème de la crème*, if there is *any* thing so superfine discoverable. . . . . . Drop me a line, pray, so that I may know, the p'c'k *did* not miscarry.

Always Faithfully, Paul H. Hayne.

[Written lengthwise in the margin on the first page of the letter:]

* Always excepting the longer poems, called *"Muscadines" "Unveiled" & "Ode to Wm Gilmore Simms"*, together with *"Underground"*, "Twilight Monologue" and *"Shadow* of *Death"*, which I'm sure, however, *you'll* like —&c[.]

[In his own day Stedman's reputation as a poetry critic was very high indeed. Hayne's opinion was the general one.

The poems (in the order mentioned in the marginal note) appear in *Complete Edition*, pp. 222–4, 219–22, 315–20, 227–8, 333–4, 334.]

No. 196

PAUL HAMILTON HAYNE to MOSES COIT TYLER

"Copse Hill," Georgia Rail Road,
December 28*th* 1878

Address:

P. O. Box 275,
Augusta, Ga.

My Dear Friend;

Both my wife & self are *profoundly* touched by the *genuine* interest you have displayed in regard to my Poems. There is only *one other besides* yourself, who has taken such a *practical* interest in them.

But first, allow me to answer your *two* most important questions.

My vl*s* have *none of them* been *"Copyrighted"*. I will mention their Publishers.

1*st* a small vo*l* issued by *Messrs Ticknor & Fields Boston* 1855—(a *mere juvenile* affair!).

2*nd* *"Avolio & other Poems"*, issued by same Publishers, Boston 1859–60 — (containing *all* I would preserve out of 1*st* book).

3*rd* — *"Legends & Lyrics,"*— (*published* by *Lippincotts* Phil*a* 1872,) *containing my* very best *narrative poems, Sonnets & lyrics*),

& 4*th* *"Mountain of Lovers*, with Poems of *Nature & Tradition"*, (issued by *E. [J.] Hale & Son, NYork 1875*). Perhaps, I ought to tell you *some* of the many things that have been said of the *narrative poems, which of course*, are less *known* & popular than the lyrics. For example, Miss *Ingelowe* thought *"The Wife of Brittany"* "very beautiful", & the illustrious Chaucer. Scholar, Prof Childs of Cambridge, wrote me actually that I had made the "original Tale quite as much my own, as *Chaucer* "ever had done *any* of his!!"—

You may recollect what *Whipple* said of it, viz, that "it was *equal to anything of Morris'*, & had it *appeared under the name* of the author of *"Earthly Paradise"*, it would have obtained a recognition on both sides of the Atlantic".

He adds, "We cannot see that the *American* Poet is one whit inferior to his English Contemporary in tenderness, sweetness, simplicity, grace, & ideal charm; while we venture to say, that he has more than *Morris'*, the *true* Poetic enthusiasm, the unwithholding self abandonment to the sentiment suggested by his theme!"—

B. Taylor said, that *he* preferred this poem to Morris'! I forget his exact words, because his letter is not by me; but he thought that I had more of the imaginative faculty, "my mood being *more* of May, while *his* is Novemberish".

Longfellow thought *"Daphles"*, *"very beautiful"* & Mr Whipple pronounced it a "flawless pearl"!

I will not weary you by more quotations from authors of distinction, & *only mention* what has been said of the *"narratives"*, because (as previously remarked), *they are less known.*

It is needless to inform you *Dear Friend* that these criticisms are *not alluded to in egotism,* or *vanity,* but merely, that they may further my interests with *Publishers.*

¶Now, as to your *next question,* I *would* myself *infinitely* prefer *a complete Edition of my Poems, if that were possible, viz all,* or most of these contained in *"Legends & Lyrics",* & "The Mountain of Lovers", together with the unpublished Poems (unpublished in book - form I mean), which you have in hand.

. . . . . If *not possible* (—*"beggars can't be choosers*["]—), *then,* I would be *satisfied perfectly* with *such* a *selection as you propose.*

As to the sketch of my life which you would like to have attached to vo*l,* there have been *four* written of me, besides the *imperfect* one, contained in *"The NYork Eclectic". Two* of these are already published, & two *others* are to be published, one by *Mrs M. J Preston* which I have read in *"Ms"* & the second by Cha*s* F Richardson,— *not* seen by me —. The latter is to appear in *"Wide Awake"* as one of the series of *"Poet's Homes"* richly illustrated, in March '79. I am *sure* you would like Mrs Preston's sketch, *brief,* terse, & to the point.! Should you need a *portrait,* I can furnish you with one —, the *very best ever* taken of me —, which was asked for by *Messrs Ford & Co*, for Bryant's *"Library of Poetry & Song"*.

. . . . . . And now, I must tell you of a matter which please *keep strictly to yourself* &c. About a year since I rec*d* a letter from *Col Jno James*, (Sup: of Texas Milt: Institute") *Austin*, Texas, who said he was *exceedingly anxious* to get up by *subscription*, a *Complete Illustrated edition of my Works*; he desired it to be *"a Poet's edition"*, so that the profits *might accrue to myself*; and the *"Illustrations" be the gift* of the So People.

Towards the close of the "Yellow Fever" epidemic, that it had been his intention to make collections for this purpose during the last autumn, when Crops were gathered; but that the *demand* for fever sufferers, combined with financial difficulties, rendered that period an unfavorable one;— but he added that I would hear from him, when the right time arrived.

I know that Co*l* James is *thoroughly earnest* in this matter; but I *don't know that he will succeed in what he proposes*; — therefore I *cannot dream of losing this opportunity which your unselfish kindness has, I may say, created!* —

I would like you to tell me, if *Holt* secures a "Copyright" for *his* purposed vo*l* (for I do not understand the subject, *I'm ashamed* to *confess*), would Co*l* James be obliged to pay him *anything*, from the profits of any future illustrated edition, should he, after all, suc[c]eed in bringing it out.? (This *question is only addressed to yourself*; for as said before, Holt must not be told of *James' plan*) I am desperately poor, & my *health* very bad; so, the money - question is important;—

If *Holt* issues the book, I suppose, (as a matter of course), I could expect to make nothing thereby. But I *do* wish frankly (above all things, money or *no* money) to see this Holt plan carried thro, & before heaven I *dont* believe he will lose; for let him once definitely arrange to publish the work, & I'll go to work among my friends in So States, & secure their *practical* interest &c[.]

All here unite in *best love* to you. We value you as a *real*, & noble friend. *In haste* but

Ever affectionately yr's

Paul H. *Hayne.*

Your noble book, I shall notice as such a work *deserves!*

[The other person who had taken a practical interest in Hayne's poems was John Garland James, President of the State Agricultural and Mechanical College of Texas, who took charge of efforts to bring out a complete edition by subscription and to whom Hayne dedicated the *Complete Edition* (1882), "in which he has taken so unselfish an interest." See Hayne's letters to him in the following group. (When their correspondence began, James was superintendent of the Texas Military Institute at Austin.)

In the list of his volumes of poems Hayne omits the second: *Sonnets and Other Poems*, Charleston: Harper & Calvo, 1857.

Hayne corresponded for years with Jean Ingelow (1820–1897), English poet and story writer. See his sonnet "To Jean Ingelow," *Complete Edition*, p. 270. It appeared in the *Youth's Companion* (Boston) for April 14, 1881 (LIV, 138).

"The Wife of Brittany" (*Complete Edition*, pp. 118–37), based on Chaucer's *Franklin's Tale*, is the best of Hayne's long narrative poems.

Francis James Child (1825–1896), very distinguished Harvard scholar and professor, edited Spenser's poems and various other works, wrote observations on the language of Chaucer and Gower, and brought out the standard collection of English and Scottish popular ballads.

For "Daphles. An Argive Story" see *Complete Edition*, pp. 89–100.

Mrs. Margaret Junkin Preston (1820–1897), poet of Lexington, Virginia, wrote the sketch of Hayne in *Complete Edition* (1882) and one of the best critical articles on him, "Paul Hamilton Hayne," in the *Southern Bivouac*, II (September, 1886), 222–9. For her letters to Hayne see Elizabeth Preston Allan's *The Life and Letters of Margaret Junkin Preston* (Boston and New York: Houghton, Mifflin and Company, 1903). She had discussed *Legends and Lyrics* in the *Southern Magazine* of Baltimore (X, 377).

At the time of this letter Charles Francis Richardson (1851–1913) was on the staff of the Philadelphia *Sunday School Times*, to which he had come from the New York *Independent*, and from which he went to the New York *Good Literature*. After 1882 he was for about thirty years professor of English at Dartmouth. Mrs. Hayne's letter to Tyler dated April 24, 1879 (No. 199), says that an illustrated article on Hayne appeared in the April issue (1879) of the Boston *Wide Awake*. (I have not seen the issue.) I suppose it is by Richardson.]

No. 197

PAUL HAMILTON HAYNE to MOSES COIT TYLER

Address P O Box 275, Augusta Geo
"Copse Hill", Ga R Road.
December 31st 1878.'.

My Dear Friend;

. . . I rec*d* your last note yesterday. Its contents by no means surprised me, because I had previously calculated that the chances of the matter were about *a Thousand to one against* me!— Nor, (to be frank), do I expect that *other* Publishers will prove a whit more amenable! I can't even *blame* them; for the *Southern People,* (who call me their *"Poet Laureate",)* have *never raised a finger* to *practically help me; & how* therefore, could I expect alien *P*ublishers to adventure the *books* of a man, discouraged even by his own People, & left — as it were, by *their* cold mercy, shivering in the Market Place?—

On this point I *do* feel better [bitter?], & with reason! . . . . *Strive no more* on my *behalf,* good & earnest Friend; *"Che sarà sarà!" What* a fool is he who "kicks against the Pricks!"—

All the same, I am *grateful beyond measure,* for *your* unselfish kindness!

I could not *feel* more grateful, had your intercession *brilliantly succeeded. Believe this!!*

Certainly, I have had the pleasure of receiving the 2 magnificent vo*ls* of your *"History".* D. V. I shall give them a *rousing* notice; such a notice as they richly merit. Perhaps some few individuals in this God-forsaken South, (to *you only* would I write this), may be persuaded to purchase the work, by my honest recommendations.

. . . In a literary & artistic sense, *Southerners,* or the vast majority; are mere *children!*—

They know absolutely *nothing* of movements, in the great World of Letters; & must be furnished with their literary pabulum, as Infants are furnished with the contents of a "Candle [caudle?] Cup".

Probably, your history will prove "too "Strong Meat for Babes"! *Nous Verrons!*

Apropos of *So* literary *backwardness*, (*mild* term!), would you believe it, that the very ablest of our *living* Statesmen, one who *really* deserves credit for vast talents, and fair acquirements in political economy, actually wrote me to the effect, that he saw *wonderful artistic promise* in a tale like *"Heart Hungry"?*

(*En passant* "*H. Hungry*", is the *spurious*, disgusting abortion, in the shape of a Novel, produced by a Mrs Westmoreland of Atlanta, a woman after the *Madame "Les Hantes"* style; equally ignorant & vulgar!)—

. . . . . But to accept the *"Inevitable"* is the first duty of a man of sense! . . . . .

. . . I have been reading *Taylor's* last work *"Deucalion"*; *Parts* strike me favorably: there are *choruses* & *semi: Choruses*, of great harmony of rhythm, & force of thought. But do you know, that after all, I vastly prefer T's *earlier* to his later productions, always excepting that exquisite *dream of color*, "The Picture of St John"? His youthful *lyrics*, e.g. *"The Continents"* so highly commended by *Edgar Poe*; his simple, touching narrative of *"Min da Min"* or the *"origin of Maize"*—; a few of his *"California Ballads"*, & that *sonorous*, *majestic* piece of versification which he calls *"The Harp"*—, all these seem — *me judice* — to possess more *real* inspiration than his later, & more ambitious performances.

Taylor himself evidently thought that his *Muse* had been infinitely benefitted by her commerce with *German thought*; but I doubt *this!*— His translation of *"Faust"*, however, is a marvel!— . . . On Xmas Eve, I was sadly reflecting upon Taylor's decease; when the following lines *sung themselves* in my brain:—

To B. Taylor   Beyond us.   .
(*A Vision of Xmas Eve 1878.*)

As here within, I watch the glowing coals,
While the chill heavens without are wanly white;—

I wonder, Friend! in what rare Realm of souls,
You hail the uprising Christmas-tide, tonight?

I leave the fire-place; lift the Curtain's fold;
And peering past these shadowy window-bars,
See thro broad rifts of ghostly clouds unrolled,
The pulsing pallor of fast-fleeting stars;—

Phantoms they seem glimpsed thro the clouded deep;
Till, the winds cease; & Cloudland's ghastly glow
Gives place *above* to luminous Calms of sleep —,
Beneath, to glittering Amplitudes of snow:—

Some stars, like steely bosks on blazoned shields,
Steed [Stud?] Constellations, measureless in might;—
Some lily-pale, make fair the ethereal fields —;
In which, O Friend! art thou ensphered to night?

Where'er 'mid yonder infinite worlds it be,—
Its Souls, I know, are clothed with wings of fire;
How would'st *thou* scorn even Immortality —,
In whose dull rest thou could'st not still aspire!?

There, Homer — raised where Genius cannot nod,—
Hears the orbed thunders of celestial seas;—
And Shakespeare, lofty almost as a God,
Smiles his large smile at Aristophanes;

With earth's supremest souls — *still grouped apart* —:
Great souls, made perfect in the eternal Noon;—
There, they [thy] loved *Goëthe* holds thee to his heart,—
Re-born to youth, & all life's chords in tune!—

And, in the liberal air of that wide heaven,—
He whispers;— *"come! we share the self-same height;*

To me on earth, thy noblest toils were given —;
Brothers! henceforth, we walk these paths of light!"

Clear & more clear the radiant vision gleams;—
More bright grand *s*hapes, & glorious faces grow;—
While, like deep fugues of Victory, heard in dreams,—
A thousand heavenly Clarions seem to blow!—

The *lord only knows*, whether this be *"good, bad, or indif-*
ferent"? I sent *"Mss"* to Alden of *"Harper's"*. If not published *there;* it will possibly appear in some N Y. daily.

¶Once more *hearken!!*—

Engaged as I am upon a long series of *"Sonnets"* on *divine*
topics,— I find among those already composed, the following;—

Disappointment

A Sonnet.

Ah! Phantom pale! why hast thou come with pace
So slow, and such sad, deprecating eyes?
What! dost thou dream thy presence could surprise
One,— the born vassal of thy realm & race?—
My boyish sight dwelt on thy clouded face;
And youth — discovered [dissevered] from all cordid
    [cordial?] ties,
Heard the cold echoes of thy murmured sighs
In many a shadowy, grief-enshrouded place:—

Therefore, oh! pensive Spirit! be not coy!—
When have we lived so alien and apart,
I could not faintly feel thy muffled heart?
Till *now*, should Hope's Fruition on me shine,—
I *well might deem beneath the mask* of joy,
Lurked that dim brow, *those twilight eyes* of thine!

Basta! eno' of this!
Tell me frankly if you dislike these *verses?*

Write when you *can*, and rely upon my doing the utmost
in my power for your History.

Always affectionately yr's

Paul H. Hayne.

[Although I sympathize deeply with Hayne in his disappointment, it is
undoubtedly true that most of his poems lack "popular" and "human"
appeal, even when they are artistic and fine, and that his poems would
certainly not have enjoyed a large sale even if he had been born and bred
in Boston. But he could never forget Lowell's remark (in his review of
Hayne's volume of 1860) concerning the hostile environment in which a
Southern author had to live and write, and Hayne found this a convenient
way to explain his failure to achieve financial success. Of course he
knew that his work was better than much of the popular verse of his day,
but even in ours the poetry of Edgar Guest has enjoyed a wider sale than
has that of E. A. Robinson. Hayne was wrong in supposing that Southern
people were obligated to buy and read his poems merely because he was
a Southerner (though some of them probably did read him for that
reason, mainly). Like the readers of other sections, they preferred Longfellow and Tennyson to Hayne, or Whitman, or Emerson. Moreover, only
a few poets in any place or time have been able to live by their poetry
alone. His friends Stedman and Stoddard had discovered that it could not
be done (at least not by them) in New York.

The Southern statesman referred to may possibly be Alexander Hamilton
Stephens (1812–1883), whom Hayne knew personally, with whom Hayne
sometimes corresponded, and whom he praised highly in a sonnet (the
American, III, 312; *Complete Edition*, p. 293).

Maria Jourdan Westmoreland (born in 1815) was the author of several
sentimental plays and novels (*Heart-Hungry*, New York, 1872; *Clifford
Troupe: A Georgia Story*, New York, 1873). See *Lib. of So. Lit.*, XV, 463,
and Aubrey Starke's note on her in *Am. Lit.*, I, 36 and 36n. I do not
know what is meant by the *"Madame 'Les Hantes'* style." Possibly Hayne
is referring to a pseudonym(?).

Bayard Taylor (1825–1878) was sent by President Hayes as minister
to Germany in 1878, where he died December 19, 1878. Hayne's poem to
him, slightly revised, may be found in *Complete Edition*, pp. 320–1. It
did not appear in *Harper's*. In the next letter Hayne says it appeared in
the New York *Tribune* (on the staff of which Taylor had worked and
for which he had gone to California in 1849 to report on the gold rush).

The sonnet, revised with respect to punctuation and about a dozen
words, appears in *Complete Edition*, p. 264. It was published earlier in
the *Youth's Companion* (Boston) for June 24, 1880 (LIII, 214).]

No. 198

PAUL HAMILTON HAYNE to MOSES COIT TYLER

"Copse Hill," Georgia Rail Road,
January 17th 1879
Address:
    P. O. Box 275,
        Augusta, Ga.

My Dear Friend;

Iö Triumphe! your Book has already made its mark gloriously!

Enclosed I send you *two* Notices; one from the captious "Nation", which *perforce* has to acknowledge its merits.

I have been *so* sick *again* since I last wrote, & so crowded with work, that I have had no chance to do more than glance over your vol*s* which I value *so highly. Have patience with* me! Please send back *"Mss"* of my Poems *per* Express, directed *to me*, as follows.

                    "Per Express,
                        Grovetown,
                            Columbia Co
                                Georgia.

You need *not* pre-pay the Pc'k.

After all it [is] *as well that Holt* did *not* take the *vol* he contemplated.

It would neither have been my *entire Poems*, nor yet my *last;* & I can perceive by my friend Col James['s] letter that he thinks it would have *interfered* with the large "illustrated edition" he desires.   Of *this* edition he is most sanguine; but does *not care to have it spoken about*, until his plans are *matured*.

Now, if I could have my Poems, written *since* the publication of "Mountain of *Lovers*" came out,—it would so far from interfering with *his* edition, prove rather an *"Advertisement"!*

I hope that you saw my Tribute to B. Taylor in "NY Tribune".?

His death was quite a *shock* to me!

About your *noble work* I shall prepare a review as soon as possible.

At a *single bound* you have attained a lofty position in out [our?] *literature.*

God bless you, my friend!

Ever yr's

Paul H. Hayne.

P. S. *Don't forget* to return my Poems when convenient— I might need them!

No. 199

MARY MIDDLETON MICHEL HAYNE to
MOSES COIT TYLER

"Copse Hill," Georgia Rail Road,
April 24th 1879

Address:

    P. O. Box 275,

      Augusta, Ga.

My dear Mr Tyler,

Among a large number of unanswered communications addressed to my dear husband—which he begged that I would answer during his absence from home—I find your most affectionate letter dated April 9th. You will be pained to hear that we were obliged to summon a physician from Augusta about two weeks ago to him—so entirely had work become impossible—& even reading too much of an effort. The Dr gave us some comfort, but said that Mr Hayne was suffering from complete nervous prostration brought about by continued loss of blood (for nearly a year), together with unremitting mental toil. He recommended perfect rest— freedom from care, as much as possible, & a change. Europe was impossible—so he has gone to Charleston, where he will be under the care of my brother, Prof Middleton Michel, who is an eminent physician, & tenderly attached to Mr Hayne. A sight of the ocean, so very dear to my husband, I trust will be of great service. My brother wrote of Mr Hayne's safe arrival (a week ago) although "greatly fatigued": and day before yesterday we had a pencil note from himself. He says— "Middleton thinks far More favorably of my case than I *dared* hope—Let me thank God for this! Friends are gathering about me—& I am enjoying a sight of the ocean—its sweet breezes make me feel a little better already"—We are expecting further News this evening—Pray God it may be good News!

It was *hard* to remain behind—but the freedom from care which. is *needed*—can best be accomplished by my doing so. My husband's Mail is so large a one, that I am kept constantly writing with my son's assistance at times. I have been thus circumstantial because Mr Hayne regards you with true affection—& your letters indicate a like sentiment for him—

Your wife & self I feel sure will sympathize with us; & pray the Merciful Father to take my gentle hearted husband under His special care. Please take a look at "Wide Awake" for April, & you will have a glimpse of "Copse Hill". Your invaluable work on American Literature I have only had time to glance at, but some day hope to read, & enjoy. It has delighted my husband to see all the favorable Notices of your work—& to know of its very great sweep.

With kind regards from my son & self—to Mrs Tyler & yourself—I remain yours truly M. M. Hayne.

[Mary Middleton Michel Hayne was "the daughter of an eminent French physician, who received a gold medal from Napoleon the Third, for services under the first Napoleon at the battle of Leipsic [1813]." See Margaret Junkin Preston's sketch of Hayne, p. vii, in *Complete Edition.* Her two brothers, Dr. William Middleton Michel and Dr. Richard Fraser Michel, were prominent physicians in Charleston and Montgomery, respectively. The former was on the faculty of the Medical College of South Carolina, at Charleston. By all accounts, Mrs. Hayne was a beautiful and charming woman and deeply devoted to her poet husband.]

No. 200

PAUL HAMILTON HAYNE to MOSES COIT TYLER

"Copse Hill," Georgia Rail Road,
November 15th 1880.'.

Address:

P. O. Box 275,
Augusta, Ga.

My Dear Old friend;—

I feel, in taking up my pen to write you once more, as if *many years*, instead (as I think), a *single* year, had elapsed, since I addressed you last. But, until *recently*, my health, impaired by continued & distressing hemorrhages, absolutely forbade my corresponding, even with valued friends like yourself—

Now, as I am somewhat better, one of the *first* among the tangled & unravelled threads of correspondence, I endeavor to re-adjust, is your own; & moreover, please credit me fully when I affirm, that *silence* with me, has *never* meant *forgetfulness!*

I have held you often in my thoughts, & very faithful, loving thoughts, these have *always* been!

Imagination has carried me over the great wastes of land & water to your *studio*, near *"Anne [sic] Arbor"*, & painted you vividly among your books, composing the new vols of your great work upon *"American Literature"*,—a work destined to perpetuate your name & fame for ages to come.

When you arrive at the *final* paragraph of that important performance, you will feel, I doubt not, much as *Gibbon* felt, when he laid down *his* pen, upon the completion of the *"Decline & Fall"*,—for *your* work—if far less complicated than his life-long labor—, nevertheless is complicated eno', & presents difficulties peculiar *to itself,*—difficulties *unique,* & hard indeed to overcome!

The success of your *2 first* vols, argues (*I think,*) *conclusively* the success of those to follow; because these *initial* ones, were beyond question, the most difficult of the entire series.

How you managed *such material*, & continued to make such "dry bones" live, is wonderful, *wonderful!!* (I mean in the purely *literary & critical* parts); the material is rich, indeed, *elsewhere!*

For example, your *2nd* vol dealing with the early V*a* settlement, & early V*a* writers is ripe with romance! The chapters on *John Smith*, (oh! plebean name heralding grand exploits!), are singularly entertaining. Only, one *must* regret a *little* the total explosion, & utter scattering into thin air of the exquisite story of the woodland Princess, & her rescue of Smith from under the very clubs of his Executioners.

It *now* appears from your graphic narrative that the gallant Captain's experiences in old Powhattan's territory were *gastronomical*, rather than romantically dangerous, or tragic! It is edifying to discover what an enormous appetite & splendid digestion he possessed; and upon my soul! his vivid picture of the *"huge platters"* of farinacious food daily placed before him, ("eno' for ten men"), flanked, or preceded by superb *"haunches of Venison"*, make one's mouth water. Tame however seems the *denoucément*[?], which consigned Cap*t* Smith in absolute safety & honor, *not* a pin scratch upon him, to his own people; & *Pocahontas!* dear me! She appears to have been but a pretty, hoydenish, slightly coquettish damsel, after all, as unhaloed by a great duel, as any well-conducted *debutante* of *5th* Avenue, or the London "West End", gleefully pirouetting with *"Snobbs"* or *"Nobbs"* of her Majesty's *"Guards"*, after due presentation, under Mamma's wing, at the latest Royal "Drawing room" reception!!

Disenchanting! but "what would you?"—as the French say—? The time for pretty myths has gone by!—Seriou[s]ly, I must repeat my admiration of all *but perfect* manner, in which your task thus far, has been performed. x x x x x x x

x x x x For myself, I have only been able to work in a literary way, during the last month or two; and often, *even*

then, I've labored with a weak frame, & throbbing brain.—
One *longish* poem of mine, I enclose for your examination.

Let me hope that the Ballad may please you!—My poetical
"Mss" still remain by me, *unpublished;* the collected performances of the last *lustrum;*—alas! no Firm can be procured
to undertake them; & to issue them on my own account, (i e)
at my *own expense*, is out of the question!—Well! *"to bear* is"
(in some measuré) "to *conquer one's fate*," but *my friend*, it
is *bitter bitter!!!*

How *delighted* I shall be to see your familiar handwriting
again.!! *Don't delay to give* me this *heartfelt* pleasure, remembering that my *own dilatoriness* in writing you, was altogether
involuntary!

My wife sends her kindest regards, & believe me, now as
Always.

Faithfully & affectionately yr's &c

Paul. H. Hayne.

[Tyler's *A History of American Literature During the Colonial Time,
1607–1765* (2 vols.) had appeared in 1878. His *The Literary History of
the American Revolution 1763–1783* (2 vols.) did not come out until 1897.
They are still the standard works on the periods covered.

Of course Hayne refers to Edward Gibbon (1737–1794), the English
historian, and his *The Decline and Fall of the Roman Empire* (6 vols.,
1776–1788).

Pocahontas (c.1595–1617) was the daughter of Powhatan (c.1550–1618),
Indian chief in Virginia. Captain John Smith (1580–1631) was the founder
of Virginia.

The *"longish* poem" enclosed, "The Battle of King's Mountain," had
appeared in *Harper's New Monthly Magazine* for November, 1880 (LXI,
942–4). King's Mountain is on the boundary line between the Carolinas.
The battle was fought October 7, 1780. In March Hayne had received
from Colonel Asbury Coward, of Yorkville, South Carolina, an invitation
to write a poem for the centennial. Apparently Hayne was very proud
of the poem. In a correspondence journal of his which I have seen he
says he sent copies of it to Swinburne, Whittier, George Bancroft, Tyler,
George H. Calvert, Miss C. F. Bates, R. G. Hazard, and others—including
one judge, one chief justice, and one senator. It was reprinted in a number
of newspapers.]

No. 201

PAUL HAMILTON HAYNE to MOSES COIT TYLER

"Copse Hill," Georgia Rail Road,

January 8*th* 1881.

Address:

P. O. Box 275,

Augusta, Ga.

My Dear Friend;—

Altho I have just come from a sick Chamber,— within the narrow walls of which I was confined for many days, by *another* attack of Hemorrhage, brought on by the unexampled Cold —, I feel impelled to write to you, some few words of remembrance & affection. Recently, (*en passant* —) I mailed you a Ballad of mine (accompanied by a note), upon the Centennial Celebration of the Battle of *"King's Mountain"*, which, let me hope, reached its destination in Safety. Your interest in all matters connected with American History, would give to such a piece an importance wholly apart from any artistic merit it may possess.

And now, my *dear old friend*, (I may surely thus address you?), how are you progressing?— *personally, professionally, and literarily?* (if there be *such* a phrase!) The *brilliant* success of the earlier vol*s* of your *"history of American Lit &c"* must have stimulated you to exertions of no ordinary sort;— and I am anxiously waiting,— (in company with *some thousands* of other folks), to hail the advent of vol*s 3 4 & 5!!*

You are right, however, pre-*eminently right*—, to take your time, in their preparation; to *digest* your *material;* and elaborate it, in the best & clearest fashion. *Hastily - written works* are for a day, or month, or year;— while works which contain the *brain - blood & heart - blood* of an author, properly fused, & amalgamated with the truths of history, or the lessons of philosophic wisdom,— are for *all Time;*— the only monuments Strong eno' to defy the slow, cruel, corroding Centuries!.

Labor on, therefore in patience, and in hope.

Think of *Gibbon;* as step by step & stone by stone, he built up the majestic edifice of *his "Decline & Fall";* a production, *chiefly* because of the conscientious toil it involved, *never* likely, (pardon the vile pun), to "decline" in value, or "fall" into disrepute, or oblivion!—

x x x x x For *myself,* despite chronic ill-health, and innumerable discouragements of every kind & degree, I have struggled & fought onward, along my chosen path—, until *at last* the *goal* of my life-long efforts, may be said to have come fairly into view!

Remembering with profound gratitude, *your* endeavors in my behalf, when you so nearly succeeded in persuading *Henry Holt & Co* to undertake my *Later Poems,* I am sure you'll be pleased to learn, that *D. Lothrop & Co* of *Boston* are now publishing my *"Complete Poetical Works",* to be accompanied, or followed, (I know not which), by a vo*l* of *Verses for Children,* &c &c.

The *adult poems,* (if one may so style them), will occupy a large sized vo*l,* including as they do — a vast variety of pieces, ranging from the performances of youth, to those of my mature manhood, bordering *now* alas! upon old age! x x x x Ah! *by Pluto!* how suddenly this same *Old Age* comes upon us!

Don't you remember what Juvenal says, or sings?—

. . . . . "dum bibimus, dum serta, unguenta puellas,
Poscimus, obrepit non intellecta Senectus"?—

which I freely (!!) translate thus;—

While we drink, pottle-deep, loud & lusty,
An[d] array us, to worship the Fair;
Old Age —(d— n his eyes!), mute & musty,
Hath pinioned us All,—*unaware!*—

Drop me a line *old friend,* soon, *very soon,* & believe me

Now as Always,
Yours Faithfully

Paul H. Hayne.

[In *Complete Edition* the last section is entitled "Poems for Children." The passage quoted from Juvenal is from *Satires,* IX, 129.]

No. 202

PAUL HAMILTON HAYNE to MOSES COIT TYLER

"Copse Hill"
Nov 6*th* 1882

Address:
P. O. Box 275,
Augusta, Ga.

My Dear old Friend;

It seems to me an age Since I last heard from you!— Of course I knew that you had become a Prof. In "*Cornell University*" & long ere this I would have written you concerning your removal from "Anne [*sic*] Arbor", and asked for *some* particulars touching the new appointment; had health & opportunity permitted.

x x x x x x x x x x But really for some years, I have rather *vegetated*, than *lived*, in the proper sense of that term. *Frequent*, tho not violent hemorrhages; and a most distressing shortness of breath, (a sort of nervous asthma), combined with *other* physical ailments, have reduced me often to a sad condition; and made all re gular correspondence next to impossible. But believe me, I have never forgotten *you*; nor ceased to think of your kindly courtesy, and your friendship as genial, as sincere.

And now, I *must* try, and hear something definite *of*, and *from* you once more! Tell me of your position & prospects. Having your professional duties, it is hardly to be supposed that you officiate in a *regular* Church; tho doubtless, since your installation as a Minister of the Episcopal denomination, (of *which event* both my wife & I gladly heard), you must preach at certain intervals.?

¶ Again, how does the "*Magnum* Opus" progress?—You are *right* to take time in the completion of a work so *very important* as yours! a "Literary History", the first volume[s] of which may already be justly pronounced permanent authorities.

If memory serves me, you design bringing your Work down to the year 1850—or '52; a tremendous task upon the scale primarily, & very properly adopted.

May all possible success attend you!

You have, (in the 2 vol*s* already issued), managed with *infinite* tact, & talent, to hit the *"juste milieu"*, the very "golden mean" of discriminating treatment, both as to presentment of *characters & events.*

x x x x x x For·*myself*, despite ill health, which has *fatally* interfered with my composing *prose*, (as I used to do), the *Muse* has not deserted me;— and consequently, my *poetical* record, during the last 2 or 3 years has by no means been barren; (as to *quantity* at least).

Moreover, you'll be glad to learn that the *Lothropes of Boston*, have *just* published a *complete edition* of my works, (poems); in a handsome vo*l* of large duodecimo size double-columned—, & with 61 *Illustrations*, many of them by our ablest *artists.*

The labors & the patience of years have thus been rewarded, at last! x x x x x Please my *honored & beloved friend*, *answer this*, as soon as you *conveniently* can!

I *long* to see that clear cal[l]igraphy of yours once more; & to learn how you are progressing in *every* particular.

x x x x x   With my wife's remembrances, & my own affectionate regards,

Ever Most Faithfully &
Cordially Yours,

Paul H Hayne.

[I find this entry in Hayne's correspondence journal:
    "Saturday, April 9,.1881
        Long letter to Prof. Coit Tyler
        (dwelling especially upon
        Hamilton & Burr) &c[.]"
Tyler went to Cornell as professor of American history in 1881.

In the earlier part of his career Tyler had been a Congregationalist minister, and in 1881 was ordained deacon and later was ordained priest in the Protestant Episcopal Church. This was the church which Hayne

joined. The rite of confirmation was administered to him at Copse Hill
by the Right Reverend J. W. Beckwith, Episcopal Bishop of Georgia,
some years before his death, at a time when he was too ill to go to church.
See the Augusta *Chronicle*, July 13, 1886.]

No. 203

PAUL HAMILTON HAYNE to MOSES COIT TYLER

"Copse Hill" Geo
Dec 11th 1882

My valued & Beloved Friend;—

It is *something,* nay! it is a *great deal,*— a blessing beyond
price to possess *such* a *friend* as you are!, a man whose *heart*
is as warm, as his *brain* is brilliant & comprehensive!

I never think of *you*, without *feeling, what* I must now
earnestly, & sincerely express — a conviction, namely, of my
good fortune in making your acquaintance nearly 10 years
ago, in NYork.

Do you know that we had not conversed for a quarter of
an hour, *before* I seemed to myself to have known you all
my life?— Perhaps after all, there was *more* in the feeling
than the practical 19*th* Century mind would be willing to
admit! Perhaps it points, however vaguely, to an existence &
communion *in some other world!* Who shall say?—

(*Apropos*, read my little poem called *"Pre Existence"*, page
204 *complete* edition!"—)

x x x x x Your affectionate letter of the 22*nd* ul*t* reached
me in due season. Surely if my *own* epistle, (to which yours
is a reply) *"cheered you greatly";* you'll comprehend how
your answer has *encouraged & cheered* me!.

Firstly, it breathes *throughout;* an unabated affection for
your *"old friend";* & *secondly,* the manner in which you
write of my *Poems,* would *stir* the *heart* of a stone. *You* judge
a work of *art* not merely with the analyzing & dissecting
Brain; but with all the subtle forces of the *Soul! Thus,* I
value *your* commendation to a degree, which it would be
difficult to exaggerate.

Enclosed, I send *"Errata"* (touching my Book), which I've had struck off for private use, & which you can easily arrange in the flyleaf — &c.

These, I have *sent to only a few friends & scholars.* It would *never do* for the *general Public to imagine* the *"Edition incorrect"*, else it would prevent sale, & the possibility of a *2nd* edition. Nor would it be just to my *plucky* & gallant Publishers who have spent a vast deal on the work. I saw a letter written to the Geo Agent by them in which they declare that $6000 were spent on the *illustrations* alone(!!)

After all, the *mistakes* will only attract the notice of very careful & scholarly readers!!

x x x x x x x x x x *Meanwhile,* my *friend,* you have said *absolutely nothing* as to the progress of your own great *"History"*.

Everything associated with that *important* work deeply interests me.

I *am about,* by the way, *to re-peruse* both of the 2 vols already published; after an old fashion of mine, which leads me to read & read again what I particularly like.

When a boy, I actually *wore out* my *"Robinson Crusoe"* by *eternal* handling; and believed as firmly in the veritable existence of *"Robin"* & his *"man Friday"*, as I did in my *own*. *Scott's novels,* (the *best*) I read again & again; and old *Burton's "Anatomy"* is—I *won't* say, *in Byron's* phrase, my *"vade mecum"* *"of the true sublime"*,— but at all events, it *is* a *"vade mecum"*; & of *scholarly* works the profoundest, & most entertaining!! *Could* I procure a moderately *small* edition, I would carry it always in my pocket!!

x x x x From a sentence in your letter I judge that *(physically)* you are not quite as strong as you were! — *Pray be careful not to over work yourself!* Americans, espècially our literary men, are too apt to commit this fatal mistake! They *"burn the* candle" *"at both ends"*, and *fall* when life's *sun ought to be* at its highest merid[i]an heat & power.

I *don't* like to hear *of your* having been so *"worn out last spring"*; altho the *remedy* must have proved *delightful;* I mean your visit to *Europe*.

Would that you & I could visit *"England" together*!!— in which connection of ideas, please turn to pages 263, & 307 of my *works*!! &c

x x x x I can well understand how trying you must have found it to leave your home in *"Ann Arbor"*. But of *course* you were right to *move!*

Ready access to the *Boston Libraries*, in your case, would *alone* have justified such a removal.

— About my *health*, which you kindly refer to, it is *generally worse* in *winter;*— but there's *nothing*, like trying as far as possible, to *ignore* one's *physical ills*, to *stifle*, if we can't *forget* them!

No *doubt* the publication of my Book *has* helped me; because when the *mind* is encouraged & exhilarated, *bodily pains* are apt to be *modified at least*.

— All my Household, (*not* a very *tremendous* one as you know) join me in the most cordial greetings to *Mrs Tyler* & *yourself*— . . . *When perfectly convenient, you'll* answer me; *but on no account, hold ceremony*, with *Your faithful & affectionate friend*

Paul H. Hayne.

[My copy of the *Complete Edition* does not contain the *"Errata,"* but the proofreading was rather carefully done. (There are some errors in punctuation, and I noticed "I" for "J" in "To M. I. P." (p. 270). The poem seems to refer to Mrs. Margaret Junkin Preston. Hayne's *I*'s and *J*'s usually look exactly alike.)

The volume was partly a subscription edition, but only about two hundred subscribers had been obtained when D. Lothrop & Co. agreed to undertake the publication. John Garland James, of Texas, had made up the subscription list.

The Byron allusion is to *Don Juan*, Canto I, stanza 201.

Hayne has two poems on "England" in *Complete Edition*—he gives the page references. His ancestors had lived in Shropshire, and in these poems he expresses his love of England and his desire to visit the Mother Country. He had published "Sonnet—On the Emigration of the Author's Ancestors from England to America in the 17th Century" in the *South-Atlantic* for September, 1880 (VI, 138). In it he expresses regret that they had left England. No doubt the poem was composed in a mood of depression over the effects of war and reconstruction. He did not include this sonnet in *Complete Edition*.]

No. 204

PAUL HAMILTON HAYNE to MOSES COIT TYLER

"Copse Hill" Geo.·.
Jan 31st 1886.·.

My Dear Old Friend:—

I *cannot* tell you how *gratified* I was to receive your cordial, affectionate letter of the 26*th inst!!!*— *Time* & *Space* have divided us, but nevertheless, I *often, think of you*, and always with feelings of *tender* admiration!

My conversations with you in N York, many years ago, & our correspondence subsequently, made a deep impression, not merely upon my *mind* but *heart*.

Conceive therefore, my delight when I recognized your well-known handwriting once more!

That the *"Sesqui-Centennial Ode"* should so strongly have impressed you, is a matter of *rare congratulation* to the author.

It has *amazed* me to discover how little the genius, the life, & the magnificent services of *Oglethorpe* are known, even among *generally* learned & intelligent men in this Country.

And now, about *yourself*—!

Tell me something of your health, your prospects, and the manner in which you are progressing in the prosecution of your *great life-task*,—the completion *namely*, of your History of *American Literature*.

When will the next 2 vol*s* appear?

A colossal undertaking! and very *properly* your motto is, *"festina lente"*!! Your multiform college duties I am afraid must interfere with the labors of the Historian.

Somehow, I cannot help feeling that you, (like so many of your Northern contemporaries), are working too hard.

Work is a grand thing; but it *may* be *overdone:* and *is fearfully* overdone in your section.

The Winter here has been unexampled in severity. Not for a Century has the *South* been given such ar[c]tic experiences. Think of the Savannah River having been completely frozen over! So hard & solid was the ice that an adventurous person walked to the middle of the Stream, & perched on a huge ice-block, had his photo: taken!

The effect of such a temperature has been disastrous to many; *myself* emphatically among them.

I have felt as if I were being converted into an *iceberg*, having sense & feeling congealed, frozen up forever!

None of our Southern houses are constructed for such Boreal spells; & as for my miserable little *Shanty*, why, the winds enter by a hundred cracks & crannies; and one feels sometimes very much as if one were in the open air.

Apropos, here is a *Sonnet!* (as yet unpublished), descriptive of this cold spell, and of the atmospheric effect upon the aspect of the sun &c!

Like some great *Soul*, defeated, half undone,—
Shorn of his splendor, baffled in his aim,—
Throbs in mid-heaven with slow, discouraged flame,
And aching forehead, the sad, noonday *Sun:*—
Like taunting knaves across his pathway run
Some vagrant Cloudlets, making impish game
Of this sick Titan, whose late fiery fame
All *such* had withered, that durst gaze thereon!—

Meanwhile, the banded winds are wolves that bay
This pallid, moon-like Sun, or rage beneath
Our Cottage eaves by casements, frail, & thin—;—
What puffs of brutal breath are swept within—;
What snarling gusts, that smite with cold dismay,—
Or nip the nerve-strings, like keen-grazing teeth!—

Have you ever met in the course of your experience a man who seemed *haunted?*—one whose eyes seemed gazing upon some awful phantom?— *I* have, & here is his picture.

Haunted.

What haunts him now?— (behold, *that* anguished face!),—
What haggard Horror? or malign Disgrace?—

His *own* Soul's evil Shadow *outward* cast,
Limned on the ghastly background of his Past!—

———————— . ————————

You have read I presume Tennyson's *"Tiresias?"* or
has the leisure been wanting? A wonderful book for a man
who will soon be an Octogenarian! Verily this grand Poet
maintains his position as the noblest *Singer* of our Century
with a royal force & amplitude of imagination & art.

I have 3 letters from his own hand in my desk, penned during
the last 18 months *apropos* of certain verses I had addressed to
him. They are *very* precious to me!

x x x x x *To return* to *Oglethorpe.*

I am glad to learn that "the *next time* "you come to the
subject" you design "reading to your students" parts of my
"Ode". *Every American* ought indeed to be acquainted with
the *"great Colony—*Founder", as you justly call him nor ought
that majestic Indian Chief, *"Tomo-Chi-Chi"*, to be forgotten.
He *was,* (considered in reference to his race, opportunities,
environments &c[)], the most *exceptional* of semi-Barbarians.

In fact he *stands alone!*

"Red Jacket" "Powhattan", *"Osceola"*, &c &c, *these* were all
mere Indian warriors—, distinguished by the characteristics
of their blood & training—gallant, indomitable, not to be
subdued by any mortal force;— but *"Tomo-Chi-Chi"*, was a
superb *Statesman,* yes, and a *Prophet!!*

He *alone, of his People,* comprehended the vast superiority
of the *English settlers, and for his People's* sake, became England's friend & ally.

A few days from the present date will constitute the *3rd*
anniversary of the *"Savannah sesqui Centennial Celebration".*

How I wish that *you* could have been with us upon that
great occasion!! In the Savannah Theatre *then* Alex—*H
Stephens* made his last *public* appearance upon earth.

He spoke clearly & philosophically in reference to the tremendous difficulties which surrounded the Settlement of the
Colony of Georgia, giving fullest credit to the influence of
Oglethorpe. When he had finished, Genl *Henry R Jackson*
—(*now* our Minister to Mexico), arose, and delivered certain

portions of my "Ode", (since I was, *because* of *a throat-affection*)—, unable to deliver it myself—, in admirable style.

We dined with him that day; and *Governor* Stephens was in full *force.* He spoke of his illustrious companions of 20 & 30 years before; & could never have been more brilliant. Only a fortnight after, they buried him in *Atlanta!!*

He had caught a cold travelling *at night between Savannah & the Capital.* This finally killed him.

x x x   *Old friend!* write to me *when you can.* Write at as much length as *practicable.*

There are few men in America, whose friendship I value as I *do your's.*

But you *must not delay*, for my health is failing fearfully.

If *I* see *the end of the present year, it will amaze me! This in sacred confidence!*

My wife joins me in *cordial* regards; & *good wishes.*

Always affectionately yours,

Paul Hamilton Hayne.

[The sesqui-centennial of the settlement of Georgia was held at Savannah in February, 1883. Hayne wrote an ode for the occasion by request. From his correspondence journal I judge that he obtained some of the historical background that he needed from Colonel Charles Jones, Georgia historian. He wrote Jones for information on December 29, 1882.

James Edward Oglethorpe (1696–1785), British general, was the founder of Georgia.

Hayne frequently advised others not to work too hard, but he himself worked as hard as any man in his state of health could have done.

Tennyson's *Tiresias and Other Poems* appeared in 1885.

Tomo-chi-chi (c.1642–1739), Yamacraw Indian chief in Georgia, effected a treaty of peace between the Indians and Oglethorpe and the ceding of territory by the Creek Indians. In 1734 he visited England with Oglethorpe and saw the king.

Red Jacket, or Sagoyewatha (c.1750–1830), was a chief of the Senecas, in New York. Powhatan (c.1550–1618), father of Pocahontas, was an Indian chief in Virginia. Osceola (1804–1838) was a chief of the Seminoles.

Alexander Hamilton Stephens (1812–1883) is best known as Vice-president of the Confederacy and as author of *A Constitutional View of the Late War Between the States* (2 vols., 1868–1870).

Henry Rootes Jackson (1820–1898) is probably best remembered today as the author of "The Red Old Hills of Georgia." He was one of Georgia's most distinguished citizens as lawyer, soldier, judge, journalist, editor, and diplomat.

Hayne died at Copse Hill July 6. 1886. For an account of the circumstances and the funeral see "Paul Hayne's Reputation in Augusta at the Time of His Death," University of Texas *Studies in English*, 1938, pp. 163–73.]

No. 205

MARY MIDDLETON MICHEL HAYNE to
MOSES COIT TYLER

Copse Hill
Sep 30*th* 1886

My dear Prof. Tyler,

I thought that you would "grieve" for the loss of my precious husband—"What must he have been to you!" Seems to be the echo which comes back to me from Mountains, and rivers, and across the Sea's. He was my life—"Soul of my Soul"—"Always remember *this*—forever! & forever! & forever! and *this* should make you content"—he said to me. And I am "content" to remain behind, because he is spared the agony through which I am passing. "Content", because "it is the will of God"—My dear one's faith was sublime, yet simple—"Thank God!" I told him, "for your child-like faith"—"Yes," he said—"there are some things hard to understand; but we enter the Kingdom of Heaven as little children, & as such I go to my Father. I know that I have sinned, but I lay my sins at the feet of Christ & He lifts them". I wish there was strength given me to tell you of his glorious passing away. He did not die, but was translated. One, of the three physicians, who never left his side, said to me. "I feel as if I were standing upon holy ground—and will be a better man for the privilege I enjoy of witnessing such faith". If sympathy for my son & self—and deep appreciation of my husband's character & genius, could lighten our sorrow it would be—lessened. Our son has his life before him, & in God's good time this crushing

grief must become a subdued, if lifelong pain. But for me—
"I know, where'er I go, That there has passed away a glory
from the earth[.]" Patiently must I live until we meet in the
better land. Such a grief as mine must remain mine, until
then. Willie appreciates your remembrance of him. He has
endeavored to voice his grief in the following lines which we
thought you would like to see. In deep sorrow—sincerely
yours

M. M. Hayne.

The Angel and My Father.
("*The Angel Men call Death*")

The tender Angel that he knew
Came to him from the starlit Blue,—
And when his last life-force has sped
Loft heavenly fingers touched his head!

The Angel spake: "Behold in me
God's herald from Eternity!—
On Earth thy spirit saw in mine
Clear guidance to the Love Divine;

"Therefore I bless thee ere we go
To realms no mortal man may know;
To heights beyond the utmost reach
Of yearning human thought and speech".

My father's voice grew clear and sweet,—
He knelt beside the Angel's feet,—
"All hail", said he—"Show me the goal"
Where Sin is lifted from the Soul".

Oh! take me thro' the void of space
To meet God's mercy "face to face";—
Long have I heard thy sacred call,—
Lead me to Christ—He died for all"!

"But heal, dear Angel, this deep woe
From wounds of parting ere I go;
Let those who love me when unseen
Keep in their hearts my memory green".

The Angel answered: "O'er thy dust
True Love abides and changeless Trust". . . .
Then clad in Faith's unfaltering light
They journeyed upward thro' *the night.*

W. H. Hayne.

Threnody of The Pines
(*For The Passing Of Their Poet.*)

The guardian pines upon the hill
Were strangely motionless and chill;
As if they drew his last loved breath
From the uplifted wings of Death. . . . .
And now their mingled voices say,
"The passing of a soul away,—
The tenderest of the son's of men—
Our dead King Arthur of the pen!
Oh! kindred of the sea and shore
Our grief is yours forevermore!
His body lieth cold and still
For Death has triumphed on the hill".

W. H. Hayne

In "Lippincott"
for October—1886.

[One of the physicians who attended Hayne at the last was Mrs. Hayne's brother, Dr. Richard Fraser Michel, of Montgomery.

The first of the two poems alludes to Hayne's "Face to Face," which appeared in *Harper's New Monthly Magazine* for May, 1886 (LXXII, 884).

William Hamilton Hayne (1856–1929) collected one volume of his poems (*Sylvan Lyrics and Other Verses*, New York: Frederick A. Stokes Company, 1893). These two poems appear in it (pp. 110 and 112). The whole volume is dedicated "To the Memory of My Father."

Mary Middleton Michel Hayne (1831–1892) continued to live at Copse Hill with her son until her death.]

XII. LIBRARY OF THE UNIVERSITY OF TEXAS

(NOS. 206–245)

No. 206

PAUL HAMILTON HAYNE to JOHN G. JAMES

\# *Address me P O Box 275, Augusta Geo*
"Copse Hill" Geo R R.
Sep 15th 1877

My Dear Sir;

It gave me *peculiar* pleasure to receive your letter of the 11*th* inst.

Your courteous allusion to my own writings I deeply appreciate; and the *more* so, because among our *So* people so few seem to be alive to the importance of *Art & Literature* as distinct & powerful agents in the creation of a true Civilization. It is simply *amazing,* the extent of this Boëtian blindness.! All sorts of trumpery Politicians; fellows only fit to form material for the wit of an Aristophanes, or the keen sarcasm of a Juvenal—, are "app[l]auded to the echo," while every literary worker is (as a general rule) neglected, if not ridiculed. Twenty five years of labor in the South as a professional *Litterateur,* has afforded me too many examples of this despicable spirit.

Yet, mark you! if some *third* or *fourth* rate Yankee *author* chances to visit our Section, the Southerners throng around him, flatter his vanity, and (should he be a Lecturer), fill his pocket with their hard-earned Greenbacks.

Our very school-books & Histories are *manufactured* so to speak, in the Yankee mills! On many accounts, therefore, I hail *your* patriotic & judicious scheme with delight. It is positively the *first* time in my long experience that I have heard of a Southern man determined to prepare "a School Speaker for use in *So* Schools & Colleges, to comprise *only* pieces of *So* origin". If we have any self-respect left, such a Compilation *ought* to succeed.

Of *course, Dear Sir,* you have "my permission to use an extract from my "Legends & Lyrics"."

Upon the *whole,* I think there are more pieces in that vol, suited to *elocutionary* purposes, than in my last work ("*The*

Mountain of the Lovers," published by *Hale & Son* of NYork in 1875).

"The Macrobian Bow" would be *most* suitable, perhaps, for advanced youths; but should you desire something simpler for school boys, why, there is "Bonny Brown Hand," "A Dream of the South Wind", *"Will &c"* from which to choose.

I suppose you are acquainted with the poems of the late Dr Frank. O. Ticknor of Columbus Geo. He was a lyrist of *great* genius, & something of his (*"Little Giffin"* for example) should by all means adorn your pages. Let me send you a copy, if you have not one yourself. I enclose a brief notice I have just written of him. x x With the writings of Mrs M. J. Preston of *Lexington* Va you must be familiar. She certainly ranks, — in some respects—, *first* among the female Poets of this Country. If you possess nothing of her's [*sic*] I take the liberty of furnishing her address, so that you may write & consult with her, if you so desire.

Here it is,

> *Mrs Margaret. J. Preston.*
> *Care Col John Preston.*
> *Lexington;*
> *Virginia.*

Hoping to hear from you soon,
> Believe me
> > *Most Truly & Respectfully,*
> > *Paul. H. Hayne.*

—P. S. — Also, I enclose the copy of a lyric, (of mine) composed last year, *before my* native State, S. Ca, was redeemed by Hampton from the foul brutes who defiled her. This lyric came from the very depths of my soul. It was written in heart's blood.

Please, when you have *completely done with it, return* the copy, as I own *no other. Keep* it *however, as long as you please.*

By the way, in mentioning the poems, I did in the body of this letter, I mentioned them merely in a *suggestive* manner. You will exercise your own judgment in the matter.

[Written in the margin of the last (third) page:]

If you will send me the early proof sheets of your book, I will *notice* it in half a dozen *So papers* — —

Am I not right in supposing that during the War, *you* were on *Beauregard's* Staff? I rec*d* a pleasant letter from the General *last month.*

[John Garland James (1844–1930), educator and banker, was born at Chatham, Virginia, attended Virginia Military Institute at Lexington, served in the Confederate Army, taught a year at the Kentucky Military Institute, and moved to Texas in 1867. Assisted by his father and two brothers, he established the Texas Military Institute at Bastrop in 1868. James was superintendent and professor of mathematics and civil engineering. In 1870 he moved his school to Austin, where he continued to conduct it until near the end of 1879, at which time he was elected president of the State Agricultural and Mechanical College of Texas at College Station. On April 1, 1883, he resigned to assist his brother, Fleming Wills James, in operating a bank at Colorado, Texas. By the end of the year he was a banker at Wichita Falls, where he founded the Panhandle National Bank and served as its president. The rest of his long life was spent as a banker and dealer in bonds and mortgages, mainly in Wichita Falls, Austin, and Roff, Oklahoma. Because of poor health, he left Roff in 1929 and went to Dallas for medical attention and died there after an extended illness on February 11, 1930. His funeral and burial occurred two days later in Austin. (The inscription on his tombstone in Oakwood Cemetery says he died February 12, and so do the Dallas *Morning News* and the Austin *American* for February 13, 1930. But one of them also states that he died on Tuesday, which was February 11.)

His correspondence with Hayne began on September 11, 1877, when he wrote to praise Hayne's work and request permission to use a selection for a school speaker which he was preparing for use in Southern schools, adding that Northern bookmakers did justice to their own authors but not to "ours." Hayne rendered James valuable assistance in deciding which Southern authors should be included and in preparing short biographical and critical sketches of Timrod, Margaret Junkin Preston, Simms, and Ticknor. After the appearance of the book (*The Southern Student's Hand-Book of Selections for Reading and Oratory*, New York, Chicago, and New Orleans, A. S. Barnes & Co., 1879), Hayne reviewed it in various newspapers and tried to increase its sales and school adoptions. James was grateful. Moreover, he was touched by Hayne's account of his neglect by Southerners and promptly determined to do what he could to remedy the matter. He made up a club of fifteen purchasers for Hayne's *The Mountain of the Lovers* (1875), and in January, 1878, wrote that he had planned to bring out by subscription an illustrated edition of Hayne's complete poems. There were numerous delays on account of the press of other duties, ill health, bad crops, and yellow fever epidemics, but James was persistent and did not give up hope. He found the task of securing subscribers much harder than he had anticipated. He sent out nearly four thousand circulars and subscription cards and finally obtained only about two hundred subscribers. This disappointing response ruined his plan of acting as publisher himself so as to have all the profits go to Hayne. But on the basis of the two hundred subscribers and the promise of securing a good many free illustrations, he finally, in December, 1880, persuaded D. Lothrop & Company of Boston to undertake the publication. Had it not been for James, it is practically certain that Hayne's *Complete Edition* never would have appeared. When the handsome volume, dedicated to Col. John G. James, came out in November, 1882, it brought nearly as much pride and joy to James as it did to Hayne himself. But both were disappointed later when Hayne failed to benefit financially from the publication.

James's letters reveal him as a kind, generous, idealistic, optimistic, cultivated Southern gentleman. His letters continued until Hayne's death, and he corresponded with Hayne's wife for some time thereafter. Over sixty of his letters and postal cards to the Haynes are preserved in the Hayne Collection at the Duke University Library. I am indebted to Miss Nannie M. Tilley, Manuscript Librarian, for microfilm copies and for permission to quote therefrom.

Apparently only about half of Hayne's letters to James have been preserved, mainly the first half. Both James's letters and Hayne's journal indicate that Hayne wrote to James at least as often as James wrote to Hayne. In 1942 Mr. Lutcher Stark purchased the Lanier and Hayne letters to James and presented them to The Miriam Lutcher Stark Library of The University of Texas. To Mr. Stark and Miss Fannie Ratchford, Librarian of the Rare Book Room of The University of Texas Library, I am indebted for permission to publish the Hayne letters to James.

James's book contains four poems by Hayne ("Cambyses and the Macrobian Bow," "The Bonny Brown Hand," "A Dream of the South Wind," and "The Mocking-Bird in the Jasmine Vine"), two by Francis Orray Ticknor ("The Virginians of the Valley" and "Little Giffen"), and five by Margaret Junkin Preston. In James's letter of October 1, 1877, he said that he knew Mrs. Preston personally and that her husband had been one of his teachers. In the same letter he said he had not served on Beauregard's staff but in his native state of Virginia. He also asked Hayne for a list of authors between Virginia and Louisiana who should be included in his reader.

Hayne's lyric referred to is "South Carolina to the States of the North" (*Complete Edition*, pp. 297-299). It is dedicated to Wade Hampton, who became governor of South Carolina in 1877.]

No. 207

PAUL HAMILTON HAYNE to JOHN G. JAMES

Address me always P O Box 275
Augusta (Ga)
"Copse Hill", Geo R Road
October 8th 1877.:

My Dear Col: James;

Your letter of the 1st inst gave me the *sincerest pleasure.*

Believe me! I *deeply* appreciate your courtesy & kindness in reference to myself, and my Poems. It was *unexpected* too; for to be candid—, the Southern People, to whose interests I have devoted 25 years of life; striving to build up amongst them a taste for literature; & literary *Art*, have shown themselves quite as callous (generally), to *my* efforts, as to those of my more illustrious pre-decessors in the same line of endeavor.

How refreshing is it then, to encounter a generous enthusiast *like yourself!*—one who exerts his influence & authority in a really great Cause; throwing by with Scorn, those mere Conventional trammels which have so long bound (as in wretched swaddling bands), the system of Southern Education! May every possible success await your new Policy!

I feel proud to think that henceforth, certain Works of mine are to form a portion of the course in study "prescribed to your Senior Class". Would God they were worthier!

About your contemplated book, ("the So "*Reader*" & "*Speaker*")—'tis pleasant to see how determined you are to carry the plan thro to a successful conclusion.

Any help of mine you are heartily welcome to. As to the "summary of So Authors" whose genius "ought to be represented—; authors living "between La & Va"—, let me suggest the following names;—(including the States mentioned—:— *Charles Guarré* [sic] of La; *Harry Flash, an Alabamian* (I think) now residing in Texas at Galveston;—*Agustus* [sic] Requier, a So Carolinian living in NY City—. Henry Timrod of S. C. (deceased), Herbert Sass of Charleston S. C. (whose *nom de plume* is "Boston Gray"). Wm Gilmore Simms, (one or two of whose poems I'll endeavor to send you)—; written *since* 1861)—;

James Randall of Augusta; (whose magnificent lyric *"At Arlington"* is enclosed).

F. O. Ticknor, (I send his *"Little Giffin,"* & *"Virginians in the Valley"*)—; —James Barron Hope—(Editor of the "Norfolk (V*a* Landmark"), Jn*o* R Thompson; and need I say, Mr*s* M. J. Preston? (Have you read her *two* representative vol*s*, *"Old Song & New"*, and *"Cartoons?"*) *Mrs Annie Ketchum*, of (Ky) [.]

This *list* is *imperfect;* but I'll try & think of other names, when the opportunity offers. Just now, I am unluckily *very much occupied.*

You say, that you propose *"limiting* your selections to pieces *written since 1861; & if possible, since the War!"* Now, frankly, I think that to adopt the *last* of these resolves; (viz) to "limit the selections to poems written *since the war"*, would be *most unfortunate!* Only see! By that plan, several of our truest Poets would scar[c]ely have a "fair showing". — (*Timrod* for example).

Of course, I would retain as few *war poems*, as practicable; but *some* such certainly ought to be included.

Of course, *all* these men are not men of *genius;* but each one has written *some* poem worthy of your book.

Great discrimination in choice, however, will have to be used. Remember I only *suggest!* You will strictly employ *your own taste;* & pray *never dream that, thro courtesy, you are bound* to *include names* or *poems, because I chanced* to mention them!

[At this point—end of p. 4—the following is written in the margin:]

Let me hear from you soon. I take a *great interest in this matter.*

Always Faithfully
Your obliged Friend,

Paul. H. Hayne.

[James's book contains nothing by Gayarré, Flash, or Requier. It contains one prose piece and three poems by Timrod, but they are not his best work: as Hayne had predicted, James's plan prevented a "fair showing" of Timrod's work. The book also contains one poem by G. Herbert Sass, one poem and one prose piece by Simms, one poem by Randall, one by James Barron Hope, three by John R. Thompson, and two by Annie Chambers Ketchum.]

No. 208

PAUL HAMILTON HAYNE to JOHN G. JAMES

Address me P O Box 275, Augusta Ga
"Copse Hill", Geo R R.
Nov: 14*th* 1877

My Dear Colonel;

Your exceedingly kind letter of the 25*th* ul*t*, *should have* been answered sooner;—but, upon my word, I have been "pressed to the wall" by unexpected engagements.

Now, let me thank you for *it*, and also for all the courtesy, and consideration voluntarily shown me in your correspondence from the commencement of our acquaintance. I feel these things, *Colonel*, deeply! Not often does a *practical* man of high position like your own, — (i e) if a Southerner—, turn aside even for *one* moment, to extend the hand of fellowship & appreciation to his brother who labors in the realm of *Art*.

Art! the real significance of that word appears unknown amongst us.

As for *Poetry*, — the scorn with which it is continually being treated by Southern Lawyers, Politicians, Merchants, and "men of affairs" (to use a Gallicism) —, has often amused, when it did not utterly disgust me!

A great bloated County Advocate, and distinguished Stump-Speaker of middle Geo, was once introduced to me in Augusta.

"Hayne! Paul Hayne!" said he musingly; "oh! now I remember! *You* are the *poetry* man, ain't you? Ho! ho! ho! why the devil don't you give up all that d—d nonsense; and take to planting *potatoes! Potatoes stand by a man!* but *poetry!* — —- *bosh!!"* You ought to have heard the emphasis of that *"Bosh!"*.

Now, it chanced that our fat friend's fame as a *politician* and *electioneerer*, was none of the *purest;* so I replied to him, "Your advice is injudicious!

"*Potatoes* are somewhat like *Politics;* they often have filthy roots, and if much handled leave devilish foul stains behind!"

"*What* do you mean by that?" queried the gentleman flushing angrily up.

"Precisely what my words convey, Sir!"

"Do. you intend to insult me, Sir?" (in great pother & excitement)—:

"By no means;—I have *merely answered* a *fool according to his folly!"*—

The face of our grand local Dignitary turned all colors of the rainbow; but he subsided finally, contenting himself with a private remark to the person who had introduced us, & who afterwards communicated it to me, laughing "Well, that fellow *Hayne* is a d—d ill natured dog! I d'ont care if I never see him again . . . d—d him!!"——

Pardon so egotistical an anecdote. It illustrates what you so justly remark concerning the artistic ignorance & stupidity of our section.

x x x You will send me, you say, "the Index to pieces & authors of your "Speaker" "hoping that I may revise, and make suggestions &c &c".

By *all means remember* to do this; and do not hesitate to command my small services at any time whatsoever.

Thanks for your *real*, practical kindness about *"the Mountain of Lovers"*. *En passant*, let me confess that I made a grave mistake in placing that *narrative poem* at the *head* of the vo*l*. 'Twas composed in a luckless hour; and shall never be re-published.

"The Vengeance of Diana" (with many faults), is still superior to it. But what I chiefly value in the last book is *the Poems of Nature*. Read them!! for example, *"the Voice of the Pines"* &c &c.

Just now, I am negotiating with a Northern Publisher, about the issue of *another vol of verse*, to consist only of 80 pages, or thereabout; the poems to be *chiefly lyrical.* Do you think it likely that I could sell from *20 to 30 copies* in Austin at *75cts* or a dollar? — I merely *inquire.* x x x Send me *not merely* the "Index" of your *"Speaker."* but *early proof sheets, (if you choose),* so that I may *have the very earliest notice of your book afield. And pray write to*

[Written in the margin, lengthwise:]

me as *frequently as possible.* Your letters will prove I *do* earnestly assure you, a *benefaction, not a trouble.*

Ever Yrs

Paul H Hayne.

[In James's letter of October 25, 1877, he expressed his gratitude for Hayne's help with his reader and his eagerness to serve Hayne in any way, adding that he had already secured fifteen purchasers for his *The Mountain of the Lovers* and had sent the order to the publisher (Hale & Son).

Hayne's poem "The Mountain of the Lovers" was republished in *Complete Edition* (pp. 166–178). Hayne is right in suggesting that his nature lyrics are vastly superior to most of his long narrative poems, especially this particular one.]

No. 209

PAUL HAMILTON HAYNE to JOHN G. JAMES

"Copse Hill," Georgia Rail Road,
January 31*st* 1878

Address:

P. O. Box 275
Augusta, Ga

My Dear Colonel;—

You are so true a Southern man; and so genuine a Patriot in every way, that I'm sure nothing connected with the great men of our Section, whether they be alive, or dead, can be a matter of indifference to *you!*

Therefore, I enclose for your perusal, a *Poem* which sufficiently explains itself.

Of course, to those familiar with *Gilmore Simms only thro his writings*, my tribute will seem exaggerated; and so in a *certain sense*, I acknowledge it to be! That is, I have treated his genius, rather *potentially*, than *practically*; rather in reference to its *latent capabilities*, than its *absolute performances*.

Fate & Circumstances were against *Simms*. His whole life was a *battle!* He had really no leisure to cultivate the finer amenities of *Art* in composition.

But—as *Edgar Poe*—once said—, of his *genius* there could be no doubt. And a nobler, larger-hearted Comrade never existed . . . — . Old eno' to be my *father*, I yet enjoyed the most *unrestrained social & literary* communion with him for upwards of *15* (!) years!!

Full of faults, he was nevertheless "a *man*, every *inch of him!*"—

Perhaps you will not object [to] noticing my "Monody" in some Texas paper, (however briefly), *not* on my *poor* account—, but because the introduction of the topic, *may* procure some aid from individuals in your State, towards the making up of the small sum, ($500 I think), *now* needed for the completion of the *Simms monument*.

Regarding you as *a friend*, I write to you frankly, & without any reserves.

Pray drop me a line, upon the *receipt* of this note, & say how your "*Speaker*" is progressing. If I *can help your work* in any *manner whatsoever, command me!*.

Always Faithfully

Paul. H. Hayne.

[Hayne's memorial poem to Simms is found in *Complete Edition* (pp. 315–320). The headnote says it was delivered at the Charleston Academy of Music on the evening of December 13, 1877, as prologue to a dramatic entertainment in aid of the Simms Memorial Fund.]

No. 210

PAUL HAMILTON HAYNE to JOHN G. JAMES

"Copse Hill," Georgia Rail Road,
February 8*th* 1878

Address:
    P. O. Box 275
    Augusta, Ga.

My Dear Sir;—

I have just rec*d* your courteous note, & thank you for it.

In response, I am luckily enabled to furnish you with an article, or *series* of articles which contain the very information you need, conveyed in the clearest possible manner.

These belong to my *wife;* and the *"bonny Brown Hand"*, charges me, (with the *profoundest earnestness*) to say, that *when* you have completely done with them, she begs you to return the same by mail.

It is encouraging to learn that *Barnes & Co*, (an excellent & responsible Firm), have accepted your Work, & purpose bringing it out so soon.

Now, in regard to *James R Randall*, let me frankly remark, that I would prefer *not* speaking to him, "urging his co-operation" upon the subject mentioned by you.

I have *already* referred to the topic, telling *him* that I had sent you his *"At Arlington";* and would prefer *your* writing the Biography of myself.

I have only known Randall since my residence here, and often do not meet him personally for a *year or two.*

In fact, *I by no means find* him as anxious to extend courtesies toward me, as I have ever tried to do towards *him*, no less than all my other fellow workers in the Literary Guild.

He seems terribly soured & disappointed, *(entre nous)*, and I feel very sorry for him; I thus make the *largest allowances;* but all the same, would steer clear, henceforth, of asking him even the shadow of a favor.

    #   Did you receive my *"Memorial* Poem upon *W Gilmore Simms*["]?—

It has had a wonderful success; even at the *North*. Bryant re-published it in full—, in his *"Evening Post"*.

Write when you can.

Command me always; and believe that I am Most Truly Yr's

Paul. H. Hayne.

[In his letter of January 31, 1878, James requested data for a brief biographical sketch of Hayne, saying that he had requested Randall (who was a newspaper editor in Augusta) to send it but had heard nothing —nor anything in reply to his request for permission to use one of Randall's poems in his reader. He added that A. S. Barnes & Co. had accepted his reader and wanted the manuscript by June.]

No. 211

PAUL HAMILTON HAYNE to JOHN G. JAMES

Address me P O Box 275,—

Augusta Geo—

[no date]

My Dear Sir;

Did I answer (as I certainly intended), your kind P. C. of some weeks ago, concerning the *"Simms Memorial Poem"?*—If not, allow me to *cordially* thank you *now*, for the *deep interest* you have evidently taken in this piece, and indeed in my *poems generally.*

Nothing could have been more *grateful* to my *feelings, saddened,* if not *embittered,* as they sometimes have been, by the *strange coldness* of the South, (that Country I have tried so hard to celebrate in its history, sociology,—Natural scenery, &c,) towards all *Literary men;*—myself, of course, *not* excepted!

Meeting with a man like *you*, is verily, like the weary heart-sore Pilgrim's encountering some "good Samaritan" amid desert wilds, after an attack from Robbers & Ravishers. . . . Need I say, how delighted I shall be to receive *"the Galveston News"*, in which paper you purposed noticing the "Simms' Ode"?—

> *Always my good friend*
> *Sincerely Yr's*
>
> *Paul. H. Hayne.*

[Though undated, this letter was written between February 14, 1878, and about March 15, 1878—probably early in March.

In his postal card of February 14, 1878, James thanked Hayne for the poem on Simms (which he praised highly), for the data concerning Hayne's life, and for his frankness about Randall (whom he said he would not trouble further). He added that he would write an article on Simms and Hayne's poem for the Galveston *News* and send Hayne a copy.

Hayne's expression of gratitude was not merely for the proposed article but also for James's earlier letters (such as that of January 7, 1878), in which he said he planned to bring out by subscription an illustrated edition of Hayne's complete poems, the profits to go to Hayne.]

No. 212

PAUL HAMILTON HAYNE to JOHN G. JAMES

> Address me P O Box 275,
> Augusta Geo
> *March 26th 1878*

My Dear Major;

I recd your long & *exceedingly* kind letter of the 17*th* [13th?] inst, and *heartily* thank you *therefor!* As for *"the Galveston News,"* let it go by the shortest route, to the Devil!

These *ultra-materialists really* do manage in the end, to cut their *own throats;* and even while congratulating themselves upon the persecution of some particularly sharp *plan,* (*conceived* in meanness, and born in disgrace!), the *seeds* of their discomfiture have been sown, to produce their *legitimate* harvest *after a time!*

And *now,* (think me *not unconscionable,* a man without "bowels of reason or compassion"), if I venture to enlist your sympathies, and practical help, in *another* subject closely *associated* with *So honor!*

. . . Some years since, I composed *two* Biographies of the *distinguished Carolinians R Y Hayne*, my uncle, & *Hugh. S. Legaré*[.]

These *"Lives,"* we desire to publish in *pamphlet*-form, (all proceeds *of sale to be devoted* to *Charity*), and already *subscription-lists are* being opened in Charleston!

Only $150.*00* are required to pay the *Printers,* and surely *such* a sum (for *such* a purpose), *ought* to be collected in *Charleston alone.* Yet, we cannot trust to this; and *if* you choose to mention the matter & exert your influence in Austin, need I say how much obliged I shall be?—

All the same, (if your recent appearance as a Canvasser in *Simms'* behalf precludes your taking hold of another scheme glancing towards the popular purse), you'll *frankly tell me so!*

It is, of course, *the very last time,* I could dream of troubling you in this way. You've done your *full part* already, concerning the South, & her intellectual advancement.

I write *my friend* in great haste.

Drop me a line, & believe that I am Always Faithfully

Paul. H. Hayne.

P.S. Don't view this as an answer *to your last.* 'Tis merely an *acknowledgment.*!!

[On March 13, 1878, James wrote Hayne that the Galveston *News* had had his article on Hayne's poem on Simms for three weeks but had not printed it. He added: "The truth is the News is owned by a set of money-worshiping, money-making men, of Yankee instincts and proclivities, and with no principle beyond that one, of 'Put money in thy purse!' " (Later James retaliated by withholding his usual forty-dollar advertisement of his school.)

Hayne sometimes addressed James as "Major" and sometimes as "Colonel." The catalogues of the Texas Military Institute assigned to faculty members whatever rank seemed appropriate to the position they occupied. At one time James's brother, who was a professor in the school, was called "General" when he was commandant of cadets. In James's letters he says he served in the Confederate Army, but he does not say whether he had a commission. He was only 20 (b. December 1, 1844) when the war ended.

Hayne's biographical sketches of Robert Young Hayne and Hugh Swinton Legaré had first appeared in Albert Taylor Bledsoe's *Southern Review* (Baltimore) in 1870. They were published together in a small volume in Charleston in 1878. The edition (1,000 copies printed at a cost of about $194) was sold before the end of the year. The profits, I believe, went to the Simms Memorial Fund.]

No. 213

PAUL HAMILTON HAYNE to JOHN G. JAMES

[Postal card]

(Address P O Box *275*,
Augusta Geo)
March 29th 1878 . .

My Dear Friend;

Your *glorious* letter of the *26th* arrived safely! *Many* sincere thanks! Shall *reply in full* to *morrow.*

Meanwhile, allow me to *withdraw the request made* in my last communication.

I find that the matter of the publication (I mean of these *Lives* of Hayne & Legaré) can be arranged in Charleston: so please d'ont *bother* about it.

Ever

P. H. H.

No. 214

PAUL HAMILTON HAYNE to JOHN G. JAMES

"Copse Hill," Geo R R. April 3rd 1878.:

My Dear Friend;

Your letters are a great benefaction to me! It warms my heart to find a man in *your* position so full of *artistic* enthusiasm, and genuine literary impulses. Many thanks for the *generous* interest you have displayed in my own career.

Verily, I can't help muttering to myself a dozen times a day, verily if we had at the *South ten men* like Maj James, the building up of a Southern Literature would be a foregone conclusion, a matter of definite calculation, & absolute assurance!

But, alas! you stand among the millions of So "professionals", and so-called *practical* persons, almost alone. Nevertheless, as a "little leaven leaveneth a large lump", thus, the exertions of a single honest, enthusiastic, intelligent man may bring about unexpectedly important results.

Just look at what you yourself have already done! In the course of a few months by the exercise of a *discreet fervor*, you have, to a certain extent, interested a whole Community in topics which previously they had ignored, if not actually despised!

But being hurried, let me come to the main point of your last communication at once.

First, as to your suggestion in regard to a complete (illustrated) Edition of my works &c.

At this particular time, when all the industries of the Country are prostrated, *both North & South*, but *especially North;* when *Publishers* are "drawing in their horns" everywhere, and economizing, — the scheme of a full edition of my Poems, could *never be successfully carried out.*

— — But, a *humbler* scheme *is* practicable; & if successfully prosecuted, must *per necessitatem rei* —, become a powerful "factor," (if I may so express myself) towards the realization of the *complete edition* at some future, & more *favorable period*; because it will act as an advertisement, and make me better known in *the West*, at all events, than I am now.

Estimating the number of Poems, I have written since 1875, I feel convinced that there is sufficient material on hand to fill a *(duodecimo) volume* of from 125, to 150 pages. These poems are among the *best* & most artistically finished of my productions; & being all comparatively *brief lyrical pieces*, are *apt* to attract the notice of readers who have neither the leisure nor inclination to "tackle" elaborate narrative or dramatic compositions.

A neat vo*l* containing these verses, and headed by a good likeness of the author, really, might, (with the exertions of friends), prove a *great* success;—and if my friends in different localities will canvass for me, and report from authoritative Book-sellers, their willingness to send the Publishers — (whoever they may prove to be —,) *definite orders, beforehand, for* a *certain* no of *copies of the book*, so that the former can make precise calculations, why, the matter is about as *good as done already!*

To accomplish this, however, *private canvassing* is *indispensable.*

Your chief Bookseller, for example, in in [repeated in beginning a new page] Austin, must receive a certain number of *reliable Subscribers*, to authorize *his risk*, and then he, (the Bookseller) must address my Publisher *directly*, and say as it were, in black and white, the moment Mr Hayne's book appears, mail me *so many copies!*

Of course, should your Bookseller refuse to have anything to do with the scheme, *then*, a subscription list, vouched for by some prominent Citizen, or Citizens, & furnished the Publisher under conditions which shall satisfy him that the money is all safe—, would be the *next best* mode of proceedure[*sic*].

I am aware that the *collected edition of my Poems* would make me stand higher as you say, at the South; but I know that no Publisher would undertake it, without being *assured from loss.* They say as a *general* rule that *Poems* don't pay; for example Mr Bunce, now Editor of *"Appleton"*—, once undertook an *illustrated* edition of a single narrative Poem by *Stoddard;* and was actually *"broken"* in consequence!! You see the difficulty is to get *subscriptions* for any *Art-Work at the South.*

Perhaps you'll be surprised when I inform you that the *Hales*, my publishers, wrote me after *"The Mountain Of Lovers, with Poems of Nature & Tradition,"* had been out about 3 months, that *nearly all the orders for my book came from North of Philadelphia!!!—*

For a *quarter of a Century*, from my earliest manhood, indeed, I have worked *hard* for my People, & their *literary advancement;* sacrificing *myself* & all plans of material wealth, or aggrandizement, to one *great, central purpose;*

never flinching, or discouraged by "the scorns & whips" of malignant Opposition;— and *behold! my reward*!! . .

To *you* I may open my heart! *You* will not miscomprehend me.

Write, when you can, and tell me whether you think it will be possible to obtain the subscribers needed in *Austin* (for this last, modest little book), or rather I mean a *fair quota* of subscriptions; and how about your chief Bookseller. x x x x

x x   You advise me to get up an edition of *Simms' Poems,* which, you believe, would sell well. Reluctantly I am forced to differ with you here.

During my old friend's life, a very *neat edition* of his collected Poems appeared; and it fell literally *"still born".!*

In fact, — tho I once tried *hard* to think *otherwise* —, Simms can scarcely be called a *Poet!* He has written some *sweet individual* pieces, and *passages* of *force & suggestiveness* may be culled, here & there, from his longer compositions; but Somehow, he lacked the *higher inspiration;* & even his abler passages must be *painfully* sought for, amid huge masses of commonplace, &c.

No! his *true Genius* was *essayical, controversial,* (as his *superb political* treatises show), and also conspicuous in the more characteristic of his novels & romances! You ask me to keep you advised of any poem &c of mine coming out in the mag*azi* beforehand.. Now, *this* unluckily I cannot do, because I am myself in the dark as to the precise time of their appearance.

But, I enclose you a lyric which has just come out in the *April Lippincott.*

Probably you saw my *"Unveiled,"* which was issued in the *Jan "Scribner"* (illustrated), & which *Bryant & Stedman* thought very highly of &c.

I also enclose you a piece, (wholly out of my *general* vein), called *"Valerie's Confession"* lately published in *"Harper's Bazar".* 'Twill please the *young girls,* at all events.

Most Faithfully Yr's

Paul. H. Hayne.
P O Box 275 Augusta Geo.

P. S. The *good* prospects of your *"So School Reader,"* may, I devoutly trust, be *fully* realized! It would be hard to exaggerate the excellent results likely to be attained by works of this sort. They make the rising generation acquainted with their *own writers,* & stand in the place of those Everlasting Yankee Compilations the main purpose whereof is to teach that "nothing good can come out of our Nazareth."

Should the 1*st* of your books succeed, by all means, follow it up with other similar compilations.

And don't forget to send me an early *(unbound)* copy of your *"Reader"*, so that I can notice it before anybody else.

[Written in the margin and at the top of the first page of the letter:]

\# As a mere *curiosity* I send you a *dialect poem* which accurately preserves the *patois* of the rice field Negro of our sea board— I *don't want this* re-published; but with the others do as you please.

[In the surviving James letters to Hayne, he first mentioned his plan to bring out an illustrated edition of Hayne's complete poems in January, 1878. For further information concerning Hayne's efforts to bring out a volume of his poems written after 1875 see his letters to Moses Coit Tyler.

Oliver Bell Bunce (1828–1890) was coeditor of *Appleton's Journal* from 1872 until 1881. Richard Henry Stoddard's *The King's Bell*, with illustrations by Alfred Fredericks, was published by Bunce and Huntington (New York, 1866).

In James's letter of March 13, 1878, he wrote: "Would it not pay for you to edit an edition—*complete*—of Simms Poems? Many of his later pieces are not in book form, and have only appeared in Mag*s* &c. I believe. it would sell *well*." In his letter of April 17, 1878, he wrote: "You are right about Gilmore Simms poems. When I wrote you, I had seen only his latest pieces, '*Sketches from Hellas*' (in So. Mag.), but afterwards I found a two volume edition of his earlier ones in town (an old work) and drearier stuff I never read. I felt ashamed of having said what I did."

Simms's *Poems Descriptive, Dramatic, Legendary, and Contemplative,* two volumes, was published in 1853 (J. S. Redfield, New York).

Hayne's poems that had recently been published are these:

"In Ambush," *Lippincott's Magazine*, XXI (April, 1878), 424

"Unveiled," *Scribner's Monthly*, XV (January, 1878), 383–386

"Valerie's Confession." *Harper's Bazar*, XI (March 9, 1878), 158
The dialect ballad was "The Hanging of Black Cudjo" (*Complete Edition*,
pp. 278–280).]

No. 215

PAUL HAMILTON HAYNE to JOHN G. JAMES

Address:
> P. O. Box 275
> *Augusta, Ga.*

April 10*th* 1878

My Dear Sir:

In accordance with your kind request that I should send,
you, from time to time, any new pieces of mine, I enclose a
brief lyric which sufficiently explains itself.

Does not this *"Fantasy"* stir a certain vague sympathy in
your heart? —

How often amid life's *turmoil*, or its bitter *ennui & dull-
ness*, the thought so subtly embodied by *Shakspeare will*
come up!

"Our *little life is rounded by a Sleep!"* . *Some* Critics have
maintained that *Shakspeare's* "sleep" meant *"annihilation!"*.
God *forbid!* I *d'ont* believe a word of this *sciolist-interpre-
tation!*

But certain it is, that *"rest"* we *all* must long for;— a
species of *Twi-light peace I should like,—indefinitely prolonged* & visited by dubious, yet charming *dreams; — who is*
or *can* be *satisfied* with the *present* existence?—

It was an old *Talmudic idea* that men after death, slum-
bered deeply & insensibly in the grave, until the opening *of a
certain Epoch;* & even some of the *Earlier* Christian Fathers,
taught that *Christ's* followers knew *nothing* after the death
angel had sealed their eyes, until the ring of the Archangelic
Trump.

. . . . . . I am *very sick, Major,* (i. e.) in *chronic &
hopeless ill health;* and (naturally) my thoughts turn *continually* towards the world beyond our own.

Tremendous imaginations occur to me at times, on this
topic!

But I must *not* trouble you!!

By the way, d'ont allow the pieces I send, to put you to any inconvenience in the way of having them re-issued &c.

If they serve to interest you personally, 'tis quite enough. — Tell me of the progress of your *"Speaker"*, & command my *small* services in its favor.

> Always Y'r *obliged & sincere*
> *Friend,*
>
> *Paul. H. Hayne.*

[In his letter of April 17, 1878, James expressed appreciation for a poem entitled "Fantasy" which Hayne had sent. I do not find that title in *Complete Edition*, but Hayne revised the titles of some poems and rejected others.]

No. 216

MARY MIDDLETON MICHEL HAYNE to JOHN G. JAMES

> "Copse Hill," Georgia Rail Road,
> [No month or day given] 1878

Address:

P. O. Box 275,

Augusta, Ga.

My dear Mr James,

First, let me thank you for sending "The Bonnie Brown Hand"—Miss Mendenhall's verses—which were re-published in the Austin State Gazette— through your courtesy. And then I can the better express my appreciation for larger services rendered me through my husband. Your Notice of "The Southern Poet" was a labor of love I feel sure, but never the less it was an additional tax upon your very busy time, & will be valued accordingly.

I read it first with my heart & saw no fault at all in it— And then I read it with my understanding, & thought the writer estimated his work far below its merit. Indeed intellectually the article is admirable altogether! I have it carefully pasted in a book devoted to tributes in verse & prose in honor of *Our* Poet—ranking with the best of them in his

& my regard. And now, *how can I* thank you *sufficiently* for the love, the thoughtfulness, and the pride, which prompted your suggestion of an illustrated edition of Mr Hayne's collected works! This was the dream of my early wedded life, when there were no works as yet in existence, but I *knew* that there would be. This hope has never left me in all these weary years of discouragement which my husband has had to pass through in his literary career.

Discouragements none could fully know but myself. When you proposed it in the first instance I told Mr Hayne how much better it would be than his idea of a small volume of the later poems— But he thought there would be no chance for the sale of so large a book, & no possibility of getting a publisher to take it at his own risk. We never thought of a subscription volume at all— as the South (even his native city Charleston) appeared to appreciate his poem so slightly. When your second communication reached us, my heart was *so full* that the only expression I could give to my feeling was this— "Mr Hayne if this illustrated edition ever becomes an accomplished fact, I know you feel as I do, that the book *should be*, & *will be*, dedicated to the warm literary admirer, & *true* friend who first gave the dream of my life a tangible form"— You should have seen the sweet smile of approval which trembled about the mouth, & lit up the dark soft eye of your Poet, as he replied—"Of course I do." And so you see it will be your book if it is ever a book at all.

But if you fail to accomplish what your generous warm heart so earnestly desires, this book will still be dedicated to you in spirit. Mr Hayne will write you fully his first leisure moment (for he is a hard worker) with reference to your suggestions. The photograph enclosed please accept from me— It was taken for W. C. Bryant— "Library Of Poetry and Song"— The steel engraving is very fine—an improvement on the photo— which has given Mr H— light hair. The publishers Ford & Company were obliged to inquire what the real color of the hair was? It is very dark brown naturally— but now turning grey. The engraving in The Eclectic is not at all like my husband. I think you are right in supposing that Mr H—' book would be subscribed for at the North: for

the Editor of The Eclectic, I remember—mentioned when he
wrote to ask permission to insert the likeness in the Magazine — that it "would give great pleasure to hundreds both
North & South if they could see it there". A great many
demands have come from the North too for an Autograph—
And many letters of appreciation with reference to various
poems & to his work in general. Mr Hayne wrote (by request) with Mr W. C. Bryant an ode to Washington on the
22 Feb. for "The Sunday School Times" of Phil. Would it
be too late if I sent it now for your Book? The Ed of The
S. S. Times wrote of it—"Your Poem is better & grander
than Bryants"— Indeed I agree with him! The poem is Noble
& would be I think fine for delivery. But do not take it if
your work would be retarded thereby. I do not expect you
to answer this letter but merely to acknowledge it when you
next write my husband.

[Written vertically across the top of the first three pages:]

Mr Longfellow who is editing "Poems of Places" wrote to
ask Mr Hayne to aid him in selecting from Southern writers
as he "wished to do the South full justice"— So we have
both been busy I copying & Mr Hayne correcting some of his
own poems. I am glad Mr Longfellow wishes to do justice
in this matter but he will not be able fully to do so—unless
he will take some war pieces For most of our poems of
places are war poems. Excuse the use of a pencil and believe
me Your true friend

M. Hayne

[This letter is undated except for the year, but it was written by
Hayne's wife (since Hayne was very busy) with reference to James's
letter to Hayne dated April 17, 1878, in which he had again spoken
optimistically about his plan for a complete edition of Hayne's poems.
The Miriam Stark Library contains a dozen other letters from Mrs.
Hayne to James. The one above is the earliest. The last is dated
January 4, 1881 (though Mrs. Hayne continued to write at least as late
as 1887). Four of her letters to James are published in the present
collection. In James's letter of May 11, 1878, he refers specifically
to the letter above; so does Hayne in the letter below (dated May 3, 1878).
The *Eclectic Magazine* (August, 1877, p. 247) of New York had an
article on Hayne (with portrait). *A Library of Poetry and Song*, edited

by Bryant, appeared in 1870 (New York: J. B. Ford and Company), and a good many editions appeared later. I have examined four of the editions but found no portrait of Hayne. It must have appeared in one of the other editions—probably that of 1878 (see Hayne's letter of February 9, 1880, to James).

Hayne's poem on Washington is found in *Complete Edition* (pp. 296–297). For other references to it see Hayne's letters to Stanford.

For information about Hayne's aid to Longfellow in connection with *Poems of Places* see his letters to Longfellow.]

No. 217

PAUL HAMILTON HAYNE to JOHN G. JAMES

"Copse Hill," Georgia Rail Road,
May *3rd* 1878

Address:
P. O. Box 275
Augusta, Ga.

My Dear Friend;

I hope you recd my *wife's letter*, which will serve to explain why I have been so long silent, in the face of *two such* letters of yours, as lie before me; and also of your P. C. which reached me on the evening of the *20th* inst.

First, allow me to thank you for the *warm* notice of myself in the San Antonio paper; for which my wife has already thanked you in her *own* name.

She sent it to our son who is at present in Charleston, & he too appreciates it *very highly*; & says "he never *can* forget the *true friend* who wrote it!".

By the way, I should like much to see some of the "school boy criticisms," (as you call them), of *"The Mountain of Lovers"*,—.

Please extend to your *Class* my *thanks* for their kindly interest in, and appreciation of, their Poet.

I value inexpressibly too your *"well done"* as to the work I have been able to accomplish. Such words *always* cheer an artist.

I am glad to say that I feel *somewhat* better than when I wrote you so despondently in regard to my health. . . . . . And now, to the main purpose of your longer communication.

You have thoroughly convinced me that "business *is* business"; & that the *main* trouble,—as you express it—, lies just *where* you have placed it, in a want of adequate *advertising*, on the *one* hand, & an ignorance of magz literature, (throughout the South), upon the *other*.

I have previously recognized the necessity of having a complete Edition of my Poems; but never applied to the Publishers for such an edition, not feeling authorized to state that a full *subscription list*, at the South, would secure them from loss.

I agree with you likewise, that there are perhaps 5000 persons able & willing to buy an illustrated Edition of my Works; —but these 5000 will be found *farther* from where I reside, than in my neighborhood. For example, in Augusta I d'ont believe that 10 copies (!!!) of my last vo*l* were sold; tho the Augusta journal had a long & favorable notice of the book!.!

I think too, that it might prove a "matter of pride" *with Southerners* to purchase a larger vo*l* rather than *"parts* of my writings"*.

Therefore, I will *abandon* the idea of issuing a *small* vo*l now*, if you advise me so to do; and embody my later verses in the *illus:* Edition.

You perceive that I am consulting you as a *business man* in this matter.

I have, unluckily, no business capacity *whatever;* and will *depend* upon *you* for the *feasibility* of such an undertaking.

If you agree, we will turn over the Subscription, touching the 4 dozen copies, to the contemplated larger publication; and I thank you, *from my soul*, for your efforts thus far.

Indeed—as you suggest, "if every Southern town the size of *Austin* does as well," we would have very little trouble in this affair.

Of course, I feel warmly grateful to you for the suggestion of a "Poet's edition", where the profits would go "chiefly to myself"; since, I need sadly a larger compensation from my productions than I have yet rec*d*, everything of mine having been lost during the war.

Indeed, you argue rightly that *all* the profits of my verses, have "gone into the pockets of Publishers." True! I *am* paid for contributions to periodicals; but as it was with *Poe* so it is with myself; (i. e.) *Longfellow*, *Whittier* &c get 10 times as much for a poem as comes to me.

There is *one* thing, however, about which I cannot agree with you. While generously saying what you would do for me in *Texas*, you add, "there certainly *must* be at least *one* person of literary taste in each State, who would heartily aid the movement, and do as much as *I* can." Ah me! had *I* a few *such* friends as *Maj: James*, & the South a few *such noble* sons, what *could not* be accomplished, *both* for *her*, & for *me?*

But alas! *I, at least*, know of no such. *Agents* no doubt, could be procured, who would take their full per-centage on the work; & *this* I *presume*, would have to be done.?

You ask what 12 or 15 illustrations would cost,? (there are about that number in Longfellow's Poems which I possess)—;—

I do not *know;*—but if you advise, (as a *business* man), I could write to the different Publishers, asking what they *would charge* for *15 engravings;* & mentioning that an illus: edition of my works—(a "Poet's edition"—, *by subscription,*) *might be called* for, if the *South* had a prosperous season, during the next winter.

Then, we would have the estimate of the several houses.

God bless you for all your generous thoughtfulness; *both* in *performance & intention.*

In *no* event am I likely to forget *you.*

With earnest regards from my wife, believe me *Always Your Faithful & Obliged friend,*

Paul. H. Hayne.

P. S. Needless to say, that *whatever* I can do

[continued lengthwise in the right margin of the last page of the letter:]

to advance the *interests* of your *"School Speaker"*, I stand ready *to perform heartily.*

[In James's letter of April 17, 1878, he wrote: ". . . I do not hesitate to say that there are *5,000* persons today *in the South willing and able* to buy an *illustrated* edition of your complete works, if brought properly before them. . . ." (He found out later how badly mistaken he was: he got only two hundred subscribers after sending out nearly four thousand circulars and subscription cards to all parts of the country.) On April 25, 1878, James wrote with reference to Hayne's proposed volume of later poems: "As soon as you announce your publishers of the proposed new volume our *booksellers here* will forward orders for *four dozen copies.*"

"You perceive that I am consulting you as a *business* man in this matter": James had written (April 17, 1878): "You see it from the *poet's* stand-point, I from a *business* one. I am convinced that the trouble has been simply that your publishers have never *properly advertised* you in *our Section.* . . ."]

No. 218

PAUL HAMILTON HAYNE to JOHN G. JAMES

May 20th 1878 . :

My Dear & Honored Friend;

The perusal of your last letter has *profoundly affected* me.

Little, ah! little indeed did I ever anticipate that Providence would raise up for me *such a friend* as you have *already* proved yourself to be!

And you have won a place in my *wife's heart—, forever.*

I am so sorry that I have *not* those political pamphlets &c of *Simms.* They were destroyed with my Charleston library.

I would send you at once by mail Longfellow's illustrated edition; but it was brought out in 1871,—& my son thinks there has been a *later* one.

I've just dropped a P. C. to Longfellow himself to inquire if there be such another. Should I find my son mistaken, I will mail you *my copy.*

The Edition of Whittier I possess is not illustrated. *Bryant's & Longfellow's* are *bound* alike, & of the same sized vol *(duo-decimo)* [.]

Longfellow's contains *12* illustrations, and Bryant's 24!.; but the *print* of Bryant's is much better; Longfellow's pages being in *double-columns,* a *great objection* I think.

. . . I would answer your *long, invaluable* letter as it deserves; but am really too sick to do so.

But you will know, *I am sure,* how fully we both, (my wife & I) appreciate it!

Yet one thing I must reply to; i e, in regard to the *"Dedication".*

I have decided that *you, and you only* shall have "that honor". (to quote from yourself) [.]

Even if in a "business point of view", it did not succeed as well. But *fear not* about that; your name could not interfere with the popularity of the work in the *remotest degree!* . . . . . In sending you the enclosed *"Prospectus"* I only mean to show you how I am working for the *"Simms'* monument" &c—*You are to* do *nothing* in the *matter.*

Always Yr's

Paul H Hayne.

I am rejoiced to be able to furnish you with all needful facts in relation to Dr F. O. Ticknor—

In addition to the printed articles sent you, I have contributed an elaborate *"life"* of *Ticknor,* with critical remarks upon his genius & poetry, to the "NY Independent", and *this* I expect to appear *soon.*

Dr Ticknor was as *true* a Poet as ever lived!

Do him *all the* justice you can in your *"Speaker".*

Ah! he was a magnificent fellow! *every inch a man!*

. . Altho we never *"met in the flesh,"* still I *knew* him, *from correspondence & otherwise;* knew him *thoroughly.*

[Written in the left margin, lengthwise, of page 1 of the letter:]

My wife sends the printed slip. You perceive the writer agrees with you as to the sale of Southern books, & the revival of some [sane?] interest in learning &c.

[The following sketch of Ticknor is on a separate folder, but was probably enclosed in the letter above:]

Dr Francis Orrery Ticknor, was born in Baldwin Co, Georgia, in the year 1823; and died in Columbus Ga (*where* he had resided for the larger portion of his life)—in Dec 1874.

. — — A scientist of high attainments, and a practical Physician, trusted & beloved by all who knew him—, he devoted his leisure hours to *art;* particularly to music & poetry. As a Poet, his genius is essentially lyrical. Its originality and fervor are remarkable.

It has been well said, that his style is best suited to forceful ballads.

Look, for example, at that superb lyric "The Virginians of the Valley".

Something in the direct, clear-ringing expression of this song reminds us of—

> "Mais quand la pauvre champagne,
> Fut en proie aux etrangers
> Lui, bravant tous les dangers,
> Semblant seul tenir la Champagne"—

With Ticknor as with Beranger simplicity is strength!—

How admirably is this illustrated also, in "Little Giffin!"— We pity the person who can peruse it without a certain throbbing at heart, and a moisture in the eyes.

Few men of Ticknor's poetical gifts ever existed, so careless of what is generally called fame.

His noblest productions appeared in obscure local periodicals; and after their being issued thus, he seemed to dismiss them from his mind with a lordly sort of carelessness, which proved how affluent were the man's artistic & imaginative resources.!—

[In James's letter to Hayne dated May 11, 1878, he expressed great appreciation for Mrs. Hayne's recent letter and the photograph of Hayne. He said he was convinced that he would eventually be able to bring out Hayne's complete poems by subscription, adding: ". . . and (though you are so dubious on the subject) *I know* you have more warm admirers and friends in the South than any other one Southern author."

Hayne's son was right: Longfellow's poems were issued a number of times between 1871 and the date of this letter—for instance, *The Complete Poetical Works of Henry Wadsworth Longfellow*. With Numerous Illustrations. Boston: James R. Osgood and Company, 1876. The Whittier volume referred to was probably by the same publisher. The Bryant volume may have been that published by D. Appleton & Co. (New York, 1872)—at any rate Hayne's description fits it.

James wrote in his letter of May 11, 1878: "Mrs. H. spoke of your dedicating the proposed Edition to *me*!! The very great pleasure that the suggestion even of such an unexpected honor gives me, does not prevent me from feeling that (even did I deserve it, which I do not) you might do yourself injustice thereby. I am perfectly aware that outside of Texas I am unknown, and . . . my small name would not be a large enough tail for such a comet! Seriously and as a man of business, I think you would advance your own interests by complimenting someone more worthy and more influential than I am. Dont believe, Dear Sir, that I am for a moment insensible to the high honor—indeed, it would be the proudest day of my life to see such a work dedicated to me, if I could feel that I really deserved it." When *Poems of Paul Hamilton Hayne* (Complete Edition. With Numerous Illustrations. Boston: D. Lothrop and Company, 1882) did finally appear, the dedication page read: "To Colonel John G. James, President of the State Agricultural and Mechanical College of Texas, These Verses, in which he has taken so unselfish an interest, are Affectionately Dedicated."

In his letter of May 11, 1878, James asked Hayne for a brief sketch of Ticknor. In his book (p. 231) James merely quoted this sketch by Hayne (with minor changes) and signed Hayne's name to it. See also *The Poems of Frank O. Ticknor, M. D.* Ed. by K. M. R. With an Introductory Notice of the Author by Paul H. Hayne. (Philadelphia: J. B. Lippincott & Co., 1879.) Ticknor's given names were Francis Orray, but his friends called him Frank.

Enclosed in the letter were two clippings from a Charleston newspaper about Hayne's lives of R. Y. Hayne and H. S. Legaré. One thousand copies were to be printed at a cost of $193.60.

Pierre Jean de Béranger (1780–1857) was a popular French lyric poet. The quotation is from his *Les Souvenirs du Peuple.*]

No. 219

PAUL HAMILTON HAYNE to JOHN G. JAMES

"Copse Hill," Georgia Rail Road,
July 9*th* 1878

Address:

P. O. Box 275
Augusta, Ga.

My Dear Friend;

My heart has *again* been *deeply* touched by yours of 16*th* ult, to which I have not been able, (& *still* am not able) to reply in *full*. To your family & self I owe my *heart-felt* thanks for the appreciation in which I am held.

Of whom (may I ask?) do your family consist? Have you any *wife* to lighten your toils? and oh! I *must* hope that your brother, about whom you seem so anxious, will be spared to you!

Pray be careful not to *overwork*, this summer in my behalf, but take that rest which nature requires.

Tender to Mr Dinwoody my *warmest* thanks for the interest he has manifested in my literary work. I enclose a copy of *"Muscadines,"* a poem well adapted for illustration. Please hand it to Mr Dinwiody [Hayne wrote *Dinwoody* and then wrote *i* for the first *o* but failed to change the second *o* to *d*], with my complt*s*.

If you have *any likeness* of *yourself, you can spare,* send it to me; that I may look upon the face of so true, noble, & generous a friend.

x x x x x I am *not* acquainted with Col R M *Johnston,* except by reputation. And now, I must answer your *2nd* letter rec*d* last Evening . . . . I send you an article on *Simms,* which will *precisely* answer your purpose; and *one* also upon Mrs Preston's first vol, which embodies a *careful estimate* of her very remarkable genius, lyrical & dramatic. You can *easily* compress *both papers,* and as for *credit,* do *just as you please in that matter.*

When you have *entirely finished* with them, *return* the articles; but do *not hurry.*

Alas! I cannot write more; since I continue *quite weak!* you'll understand, and pardon me.

Best regards from Mrs Hayne, & all here.

Anything I have done for *you,* has been *unalloyed* pleasure. *Never.* therefore, apologize about *"trouble* &c &c" !!

> *Always Most Faithfully,*
>
> *Paul. H. Hayne.*

[In his letter of June 16, 1878, James said that he had lost his father and eldest brother since he had founded the Texas Military Institute and that another brother, a teacher in the institute, was in very poor health, would probably have to give up teaching, and would spend the next six

months with relatives in Virginia. The brother who was ill was probably
Fleming Wills James, who later went into banking. In the same letter
James spoke of some illustrations for Hayne's book which were being
made by the professor of mathematical science and drawing. He was
Hardaway Hunt Dinwiddie, of Virginia, a professor at the Texas Military
Institute from the beginning (1868), and later a professor at the State
Agricultural and Mechanical College of Texas.

For "Muscadines" see *Harper's New Monthly Magazine*, LIV (Dec.,
1876), 127–128 or *Complete Edition*, pp. 222–224.

Richard Malcolm Johnston (1822–1898), of Georgia, was a lawyer, professor. author, and a colonel on the staff of Governor Brown. After the
war he lived mainly in Baltimore. He and William Hand Browne
collaborated in several works, including a *Life of Alexander H. Stephens*
(1878). He was an intimate friend of James, and his home was James's
headquarters whenever he visited Baltimore.

On July 3, 1878, James wrote Hayne for sketches of Simms and Margaret
Junkin Preston for his reader.]

No. 220

PAUL HAMILTON HAYNE to JOHN G. JAMES

"Copse Hill," Georgia Rail Road,
October 8*th* 1878.˙.

Address:

P. O. Box 275
Augusta, Ga.

My Dear Friend;

Your long & truly courteous letter of the 27*th* August *ought*
certainly to have been answered before; but *chronic* ill health
combined with certain items of *imperative* business, (in the
literary line), has delayed its proper acknowledgement. I was
glad to hear of the completion of your "School-book"; & do
not wonder at your resolution never to attempt *anything* of
the sort again. These compilations demand an amount of tact,
taste, good judgment, & patient labor which to *one* engaged in
other practical toils of life, must be *exceedingly trying*.

Nevertheless, the book in question, *may* bring you a rich
reward.

I am *touched* by your reference to what you call my "kind
asssistance" in your work, & the "friendship" resulting therefrom.

This "friendship" *I* too *especially value.*

. . . . And so, you are a "Bachelor on the shady *side of thirty*"; & *one* moreover, likely to occupy for an indefinite period to come, his bachelor *status,* since in your own language, *"you can see no* no [*sic*] prospect of bettering (!) your condition!"

Is *that* phrase "bettering" to be interpreted *"sarcastical"* — as *Artemus Ward* would say.?

Seriously, my friend, I perceive from what you write, that you have *deliberately sacrificed* all your *personal* feelings & projects to a *higher duty,* as you consider the matter; & that you occupy now, *precisely* the same honorable place, which Miss Mulock gives to her noble hero, *"Ninian Graham"* in the novel entitled, *"The Head of the Family".*

My *wife,* in fact, as soon as she read your letter, said that this character of Miss Mulock's was suggested by your noble sacrifice of self! — — so that you should peruse the book *("Head of the Family"),* if you have not *as yet done so.*

I *rejoice* to hear of your *brother's* improved health; and trust that he may be *permanently restored;* & I hope that your *own* health is *good.*

Let me say that I am *heartily obliged,* of course to *yourself* first, & likewise to *Major Dinwiddie,* for your *practical demonstration* of *interest* in the illustration of my Poems! Certainly, we shall *all* be *delighted* to see these "illustrations", when you have a "number completed to send on".

I have *no doubt* whatsoever that *"you* will receive as much pleasure as I shall, to see the contemplated work accomplished"; but you *must* not *overexert yourself* in my behalf.

By the papers, I see, that the *Texas crop* is a fine one, & that the *"Texians"* are much Elated thereby; but I fear that the suffering from *"Yellow Fever"* has injured *So* trade awfully. *Tell me what you think?—*

Apropos, I have composed a *Poem,* called *"The Stricken South to the North",* expressive of our gratitude for their generosity to the Yellow Fever sufferers. x x x x

x x *Indeed* I *did "mean* it" when I expressed a wish for the photo of *one* who has *proved* himself so *genuine a friend.* We shall *all* value it very *highly.*

I hope that you rec*d* a copy of my *"lives"* of *"Hayne &
Legaré"*;— the Edition has nearly *sold out*, and the little book
has been honored with unusually warm praise. My wife sends
you a few *"autographs"*. You acknowledged the one of Longfellow; & afterwards she (my wife) mailed you *Whittier's.*

They cannot always be cut from the letters; because important reading matter on the other side would be destroyed; —
and I have a wretched habit of tearing off envelopes, or she
might have sent you many more.

Sherman's ruffians destroyed many *invaluable "MSS,"* autographs &c belonging to me, when they passed thro Columbia.
. . . By the way, the Photographers came up *here* on Sa*t*
to take *"Copse Hill"*, including my study, at the request of
Messrs[.] *Lothrope & Co, Boston,* to illustrate *"the Poets
Homes"* in *"W. Awake"*. These articles will be *collected,*
finally, in· *book-form*... . . . . . *Our* household too, join in
best wishes for yourself & family; & my love to *that "dear,
venerable old Virginia mother of yours,"* whom I should so
much like *to know.*

With warm regards from *my wife,*
I remain *Ever Faithfully,*

Paul. H. Hayne.

[In his letter of August 27, 1878, James wrote: "I am sorry to have to
confess that I am a bachelor, on the shady side of thirty, and so far as I
can see with no immediate prospect of bettering my condition. . . . My
family consists of my mother (a real old Virginia lady whom I know
you would love), a young brother—a cadet in school—and the widow of
my eldest brother— My father died about two years ago, leaving me the
head of the family— My brother (about whose ill health I wrote you)
and his wife & child live just across the street, but take their meals with
me, so that we really form one family— Now you have us all, and you
can readily see that I have *family enough* without marrying. I feel it
my duty, indeed, not to marry, but to devote myself to the care of those
left to me, and to find my happiness thus."

The James burial plot in the Oakwood Cemetery in Austin contains
the graves of Henry James (1814–1876), Eliza M. James (1819–1904),
Ashby Stuart James (1862–1909), and John Garland James (1844–1930).
Ashby graduated in law in 1882 at the University of Virginia and returned
to Colorado, Texas, to practice. For a time he was cashier in his brother's
bank at Wichita Falls. Later he practiced in Austin and was one of O.
Henry's attorneys in his trial.

Dinah Maria Mulock (Mrs. Craik, 1826–1887), English novelist, brought out *The Head of the Family* (the hero of which is Ninian Græme) in 1851.

For "The Stricken South to the North" see *Complete Edition* (pp. 299–300).

D. Lothrop & Co. of Boston published the juvenile magazine *Wide Awake* (to which Hayne contributed) and later (1882) published Hayne's *Complete Edition*.]

No. 221

PAUL HAMILTON HAYNE to JOHN G. JAMES

"Copse Hill," Georgia Rail Road,
December 17*th* 1878. :

Address:

P. O. Box 275
Augusta, Ga.

My Dear Col:

Let me thank you *most* warmly—though at this abominably late date—, for your truly interesting & affectionate letter of Oc*t 6th.*

You would pardon my *long* delay in replying, if you had any idea of the multitude of literary engagements, which daily oppress me.

You have been *very near* my thoughts, however; & I have looked, every 24 hours, for the *receipt* of your *"Speaker?" What has* become *of it?*—

Before reverting to my *own* affairs, let me tell you how much my wife & I were interested in the little episode connected with a certain nameless widow, (*"O! Samivel, Samivel, beware of the vidders!"*)—, and *we both* decided that she was *not worthy of you;* while our satisfaction was great to learn that "your appetite had returned, & that *henceforth,* you were going to give all widows a wide berth!"—

Seriously, I *do* trust that this disappointment was *not* a heavy blow.

Do you recall what manly *George* Wither once wrote, *apropos* of a *heart* affair?

"Shall I wasting in despair,
Die, because a woman's fair?
Or, make pale *my* cheeks with care,
Because another's rosy are?—
Be she fairer than the Day,
Or, the flowery meads of May—,
If she be not so for me—,
What care I *how* fair she be?"

————————— . . —————————

Now, *you* seem to have accepted your fate, in the same heroic, independent temper!—

By Venus, Cupid & all their family, if *women* were more frequently treated *thus,* instead of being lackadaisically humored, and worshipped even in their cruellest whims—, how much more they would respect the sterner sex?—

Concerning your lyric, you *certainly undervalue* it! It is *graceful* in conception, and *harmoniously executed;* and I promise not to send it to *"Scribner",* *unless* he offers me *$3000,* instead of *"One"!!*

x x x. In regard to your kind suggestion about a "Compilation of Poems", (like *Bryant*[']*s* e. g),—(by the way, the steel engraving of myself in *his "Library of Poets,"* I'd like you to see, since it is incomparably the *best* likeness ever taken), you know that Bryant's work, Whittier's *"Poems of 3 Centuries",* Longfellow's *"Poems of Places,"* with various *others* I could name—, were *all direct* suggestions of the *Publishers,* for the *Editorship* of which they (*the Poets*) were handsomely paid. Indeed so *many similar* compilations, have been made, that I fear there would be *no profit* in such a speculation.

. . . . You ask after my health.? It *continues very feeble; &* therefore, I cannot tax myself with *more* work than I have on hand. A Poet, you see, *must* compose original verses, whenever the inspiration seizes him; & should I cease writing *"Book Notices",* *how* could I receive the new *Publications.?* You judge rightly in supposing that I have done enough *"gratuitous work for others* during the last year or two, to fill a vo*l* like the one proposed!" Touching the "dollar question," it is not that I "ignore it" altogether as you suppose, (yet thank God! I *can* truly affirm that I *have* always written disinterestedly for the good of my section, & the love of my art). At the *South,* you are aware, *Art* is not appreciated at any *monied* or *practical value;* & at the *North,* of course, I am *not paid,* as I *would have been,* if a *born* Yankee! . . . Verily, I am *too poor in* this world's goods, not to be rejoiced to receive *my due.* (Then *old age* is approaching, with all its ills added to *chronic* disease).

As to a vo*l* of "Lyrics", if the hard Times do not prevent the N*o* book (Publishers) from bringing out my unpublished verses, I *shall certainly issue the little work* of which I spoke to you; but in *that case, I'll inform you in due season.*

Our grand *"illustrated edition",* I *leave* in *your hands, knowing* that you *will* attend to the *matter diligently, when you deem* the *time propitious.*

x x x x x *Do not forget* the *promised likeness of yourself,* as *my wife & I earnestly* desire to see the *friend* who has *indeed proved* himself worthy that sacred name.

With warmest regards from my entire household to *your family & yourself,* & *hoping* that your brother has quite *recovered his health,* I remain

Yours Faithfully & affectionately &c

Paul. H. Hayne &c.

Strange!! only a few weeks ago, a letter reached me from *Augusta,* asking *where* a *complete (illustrated) Edition of my Works* could be procured! As I have been *scrupulously careful not to mention your design, abroad,* perhaps we may regard this as a *"good omen"!* Enclosed, is a piece on *H* [.] *Benner,* from *NYork Sun.* It has had *immense success!*

[Written at the top of p. 1 of the letter:]

Do *send* me your *"Speaker"* at once!

[Written lengthwise in the margin on page 4:]

I send you a *"Sonnet"* addressed to myself in *French,* by a gentleman of NYork, who, has published *one* vo*l* of Poems, & travelled all over the world, & whom I have *never* seen. This comp*t* is doubly appreciated, because the writer belongs to the school of *"Evolutionists,"* so different from my *own!*

[Written on an extra sheet:]

(P S No 2)—

A word *in confidence,* about the small vo*l* of Lyrics, which I contemplate publishing. Friends in NY. are now canvassing among Publishers, to find (if possible), one who will undertake the *"affaire"!*

It is a very dubious undertaking. Indeed (to be frank), I *d'ont believe that* any *Pub: will be found, unless I can convince him that all loss on his part is impossible; nay,* that *some definite gain is certain.*

How is this to be done? Why, in only *one* way! I must *address friends everywhere,* and *procure* from them assurances, that the *book-dealers,* in their respective *towns, or cities,* are ready to send on *"orders"* to the *Publisher,* the moment the work appears; or *'twould be better* to have the *"orders"* prepared & fixed up, so that they can be despatched *immediately.* *More plainly;* if from some of the chief *So towns* &c, I can procure book-sellers' *"orders",* some for *20, some 50, some 70,* or 80 copies of the contemplated work, and my friends—(each in his section), will so interest themselves, as to see that such "orders" are prepared—, it will all be right. What I would have my friends do is *this. viz, let each* go to his book-seller, and say, "how many copies of *Mr H's work,* (a small vo*l* worth about *a dollar,* or at *most* a *dollar & a half),* are you willing to send for, when I tell you the name of his *publisher?"*

. . . . *Here's* the whole matter in a *"nutshell"—!!*

. . Now, *mon ami, if you think,* the mention of the *present* vo*l* is *calculated to injure* the prospects of the *other more important (complete) edition, d'ont breathe, I entreat,* one *syllable concerning* it. But if *not,* perhaps the *Austin "Stationer*[?]*"* might be *addressed! When you reply, answer this portion* of *my letter* on a *separate sheet, addressed to me privately.*

Will explain *hereafter.*

[In James's letter of October 6. 1878. he confessed that he had not been entirely honest in his last letter in saying that he had no interest in marriage. He confessed that he had just passed through what for a time had seemed like a serious love affair with "a very charming lady neighbor"—the widow of one of his old college classmates. She had spent the preceding summer in Virginia, and it was during her absence that the romance had waned. James said he had written her a *"pome,"* which he enclosed to Hayne with this comment: "These lines are not for sale! So dont let Scribner have them, if he offers a thousand dollars, as he doubtless would if he ever saw them." The poem follows:

Out of Tune!

O mocking-bird, you are out of tune!
    Pray, cease your senseless roundelay:
You sing no more as you did in June,
    When my heart beat time the livelong day.

My heart beat time as you led the tune,
    In a measure always sweet yet gay,
For we both were happy in that lost June,
    While you alone are happy today.

O Love, once more put my heart in tune!
    (Its chords own ever thy magic sway.)
That again I may live in that vanished June,
    And banish forever the pain of today.

James said the charming widow said "she wasn't in the *tuning business,* but advised me to call on a *piano tuner* in town." He assured Hayne, however, that his appetite had returned.

Sam Weller in *Pickwick Papers* was frequently warned against widows by his father, who, late in life, had married one.

In James's letter of October 6, 1878, he suggested that Hayne might make some money by editing such a compilation as Bryant's *A Library of Poetry and Song* (New York: J. B. Ford and Company, 1870, etc.). Hayne also refers to Whittier's *Songs of Three Centuries* (Boston: James R. Osgood and Company, 1875, etc.) and Longfellow's *Poems of Places* (31 vols. Boston: Houghton, Osgood and Company, 1876–79). James said Hayne had done too much free work for others who had profited thereby—probably referring to aid which Hayne had given to various compilers of anthologies.

For Hayne's poem "Hiram ·H. Benner" ("Dedicated to the Wife of this Hero and Martyr") see *Complete Edition* (pp. 314–315). Benner, of Illinois, was an army officer who volunteered to take charge of the relief ship taking supplies down the Mississippi to yellow fever sufferers at Memphis, Vicksburg, and other points south. He caught the fever and died. Many Southern newspapers at the time published editorials in praise of him.

The sonnet in French, "À Paul H. Hayne," was by Francis Saltus Saltus (1849–1889), traveller, linguist, and poet, of New York. He and Hayne corresponded for years.

Moses Coit Tyler was interviewing New York publishers about a proposed volume of Hayne's poems. See Hayne's letters to Tyler.

The newspaper referred to near the end is the Austin *Statesman*.]

No. 222

PAUL HAMILTON HAYNE to JOHN G. JAMES

"Copse Hill," Georgia Rail Road,

December 28*th* 1878

Address:

P. O. Box 275,

Augusta, Ga.

My Dear Co*l* James;—

I hope you *received* my reply to your last letter.? Now, I can merely write in *great haste* touching a business matter.

Only last Ev*n*g l rec*d* a communication from my *dear* friend, Prof Coit Tyler of the "University of Michigan," author of that admirable work, (two vol*s* of which have just appeared from the press of the Putnams), called a "His: of American Literature".

He has been kindly trying to negotiate with some Publisher for me, in regard to my *unpublished Poems;*—but *thus far,* he has *not* been successful.

He tells me, however, that there is *one* Publisher, (who shall be nameless), & who *objects* to the issuing of a small vo*l*—*(viz)*, my *last Poems,*—but *perhaps, may* be *induced to bring out a handsome large* vol*; selected carefully from* my *works.* He wished, first, to know who held the *"Copyright",?* but indeed, they *never* have been "copyrighted"! An immediate answer was requested to these *two* inquiries, namely, *about* "Copyright", & whether I was willing to have the *"selection,"* (conducted on a *most liberal* plan) made from the mass of *what* I had written.

I have just finished a reply to *Prof Tyler*, in which I told him (in *strict confidence*), of *your* generous design concerning

an Illustrated Edition, saying, you wished a ["]Poet's Edition,"
in order that I might make something, & asking if this Publisher
secured Copyright, *you* would be compelled to pay him any of
the proceeds from the *Ill: edition* you contemplated.

Also I said, that I would *prefer* a *Complete* edition instead of
a *"selection* &c"[.]   But remember "beggar's [*sic*] *can't* be
Choosers," and should the mysterious *Pub:* not be willing to risk
so large a book, in face of the Monied difficulties, I *must be
satisfied to do the best possible under the Circumstances,—
don't you think* so?—

I may not enjoy such a chance again.   x x x How are the
"Widows"? Lively I presume, in this excessively lively
weather.? *We* are being half frozen over here, in the remote
South!.

'Tis damnable to have "ice-fingers" down one's back, and a
general creepy sensation of Arctic desolation &c!   *Best love
from all* the *family! Do write a reply at* once!

Ever Yr's

Paul H. Hayne.

[Written in the margin of the second page of the letter:]

Dec: *Dec 28th 1878.* Would you credit it?. the very *oil* is
frozen!

[See Hayne's letters to Moses Coit Tyler and the notes thereon.

In a letter dated January 1, 1878, James wrote: "My *widow*, after whom
you kindly inquire, *is* lively, and as pretty and plump as a partridge,
though I do not believe I am still in love."   Obviously the date is an
error for January 1, 1879.   In the same letter he spoke of his plan to
bring out an illustrated edition of about one thousand copies of Hayne's
complete poems by subscription—with the profits going to Hayne.   He
complained of the "niggardliness" of Northern editors toward Southern
writers and added: "But, alas! we are in the hands of the Philistines,
and must get out as best we may."]

No. 223

PAUL HAMILTON HAYNE to JOHN G. JAMES
[Postal card]

Jan 25th—1879

My Dear Friend;

A letter from *Henry L Flash*, (the Poet) shows me that he has changed his address to No *44 Canal*, & *63 Common* Sts N. Orleans.

Mr M R Tunno's address *P. O. Box 255*
Savannah Ga.

He is a *S. Carolinian.*

Mr Wm Duncan's address *is*

Cor: Bryan & Abercorn S*t*
Savannah Ga

Miss Sarah Hobby, Cor: Perry & Bull S*ts*
Savannah Ga

Dr John Darby, No *39* W. 20*th* St *NY*

(He is Prof: in *"Med College,"* o[f] So C*a* and knows *many Southerners* in NY. He is a *Connection of my wife's*, & may do *much*. x x H. Flash says, he "takes interest in all *things that concern me.*["]

[Written in the margin:]

I rec*d* your P. C. of 18*th*. *Kindest* regards!

Ever Yr's

P. H. H.

[In a number of letters both Hayne and Mrs. Hayne, at James's request, sent names of people who might be interested in purchasing Hayne's poems or in securing subscriptions.

The Medical College of South Carolina is in Charleston. One of Mrs. Hayne's brothers, Dr. William Middleton Michel (1822–1894), was a professor there for a number of years.]

No. 224

PAUL HAMILTON HAYNE to JOHN G. JAMES

"Copse Hill," Georgia Rail Road,
March 4th 1879

Address:
P. O. Box 275
Augusta, Ga.

My Dear Friend;

What can I say to you for all your *generous, unselfish* kindness on my behalf? I can only repeat again & yet *again, that I thank you from the bottom of my soul!*

It *grieves* us to read in yours of the 21st ult that you have been *"seriously unwell;* broken down by press of work as much as anything else", but we observe with great relief in the same letter that you have *measurably* recovered.

You must *not,* (I *pray) over exert* yourself in reference to the *Book.*

Last Evng's mail brought me yours of the 24th & 26th Feb, together with *Miss* Lathbury's, & Mr Pratt's letters.

The *latter* I return according to request.

Now, I'll take your 1st communication. My wife is on the alert looking for every, *even* the *briefest* notice of your School Reader. (She attends to my mail). We rejoice to observe how bright the prospects are, for its success. Of *course* I read the "Circular" with *deep interest, and will notice the work particularly, so soon as I receive it from Barnes & Co*[.] (It has *not yet* "put in its appearance"). As for the *"bound* copy", you so liberally, & kindly promise, it shall surely have a prominent place in my *library.*

I think your plan as to "Circulars" *just* the right one; and *cordially* do I join in the wish that you lived near me. *If* you *can come* to us, how *very warmly* you will be *welcomed* in our plain little Country home;— *none on this Earth more so!*

Now, for your's of 26th [.]

I think with you that the outline given in Pratt's letter is indeed *"admirable"*, but *beyond* your possible subscription list, I *feel* assured. I *have* written to Lothrop & Co for Miss Lathbury's book for review; & if it comes, I will re-mail it to you in a few days.

Personally, I do *not* know the Firm, nor have I ever had any *personal dealings* with them. I send my contributions (to *"Wide Awake"*) to Mrs Pratt, who, under the name, of *"Ella Farman"*, Edits *that* Magz.

I have always been promptly paid for my pieces; and *certainly* she seems to take an interest both in Mrs Preston & myself, as *So Writers*.

I think Miss *Lathbury's* advice should be followed; & you perceive that she courteously offers to *aid* you in getting estimates from New York Publishers. But I've *no doubt*, as she says, that *Lothrop & Co will do it as reasonably as any Firm North* of good standing.

. . . . . They tell me that I am *popular* in *Boston*, and *really* I *believe* that Mr & Mrs Pratt *will*,—as they promise, "gladly distribute *Circulars* among literary people we (they) are daily meeting, & are in correspondence with! We (they) can doubtless help *not* a little in *this* way".

. . . . I see that Mr Pratt writes, "I send Col James copies of *"W Awake" referred* to. ["]

Has he sent you the monthly, with *"Katie"*, & *"Motes,"* or does he refer to the Jan & March nos, containing specimens of Mr Dana's work?—

Please *glance over* Mr Pratt's letter *again*, & you'll observe that I have made a few *marginal* comments. He (Pratt) says, "if Col James would send us the *collection* (*of my Poems*) *complete*, I'm sure *you*, (Miss Lathbury), or, *we here* would gladly examine and sketch *an outline plan of illustration"*.

This is *an exceedingly kind offer*, since it would involve a *good deal* of trouble. Don't *you think* so?.

My Poems written *since "The Mountain of Lovers,"* are now in the vault of *Putnam & Co*, NYork. You remember they were despatched to *Prof. Tyler*, to see whether he could have a small vol issued at Publishers' expense.

(I enclose the Professor's *last letter* to me) Just *before* receiving it I had written to ask Mr Longfellow to use *his* influence touching their publication with *Houghton & Osgood*. I've *not* heard from him *since*, but the papers say he *is quite sick* with *Influenza*.

Now, what shall I do in regard to this matter? Give up the idea of having the little work issued (even if it should be accepted on the terms *specified*), & *concentrate all interest & effort on the Ill: Edition?* I think this would be by *far the best course; d'ont you think so too?*

Drop me a P. C. embodying your opinion, *as soon as possible*, so that I can *act* in the affair.

With *truest love* from all, &c
      I *am Ever Yrs'* &c

      Paul H Hayne

[In his letter of February 24, 1879, James wrote: "I will print this week circulars [of Hayne's proposed volume] and postal subscription cards, in proper form, which will be put in the hands of every body of note North and South. . . ." In the same letter he wrote: "Would that you lived here near me! I do hope that I may be able to see you this year—perhaps may visit the North, & take Copse Hill on the route." In later letters he also spoke of his desire to go to the North, partly on business connected with the college but mainly to interview publishers about Hayne's book, and to see Hayne at Copse Hill on the way. He was never able to visit Hayne, however, and the two friends were never to meet in the flesh.

Mary Artemisia Lathbury (b. 1841) was a prolific author of New York. Most of her work (verse and prose) was juvenile or religious. In a later letter Hayne mentions her *Out of Darkness into Light*.

Ella Farman was the maiden name of Mrs. Charles Stuart Pratt, editor of *Wide Awake*, a magazine for boys and girls published by D. Lothrop & Co. of Boston. Charles Stuart Pratt (her husband) was associate editor.

In his letter of February 26, 1879, James wrote: "I do not know the house of L[othrop] & Co by personal dealings—you do. What do you think of letting them manufacture the book, if I approve of the prices they may give me? I will write them by this mail, for full information, and see just exactly what they will do, & what we must do—" This is James's first mention of Lothrop & Co. Apparently he hoped to distribute the book himself by subscription, pay Lothrop & Co. a set sum for the printing and binding, and send all profits to Hayne. But the plan did not work. On March 28, 1879, he wrote that Lothrop's prices were too high.

In December, 1880, James wrote Hayne a joyful letter stating that D. Lothrop & Co. had finally agreed to publish the book, mainly at their own risk, since James had only two hundred subscribers. Just before D. Lothrop & Co. agreed to publish the book, James had written them twice making a "proposition." He does not say what the proposition was. He probably mentioned not only the subscribers but also other efforts to secure subscribers, the use that could be made of agents, and certain illustrations that were available without cost.

In his letter of February 24, 1879, James said he had not yet received from Barnes & Co. a copy of his reader but had requested the publisher to send to Hayne an early copy, "which I hope you will Kindly notice for me in some of your papers," and promising to send Hayne a specially bound copy at a later date. He expected general adoption in Texas and other states and added: "The leading men of Charleston manifested more interest in my-enterprise than did the people of any other city. . . . It would be splendid to have the book adopted by that city and Augusta!"

"Kiss Me, Katie" and "Motes" are both juvenile poems by Hayne. See *Complete Edition* (pp. 368–369, 376).

I have not seen the issues of *Wide Awake* "containing specimens of Mr Dana's work," but the reference may be to Richard Henry Dana, Senior (1787–1879), New England author, whom Hayne had visited years earlier. See the letters to Longfellow for other references to him. Hayne wrote a memorial poem to him after his death (*Complete Edition*, pp. 321–322).]

No. 225

PAUL HAMILTON HAYNE to JOHN G. JAMES

"Copse Hill," Georgia Rail Road,
March 7*th* 1879

Address:
 P. O. Box 275,
  Augusta, Ga.

My Dear & Valued Friend;—

— — It is *simply impossible* for me to express to you the feeling of *profound appreciative gratitude* which warms my *soul* thro & thro, when I reflect upon your *unparalleled* kindness towards *myself!*—Perhaps, I may have used the illustration *before;* but no matter! — I *must* employ it *again!*

I *must* say, that I feel like "Midwinter", in W. Collins' strange romance of "Armandale", when he found that young

Armandale truly designed to *"stand by him"*, in "good report, and Evil," to help, support, encourage, — and in *every possible* manner, *exalt him!* —

Socially before his new acquaintance took him up, poor Midwinter (as his *very* name *implies*), had been an *outcast;* — *Every* man's *hand* & *heart* appeared against him!! What marvel that when sudden Social Sunshine burst upon him thro Allan's frank blue eyes, he hailed it as well nigh *miraculous?*—

Now—in a *literary sense, I* hav[e] been *newly,* if not quite an *"outcast"*, among my *own* People, — the people for whom I have *"agonized"*, (*that's* the term), during 30 long, weary[,] bitter, — *inconceivably bitter years!!*—

— — — But *when least expected,* light dawns, *not* in my *East,* (mark you!) — for the *Orient* of *my* existence had long ago faded—, but along the *slopes,* & *declivities* of my *Western* life—;—almost in the *gloaming,* next to *night!*—

—All this imagery seems— God help me! *fantastic;* yet I am *certain* of being comprehended by a *Heart* so *deep,* & *broad* as your *own.*

— — — Nor will you any the less fail to understand, if I venture to ask of you the *most solemn of favors!*—

— —The *life* of Every man is *uncertain!*— But *doubly, trebly uncertain* is the life of one, who like—myself—, has suffered from *chronic sickness* for a quarter of a Century!

———The persuasion, the *presentiment,* (*whatever* we may term it), is *Strong* upon me, that a year or two,—(perhaps even a few *months*), will round the sum of my *Earthly* days—;—

————*Should* this *prove true; do not allow your contemplated Edition of my Poems, to fall through !!* ———

———I, indeed, *would* (in the case anticipated), be far *beyond* the tickling of mortal vanity; — but there is one connected with me, (my poor *wife* I *especially* mean) — whose *heart might be Saved from a broken condition,* by your *forcing* her to *further interest* in the *Scheme* of an *illus: Volume!!*—

x x x x x   *Per Hercle!*— these be Sombre intimations!

— — Well! well! — I *may* be *all astray;* but (in *any* event), *no harm* can be done by my *letter to you.* Even beyond the bounds of the *present life,* I verily think, that I would, (so far as my *deepest affections* are concerned), be enabled to communicate with the few Beloved ones from whom I had been Separated. x x x

————Forgive the *wildness* of this communication.

———— I could *not* subdue the impulse which almost *constrained* its composition.

Of course I address you in *sacred privacy.*

Don't Ever— in writing— allude to this letter — however vaguely.

God be with you—
Ever Yrs' — in *this world, or any other.*

P. H. H.

[Written lengthwise at the bottom of the letter:]

I *don't* ask you to *destroy;* I only beg that you would keep this letter where no Eyes but your own can see it!

x   x   *One of these days, you may turn to its pages,* with a *strange feeling* that there are *indeed* "more things in heaven & earth, than *we,* (poor blinded fools!) dream of, in our *circumscribed philosophy!"*.

[Written at the top of the first page of the letter:]

Private & Confidential.

[William Wilkie Collins (1824–1889). English novelist, brought out *Armadale* in 1866.]

No. 226

PAUL HAMILTON HAYNE to JOHN G. JAMES

[Postal card]

March 12th 1879

Dear Friend;

I send you by to *day's* mail Miss *Lathbury's book,* which please *return,* when you have *entirely finished* with it. She is a woman of a *great deal* of *talent.* x x Have you seen her *illustration* of my poem, called *"Katie"?* 'Tis *perfect!* x x

Your book *has reached* me; — I think *you have done your work admirably;* and I shall notice this very *important work as soon as possible.* Many *many thanks* for what you have so kindly *said of myself. We deeply appreciate* it!

In haste, but Ever

P. H. H.

[In *Complete Edition,* opposite page 368, there is an illustration of "Kiss Me, Katie!" This may be the one to which Hayne refers. He and James tried to secure some of the illustrations of his poems that had appeared in various magazines for his volume.

James's book (pp. 7–8) contains a sketch of Hayne. The last sentence reads: "In delicacy of imagination, sweetness, simplicity, and grace of style, melodious movement, purity and elevation of thought, exquisite sensibility to the manifestations of beauty under all its forms, and in sympathetic interpretation of Nature, he is not behind any singer in the modern American choir."]

No. 227

PAUL HAMILTON HAYNE to JOHN G. JAMES

"Copse Hill," Georgia Rail Road,
March 14*th* 1879

Address:

 P. O. Box 275,
 Augusta, Ga.

I have *just completed* a notice of your Book *My Beloved Col,* and will send it *per mail* this *evng,* to the *chief Augusta* journal.

I did *not* put my name to it, *because* I am so prominently represented in compilation.

(Will send *you copies* as *soon as article appears*).

I *purposely* alluded to your having *accidentally,* left out *Henry L Flash; so as not* to appear *too partisan* by *finding no fault at all.* Now this omission is *upon* my shoulders, rather than *yours,* since I ought to have remembered him myself.

Until *hearing* from him within the last few months, he had escaped my mind.

How rejoiced I am to learn that your "Speaker" is having *such* a success in *Texas;!* while *au contraire*, I grieve that you have been sick again. Let me *repeat* my injunction; do *not overwork* yourself.

I trust that 'ere this you have recd my letter containing *Lothrope's & Miss Lathbury's* letters—, also the latter's work, *"Out of Darkness into Light"*, which I sent by *mail.?*

Am *much pleased* that you liked the Taylor poem.

Your criticism of *Lanier's piece* is just what my wife said of it; & *therein*, I agree, upon the whole.

—*"Conceits"*, and eternal *straining after effect*, are the radical errors of his style;—. 'tis pitiful, for he has *real genius*.

Thanks *again & again* for all you are doing in my behalf. I send *several other* names, *viz—*;

> *President N. Russell Middleton*
> *Pres: of College of Charleston S. C.*
> *Wm Tunno & Co 55 Gaston Street*
> *Savannah Ga*
> Chas E. Hurd (Ed *"Evng Transcript"*
> No 324 Washington S*t*
> Boston Mass
> W W. *Screwes Esq Ed: "Montgomery Advertiser"*
> *Ala*
> Mrs Louise Chandler Moulton
> *"28 Rutland Square*
> *Boston* Mass

[Written lengthwise in the margin of the second (and last) page of the letter:]

Have noted in my review of *"Speaker &c"* what *Barnes suggested*.

My *private* note reached you I hope. Never notice its contents in writing me.

Always Yrs'

P H H.

[Hayne had not forgotten Flash. See his letter to James dated October 8, 1877.

On March 8, 1879, James wrote that nearly every mail brought him orders for his reader from Texas teachers. In his letter of March 28, 1879, James thanked Hayne enthusiastically for his "notices" of his book.

For two poems on Bayard Taylor (he died in Germany, December 19, 1878) see *Complete Edition* (pp. 320–321).

James's letter of March 8, 1879, contained his criticism of Lanier's poem on Taylor in *Scribner's* for March. He found Lanier's poem "very beautifully expressed" but pagan in tone and lacking in "true feeling." He said it "seems to occupy itself more in the studied search of quaint & novel figures with which to adorn itself, than with the expression of *true feeling*." He added that Hayne's poem on Taylor was "so much more *natural!*" James's book contains selections from Lanier's "Corn" and "Psalm of the West" and "The Symphony," and "The Power of Prayer; or The First Steamboat Up the Alabama." Lanier had made the selections himself. See Margaret Lee Wiley's *Letters: Sidney Lanier to Col. John G. James* (The Miriam Stark Library, The University of Texas, Austin, 1942).]

No. 228

PAUL HAMILTON HAYNE to JOHN G. JAMES

[Undated and without heading or signature.]

\# I send you some *additional names.*

In England

Arthur P. Stanley—*Dean of Westminster*

Jean Ingelow, "*No 6 Holland Villas Road,
Addison Road
Kensington. W——
London*

Miss Ingelow is a *kind friend* & *Correspondent* of *mine.*

—William Black—*author* of "*Princess of Thule* &c"
(*Care Messrs Harper & Bros*)

*Algernon Charles Swinburne (Care of Messrs
*Chatto & Windus 74 Piccadilly
London . W.*

(*I *correspond* with *Swinburne* who is *very friendly.*)

Mrs Mulock Craik (*Care Macmillan & Co* London)
Justin M'Carthy *No 48 Gower St Bedford Square*
London—
—Hon John Welsh, *U. S. Minister to C't of St James*
37 Queen's Gate S W London
(# *Mr Welsh* has just written me a *very friendly* letter, send-
ing with it half a dozen copies of the *"Anglo American"*, in
which *he had* re-published my *"Stricken South to the North"*)—
John. H. Ingram—*"Engineer in Chief's Office*
Genl P. Office London"
Ingram is *Edgar Poe's Eng: Biographer.*
Dr J. Marion Sims, (*a So Carolinian*)
(his address is—*Care of Munroe & Co Bankers*
No 7 Rue Scribe Paris—
Martin Farquhar Tupper,
"Western Villa, North Park, West Croydon
Suffolk England [*"*]
Tupper knows my poems *well*, & professes a *great interest*
in the *South*. We too have *corresponded.*
Philip Bourke Marston . (address him as follows;
Care of *Mrs Louise Chandler Moulton*
Pomfret—Connecticut

America

Gen*l* George McClellan Gov: N. Jersey (*Trenton N Jersey*)
I rec*d* a *warm* letter of appreciation from him touching my
"Stricken South to North"—
Richard Henry Dana, (Care Henry W Longfellow *Cambridge*
Mass.
John. S. Dwight, address *"Dwight*[*'*]*s Journal* of Music,[*"*]
Care *Houghton & Osgood Boston Mass*
George H. Calvert, Newport R. Island
Mrs Elizabeth Oakes Smith,
Patchogue, Suffolk N. York State
(# I think *she* will help you; for she has *just* written me a
letter calling me "her *one true Poet in these* days of *namby-*
pambyism". Mrs S—. was very highly esteemed by *Poe*—)

\# Father Cochran,
"Principle [*sic*] *of R. Catholic Institute",*
"Overbrook, Montgomery Co Penn
\# *A strong Southerner—; originally* a *Charlestonian—*
Gen*l* Holtzclaw— ⎰ *Montgomery (Ala)*
Maj T*hos* Jones ⎱
Cap*t* Sam*l* Mays, Belair,
            Richmond Co Geo
Ella F Moseby—*Montreal P. O. Nelson Co*
            Virginia
Geo Houghton, *"Lotus Club"* N*York City*
Miss Frances C. Fisher, *Salisbury C. H Rowan Co No Ca*
Miss Marian L. C. Reeves,
            New Castle, Delaware
Hon W*m* Porcher Miles, Care W*m* Henry *Trescott*
            Washington D. C.
W*m* Henry *Trescott* " do "
Co*l* Ben*j* Rutledge & ⎰ *Charleston, S. C.*
    Prof. Francis Holmes ⎱
Ex Go*v* Hampton—*Columbia S. C.—*
        \# *Bishop Beckwith of Georgia* & the *Rev* Mr Weed—
        "Church of the "Holy Shepherd,"
        Summerville—near Augusta Ga
D*r* H. H Steiner *Augusta* Ga.
D*r* Roland Steiner (Care D*r* H. H Steiner
            Augusta Ga
Mr*s* Marie B. Williams, *Opelousas* St Landry *Louisiana*
Co*l* B. F. Sawyer, Editor *"Rome Tribune"*
    He is an influential man in *Rome, Rome Geo* & he has
    just written to say he is ready to serve me in *any*
    way.
    * E. Law *Esq—Bainbridge,*
            Decatur Co Geo
\# M*rs* Dahlgren Washington D. C.
\# I d'ont know M*r* Law, but *hear* that he is *interested* in my
Poems. He's a son of Judge Law of Savannah; and you might
ask him about your "Speaker", since he *has been,* & I believe
still is "School *Commissioner"* [.]

\# Now, I have exhausted my list for the present, and am *exhausted myself,* &c.

Yet, in *conclusion* I must *entreat* you to *remunerate yourself* out of the *proceeds* of the *Book* for *all expenses incurred in its behalf;* since *your Purse* must *not* be taxed as well as your *time & Strength.*

And d'ont fatigue yourself in writing me letters, *except* when necessary, for I shall *never misunderstand* your *silence.*

[Of course this is a list of prospective subscribers for Hayne's poems. No doubt it was enclosed in one of Hayne's letters.]

No. 229

PAUL HAMILTON HAYNE to JOHN G. JAMES

"Copse Hill," Georgia Rail Road,

March 19*th* 1879

Address:

P. O. Box 275,
Augusta, Ga.

Dear Friend;

I hope you have rec*d* my *two* letters mailed since I heard from you last, together with Miss Lathbury's work.?

Enclosed, you'll find my notice of your "Speaker &c" which appeared, *Editorially* & prominently in yesterday[']s Augusta *"Chronicle,"* & trust you may like it.?

I asked for *several* copies, but only one has reached me so far.

Of course I'll mail one to Barnes & Co as soon as possible.

Have penned another notice, which has been sent to a Columbia S. C. journal.

In haste, *but Ever Yr's*

Paul H Hayne
Hope you are *better.*

No. 230

PAUL HAMILTON HAYNE to J. H. ESTILL

"Copse Hill," Georgia Rail Road,

March 26th 1879

Address:

P. O. Box 275,

Augusta, Ga.

Dear Sir,

There is a French proverb to the effect that a man "who has reached his fortieth year, ought to be *surprised at nothing in this best of all possible worlds*"! Nevertheless, I must confess to having been *greatly astonished* at the *tone & matter* of your note of the 24th inst, just received. That *such* a work as the one noticed: a careful Compilation by a prominent Southerner at the head of a So Institution of Learning;— representing, (tho in a liberal Catholic way), the genius of the "New South", & thus supplying a *desideratum* long painfully felt among intelligent & thoughtful Teachers—; a Collection which *largely illustrates the genius of Georgia*, from the political philosophy of her Stephen's[,] Gordons[,] &c, to the *fine* poetry of your own illustrious fellow citizen Henry R Jackson — that *such* a book, I say, or any notice of it, would possess "no interest" for the readers of your journal, — is certainly an extraordinary statement, & hardly complimentary to the patriotism of your Patrons!

Allow me, if only for the *credit* of Savannah & its vicinity to express the *hope* that you *may be mistaken!*

It is, indeed, fortunate for our Southern writers that *Southern* Editors of newspapers do *not* regard appreciative notices of their books in the light of "*advertisements* for *their Publishers.*"

It strikes *me* that *Barnes* & Co in this case at least *deserve* to be commended for the publication of a work calculated to bring upon them the reprobation of some portion of their *own* People; for in doing *justice* to Southern Literature, they have already provoked the antagonism of *Extremists*. In regard to "specimen copies" of your "weekly News", pray do *not* trouble yourself to have them mailed me. Your Edition I conclude is a small one, & the sending of these "specimens" might seriously incommode you. I am glad to be able to remark in conclusion, that after a professional literary experience of more

[Written lengthwise at the top of page 1 of the letter:]

than a quarter of a century I do not remember ever having received from any Editor, *Northern* or Southern, a communication — under the *circumstances* — so *curtly & coldly* discourteous as your own.

Your obt. Servant

Paul H Hayne

[The letter to which the letter above is a reply is given below.

The Savannah Morning News,
Daily, Tri-Weekly and Weekly

J. H. Estill,
Proprietor. *Savannah, Ga.*, Mar 24   1879

Paul H. Hayne, Esq.
P. O. Box 275, Augusta, Ga.

Dear Sir: Yours of 22*d* at hand & contents noted.

The article on "James' Speaker & Reader" is of no interest to our readers, & is properly an advertisement for A. S. Barnes & Co. The proper place for it is our advertising columns.

I send you specimen copies of our publications, it would afford me pleasure to comply with your request & send papers free, but our list of complimentary exchanges is already full.

Yours very truly

J H Estill

At the bottom of the letter and in the right margin Mrs. Hayne wrote in pencil: "M*r* Hayne wrote to ask M*r* Estill to republish the article in 'Chronicle & Sentinel' on your book. I enclose a copy of M*r* H—' reply— We thought you would like to see it—& that it would amuse you a little."

The copy of Hayne's reply is in Hayne's hand.

James's book contains selections from twelve Georgia writers, including Alexander H. Stephens, Linton Stephens (brother of Alexander H.), John B. Gordon, and Henry R. Jackson (a distinguished lawyer of Savannah).]

No. 231

PAUL HAMILTON HAYNE to JOHN G. JAMES

April 6th 1879

Kindest of Friends;

How *can* I thank you for the labor of love you have taken upon yourself—? This Card, you send, is simply *perfect*, I think; & beautifully printed. Do thank your Printer in my name, & tell him how highly I appreciate seeing his name first on my list. It *is* "a good omen"!

I am *utterly* broken down by overwork, and my constant attacks of sickness—

My son goes to Augusta to morrow, for a Physician to see me—

Please d'ont break *yourself* down in my behalf—

Ever Yr's

P H Hayne

[In his letter of March 31, 1879, James enclosed the first subscription postal card that he had received from his printer—and the printer had signed it himself, ordering a copy of Hayne's book, unsolicited.]

No. 232

MARY MIDDLETON MICHEL HAYNE to JOHN G. JAMES

"Copse Hill," Georgia Rail Road,

April 25*th* 1879

Address:
    P. O. Box 275,
        Augusta, Ga.

Dear Col James

Your circular with highly prized letter arrived in last evenings mail—It is *all* that it should be—simply perfect; *especially* in the self abnegation of the *three* last lines— God bless your generous Nature! I will send it this evening to my husband— but I can answer for him that it will *thoroughly* suit him. Our Son too is delighted with it—he takes great pride in his father, & bids me thank you for all you are doing for him— Mr Hayne's Mother too appreciates your unselfishness— & has read every word of your Speaker with much pleasure. We are *sincerely* rejoiced to hear of its unparalleled success. I received a P. C. from my husband, & one from my brother last night; the former [latter] writes

"God has given me in our dear Paul's case judgement to discern disease & skill, I trust, to treat it. He is decidedly improved under my direct care, and in faith in me, & in all I can do for him, great improvement is looked for confidently.
Yours in Love
Middleton["]

This is comforting is it not? You see I still take the liberty of writing you in pencil— letters crowd in upon us from all points, & I should *despair* of ever being able to clear them away, did I not write rapidly— for I cannot use my eyes at night *at all.* Are you going to *add* any more poems, or prose articles to this Second edition of your Speaker? I only ask because if this is your *intention—*& if *you* would not *incur any fresh expense, or lose in any way*—I would suggest a piece of Mr H—' prose— say the peroration in R. Y. Hayne's B. Sketch— or any other that might suit you better— I heard Mr Hayne say he regretted not suggesting something in prose from himself, but did not remember it in time. But you will be *frank—*& not fear to *offend?*— Indeed it would *pain* me if I thought you would not be frank in view of what you have done, & are now doing for my husband. You need not *even answer* the above question if you do not mean to *add to the Speaker*— or can only add from any one you

[Written vertically at the top of the first page:]

may have neglected in the *first* Edition. I hope you received my last letter. *Very truly*
Your friend—
M Hayne

Do not trouble to answer this)

[At the time of this letter by Hayne's wife, Hayne was in Charleston in the home of his wife's brother, Dr. William Middleton Michel. He was ill and overworked and had gone for medical attention and for rest. Mrs. Hayne had to stay behind to take care of Hayne's correspondence.

In James's letter to Hayne dated April 19, 1879, he enclosed a circular which he had had printed concerning Hayne's proposed volume. He sent out a total of nearly four thousand circulars and subscription cards (printed on the backs of postal cards). In the same letter (April 19, 1879) James said the first edition of his reader had been exhausted and a second would be out soon.]

No. 233

PAUL HAMILTON HAYNE to JOHN G. JAMES

"Copse Hill," Georgia Rail Road,

Address:

P. O. Box 275,   July 9*th* 1879
Augusta, Ga.

My Dear & Valued Friend;—

I have been at home a little over a week; and tho quite feeble still, & only equal to a few lines (in pencil), I *must thank* you *again & again* for your chivalric devotion to me.

I *do* hope your trip may prove of benefit to you; & that you may come back refreshed & strengthened; but in *future* you *must* not work so *hard*.

I have suffered so much, myself, in *body;* and my mind is so exhausted (from years of excessive labor), that I am unable to do any writing. My Physician *imperatively* orders me to make a change this summer, and truly I feel the absolute need of it, if I am ever to accomplish anything more in my profession.

I'll have to take my "winsome Marrow" with me; — she has had *fever* for a long time, & needs some change *very* much on her own account. In fine, I am only waiting for my wounded leg to heal sufficiently to enable me to start Northward; which I *hope* may be in about 2 week's [*sic*] time. Have already written to inquire about *board* somewhere near Boston.

Of course, I feel a strong desire to see *once more* Long-fellow & Whittier, (they are old men now) before they pass away.

Probably we shall go, for the summer to the White Hills of N. Hampshire, as the best climate to be obtained.

How I wish that *you* were in that direction!—

My vol*s* of published Poems, and miscellaneous pieces I shall take along with me, so that when I have recovered sufficiently, I can begin to revise, and arrange. For the *present*, I have an absolute *loathing* for pen, ink & paper. But this morbid condition must pass after a while.

I am compelled to take *Capital*, in order to make this trip; — but *health* is more important to me now than *anything* else; and I must trust *God* for the *rest!*

x x x x   I sent a few lines to M*r* Sam*l* Bancroft, as you suggested; and will do the same to Flash.

If you have a "Circular" with you, please mail one to Cap*t* W*m* *Ashmead Courtenay*, *Charleston*, *S. C.* with *just one* line, requesting him to get up a good subscription list in *Charleston*, as Courtenay is a prominent man, a good fellow, my personal friend, and one who will do much for the book.

Did you remember to send a "Circular" to M*r* *B. F. Sawyer* of Rome Geo, since I *think* he will help you. *En passant,* my *wife* begs you to send her 3 or 4 (Circulars), if convenient, together with Cards.

She encloses an attack on your school book, (from "Harper's Weekly ["]), wherein, they are evidently trying to make political capital; but *this*, & the assault in the Ohio paper will only do you *good*, I'm sure.

Love from my wife, & *may God bless* you & *yours*.

Should you ever be at a loss as to my address, (during the summer), send your letters to *"Copse Hill"*, or rather to my *old Augusta* address

P. O Box 275 Augusta Ga

and they will be forwarded by my son.

Always *Most Faithfully* & *Gratefully* &c

Paul H Hayne.

This execrable pencil-writing will show you (in part), what I have been through.

My wife heard from her Brother Dr Fraser Michel of Montgomery a few days ago; and he tells her that he sent you a list of 80 names of persons there, to whom you could send "Circulars"; & that when a "Circular" reached the book store man (of Montgomery) *Mr G. White*, why *then* they would begin work in that City.

[In two letters (May 21 and June 11, 1879) and an undated postal card to Mrs. Hayne while Hayne was ill in Charleston, James said that by June 11 he had obtained only eighty subscribers from about eight hundred circulars and subscription cards sent out, that the North was responding more generously than the South, and that he was beginning "to realize the extent of Southern apathy on the subject of Southern literature." He mentions the following subscribers: Longfellow, Whittier, Stedman (two copies), Boker, Bunce (five copies), Child, Holmes, Henry R. Jackson, Harvard College Library, Whipple, F. S. Saltus (with five subscribers), George Bancroft, General Smith (Superintendent of the Virginia Military Institute), Professor Price (of the University of Virginia), two members of the James family, Dr. Arthur Hayne (Hayne's cousin, the son of Robert Y. Hayne), Mrs. Toland, Moses Coit Tyler, George B. McClellan, Col. W. C. P. Breckinridge (of Kentucky), Kemp P. Battle (President of the University of North Carolina), and others. On July 21, 1879, James wrote Hayne that Major Hill (Hayne's neighbor) had sent a list of forty subscribers, and that the total number of subscribers was then 150.

In the letter to Mrs. Hayne dated June 11, 1879, James said his school was out and that he would leave shortly to spend a month on the Gulf coast.

Hayne and Mrs. Hayne spent three months in the North, August-October, in New England and New York City.

I do not know which Samuel Bancroft is referred to, possibly Samuel Bancroft (1840–1915), of Delaware, publisher and manufacturer.

William Ashmead Courtenay (1831–1908) was a Charleston bookseller and publisher, business man, mayor from 1879 till 1887, and later he founded a cotton mill in the upper part of the state.

B. F. Sawyer is elsewhere in these letters identified by Hayne as the editor of the Rome (Georgia) *Tribune*.

There is an editorial in *Harper's Weekly* for July 5, 1879 (pp. 522–523), entitled " 'Southern' School-Books." It is a vigorous attack upon James's book on the grounds that it would make students hate their country and would produce Southerners rather than Americans. In James's letter to Mrs. Hayne dated June 11, 1879, he said he had just received from the leading Republican newspaper of Ohio, the Cincinnati

Commercial, an issue containing an attack "of most venomous character" upon his reader. He added that it would increase the sale of his book in the South if Southern papers would copy it.

Both of Mrs. Hayne's brothers (William Middleton Michel of Charleston and Richard Fraser Michel, who moved from Charleston to Montgomery, Alabama, after the war) were physicians. Their father was "an eminent French physician, who received a gold medal from Napoleon the Third, for services under the first Napoleon at the battle of Leipsic," according to Margaret Junkin Preston's sketch of Hayne in *Complete Edition* (p. vii).]

No. 234

PAUL HAMILTON HAYNE to JOHN G. JAMES

"Copse Hill," Georgia Rail Road,

Address:

P. O. Box 275,   *29th* July 1879

Augusta, Ga.

Dear Friend;

Detained a day or two from starting Northward, I take this chance of acknowledging your truly welcome, & noble letter rec*d* yesterday.

'Tis useless to *repeat* what I feel upon the subject of your *unparalleled* generosity, unselfishness, and devotion; but I only feel the more *profoundly*, for not giving my sentiment *full* expression.

x x x Now ab't Charleston my native City, let me suggest that you mail Circulars to the following persons.

———. If I repeat names *already* given, pardon me.

D*r* Parker . . Roper Hospital . .

D*r* R Barnwell Rhett J*r* Roper Hospital

If you can drop a line to these two gentlemen 'twould be as well.

Hail them as kindly acquaintances of my own, and as cultivated gentlemen who must take some interest in the welfare of a compatriot &c. Ask them to *ventilate* the matter.

D*r* Henry Fraser—

D*r* R. Kinlock

† Judge Geo Bryan—
    I. H. Hassoldt
        (send Hassoldt a Circular particularly, with
a brief note from yourself—,
He is an old friend of mine, and tho a Mechanic (a Gun
maker) has great influence, & may work in my behalf—
  # Send a Circular also to
    Dr Panknin—
      Meeting S*t* Charleston
Ask Panknin if he has no objection to put up a List in his
store to be exhibited to his Customers &c. The same suggestion
might be made to the Edt's of "Wilmington (N C) *Star*", true
friends of mine. Excuse these hints my *beloved friend*, which
you must not follow, unless they approve themselves to

[Written lengthwise in the margin of the second (last)
    page of the letter:]

your j··dgment.
    Direct your next letter to me,
      (Care *Messrs Harper & Bros NYork*)

                God bless you!
                In *great* haste, but Ever

            P H H—

No. 235

PAUL HAMILTON HAYNE to JOHN G. JAMES

Wolfboro', N Hampshire
(on Lake Winipissaugee)
Sunday 14th 1879.

My Dear Friend;
    I hope you rec*d* my answer to your letter, from "Copse Hill",
& that Prof Dinwiddie & yourself got my P. cards from Jefferson.
    We are enjoying this lovely Lake, & trust to take a sail upon
it, weather permitting, to morrow.

On Thursday next we expect to visit Mr Whittier at Danvers; & thence we shall go to Boston.

My wife & self are both improving; and I hope for greater improvement still when we return home.

We have had many kind attentions, & cordial invitations to private houses.

At Jefferson we met the Rev R. S. Storrs of Brooklin;— he is the most distinguished Congregational Preacher North; & altho the life long friend of Beecher, he gave *earnest* testimony against him, when the evidence produced in the great trial proved conclusively B's guilt.

Therefore, I have quite a respect for him. Mrs Storrs expressed herself anxious to possess my two last vols, which she was kind eno' greatly to admire.

My wife chancing to have with her your Card & Circular, she handed Mrs S—*one*, as she desired my complete Poems. Afterwards she told my wife that the Doctor (her husband) had sent for *two* copies, adding "I would like Mr Hayne & yourself to know this! *One* copy I intend to present to Roginet [?] Pryor who lives in Brooklyn."

The other day I recd a note from Miss Mary Lathbury. Among other things she remarks; "I shall be glad to know you are better, & able to further the plan, which of course is no longer a secret, that Col James, & other friends have been putting forth. I was grateful for his confidence in the matter, & *will be glad to help in the consummation of the work!*"

I thought perhaps she might give you an illustration.

Again, may God bless you for all your *noble* Kindness to me. Let me hope that *everything* goes well with you.

My wife joins in love.
Excuse this scrawl.
Pen & ink are both *horrible*.
Ever affectionately

Paul H. Hayne.

[This letter was written on September 14, 1879, which was Sunday (neither August 14 nor October 14 was a Sunday).

I am not certain that Hayne spells the name of the lake correctly— but who can?

For Hayne's opinion of Henry Ward Beecher see his letters to Moses
Coit Tyler.

For a poem ("A Mountain Fancy") which Hayne inscribed to Mrs. R.
S. Storrs in September, 1879, see *Complete Edition* (p. 248).

The Pryor referred to was probably Roger Atkinson Pryor (1828–1919),
Virginia lawyer and editor and Confederate soldier, who lived in New
York after the war. He became a distinguished lawyer there and was
counsel for Theodore Tilton in his suit against Beecher.]

No. 236

PAUL HAMILTON HAYNE to JOHN G. JAMES

"Copse Hill," Georgia Rail Road,

Address:

P. O. Box 275,   Nov *4th*   x   1879
Augusta, Ga.

My Dear Friend;

We have just returned from a three months['] tour thro
the Northern States, having penetrated as far as the "W.
Mountains" of N. H. From that remote Region I wrote you
twice, but somehow, fear that my communications *miscarried*.

Should *that* have really happened, you must deem me a
cold, ungrateful fellow.

Let the blame, however, be now put upon the right shoulders; those broad, impudent shoulders of "U. Sam".

Meanwhile, I long to know, (as my wife does also) *how
you* are progressing? — *Firstly*, how is your *health;* and
secondly, what of your *school?* Be as *Egotistical* as you choose;
we shall only be the more interested! *Thirdly*, as of *less* importance than the other points, what luck has followed your
enterprise thus far, concerning the Poems?— Have you become *discouraged* as might well be; or do you still contemplate prosecuting the scheme; only upon the new (& more
feasible plan) of Employing Agents; as I suggested, in writing from *Jefferson*, N Hampshire?—

When I was at Whittier's home in *Danvers* (Mass), he
asked particularly after the Book, saying that "your work
ought and *should* be [a] success," adding "I intend to write

him ab't it!" But he finds *writing* a *great* effort now; and he may *not* have done as he proposed.

The old Gentleman thought it *best* (as *inferior* Artists had spoiled so many of his *own* Poems) that only the *ablest* Artists should be employed, even if you should have fewer illustrations in consequence. Of course if you decided upon the *Agent Plan*, they would have to receive the subscriptions in advance (at *least* I presume so) in order to get their *percentage*. The *worst* of "Circulars," Mr Whittier observed is, "that many throw them aside without even examining them; and then too, many names sent on to you *per mail* might fail to reach you.

In Washington (D C) Mrs Burnett, (author of *"That Lass O' Louries"*) told me that *she* had Subscribed. Did you receive her com.?, and Dr R S. Storrs, (the famous Congregational Preacher, of Brooklyn, who bore testimony against Beecher), informed me that *he* had sent for 2 copies.

Many others spoke of having subscribed. Only a few days since, I recd a note from Judge Durfee, (Chief Justice of R. Island), Enclosing $4.*00*,) saying he had been told of the edition, and heard that *that* was the *price*!

I'll return the money to day, with the *last* of the *"Circulars"* I possess, begging him to forward his name to *you*.

You'll be glad to hear that my wife has improved from our trip. I myself feel *stronger;* yet have had several hemorrhages, & was forced to call in a Physician while in NY.

We had attentions *lavished* upon us; invitations to many private houses; & guests invited from hundreds of miles to meet us. Longfellow gave us a *lunch,* as he did Dickens & Thackeray; and we spent 5 days with *Whittier*, visits *never* to be forgotten.

Trusting that all are well with you, & with affectionate regards from Mrs Hayne, I am *as Always*,

Most Faithfully,
Paul. H. Hayne.

P. S. The report that I had *publicly abused* the *South* while away, & designed moving North, is all *fudge!!*

Will send you my *published* reply to these libels soon.

[In his letter of December 5, 1879, James said he had received one or two letters from Hayne while Hayne was in the North but added: ". . . you wrote on the wing and did not give me your address, so I could not answer." Only one letter has survived.

Frances Hodgson Burnett (1849–1924) was a prolific author whose most famous work was *Little Lord Fauntleroy* (1886). *That Lass o' Lowrie's* (New York: Scribner, Armstrong & Co.) appeared in 1877.

Thomas Durfee (1826–1901) was a member of the Supreme Court of Rhode Island for over twenty-five years. He became chief justice in 1875.

In his letters to Stedman, Hayne refers several times to his illness in New York in 1879. Stedman called a physician for Hayne and presented a basket of flowers to Mrs. Hayne.

In the Augusta *Chronicle and Constitutionalist* of November 5, 1879, appear Hayne's reply to his critics and an editorial in his defense. Hayne wrote (in part): "If I have been traveling North for some months past, it has been in search of health, not of a new home. . . . If ever I have uttered anything touching the luke-warmness of the South . . . toward her literary children, the melancholy truth has been embodied in Southern journals, frankly, openly, fearlessly, over my own proper signature, and not bruited with treacherous or embittered breath for the delectation for [of] the alien." I quote from the editor's comment: "There is no more melancholy story than that of Henry Timrod as told by Paul H. Hayne, and some day the true history of Paul H. Hayne may bring a blush to his fellow-countrymen for their neglect of a rare and noble intellect entirely devoted to art, and too ethereal perhaps for this workday world."]

No. 237

PAUL HAMILTON HAYNE to JOHN G. JAMES

[Written on paper with black borders]

\# Address me as usual
P O Box 275 *Augusta* Ga
"Copse Hill" Ga R R—
Jan 2nd 1880. .

I would, *My Dear Friend*, have written you long ago, but a dark trouble which had threatened us for months, culminated upon the night of the 9*th* Dec, in the death of my honored mother. The *blow* was a very *very* heavy one;—and so, for a *season*, I allowed all business matters to remain (as it were) in abeyance! *But* our lives have their stern duties; and these must be fulfilled. Therefore I again buckle on my armor, &

tho with a sad heart resume the load of Earth's necessary cares & labors.

Now, first *about yourself*!

It afforded us *all* real satisfaction, indeed, I may truly say, the *most vivid* pleasure to learn of the glorious change in your prospects; the Elevation vouchsafed you from the levels of unappreciated work, and stupid opposition, to the calm height of of [*sic*] honorable Trust, and dignified, profitable, & congenial toil! Then, the peculiar manner in which your present high office was tendered you, must add incalculably to your own just exultation, no less than to the pride of your friends.

In one word, all of us congratulate you *from the heart*, rejoicing that for *once* a noble man, and competent Teacher has met, *during his life*—with something like due appreciation.

In *fancy* I accompany you to your new home! I mingle with your associates, and remark the improvements your taste suggests in domicile & College, with the Environments that belong to both.

I am with you—*spiritually*—at class-time, & leisure-time; Enter into your views, comprehend your purposes, and sympathise in your just ambitions!—

My presentiment is, that your new career is destined to succeed wonderfully. You will build up probably a great, and permanent Institution; & by the way, how *inestimably* valuable *now* must your past experiences as Teacher & Disciplinarian prove!

Ah! even unremunerated & unappreciated labors "tell" sooner or later, in our favor!

No *conscientious* work is ever wholly thrown away in this world.

I am touched, beyond words, by the fact that amid your new & pressing engagements; amid all the novel & perplexing responsibilities of your position, you still manifest such unabated interest in my book.

You ask whether I saw any of the Publishers when at the North? Yes, I saw *some* of them, tho others were absent from their posts.

Do you propose turning over the Book to any of them, so as to get a first-class Publisher's Endorsement, or do you hold to your *original* plan?

I *have* written some 6 or 8 poems since I left the mountains; one rather long one now in the hands of the Harpers, (among my best I believe). Whittier thinks with you that I *ought* to be paid well for my verses; (*En passant* I've just recd an affectionate note from the kind old man), but being a *Southerner*, how could I expect such good fortune?

I told Maj: Hill what you wrote of him, & he was truly gratified; but for the last 2 mts' he has been engaged in business, in *Augusta*. Touching our health, which you so affectionately ask after —let me say that *my wife*, at least, has improved.

I had several hemorrhages at the North, the most severe in NY, but *thank* God! (for 2 mts' I have had none). Of course my mother's death terribly depressed & threw me back.

x x x   Enclosed, you'll find a letter from my Cousin D*r Arthur P Hayne*, as it concerns our book. *Please return it.* With my wife's love & our best wishes for you & yours, believe me as Ever affectionately

Paul H Hayne.

(P. S)

I have been considering this matter over very seriously; and all of a sudden a plan has occurred to my mind which I must suggest.

Entre nous my health is much shattered and (frankly) I *would* like to see my Poems in some complete form before I die. Now the *agent* system is surer than any other, & *may* ultimately succeed; but still there's doubt about it.

On the other hand, you have *already* secured *almost*, if not quite enough in the way of responsible subscribers to have *my works* put *forth* in *neat tho plain shape with* a *portrait* as introduction, and a few—a very *few* Illustrations, the latter to be furnished by friendly artists, (whose names I can suggest) for probably—*nothing!*

Were this plan adopted, 'twould be necessary to have a number of Circulars printed & mailed to subscribers stating the change of programme. & asking for the consent of each.

Tell them *silence* would be taken for consent.

In answering, do not say that this plan was suggested by me, but treat it as something obvious eno' in contemplation of the difficulties attending any other way of publication.

Of course I *merely suggest*.

You must use your own judgment *dear friend*.

The larger handsomer edition *would* be preferable; but the time is short, & our people are—fools & ingrates!

Only turn over this matter.!

Did you see *Houghton & Osgoods'* late Edition of B. Taylor's *Complete Poetical Works?*

Look at it!

Such an edition (with portrait &c) would *now* be within our means.

But *emphatically*, I say again, this is only a suggestion.

[Emily McElhenny Hayne died at Copse Hill on December 9, 1879, at the age of 74. She had been a widow since 1831, when her husband, Lieutenant Paul Hayne of the United States Navy, died at sea and was buried at Pensacola.

In his letter of December 5, 1879, James said that the public free schools had made his private educational enterprise unprofitable, that the governing board of the State Agricultural and Mechanical College of Texas had recently unanimously elected him president of the institution, that he was happy in his new work except for his regret in having to leave Austin, that his salary included $2,300 and a $12,000 residence and certain other privileges, that he had left his Austin school and property under the management of his brother, and that his mother would live with him as mistress of the "President's House."

In the same letter he said that the subscription list was still short of two hundred, although he had sent out nearly four thousand circulars and cards. He asks, "Is'nt that enough to make one lose faith in one's own people?" At great length he tells of his disappointment in Southerners because of their failure to support their writers. He also asked whether Hayne had seen any publishers on his Northern trip.

The long poem referred to is "The Snow-Messengers," *Harper's New Monthly Magazine*, LX (March, 1880), 598. (See *Complete Edition*, pp. 290–293.)

Major Joseph A. Hill was Hayne's most intimate friend in the vicinity of Copse Hill.

The Poetical Works of Bayard Taylor (Household Edition. Boston: Houghton, Osgood and Company, 1880) is probably the volume referred to.]

No. 238

PAUL HAMILTON HAYNE to JOHN G. JAMES

[Written on paper with black borders.]

"Copse Hill" Ga R. R
February 9th 1880

My *Most Generous & Unselfish of Friends;—*

Your thought for me, how *can* I fully appreciate?   But rest assured that I do my best to value *all* you are doing in my behalf!—

I *would* have answered your last letter sooner; but for a distressing *shortness of breath* which for 3 weeks has incapacitated me for work of any sort.

Our old Country Esculapius, who examined me thoroughly with the *Stethoscope* Says, the trouble is with my *Liver*, not *Lungs!* Weather permitting, I go to Augusta to morrow, in order to consult Physicians there.   I have had no return of Hemorrhage since the *6th* ult.   My *wife's* health *greatly* improved from her No trip, & she *wholly* recovered from the malarial fever; but the decease of my Mother, coupled with anxiety as to my own condition, has somewhat put her back.

Now that I have replied to your kind inquiries in reference to our respective healths,—let me answer the questions about *your* Book.

First, as to Publishers.

Messrs Houghton & Osgood are *par excellence* the Publishers of Poetry.

Next, *come Roberts & Bros & then Scribner & Co*[.]

—The *Putnams*, and Widdleton are more exclusive.

The *Harpers* occasionally issue a vol of verse;— and the *Lippincotts* of Phil*a often* bring out such books; only they utterly neglect all *So Poems, even when* bearing their own imprint.

Entre nous, Boker (Geo. H.), tho himself a Phil*a Litterateúr* of great eminence, has complained of their lukewarmness, *apropos* of one of *his own* productions!!

x x x I think that your idea "of letting the Public *alone*, until you can talk with the Publishers," is a *wise & practical* notion.

You ask me concerning the number *of Pages* I would probably have in the *complete* Edition? If the vo*l* had the *same sized print* as the *"Legends & Lyrics"*, & of the same *duodecimo page*, I calculate that from *500 to 550* pages would be needed; *including* of course my comparatively *recent pieces*, such as have *never* been issued *except* in Magazines, & newspapers. x x x There is one *steel plate engraving* (a likeness of me) in *"The NYork Eclectic"*, which is *execrable;* but a *very fine one* of me, as I *used to look before* I had lost so much flesh—, in *Bryant's "Library of Poetry & Song"*; owned by *Messrs Fords, Howard, & Hulbert*, No. 27 *Park Place* NY (this *was* their address in 1878): .

I have *one* of the "proofs" of said likeness, & should you need *that*, can furnish you with it. It is the *best likeness* I ever *had taken;*—The only *full length* portrait in existence is one Taken in my dressing, or study Gown, I being *seated* near a table; but "my idea" on the point, is *only* to have the *steel Portrait*.

It might seem *egotistical* to have more than a single "presentment" of the writer.

"Are there not", you ask, "some excellent wood-cut illustrations of my poems, which could be used, & who are the *owners* of these?". The *"Wide Awake"* Proprietors own the following illustrations of my verses for children, (viz)

"Katie Kiss me!" (Wood cut, *very fine!*

"Motes"—(pen & ink—*very fine.*)

"Ground Squirrel" (*fair*) *wood cut*—

"Lottie's Grievance, ["] (wood cut a *little too much* shaded, but still *good*)—

X   X   X   X

"The Three Copecks", illustrated in "Scribner" by a Russian Artist I send you by this mail.

Then there is the long poem *"Unveiled"* in *"Scribner"*, the illustration of which is at least, *passable!*

"McDonalds' Raid" (in *"Harper"*) has an abominable wood-cut, not even *original*, but taken from some one of Simms' Revolutionary Tales.

My son now in Montgomery sends me the Enclosed (return at your leisure), which he copied from a book called *"Landscape in American Poetry"*, edited by *Lucy Larcom*, & published by the *Appletons*.

En passant, I forgot to mention *them* as *Publishers*. They bring out *very fine illustrated* vols tho they *charge like the devil!*—

x x I feel grateful to those *"charming* Michigan ladies" for their appreciation of *"The Wife of Brittany"* & *"Bonny Brown Hand"* [.]

From the cheerfulness of your letter I argue that you are in good health; & *doubt not*, for a moment, that *"The College"* will vastly improve under your *indomitable* rule, guided by practical sagacity, and *that* imperial *Will* which *breaks*, if it cannot *bend difficulties!!*— We rejoice to learn (thro your letter to Maj Hill), that we may hope to see [you] at *"Copse Hill,"* *after* your visit North. *Who* could be *so* welcome?—

x x x My cousin Dr *A. P. Hayne* wrote some time ago, to inquire as to the prospects of your *Book;* so I forwarded him your communication (*one before the last*), and I quote what the Doctor says; — "I am sorry that the vol of Poems meets with such slow progress; but I trust that Col James will yet make a success of it. By the way, I *like his letter very much;* & can picture in my mind's eye, what *sort of a man he is.* Mrs Toland said *she* intended to subscribe for another $10.00 copy. If Col James could only get a Publisher to take risk of getting out, I believe it would sell *very rapidly.* I think a *Hundred copies* could *easily* be sold in *San Francisco."* *(Jan 25th)* Dr *Arthur P. Hayne, Resident Physician & Superintendent* of *"Home of Inebriates"*, *N. E. Corner* of *Stockton & Chestnut Sts San Francisco, Cal.*—I give this address so that if you desire to write him, it may be convenient.

With warmest regards from my wife *Ever affectionately Yrs*

Paul H Hayne.

[Written lengthwise in the margin of the first page of the letter:]

\# Please let me kr.ow, *if only* by a P. C. when this letter reaches you.?

[In his letter of January 28, 1880, James said that within about two months he would make a trip to the North in connection with his work of reorganizing the college, that he hoped to interview publishers in Philadelphia, New York, and Boston, and that he would try to get a publisher to bring out Hayne's complete poems, or at least the smaller volume which Hayne had spoken of. He asked many questions about portraits of Hayne, illustrations, woodcuts, who had them, etc. Concerning portraits, he said: "As you used to be, I have heard, a rider and huntsman, how would it do to have you with horse, dog, or gun—and out doors or in the woods? I want to have *two* pictures of you, you see, and *one* I think should show your love of nature. . . ."

In the same letter James wrote: "I have now staying with me some charming Michigan ladies, and they are reading with great pleasure my copy of your Legends & Lyrics—having never seen your poems before in book form— Your 'Wife of B—' & Bonny Brown Hand delighted them mightily." Later James married one of these charming Michigan ladies, Mrs. Clara White (Brigham) Trowbridge, of Detroit, a widow with two daughters, Kathleen and Annie. I judge that the marriage took place early in 1883. In his letters up to January 5, 1883, he says nothing about being married, whereas in his letter of March 24, 1883, he speaks of his marriage as if it had recently occurred—to a beautiful lady who is "to me the personification of goodness and unselfishness, and refinement." He had made a hurried trip to Detroit for the wedding and had returned immediately. Annie was staying with James and her mother, and Kathleen was with her grandfather, C. C. Trowbridge, in Detroit. In his letter of August 8, 1884, he says his wife was visiting in Detroit. In his letter to Mrs. Hayne dated August 7, 1887, he speaks with great affection of his wife, Clara (who was visiting in Detroit again): ". . . I *know* you would *love* my wife, she is such a noble woman, & true in all respects, & so cultivated, considerate & unselfish in all things. She often spoke of our proposed & hoped for trip to see you & Mr Hayne, for she loves you both—" He said that all her people in Detroit were wealthy, that Kathleen had just completed three years of study in Europe, and that Annie would soon go to school in Baltimore. He added: "It is a sad contrast for Clara to come back here to her little frontier home [then in Wichita Falls], but yet I know she will come back happily, for she often says she is happier here with me than she could be there with all the splendor around her. I have lived in Texas so long—where one is so free & easy in manner & dress, that I feel that I am not fit to live anywhere else—am content to live here, and so strong is my attachment to the soil & its people that I hope to be buried here."

The Lippincotts published Hayne's *Legends and Lyrics* in 1872, at Hayne's expense.

Hayne corresponded with George Henry Boker (1823–1890), of Philadelphia. In his letters to Stoddard he tells of his meeting Boker.

Hayne's *Complete Edition* has 386 pages, printed in double columns.

An article on Hayne (with portrait) appeared in the *Eclectic Magazine* of New York for August, 1877 (p. 247). Possibly Hayne's portrait appeared in Bryant's *A Library of Poetry and Song* in 1878. I have not seen that particular edition. The portrait did not appear in two earlier and two later editions that I have seen.

In *Complete Edition* there is a full-page illustration (opposite p. 369) for "Kiss Me, Katie!" The artist's name is not given, but it may be the one, referred to in an earlier letter, by Mary Artemisia Lathbury. There are no illustrations for "The Three Copecks," "Little Lottie's Grievance," "Motes," or "The Ground Squirrel." There is an illustration (p. 221) for "Unveiled," but it is not the one that accompanied the poem in *Scribner's Monthly*, XV (January, 1878), 383–386. The illustration (p. 273) for "Macdonald's Raid—A. D. 1780" is not either of the two that accompanied the poem in *Harper's New Monthly Magazine*, 53 (July, 1876), 200–203.

Lucy Larcom (1824–1893), of Massachusetts, was a poet, teacher, and editor. The book referred to is *Landscape in American Poetry*, with illustrations by J. Appleton Brown (New York: D. Appleton and Company, 1879).

"The Wife of Brittany" (a version of Chaucer's *Frankeleyns Tale*) is Hayne's best long narrative poem. "The Bonny Brown Hand" is a fine tribute to his wife. See *Complete Edition* (pp. 118–137, 106–107).

Dr. Arthur P. Hayne, Hayne's first cousin, was the son of the famous Robert Young Hayne.

Mrs. Toland was the wife of Dr. H. H. Toland, a native of South Carolina who (like Dr. Arthur P. Hayne) had moved to California (810 Jackson Street, San Francisco). Hayne's *Complete Edition* with full morocco binding sold at ten dollars a copy. Most of the subscriptions were for a cheaper binding.]

No. 239

MARY MIDDLETON MICHEL HAYNE to JOHN G. JAMES

"Copse Hill," Georgia Rail Road,

March 5th 1880

Address:

P. O. Box 275,

Augusta, Ga.

Dear Col James,

M*r* Hayne received your kind favor of Feb 23*rd* which we both *truly* appreciate; And I thought I would reply to it in his stead, while he was out for a morning ride on horse back. We grieve to hear that you have been sick again— I fear that your strength is over taxed but do hope the trip North may build you up again— How *glad* we shall be to welcome you to our rough country home, with no beauty in its surroundings until spring environs it with greenery. And now let me tell you about M*r* Hayne's horse— My dear husband had been suffering for over a Month from a distressing shortness of breath, & our country D*r* failing to afford him any relief, I persuaded him to consult a physician in Augusta, who prescribed horse back exercise as the best remedy— he thought the case one of nervous prostration— And M*r* Hayne— Now that God had taken one of our little circle into His Holy keeping— felt that he might be able to feed the horse if he could find the Means of purchasing one— It was strange that just after you had written to ask how it would do to have a picture of the poet on horse back for the complete edition of his poems—, He should receive a check from a wealthy gentleman who was our host while in R. I. (& who had written to inquire after my husbands state of health), which enabled him to purchase a nice little Ky. pony. It was singular too that this distinguished writer, & Noble gentleman, above referred to, wrote *before* we went to Augusta, & I replied the *day before* we saw the D*r*. M*r* Hayne is devoted to the pony— & I think she knows him already. She is staying at M*r* Hill's until we can get a stable built for her here: & M*r*

Hayne has improved greatly during the last few weeks, although he still suffers daily from shortness of breath— The Dr thinks there are weak points about the lungs but no tubercles. Mr Hayne is encouraged by his diagnoses, & is hopeful— I need not say how grateful to God we are (my son & I) for so much of comfort with regard to our dear one. Mr Hayne will *try* to have all the poems arranged *for publication* by the time you reach Copse Hill— He has been busy correcting *such* of the *earlier* poems—& the War verses, which he means to *republish* in *your* edition. My husband has been such a careful Artist of late years that the later poems will need little, if any, revision. We will have (as you desire) "a complete list of *all* illustrations"—and of "a dozen or so poems which he will suggest for illustration—["] We think *you* could use the Copse Hill illustrations to advantage— I have in charge all the reviews of my husbands poetic work, & you can select what you desire from them for advertising: there are a large number of *private critical* opinions, from many distinguished writers, but unfortunately these cannot be made available for your purpose. You ask how you can reach us from Augusta? If your route is through Atlanta you will reach us without going to Augusta; & (as the regular train *perhaps*, might not be willing to put you down at our door) you must tell the Conductor to stop at Forrest Station, a half mile from C. Hill & Mr Hayne will meet you, or our son Will— All the Conductors know our home, & if the train is not behind time, & has not to put any passenger down at "Forrest" or "16" — as it is sometimes called— he might land you *here*. Should you come through Augusta I enclose Schedule of R. R. The "Harlem Accommodation" or "Picayune" as it is called will put you down *at our door*— the others, at Forrest— unless disposed to be exceptionally accommodating. Within a few days Mr H— has received two letters of inquiry about a complete edition of his poems, one from Florida, & one from Vir. I copy the last as it is short.

Odom Branch, Fla. Feb 25th

"Mr P. H. Hayne.

Sir I have read as many of your poems as the newspapers have brought me. I am still unsatisfied & wish for more.

Please inform me if your works have been collected & published, & if so where I can find them. I have deeply sympathized with you in your efforts to engender a literary love in the Southern people. I have just begun a life which I intend devoting to the same

[Written vertically at the top of the first page:]

purpose. Yours W. T. Dumas—

Mr H— will tell him of your edition— Mr H— has just come in & is at work on one of the poems. He sends best love.

Ever Your friend,

M Hayne

[In his letter of February 23, 1880, James said he hoped to leave in April on a tour of inspection of agricultural and mechanical colleges and engineering schools, both in the South and in the North, and hoped to stop a day or two at Copse Hill. He added: "Let me know how best to reach you from Augusta. . . ." He asked Hayne to make a list of existing illustrations of his poems and a list of a dozen or so which he wanted illustrated. He repeated that he wanted two portraits of Hayne in the book in spite of Hayne's scruples. He also wanted extracts from notices of Hayne's earlier work to use in advertising: ". . . our Yankee friends have taught us the importance of such influences— They have actually manufactured reputations in this way—"

In Hayne's journal he noted that he went to Augusta on February 23, 1880, and bought a pony for eighty dollars from a Kentucky drover. The wealthy Northern writer who sent Hayne a check was probably Rowland Gibson Hazard (1801–1888), of Rhode Island, a retired manufacturer and philosophical writer. His mother was a Charlestonian. The journal makes clear that Hayne and Hazard corresponded. On November 13, 1880, Hayne received from him a letter containing fifty dollars. Hayne refers to him in a letter to Nathaniel Russell Middleton in this collection (No. 114).]

No. 240

PAUL HAMILTON HAYNE to JOHN G. JAMES

[Postal card]

April 15th .. .. 1880.

My Dear Friend;

I recd your valuable & interesting Report in due season; and we have been anxiously looking for you ever since. Can it be *possible* that your request for *two mnts'* "leave of absence from April *1st*", has been refused.? I *do trust not;* because great would be our disappointment in *that* case! But I can hardly fancy such a thing possible. —My *kindest* regards to Prof *H. H Dinwiddie,* who, by the way, I observe, is with you in the College.

I'd write more at length, but am still unwell, and pressed for time. With my wife's *warm remembrances,* I am,

Ever Faithfully Y'r obliged,

P H. Hayne.

[Hardaway Hunt Dinwiddie, of Virginia, was on the faculty of James's Texas Military Institute during the whole of its existence (1868–1879) and joined the faculty of the State Agricultural and Mechanical College of Texas when James became its president. He spent a summer vacation making illustrations for Hayne's volume. I do not know whether any of them were used.]

No. 241

PAUL HAMILTON HAYNE to JOHN G. JAMES

[Written on paper with black borders.]

"Copse Hill", Ga R Road
May 21st 1880..

My Dear Friend;

I wrote you a P. C, some weeks ago, but have heard nothing from you, & since your College report to the *Governor of Texas,* I'm fearful you may be suffering from ill-health, because I *cannot think* he failed to grant your request for leave of absence.

When you last wrote, you spoke of having been quite sick again; and feeling "shaky" on your legs.

You have been *such* a friend to me that I can't bear to think of your being *ill.*

For myself I'm in *chronic* ill health, & not a day without suffering; so, upon *that* ground alone, would have deep sympathy with you, if sick.

I do but little correspondence now, even the writing of a letter being an exertion.

But my good wife takes charge of *that;* tho by no means strong since the warm weather.

My son has just returned after a 4 mts' absence, seeking employment, which he has failed to get.

If too ill *to write yourself,* please get someone to write for you.

With warmest regards from our household.

Ever Yrs'

Paul H Hayne.

[James had written on May 18, 1880, but his letter had not yet reached Hayne.

William Hamilton Hayne had been in Montgomery in the home of his mother's brother, Dr. Richard Fraser Michel.]

No. 242

PAUL HAMILTON HAYNE to JOHN G. JAMES

"Copse Hill," Georgia Rail Road

Address:

P. O. Box 275,   Nov: 27*th* 1880
    Augusta, Ga.

My Dear Friend;

I sent you my *"Ballad on the Battle of King's M't,"* which I hope was duly rec*d.* We are *anxious*—Mr*s* Hayne & I—, to know *something* of you; & do *Earnestly pray* that your *health* is Stronger than when you wrote last. Thank Heaven! I am myself a trifle *better;* having had no hemorrhage for 6 weeks! Constant exercise on horseback, has done *much* for me; & I can now perform *some* literary work.

Have been just reading over our last tidings from you (*in a letter* of May 18*th*); & verily, its *pathetic tenderness deeply* moved me.

Well! *my friend!* you *certainly* did your *best* for me in the matter of the Book; and I can *never* cease to be grateful to you. *Apropos*, I send you enclosed a sketch, written by a gentleman of the North, whom I never met. He is a young Poet himself, & has done good work.

After persuing this sketch,—published a few weeks ago—, being quite unwell—, my wife wrote to thank Mr Collier for it, & begged that he would mail a copy to the *Scribners*, as she thought *perhaps* the last paragraph *might* suggest the bringing out of my Poems, from a p't of view they may not have considered.

I rec*d* a letter from *Collier* last evng, enclosing note from Scribners, of which I send you a copy. C—says, "I enclose a letter from *Scribners;*—Tho *not* successful, it may be of use, as all such items help to wear away the *stone of resistance. A good edition of* your Poems is a *Necessity, & must come!"*

Last evng, also, I rec*d* a letter from *John James Piatt* (the Western Poet) who is now editing a work on *"American Art & Poetry"* for Mr Dibble—a new Publisher—of Cincinnati, Ohio. *We* have been aiding Mr Piatt, in the So part of his collection. The 4 first installments have appeared; & are quite handsome. Mr P—speaks of this work having "already cost Dibble much more than he *expected* it would; & he is forced to move *very* slowly, lest he should become involved!".

I mention this to show how much an *"illustrated"* Edition of my works *would have cost;—too much,* you see, to be undertaken.

The *Stoddard* vol, (to which *Scribner* refers, has *only* his, (the *Poet's*) portrait, is *one* vol—*8vo extra cloth, pp. 512,—*& yet the cost is $4.*09* (!!) [.]

Mr Piatt speaks of the firm of *Messrs Clarke & Co Cincinnati;* "wealthy *& long-established Publishers & Booksellers",* he says, "& well *known East & West; but they* are *slow to move* & rather *unventurous &c".*

Perhaps you might address them, & see with your *Sub: List,* whether they would undertake a vo*l somewhat like Stoddard*[']*s,* with nothing save a Portrait &c.

Should you fail, I'll then write, & see if they will take a smaller book, (viz) my *Poems* written *since* the appearance of *"Mountain of Lovers"*. x x x I *hate* to tax your overworked brain & time; but I thought *you* could tell him of your *"List"* &c.

How I would rejoice to write you *more at length,* but I must husband my strength for such literary labors as may yet be within my power. Mr*s* Hayne sends her *best love.*

Always Faithfully

Paul H Hayne.

[On the back there is a copy, in pencil, in Mrs. Hayne's writing, of the letter from Charles Scribner's Sons to Thomas L. Collier, New London, Connecticut. They declined to undertake the publication of Hayne's poems since "the success of the Stoddard volume has not been such as to encourage us to go into another similar venture just at present."

For "The Battle of King's Mountain" see *Harper's New Monthly Magazine,* LXI (November, 1880), 942–944 or *Complete Edition* (pp. 274–277).

On May 18, 1880, James wrote that he had had to forego his trip and that both Scribner's Sons and Roberts Brothers had declined to publish Hayne's volume, but added that he was still determined to bring it out, "even if I have to be publisher myself." He said also that a Miss Carpenter [Esther Bernon Carpenter] of Rhode Island had written to him of Hayne with great appreciation and had sent a sketch of Hayne which had appeared in a Rhode Island paper. She had enlarged it and sent it to be forwarded to some Southern paper. James said he had sent it to the New Orleans *Picayune.*

Thomas Stephens Collier (1842–1893), of Connecticut, corresponded with Hayne for at least some years, according to Hayne's journal. In 1889 he published a volume of poems entitled *Song Spray* (New London: Carl J. Viets).

John James Piatt (1835–1917) was a journalist, poet, librarian, and two years later entered the United States consular service. He edited (in twenty parts) *The Union of American Poetry and Art: A Choice Collection of Poems by American Poets . . .* , with 300 illustrations (Cincinnati: W. E. Dibble, 1880).

The Stoddard volume referred to is *The Poems of Richard Henry Stoddard,* Complete Edition (New York: Charles Scribner's Sons, 1880).]

No. 243

PAUL HAMILTON HAYNE to JOHN G. JAMES

"Copse Hill," Georgia Rail Road,

Address:

P. O. Box 275,   December 6th 1880.ˑ.

Augusta, Ga.

My Dear Colonel;—

I rec*d* your *most* affectionate letter, which must have *crossed* one of my own to you; & I write now, *not* only to acknowledge all its tender regard,—but to enclose you a communication from *Mr Charles Pratt*, (of the firm of *D. Lothrop & Co*), which please *return*, when you have done with it.

I had applied to him *before* receiving your letter, to see whether *Lothrop & Co* would take a vol of my *"Child's Poems"* *at their* own risk; but I now perceive it was *too late in the season* to make such a request.

I *should* have waited till autumn; for there is no sale for such books but as Xmas gifts.

M*r* Pratt makes no mention of your letter,— as you'll observe,— but I *think* the 1*st* book alluded to, must have been *your's?*

I have just written to M*r* Pratt, to say— (with the light he has thrown upon the subject), that it *would* be best to wait till *after* 1*st* Jan, before he speaks to M*r* Lothrop.

I have but little hope, however, that he will undertake the *work*.

With *warmest* regards from my wife to your Mother & self— in which I *heartily* join,

I am as *always*,

Your grateful & attached friend

Paul H. Hayne.

[Written vertically at the bottom:]

I *deeply sympathise* with you, on account of the annoyances of your present position; but *hope on!*

[On November 23, 1880, James wrote that all his efforts with publishers during the summer had been fruitless, but that he had written twice within recent weeks to D. Lothrop & Co. "making a proposition," adding: "I interpret their silence favorably, as it seems to mean that they are figuring on it. In a few days I may be able to send you the joyful news that they have accepted! But even should they not I shall not be discouraged—"

In the same letter James said he was finding his position as college president annoying and harassing, virtual slavery.]

No. 244

PAUL HAMILTON HAYNE to JOHN G. JAMES

Dec 28th 1880—

Dear Friend;

I recd your most affct letter last night, & rejoice to hear that all is well with you & yours. Thank your honored Mother for the interest expressed in our book.

I sent on per Express to Lothrop & Co. (on the 18*th* ins*t*) those of my youthful verses I wish to retain with my last 2 vol*s;* — writing them also a note of thanks for the very courteous manner in which they had undertaken the work.

As yet I have heard nothing. Am now correcting my last poems, to be sent on *shortly*. Have you heard from Mrs Preston?— In a letter of her's, (penned months ago) speaking of our book, she said; "if Col James can bring it out, it should have a picture of the beautiful home of your *birth*, in contrast to your present abode!" (I *have* a photo! of the same[.])

Also, she expressed the wish, (if her Eyes allowed), to execute a picture of *"Copse Hill,"* which would bring it out to much greater effect.

Hope you recd a book I sent you by *mail* on Xmas; & one per Express from my wife & son, sent on the 26*th*.

With best love from our household[.]

Ever affect yours,

Paul H Hayne—

I am unluckily sick again.

Can hardly write.

[In margin, vertically, on last page:]

\#   Express was *prepaid*. You must pay nothing upon it—

[The letter which Hayne mentions in the first sentence was dated December 20. On December 7 James had written this one:

President's Office

State Agricultural & Mechanical College of Texas,

John G. James,

President   College Station, Texas, Dec. 7 1880

My Dear Mr Hayne.

It is impossible to express to you the joy I feel at having found at last a publisher for our book. The mail brought me a minute ago the enclosed letter from D Lothrop & Co of Boston, which I wish I could send you by *telegraph* for I know it will do you so much good— I trust they will make money for you, as well as for themselves. I shall write them at once, and believe they will do all that can be done for you— We will leave details of get up to their judgment, and you will supply them as rapidly as possible with all the material you have— and all information they may need. About the memoir. I suggested it as tending to make the volume more valuable, for all the buyers of the book will like to have your life in it; and I also said that I thought Mrs Preston would prepare a brief one— I Know her friendship for you, and her ability, & will write her at once— In [the] meantime bethink yourself of some other person in case she should decline.

I shall try to make Lothrop & Co allow something for the 200 sub. list I sent him— He should allow *me* (*for you*) the regular agents Commission—

I write very hastily—and can assure you that my whole heart is filled with joy at this Xmas gift which has fallen to you, and which I do so much hope may be not only a great satisfaction to you, but a real benefit— This is but little that I have done, when I have wanted to do so much more, but I am sure you will understand me and know how I have been prevented— May God bless & prosper you all.

With much love

John G. James

No doubt Hayne replied immediately, but if so, his letter has been lost.

The *Complete Edition* contains pictures of Hayne's Charleston home and of his Georgia cottage, "Copse Hill."]

No. 245

MARY MIDDLETON MICHEL HAYNE to JOHN G. JAMES

"Copse Hill," Georgia Rail Road,
Jan 4th 1881

Address:

P. O. Box 275,
Augusta, Ga.

Dear Col James,

I write from my husband's sick room where he has been confined for 9 days—At first he was taken with a cold, & then followed a hemorrhage on the 26*th* Dec—& again a slight one three days ago. This attack has been accompanied by a good deal of pain in his chest— And yet he keeps up bravely, & is so patient: he has done a great deal of work on your book in the way of correcting—particularly—the latest poems—He has only retained about *one half* of his youthful poems. To-day my precious Poet is feeling somewhat stronger but the weather is so against him—snow on the ground for a week—sleet—& ice in our chamber with constant fire through the day, & until a late hour at night. Our son too has a severe cold, & cough, which has been hanging on him for a Month— & our *only*, & faithful servant is quite out of health— So you see, My poor heart & hands are full to overflowing. But God is good to me, for I have my dear ones still with me; & strength so far "according to my day"—M*r* Hayne sends you "a great deal of love—& best wishes for you & yours". I hope you received three books we sent you as a little remembrance? Last night the Mail brought us the following letter from Lothrop & Co. & to-day I have sent letters to "Scribner"—"The Sunday Mag" —& "Southern Monthly"—asking for their illustrations of three of M*r* H—' poems for children. Is not L—& Co' offer a liberal one?

Boston Dec 30th—

"Dear Sir,

The two parcels of Ms. are at hand & already going into type. I shall send you a proof of Contents table tomorrow which you will please correct, if faulty in arrangement; placing the poems under their respective heads. In regard to the vol. of Childrens Poems, I would say that if you can procure for us the illustrations of which you speak, without cost to us we will use those we have" (five of them in "Wide Awake") "without charge—& publish the vol. allowing you a Royalty of 10 o/c on all sold.

The usual rate is 10 o/c on all sales after the first one thousand copies: but we will make this exception in your case. Please communicate with us at an [as] early a day as possible in regard to it.   We have understood from Mr James that this vol. now in preparation was to be "Complete"—

Yours sincerely—

F. H. Allen

per D. Lothrop & co"

P. S.

This letter has been answered this Morning. Last evening Mr H— received a letter from Miss E. B. Carpenter with the enclosed— I have sent on the Names to Lothrop & Co in to-day's letter. Have you heard from Mrs Preston?— She sent us two Christmas Cards which I acknowledged a few Moments ago, but of course I did not allude to the sketch— She will write it if her health permit I am sure.

Excuse these few hastily written lines
in a dark room.

With warm regards to your Mother—
Ever you friend

M M Hayne

[The last section of *Complete Edition* (pp. 355–386) is entitled "Poems for Children." No separate volume of children's poems was published. James preferred one complete edition.

A later letter of James to Hayne indicated that Josiah Gilbert Holland, editor of *Scribner's Monthly*, refused Hayne permission to use the illustration referred to, whereupon James condemned him harshly for his selfishness.

Esther Bernon Carpenter (b. 1848), of Wakefield, Rhode Island, daughter of an Episcopal clergyman, was a member of the local school board, contributed to newspapers (such as the Providence *Journal*), and wrote poetry and a number of items on New England history. In her letter she enclosed the names of two subscribers for Hayne's poems.

In James's letter of January 10, 1881, he said he had written Lothrop that Mrs. Margaret Junkin Preston would write the introductory sketch of Hayne. In his journal, Hayne noted that on January 20, 1881, he received from Mrs. Preston the manuscript of her "very fine sketch" of his life, and that on the next day he forwarded it to Lothrop with a "candid statement of facts & opinions about it."

No later letters from Hayne or his wife to James survive, but both James's letters and Hayne's journal indicate that they continued to write at least as often as James did. Hayne died July 6, 1886, and James continued to correspond with Mrs. Hayne at least until the middle of the following year. His last extant letter to her is dated August 7, 1887.

I sum up briefly some of the data in James's letters written after 1880. While Hayne's book was going through the press, James did not often hear from the publisher and had to depend upon Hayne for news about it. Between November 28 and December 8, 1882, James received a copy of Hayne's book which Hayne had asked the publisher to send and three dozen copies which he had ordered himself. He was delighted with the book and grateful for the dedication, but could not believe, he said, that "I deserve so noble-hearted a recognition of my humble efforts." He said he felt that the volume should have been dedicated to Hayne's wife. As late as August 8, 1884, Hayne's book had not yet brought him any money.

The failure of James's Texas Military Institute in 1879 left him burdened with debts for years. By the fall of 1882 James and his brother (Fleming Wills James) had embarked in a banking enterprise at Colorado, Texas. Early in January, 1883, James sent in his resignation as president of the college and wanted to be relieved as soon as possible so as to join his brother in the bank. James announced his marriage in the letter of March 24, 1883. His mother and invalid sister-in-law continued to live with him after his marriage. He was relieved at the college, at his urgent request, on April 1, 1883, and moved to Colorado, Texas. By the beginning of 1884 he was a banker in Wichita Falls. He was still there when the extant correspondence ended (August 7, 1887). He was president of the Panhandle National Bank. His brother Ashby was cashier in August, 1884. (Ashby had graduated in law at the University of Virginia in 1882 and had practiced for a time at Colorado, Texas.) In January, 1885, James invited Hayne to purchase some stock in his bank, which he said would pay Hayne three or four times what he was getting in the Southeast. The terms were $400 cash and a note for $600 for a thousand dollars' worth of stock, the dividends to pay off the note gradually. Hayne made the purchase before March 16, 1885. On January 21, 1887, James wrote Mrs. Hayne: "I had postal from Will today acknowledging *your dividend*. No thanks are due *me*—You & he strangely misunderstand the matter, it is *your* money, not *mine*—Mr. Haynes bank stock yields 6%

semi-annual dividend, and it is duly earned by *his stock*— So please dont thank *me* for what is *his*." At the time of this letter Mrs. Hayne was visiting her brother in Montgomery but planned to return to Copse Hill.

In a letter of consolation to Mrs. Hayne, July 10, 1886, when he heard of Hayne's death, James spoke of his own sorrow and said of Hayne: "God has taken to Himself one of the noblest, truest, purest, characters that has adorned humanity in our age. We are all purer & better that he has lived, and the fragrance of his life, & life's work, will sweeten Society wherever it is Known. A *man* among men, he was, no time server, nor money lover, nor man-worshipper, but one who used his great powers in the way God intended them to be used—for the elevation of humanity, and not for self advancement. No more unselfish character ever lived, nor one more worthy of the vocation whereunto he was called."

The little family of three lie together in the beautiful Cemetery at Augusta:

Paul Hamilton Hayne (1830–1886)
Mary Middleton Michel Hayne (1831–1892)
William Hamilton Hayne (1856–1929).]